Advanced Studies in Supply Management

Weitere Bände in der Reihe http://www.springer.com/series/12204

Christoph Bode · Ronald Bogaschewsky
Michael Eßig · Rainer Lasch · Wolfgang Stölzle
(Hrsg.)

Supply Management Research

Aktuelle Forschungsergebnisse 2018

Springer Gabler

Hrsg.
Christoph Bode
Universität Mannheim
Mannheim, Deutschland

Rainer Lasch
Technische Universität Dresden
Dresden, Deutschland

Ronald Bogaschewsky
Universität Würzburg
Würzburg, Deutschland

Wolfgang Stölzle
Universität St. Gallen
St. Gallen, Schweiz

Michael Eßig
Universität der Bundeswehr München
Neubiberg, Deutschland

Advanced Studies in Supply Management
ISBN 978-3-658-23817-9   ISBN 978-3-658-23818-6 (eBook)
https://doi.org/10.1007/978-3-658-23818-6

Die Deutsche Nationalbibliothek verzeichnet diese Publikation in der Deutschen Nationalbibliografie; detaillierte bibliografische Daten sind im Internet über http://dnb.d-nb.de abrufbar.

Springer Gabler
© Springer Fachmedien Wiesbaden GmbH, ein Teil von Springer Nature 2019
Das Werk einschließlich aller seiner Teile ist urheberrechtlich geschützt. Jede Verwertung, die nicht ausdrücklich vom Urheberrechtsgesetz zugelassen ist, bedarf der vorherigen Zustimmung des Verlags. Das gilt insbesondere für Vervielfältigungen, Bearbeitungen, Übersetzungen, Mikroverfilmungen und die Einspeicherung und Verarbeitung in elektronischen Systemen.
Die Wiedergabe von Gebrauchsnamen, Handelsnamen, Warenbezeichnungen usw. in diesem Werk berechtigt auch ohne besondere Kennzeichnung nicht zu der Annahme, dass solche Namen im Sinne der Warenzeichen- und Markenschutz-Gesetzgebung als frei zu betrachten wären und daher von jedermann benutzt werden dürften.
Der Verlag, die Autoren und die Herausgeber gehen davon aus, dass die Angaben und Informationen in diesem Werk zum Zeitpunkt der Veröffentlichung vollständig und korrekt sind. Weder der Verlag noch die Autoren oder die Herausgeber übernehmen, ausdrücklich oder implizit, Gewähr für den Inhalt des Werkes, etwaige Fehler oder Äußerungen. Der Verlag bleibt im Hinblick auf geografische Zuordnungen und Gebietsbezeichnungen in veröffentlichten Karten und Institutionsadressen neutral.

Lektorat: Susanne Kramer
Redaktion: Christoph Bode, Ronald Bogaschewsky, Michael Eßig, Rainer Lasch, Wolfgang Stölzle, Bianka Blankenberg

Springer Gabler ist ein Imprint der eingetragenen Gesellschaft Springer Fachmedien Wiesbaden GmbH und ist ein Teil von Springer Nature
Die Anschrift der Gesellschaft ist: Abraham-Lincoln-Str. 46, 65189 Wiesbaden, Germany

Geleitwort

Der Bundesverband Materialwirtschaft Einkauf und Logistik e.V. (BME) fördert seit vielen Jahren den konstruktiven, offenen Austausch zwischen Praktikern und Wissenschaftlern. Dabei unterstützt der Verband aktiv das Aufspüren von Trends und Innovationen, das Erarbeiten von Erfolgsansätzen, das Vermitteln von Erprobtem und das Vernetzen interessierter Menschen und ihrer Ideen. Für 9.600 Mitglieder und eine breite Fachöffentlichkeit bietet der BME exzellente Networking-Plattformen zum Know-how-Transfer.

Eine wichtige Säule der Verbandsarbeit ist die wissenschaftliche Auseinandersetzung mit den Themen Beschaffung und Logistik, verbunden mit der Unterstützung des wissenschaftlichen Nachwuchses. Dabei werden der Öffentlichkeit interessante Ansätze in der Forschung zum Thema Supply Management vorgestellt. Seit 1988 werden Verfasser von Habilitationen und Dissertationen mit dem BME-Wissenschaftspreis ausgezeichnet. Herausragende Studienabschlussarbeiten prämiert der BME seit fünfzehn Jahren mit dem BME-Hochschulpreis für Beschaffung und Logistik.

In der Buchreihe „Advanced Studies in Supply Management" veröffentlicht der Verband wichtige wissenschaftliche Erkenntnisse rund um aktuelle und vieldiskutierte Managementmethoden. Auch der elfte Band zeigt wieder Lösungsansätze für aktuelle Herausforderungen. Beispiele dafür sind die Beiträge zur Lieferentwicklung in Transportnetzwerken, zum Qualitätsmanagement mit Lieferanten in Schwellenländern sowie zu kooperativem Supply-Chain-Risikomanagement. Interessante Lösungsansätze für Praktiker bieten unter anderem Aufsätze zum Komplexitätsmanagement in der Produktentwicklung, zu Erfolgsfaktoren zur Gestaltung resilienter Supply Chains und zu Supply-Chain-Risiken in der Textilindustrie.

Mein herzlicher Dank gilt den Autoren für ihre Beiträge sowie insbesondere den Professoren Christoph Bode, Ronald Bogaschewsky, Michael Eßig, Rainer Lasch und Wolfgang Stölzle für ihre fachliche Unterstützung und ihr großes Engagement.

Eschborn, im Oktober 2018

Dr. Silvius Grobosch
Hauptgeschäftsführer
Bundesverband Materialwirtschaft, Einkauf und Logistik e.V.

Vorwort

In dem vorliegenden elften Band der Reihe „Advanced Studies in Supply Management" werden erneut ausgewählte wissenschaftliche Fortschritte in diesem Forschungsfeld dargestellt. Er ist zugleich Tagungsband des 11. Wissenschaftlichen Symposiums „Supply Management", das im März 2018 an der Universität Mannheim stattfand. Veranstalter dieser Tagung ist der Bundesverband Materialwirtschaft, Einkauf und Logistik e.V. (BME), der auch als Herausgeber der Buchreihe fungiert. Inhaltlich verantwortlich für die Durchführung des Wissenschaftlichen Symposiums und die daraus resultierenden Schriften ist der Wissenschaftliche Beirat des Bundesvorstands des BME.

Die außerordentlich große Bedeutung des gesamten Beschaffungsbereichs spiegelt sich in der seit Jahren deutlich steigenden Anzahl wissenschaftlicher Publikationen und anwendungsnaher Arbeiten wider. Das Wissenschaftliche Symposium „Supply Management" hat sich zu einer zentralen Plattform für die Präsentation von sowie den Austausch über neueste Forschungsergebnisse aus den Gebieten Einkauf, Materialmanagement, Logistik und Supply Chain Management etabliert.

Die in diesem Band veröffentlichten Beiträge wurden gemäß dieser beiden Tracks auf dem Symposium in strenger wissenschaftliche sowie stärker anwendungsorientierte Arbeiten unterschieden. Alle Einreichungen wurden in einem Double-Blind-Review-Verfahren von unabhängigen Gutachtern eingehend geprüft. Diesen gilt unser besonderer Dank für die gewissenhafte Erstellung der Gutachten und die dort angeführten Verbesserungsvorschläge für die Beiträge. Zahlreiche Einreichungen wurden abgelehnt, da sie den hohen Ansprüchen der Gutachter nicht genügten. Aufgenommen wurden zudem die Arbeiten, die sich für das Vortragsfinale des BME-Wissenschaftspreises 2018 qualifizieren konnten. Der Jury des BME-Wissenschaftspreises gilt ebenfalls unser Dank für die geleisteten Begutachtungen.

Der vorliegende Band zeigt die große Breite und Tiefe der wissenschaftlichen und anwendungsnahen Arbeiten im Bereich Supply Management auf. Es ist dem Wissenschaftlichen Beirat und dem BME ein besonderes Anliegen, Forschungen in diesem Bereich weiterhin intensiv zu fördern.

Eschborn, im Oktober 2018

Prof. Dr. Christoph Bode, Mannheim   Prof. Dr. Ronald Bogaschewsky, Würzburg
Prof. Dr. Michael Eßig, München   Prof. Dr. Rainer Lasch, Dresden
Prof. Dr. Wolfgang Stölzle, St. Gallen

Inhaltsverzeichnis

Geleitwort V

Vorwort VII

Teil A Wissenschaftliche Forschungsbeiträge

Supplier social standard (non-)compliance:
A multi-perspective approach focusing on emerging economies
Marc Müller

Abstract 3
1 Introduction to the research on supplier social standard (non-)compliance 3
2 Conceptual background of the research on supplier social standard
 (non-)compliance 5
 2.1 Sustainable supply chain management 5
 2.2 Buyers' strategies and practices to address social issues at
  suppliers' sites 5
 2.3 Buyers' vehicles and instruments to address social issues at
  suppliers' sites 6
 2.4 Suppliers' (non-)compliance with social issues 8
3 Studies on supplier social standard (non-)compliance 9
 3.1 Research framework 9
 3.2 Study A: Compliance adjustment with an externally imposed social
  standard: the influence of historical and social aspirations at early
  and advanced stages of exposure 10
 3.3 Study B: When logics extend: pursuing compromising and decoupling
  strategies to manage commercial and social objectives 12
 3.4 Study C: Socially responsible supplier selection and development for
  supplier social standard compliance: an effectiveness analysis 14
4 Conclusion of the research on supplier social standard (non-)compliance 17
 4.1 Practical implications 17
 4.2 Theoretical contributions 18
 4.3 Selected limitations and directions for future research 19
References 20

Qualitätsmanagement mit Lieferanten in Schwellenländern – Zusammenspiel aus Einkaufspraktiken und „kognitiven Karten"
Tobias Kosmol

Abstract	27
1 Einleitung	28
2 Theoretischer Hintergrund	30
2.1 Neo-konfigurative Perspektive	30
2.2 Barrieren für das LQM in Schwellenländern	32
2.3 LQM-Praktiken	32
2.4 LQM-bezogene kognitive Karten	34
3 Methodik	35
3.1 Sampling und Datenerhebung	35
3.2 Fallstudienanalyse	36
3.3 Fuzzy-set qualitative comparative analysis	37
3.4 Kognitiv-linguistische Analyse	37
4 Ergebnisse	38
4.1 Team Coaches (Konfiguration 1)	40
4.2 Hands-off-Lokalisierer (Konfiguration 2)	40
4.3 Synchronisierte Kontrolleure (Konfiguration 3)	40
4.4 Skeptische Aufseher (Konfiguration 4)	40
5 Fazit und Praxisimplikationen	41
5.1 Neo-konfigurative Perspektive für das Beschaffungsmanagement	41
5.2 LQM-bezogene kognitive Karten als wichtige Elemente in Konfigurationen	42
5.3 Theorie mittlerer Reichweite für das LQM in Schwellenländern	43
5.4 Praxisimplikationen	43
Literatur	45

Collaborative recovery from supply chain disruptions
Marie Katharina Brüning

Abstract	51
1 Introduction	51
2 Conceptual framework development	54
2.1 Multi-methods framework development	54
2.2 Collaborative recovery	54
3 Framework testing	58
3.1 Data collection and sample	58
3.2 Measures	59
3.3 The measurement model	60
4 Analysis and results	62
5 Discussion	64
6 Conclusion and implications	66

Appendix: Construct items 68
References 69

Optimal framing of scores in procurement auctions
Nicolas Fugger, Christian Paul, Achim Wambach

Abstract 77
1   Introduction 77
2   Literature review 79
3   Experimental design and hypotheses 81
4   Experimental results 85
    4.1   Beliefs 85
    4.2   Bidding 86
5   Conclusion 90
References 91

Integrated segmentation of supply and demand with service differentiation (Extended abstract)
Benedikt Schulte

Abstract 93
1   Introduction 93
2   Motivation and introduction to service differentiation 94
3   Summary of findings 95
References 97

Supplier development considering interdependencies in the inbound logistics of the automotive industry
Sönke Wieczorrek, Martin Grunewald, Thomas S. Spengler

Abstract 99
1   Introduction 99
2   Literature review 101
    2.1   Interdependencies in supply networks 101
    2.2   Supplier evaluation 102
    2.3   Supplier development 103
3   Problem setting 104
4   Solution approach 106
    4.1   Stage 1: Effects of measures 107
    4.2   Stage 2: Assignment of measures 108
5   Numerical example 109
    5.1   Data and benchmark 109
    5.2   Results and implications for supplier development 110
6   Conclusions 112
References 114

How do buyers respond to corporate social irresponsibility of suppliers? (Extended abstract)

Maximilian Merath, Christoph Bode

Abstract	117
1 Introduction	117
2 Conceptual background	118
2.1 Corporate social responsibility (CSR)	118
2.2 Substantive and symbolic management of CSR	119
2.3 Corporate social irresponsibility (CSI)	119
2.4 The fragility of insurance-like effects of ex ante CSR	120
2.5 Contrast and assimilation effects subsequent to CSI	120
3 Method	121
4 Results	122
5 Discussion	123
References	124

Specific investments in the supply chain – a literature review on the state-of-the-art knowledge with an outlook on safeguarding mechanisms and avenues for future research

Julia Burkhardt

Abstract	129
1 Introduction	129
2 Methodology	130
2.1 Data collection	131
2.2 Bibliometric analysis	132
3 Content analysis	135
3.1 Definition, background and characteristics of specific investments	135
3.2 Types of specific investments	136
3.3 Motivation and antecedents for specific investments	138
4 Discussion of safeguards	139
4.1 Summary of the paper	140
4.2 Limitation of the research	141
4.3 Implications for practice	141
4.4 Further research	142
References	143

Teil B Anwendungsorientierte Forschungsbeiträge

Single approaches for complexity management in product development: An empirical research
Wolfgang Vogel, Rainer Lasch

Abstract	151
1 Introduction	151
2 Literature review	154
2.1 Research methodology and boundary definition	154
2.2 Single approaches for managing complexity	155
2.3 Existing empirical studies in the field of complexity management and identification of gaps in literature	159
3 Empirical research	160
3.1 Research methodology and objectives	160
3.2 Questionnaire design, data collection methodology, sample description and statistical analysis	161
4 Analysis of empirical research and findings	162
4.1 Sample results and data validation	162
4.2 Results regarding single approaches for managing complexity	164
4.3 Comparison between empirical and literature results	174
5 Conclusion and outlook	176
References	177
Appendix	203

Der Faktor Unsicherheit bei ersatzteillogistischen Kooperationen auf dem Drittanbietermarkt
Stefan Drechsler, Bastien Bodenstein, Rainer Lasch

Abstract	217
1 Einleitung	217
2 Literaturüberblick	218
2.1 Kooperationen auf organisatorischer Ebene	219
2.2 Technologisch ermöglichte Kooperationen	220
3 Methodik	221
3.1 Qualitative Fallstudien und Experteninterviews	221
3.2 Inhaltsanalyse	222
4 Resultate	223
4.1 Wahrgenommene Bedeutung von Kooperationen	223
4.2 Aktuelle Relevanz organisatorischer und technologischer Kooperationsmöglichkeiten	225
4.3 Implikationen und kritische Würdigung	227
5 Fazit und Ausblick	229
Literatur	230

Erfolgsfaktoren zur zukünftigen Gestaltung resilienter Supply Chains – Konzeption eines Bezugsrahmens

Lukas Biedermann, Herbert Kotzab

Abstract		235
1	Einleitung	235
2	Kritische Bestandsaufnahme der Literatur	236
	2.1 Methodischer Zutritt	236
	2.2 Inhaltliche Schwerpunkte in der Literatur	237
	2.3 Literaturgestützte Erfolgsfaktoren zur Gestaltung resilienter Supply Chains	239
	2.4 Kritische Würdigung der Befunde	240
3	Aufbau und Struktur eines konzeptionellen Bezugsrahmens	241
	3.1 Gestaltungsansätze für resiliente Supply Chains	241
	3.2 Erfolgsfaktoren und deren Wirkzusammenhänge	243
	3.3 Kritische Würdigung des konzeptionellen Bezugsrahmens	248
4	Zusammenfassung und Ausblick	248
Literatur		249

Supply-Chain-Risiken in der Textilindustrie

Tessa Sarnow, Meike Schröder

Abstract		255
1	Einleitung	255
2	Forschungsgegenstand und -design	256
	2.1 Wertschöpfung in der „textilen Kette"	256
	2.2 Forschungsdesign und -struktur	259
3	Supply-Chain-Risiken in der Textilindustrie	261
	3.1 Prozessrisiken	261
	3.2 Steuerungsrisiken	262
	3.3 Versorgungsrisiken	263
	3.4 Nachfragerisiken	264
	3.5 Umfeldrisiken	265
4	Situation und Entwicklung der Textilindustrie	266
5	Zusammenfassung und Ausblick	269
Literatur		270
Anhang A		273
Anhang B		274

Autorenverzeichnis ... 277

Teil A

Wissenschaftliche Forschungsbeiträge

Supplier social standard (non-)compliance: A multi-perspective approach focusing on emerging economies[1]

Marc Müller

Abstract

The upholding of labor issues in supply chains is increasingly debated in the business sphere, in the political arena and within civil society. Hence, this thesis aims to study supplier social standard (non-)compliance from the suppliers' and buyers' perspectives informed by three organizational theories that guide three quantitative studies. The results largely confirm the predictions that (1) emerging market suppliers amend their social standard compliance by referring to their past and competitors' social standard compliance, (2) the intensity of the tensions between commercial and social objectives shape supplier social standard (non-)compliance, (3) socially responsible supplier selection is a key capability to influence supplier social standard compliance. The research contributes to the behavioral theory of the firm and the institutional logics perspective. It offers implications for buyers, policy makers and standard setters.

1 Introduction to the research on supplier social standard (non-)compliance

Economic activity is spread around the globe (Hofmann, 2011) creating supply chains in which labor-intensive production processes are increasingly placed in emerging economies (Buckley, Strange, 2015). The search for low-cost production has driven these outsourcing activities (Gereffi, Lee, 2012). Yet, low-cost production is often related to exploitation of workers at the production sites in emerging economies (Locke,

---

[1] This article is based on and summarizes the author's related dissertation project as contestant for the BME Science Award. For more details see Müller (2016).

Qin, Brause, 2007). The scandals on unbearable working conditions at the production sites supplying to the sportswear industry have started a public debate on social issues[2] in supply chains (Zadek, 2004) which mainly refer to labor aspects such as working conditions as well as health and safety (Yawar, Seuring, 2017).

Since the dispersion of production around the planet has yielded "buyer-driven" supply chains (Gereffi, Lee, 2012), stakeholder groups hold buyers responsible to ensure adequate working conditions at their supply chain partners' facilities (Ehrgott, Reimann, Kaufmann, Carter, 2011; Gualandris, Klassen, Vachon, Kalchschmidt, 2015; Parmigiani, Klassen, Russo, 2011). In response to the growing stakeholder demands, buyers increasingly turn to social standards and require their suppliers to fulfill the associated obligations (Anner, 2012).

Literature reviews on sustainable supply chains show that research has paid relatively little attention to social issues (Beske-Janssen, Johnson, Schaltegger, 2015; Touboulic, Walker, 2015), and studies on social aspects have increased only in the past few years (Müller, Stölzle, 2015; Walker, Seuring, Sarkis, Klassen, 2014), suggesting that more investigations are required to better understand the particularities of the social dimension (Beske-Janssen et al., 2015). Buyers have largely focused on direct suppliers aiming to ensure that these suppliers meet the labor requirements (Jiang, 2009). Yet, suppliers often do not live up to a social standard's obligations (Distelhorst, Locke, Pal, Samel, 2015; Egels-Zandén, 2014, Egels-Zandén, Lindholm, 2015). Accordingly, this research concentrates on the buyer-supplier dyad to study supplier social standard (non-)compliance from the suppliers' and buyers' perspectives guided by the following research question: *How do organizational aspirations, institutional logics and buyer capabilities for supplier management influence social standard compliance of emerging economy suppliers?*

Section 2 provides the conceptual background and summarizes the current state of the literature in the research area. Section 3 presents the research framework as well as the three studies along with the research approach, findings and contributions. Section 4 concludes this article by focusing on the practical implications, theoretical contributions as well as selected limitations and directions for future research.

---

[2] Social issues, social aspects, labor issues and labor aspects are used interchangeably referring to working conditions and related aspects specified by the International Labour Organization (ILO), Organisation for Economic Co-Operation and Development (OECD), the United Nations (UN) and national laws.

2 Conceptual background of the research on supplier social standard (non-)compliance

2.1 Sustainable supply chain management

In management research, definitions of sustainability build on the triple bottom line of economic, social and environmental issues (Dyllick, Hockerts, 2002; Elkington, 1998; Schaltegger, Beckmann, Hansen, 2013), which triggered supply chain management scholars to increasingly focus on social and environmental aspects. Today, sustainable supply chain management that draws on economic, social and environmental issues has become a focal area in the supply chain management literature (Pagell, Shevchenko, 2014). Despite that the literature on sustainable supply chain management has produced more than 300 publications (Touboulic, Walker, 2015) scholars have addressed the environmental dimension of sustainability to a considerably greater extent (Beske-Janssen et al., 2015; Kudla, Stölzle, 2011).

Accordingly, this thesis aims to concentrate on supplier social standard (non-)compliance from suppliers' and buyers' perspectives, mainly addressing the social dimension of sustainability. More specifically, it focuses on social issues in line with the requirements defined by the Business Social Compliance Initiative (BSCI) as a social standard (BSCI, 2009), and the understanding that social issues in supply chains mainly relate to labor issues (Yawar, Seuring, 2017). This positioning is informed by the argument that "research concentrating on the social performance or its relationships to only one of the other two might reveal interesting insights that are otherwise overlooked, as such an approach would possibly allow for more focused attention on specifics to the social dimension" (Beske-Janssen et al., 2015: 673).

2.2 Buyers' strategies and practices to address social issues at suppliers' sites

Buyers' strategies to ensure the upholding of social issues in supply chains can be categorized as proactive and reactive. Proactive strategies[3] are characterized as a collaborative approach, which entails to support supply chain partners meeting social requirements (Harms, Hansen, Schaltegger, 2013; Muller, Vermeulen, Glasbergen, 2012; Yawar, Seuring, 2017). Reactive strategies[4] follow a compliance orientation, according to which buyers' internally specify or externally adopt criteria and measure

---

[3] Alternative terminologies for proactive strategies are collaborative strategies (Muller et al, 2012), opportunity-oriented strategies (Harms et al, 2013), or supplier development strategies (Yawar, Seuring, 2017).
[4] Alternative terminologies for reactive strategies are prescriptive strategies (Muller et al, 2012), risk-oriented strategies (Harms et al, 2013), or compliance strategies (Yawar, Seuring, 2017).

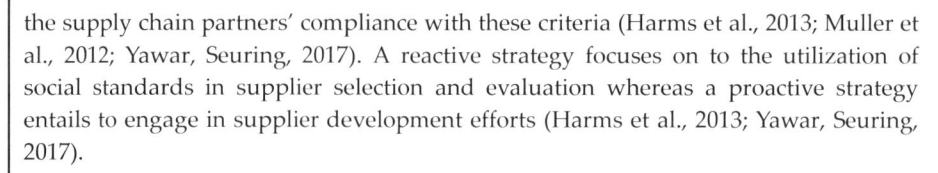

the supply chain partners' compliance with these criteria (Harms et al., 2013; Muller et al., 2012; Yawar, Seuring, 2017). A reactive strategy focuses on to the utilization of social standards in supplier selection and evaluation whereas a proactive strategy entails to engage in supplier development efforts (Harms et al., 2013; Yawar, Seuring, 2017).

Some researchers (e.g., Foerstl, Reuter, Hartmann, Blome, 2010; Reuter, Foerstl, Hartmann, Blome, 2011) refer to all three supplier management practices (i.e., supplier selection, supplier evaluation and supplier development) to uphold labor issues at supply chain partners' facilities. Other scholars mention only supplier selection and development (e.g., Beske, Seuring, 2014; Pagell, Wu, 2009) or supplier evaluation and development (e.g., Klassen, Vereecke, 2012). In conceptual studies, supplier selection and supplier development are suggested to positively influence social issues at suppliers' sites (Parmigiani et al., 2011). However, previous research lacks empirical evidence whether socially responsible supplier selection and development effectively safeguard supplier social standard compliance.

2.3 Buyers' vehicles and instruments to address social issues at suppliers' sites

The buyers' vehicles to ensure the upholding of social aspects in supply chains can be conceptualized under the construct of self-regulation.[5] The definitions of self-regulation reflect the different approaches at corporate and collective-level. Christmann and Taylor (2006: 863) focus on the corporate-level by defining self-regulation as a "firm's commitment to control its own conduct beyond what is required by the law". Bartley (2007: 298) understands self-regulation as an industry-level construct "in which coalitions of nonstate actors codify, monitor, and in some cases certify firms' compliance with labor, environmental, human rights, or other standards of accountability".

Figure 1 illustrates the overview of vehicles of self-regulation for social issues, including corporate and collective approaches and mixtures thereof. Corporate self-regulation includes company-individual activities concerning the adoption of a code of conduct, verification of compliance with the code of conduct through monitoring, and implementation of corrective actions for the areas of improvement (Andersen, Skjoett-Larsen, 2009; Awaysheh, Klassen, 2010). The successful implementation of codes of conduct depends on efficient monitoring as well as incentives and sanctions (Pedersen, Andersen, 2006), which can be integrated in supplier management practices (Kudla, Klaas-Wissing, 2012).

---

[5] Alternative terminologies for self-regulation are private regulation (Bartley, 2007; Locke et al., 2007, O'Rourke, 2003), private decentralized institutions (King, Lenox, Terlaak, 2005) and civil regulation (Vogel, 2010).

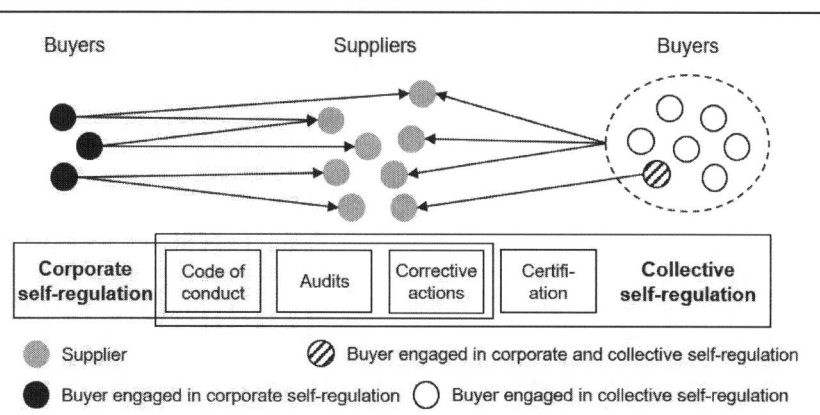

Figure 1: Overview of vehicles of self-regulation for social issues

Collective self-regulation[6] that draws on standardized codes of conduct and monitoring systems has gained popularity as a result of the growing stakeholder pressures (O'Rourke, 2006). Collective and corporate approaches are often comparable in "design, content and intentions to regulate the transnational arena" (Reinecke, Manning, von Hagen, 2012: 792). Yet, differences exist between the collective approaches with regard to the inclusion of stakeholders and the certification of audit results; Fair Labor Association (FLA) and Fair Wear Foundation (FWF) as multi-stakeholder initiatives do not offer certification whereas Social Accountability 8000 (SA8000) resembles a multi-stakeholder certification (Fransen, 2011). A mixed approach is followed by Nestlé (2016) that employs internal human rights impact assessments and internal programs to train farmers along with established standards such as Sedex and FLA.

Previous research has addressed collective self-regulation of environmental issues (e.g., Aravind, Christmann, 2011; Darnall, Sides, 2008; King, Lenox, 2001; King et al., 2005) and quality aspects (e.g., Guler, Guillén, Macpherson, 2002), and has concluded firms' response to social standards by drawing on companies' response towards quality standards (Christmann, Taylor, 2006). Yet, social standards differ from environmental (e.g., ISO 14000) and quality standards (e.g., ISO 9000) in two ways: First, social standards mainly draw on performance outcomes that are partly attributed to national laws rather than management systems (Kortelainen, 2008). Second, environmental and quality standards mainly refer to ISO certifications while social standards are more diverse. **Figure 2** shows the standards that focus on social issues in line with ILO conventions at the production sites for cocoa in Côte d'Ivoire (19 social standards), elec-

---

6   O'Rourke (2003) distinguishes collective self-regulation between "collaborative regulation" (e.g., FLA) and "socialized regulation" (e.g., FWF).

tronics in China (16 social standards) and textiles in Bangladesh (22 social standards) for goods sold in Europe.

Figure 2: *Overview of social standards applied in different production contexts for goods sold in Europe obtained from the International Trade Centre (ITC) Standards map*

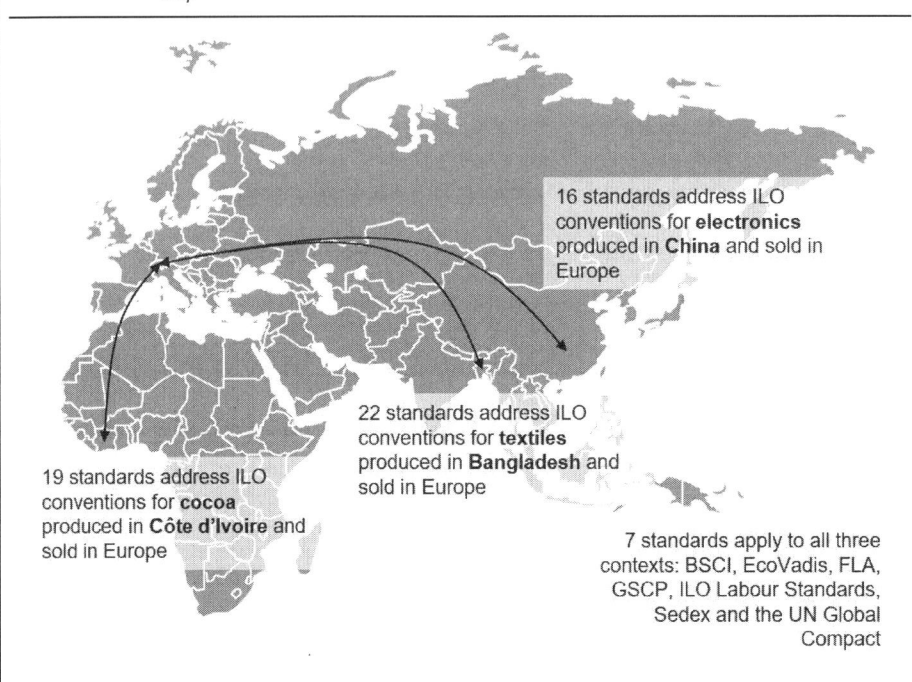

16 standards address ILO conventions for **electronics** produced in **China** and sold in Europe

22 standards address ILO conventions for **textiles** produced in **Bangladesh** and sold in Europe

19 standards address ILO conventions for **cocoa** produced in **Côte d'Ivoire** and sold in Europe

7 standards apply to all three contexts: BSCI, EcoVadis, FLA, GSCP, ILO Labour Standards, Sedex and the UN Global Compact

While previous research has focused on the institutionalization of collective approaches to address social and environmental issues (e.g., Peters, Hofstetter, Hoffmann, 2011), this research aims to investigate the utilization of collective self-regulation of labor aspects in buyer-supplier relationships.

2.4 Suppliers' (non-)compliance with social issues

Suppliers are increasingly exposed to buyer-imposed social obligations (O'Rourke, 2003) but research on social issues in supply chains has mainly concentrated on buyers as unit of analysis neglecting suppliers (Müller, Stölzle, 2015). **Table 1** summarizes the studies focusing on suppliers as unit of analysis and the observed determinants of supplier social standard (non-)compliance.

Table 1: Determinants of supplier social standard (non-)compliance

Determinants	Sources
Auditors	Reinecke, Ansari, 2015; Short, Toffel, Hugill, 2016
Buyer-supplier relationship	Egels-Zandén, 2014; Locke et al., 2007; Perry, Towers, 2013
Configuration of the social standard	Anner, 2012; Reinecke, Ansari, 2015
Country contexts	Distelhorst et al., 2015; Locke et al, 2007; Locke, Rissing, Pal, 2013; Toffel, Short, Ouellet, 2015
Factory characteristics	Kortelainen, 2008; Locke et al., 2007; Perry, Towers, 2013; Young, Makhija, 2014
Industry	Lee, Kim, 2009; Locke et al., 2013; Perry, Towers, 2013
Purchasing practices	Egels-Zandén, 2014; Jiang, 2009, Mamic, 2005; Perry, Towers, 2013

The literature on determinants of supplier compliance with social requirements addresses the functioning of the social standard, the embeddedness of the social standard in national contexts and industry characteristics. Yet, less attention has been drawn to the behavioral aspects that guide firm behavior in the context of a social standard. Exploratory research proposes that emerging economy producers amend their social standard compliance between audits (e.g., Egels-Zandén, 2014; Egels-Zandén, Lindholm, 2015), and that emerging market suppliers are in a trade-off between commercial and social goals (e.g., Egels-Zandén, 2014; Jiang, Baker, Frazier, 2009). Hence, this research aims to focus on the behavioral aspects that lead emerging economy producers to amend their social standard compliance over time, as well as their response to tensions between commercial and social goals.

3 Studies on supplier social standard (non-)compliance

3.1 Research framework

Figure 3 exhibits the research framework of this thesis, in which institutional theory serves as the main theoretical lens. This is attributed to (1) the compliance with a social standard as institutionalized means of self-regulation (Terlaak, 2007), and (2) its ability to relate to and to integrate with the behavioral theory of the firm and the resource-based view. In addition, institutional theory addresses the commercial and social dimension of sustainability (Touboulic, Walker, 2015), and it provides a suitable theoretical lens to study how emerging economy suppliers cope with conflicting commercial and social objectives. The behavioral theory of the firm allows to study how internal (i.e., historical aspirations) and external references (i.e., social aspirations) guide emerging market producers' adaptation to a social standard over time. The resource-based view allows to model socially responsible supplier selection and development as buyer capabilities for supplier social standard compliance.

Figure 3: Research framework

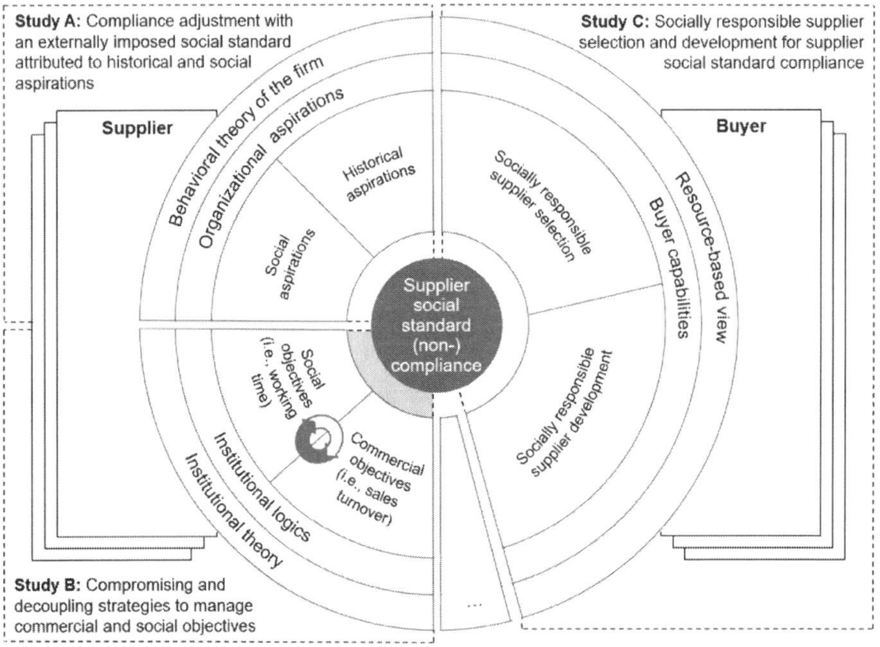

3.2 Study A: Compliance adjustment with an externally imposed social standard: the influence of historical and social aspirations at early and advanced stages of exposure

Research approach

Study A sought to investigate *how historical and social aspirations influence emerging market suppliers to adjust their compliance with an externally imposed social standard, and how the influence of historical and social aspirations on the compliance amendment differs for early versus advanced stages of exposure to that social standard.*

Hypotheses 1a and 1b suggest that suppliers' performance adaptation differs above and below historical and social aspirations. Hypothesis 2 predicts that historical aspirations serve as the main reference for performance amendments at early stages of exposure to the social standard (i.e., when few social audits have been conducted). Hypothesis 3 anticipates that social aspirations become the main reference for performance adjustments at advanced stages of exposure to the social standard (i.e., when more social audits have been conducted).

The analysis builds on social audit reports of the BSCI for 87 suppliers from Bangladesh, China, India, and Turkey in the clothing and textile industries that have undergone at least four full audits between December 2003 and September 2012. The dependent variable is characterized as supplier social standard compliance delta, which is the difference between the results of a supplier's two subsequent full audits indicating the changes of the supplier social standard compliance over time. The independent variables are historical and social aspirations, which are operationalized following Harris and Bromiley (2007). The control variables are country, industry, number of audit, year of audit, and time between audits. Similar to Greve (2003), the hypotheses are tested by employing a linear regression analysis whilst also conducting a repeated measures fixed effects-analysis as robustness test that provided similar results.

Findings and contributions

The linear regression analysis provides partial support for Hypothesis 1a, and full support for Hypotheses 1b, 2 and 3. **Table 2** summarizes the results of the linear regression analysis. Previous studies on aspiration-driven behavior have addressed economic goals of developed country firms (e.g., Baum, Dahlin, 2007; Harris, Bromiley, 2007; Mishina, Dykes, Block, Pollock, 2010), this study proves the applicability of the behavioral theory of the firm on social goals of emerging economy producers. Further, it refutes the long-standing assumption of the behavioral theory of firm that organizational aspirations act concurrently in influencing performance outcomes, suggesting that historical and social aspirations work in sequence to affect emerging economy producers' compliance adjustments with an externally imposed social standard.

This study equips buyers, policy makers and social standard setters with one major implication. After processes have been set up, which four out of eleven socially compliant producers already achieved in the second audit, the suppliers orientate towards competitors' performance levels rather than the standard's requirements. This suggests that garment producers may not live up to the requirements of an externally imposed social standard in the long run. Given the suppliers' strong orientation towards their peers, it follows that incentivizing the suppliers with a superior social

Wissenschaftliche Forschungsbeiträge

performance would create a higher-level playing field in terms of supplier social standard compliance.

Table 2:   Summary of the linear regression analysis results in study A

H	Description	p-value	Remark
1a (+)	Social performance below/above historical aspirations leads suppliers to improve/deteriorate performance relative to an externally imposed social standard.	$p < .05$ (Model: $p < .01$)	Performance below historical aspirations is not significant
1b +	Social performance below/above social aspirations leads suppliers to improve/deteriorate performance relative to an externally imposed social standard.	$p < .01$ (Model: $p < .01$)	-
2 +	At an early stage of exposure to an externally imposed social standard, historical aspirations dominate as the reference for performance adjustments.	$p < .05$ (Model: $p < .01$)	Performance below organizational aspirations is not significant; performance above social aspirations is less significant ($p < .1$)
3 +	At an advanced stage of exposure to an externally imposed social standard, social aspirations dominate as the reference for performance adjustments.	$p < .01$ (Model: $p < .01$)	Performance below and above historical aspirations is not significant

+ Hypothesis is confirmed; (+) Hypothesis is partially confirmed.

3.3   Study B: When logics extend: pursuing compromising and decoupling strategies to manage commercial and social objectives

Research approach

Study A indicated that the conflict between commercial objectives and social obligations may lead suppliers to deteriorate social standard compliance. Study B builds on this inference and intended to analyze *how emerging market suppliers respond to conflicting objectives of the commercial and the new social logic.*

Hypothesis 1 suggests that high sales turnover is negatively related to compliance with working time requirements, which constitutes the decoupling strategy. Hypothesis 2 predicts that the higher the growth in sales turnover the higher is the compliance with working time requirements, representing the compromising strategy. Hypothesis 3 anticipates that greater exposure to a social standard (i.e., more social audits) leads to a distinct pattern of choosing decoupling or compromising strategies.

The sample relates to a research project with 42 buyers that provided information on their supply arrangements. A potential sample bias was tested prior to the analysis and not of concern. The analysis builds on social audit reports for 90 suppliers from Bangladesh, China, India, and Turkey in the garment industry that have completed two full audits between September 2012 and March 2015. Compliance with a social standard's requirements on working time serves as the dependent variable; since producers were either rated 'non-compliant' or 'good', it is dichotomous and analyzed using logistic regression analysis. Sales turnover and sales turnover change are the independent variables of this study for which z-scores were computed following Bloom, Kretschmer and van Reenen (2011). Robustness tests with less conservative samples and additional predictors were conducted and did not yield significant results. A reciprocal relationship between the predictors and the dependent variable was tested and did not lead to significant results. Country, year of the audit, share of female managers to all managers, share of managers to all workers and auditing company serve as control variables.

Findings and contributions

The logistic regression analysis provides support for the three Hypotheses. **Table 3** summarizes the results of the logistic regression analysis. The study sheds light on the hybridization of emerging economy producers that are strongly rooted in the commercial logic while increasingly facing a social standard's obligations as part of a new social logic. The findings indicate that producers, in fact, pursue decoupling and compromising strategies, and the strategy choice depends on whether the conflict between the commercial and social goals is present or not, and on the stage of exposure to the social standard.

Table 3: Summary of the logistic regression analysis results in study B

H	Description	p-value	Remark
1 +	High performance relative to the goals of the commercial logic is negatively related to compliance with the obligations of the social logic (i.e., decoupling strategy).	$p < .01$ (Model: $p < .01$)	-
2 +	The higher the performance improvements against the goals of the commercial logic, the greater is the compliance with the obligations of the social logic (i.e., compromising strategy).	$p < .05$ (Model: $p < .01$)	-
3 +	The higher the extent of exposure to the social logic, the clearer is the pattern of choosing a decoupling or compromising strategy to manage the conflicting objectives of the commercial and the social logic.	$p < .05$ $p < .1$ (Models: $p < .01$)	Model that tests the decoupling strategy may suffer from lack of fit

+ Hypothesis is confirmed.

Garment producers decouple standard adoption and implementation when the conflict between the competing logics' objectives unearths and they balance the objectives of the competing logics by meeting the working time requirements when the conflict eases. These observations support Smith and Lewis' (2011) suggestion that tensions between contending objectives come at different intensities under different conditions, implying that different strategies can be pursued in response to these tensions. Further, growing exposure to a new logic leads to isomorphic strategic behavior over time, which can be described as settlement (Helms, Oliver, Webb, 2012).

This study offers one practical implication for buyers on the one hand, and policy makers and social standard setters on the other hand. First, the buyers' agreement with suppliers following the decoupling strategy indicates that buyers do not seem to "walk the talk" as they keep being associated with and keep purchasing from suppliers violating social obligations. This inhibits suppliers' motivation to live up to social standard's requirements, and buyers shall consider assuring that purchasing decisions reflect the demands imposed on suppliers. So, if social standard compliance was one of the demands imposed on suppliers, they shall reward suppliers for meeting this objective (i.e., placing orders), and they shall sanction suppliers for not fulfilling this criterion (i.e., withdrawing orders). Second, policy makers and social standard setters are ill-advised to focus their attention solely on suppliers to improve working conditions at the production sites in emerging markets. By addressing the sourcing practices of buyers towards a greater and more thorough application of social standards, they gain leverage to influence the suppliers' upholding of social objectives.

3.4 Study C: Socially responsible supplier selection and development for supplier social standard compliance: an effectiveness analysis

Research approach
Compensation, working hours and health and safety are the most often violated labor aspects (Anner, 2012; Egels-Zandén, Lindholm, 2015; Locke, Amengual, Mangela, 2009), and supplier selection and development are put forward to positively influence compliance with social issues at suppliers' facilities (Carter, Easton, 2011; Parmigiani et al., 2011). Study C aimed to link these observations and investigate *how socially responsible supplier selection and development influence emerging economy suppliers to comply with the requirements on working time, compensation, and health and safety.*

Hypotheses 1 and 2 predict that socially responsible supplier selection has a stronger positive effect than development on supplier social standard compliance with working time and remuneration requirements. Hypothesis 3 suggests that socially responsible development has a stronger positive effect than selection on supplier social standard compliance with health and safety obligations. Hypothesis 4 anticipates that buyer long-term orientation moderates the effect of socially responsible supplier development on supplier social standard compliance with the three social issues.

The sample was obtained from a research project with 42 buyers that agreed to provide information on their supply relationships and to participate in a subsequent survey on these supply arrangements. Accordingly, supplier data is obtained from BSCI social audit reports and buyer data is collected through a survey. Potential concerns for sample bias were tested for which no evidence was found. Supplier compliance with working hours, remuneration, and health and safety obligations constitute the dependent variables of this study. Since the sampled suppliers were rated either 'good' or 'non-compliant' on compliance with working time and compensation requirements, these variables are binary coded and analyzed through a logistic regression analysis. The sampled suppliers' compliance with health and safety obligations fell into the three categories 'good', 'improvement needed' and 'non-compliant', implying that this variable is categorical for which a multinomial logistic regression is employed. 88 questionnaires from 18 buyers were eligible for analysis.

Socially responsible supplier selection and development serve as independent variables of this investigation. Supplier country, supplier industry, supplier dependability, buyer country, buyer long-term orientation, buyer dependability and auditing company constitute the control variables which were partly obtained from BSCI social audit reports and partly from the buyer survey. All items assessed in the buyer survey were adopted or adapted from previous studies. Key respondent, nonresponse and common method bias were tested, none of which was of concern.

Findings and contributions

This study was first to empirically assess the effect of socially responsible supplier selection and development on suppliers' compliance with working time, remuneration, and health and safety obligations by utilizing buyer and supplier data. The logistic and multinomial regression analyses provide full support for Hypothesis 1 and Hypothesis 2, and partial support for Hypothesis 4 while Hypothesis 3 is not confirmed. **Table 4** shows the results of the logistic and multinomial logistic regression analyses.

The results support previous arguments for the crucial role of supplier selection to safeguard suppliers' compliance with social aspects (e.g., Carter, Easton, 2011; Parmigiani et al., 2011). The findings also complement the conceptual (e.g., Yawar, Seuring, 2017) and exploratory studies (e.g., Klassen, Vereecke, 2012) putting forward that supplier development is important for the upholding of social aspects in supply chains by demonstrating that this practice unfolds its influence on compliance with working time obligations when buyers consider the supply relationship as a long-term arrangement. Unexpectedly, no direct of influence of supplier development on the three social issues was observed.

Table 4: Summary of the logistic and multinomial regression analysis results in study C

H	Description	p-value	Remark
1 +	Socially responsible supplier selection has a stronger positive influence than socially responsible supplier development on a supplier complying with a social standard's requirements on working hours.	$p < .1$* (Model: $p < .05$)	Socially responsible supplier development is not significant
2 +	Socially responsible supplier selection has a stronger positive influence than socially responsible supplier development on a supplier complying with a social standard's requirements on compensation.	$p < .01$* (Model: $p < .01$)	Socially responsible supplier development is not significant
3	Socially responsible supplier selection has a weaker positive influence than socially responsible supplier development on a supplier complying with a social standard's requirements on health and safety.	$p < .1$* (Model: $p < .05$))	Socially responsible supplier development is not significant; socially responsible supplier selection is only significant for 'improvement needed' with 'non-compliant' as reference category
4 (+)	Buyer long-term orientation positively moderates the influence of socially responsible supplier development on a supplier complying with a social standard's requirements on working time, compensation, and health and safety.	$p < .1$ (Model: $p < .05$)	Moderation effect is only significant for compliance with working time obligations; model may suffer from lack of fit

+ Hypothesis is confirmed; (+) Hypothesis is partially confirmed; * Significance level of socially responsible supplier selection.

The results equip purchasing managers with two individual implications, and practitioners at buying firms, social standard setters and policy makers with one implication. First, the findings support buyers to devote their available resources to supplier management practices, which allow them to safeguard that their suppliers live up to or at least do not violate the three most critical social issues. Second, the results aid purchasing managers to adjust their take on supply relationships as buyer long-term orientation is positively related with both the socially responsible supplier management practices and the supplier social compliance outcomes on working time and compensation. Third, the observations on the effect of socially responsible supplier development on supplier compliance with the three social aspects may trigger buyers, policy makers and social standard setters to reconsider their approach on developing emerging market suppliers on social issues.

4 Conclusion of the research on supplier social standard (non-)compliance

4.1 Practical implications

This research addresses the behavioral aspects that affect emerging market suppliers to amend their social standard compliance. The findings imply that the producers' social standard compliance converges to a common level below full compliance with the social standard. Hence, suppliers are able to improve their social standard compliance level but they are unlikely to fully comply with the social obligations over time. Despite that, buyers, policy makers and social standard setters may notice that emerging market producers can achieve full compliance with a social standard relatively quickly. This suggests that the focus shall be to incentivize the above average performers to achieve full compliance as well as the compliant producers to maintain their performance level; since the orientation towards peers is strong, the average supplier social standard compliance is likely to increase.

This thesis draws attention to the the emerging market suppliers' conflict between generating sales turnover whilst complying with a social standard's requirements on working hours. The results signal that emerging market producers are rather guided by commercial objectives than by social obligations in the long run. This implies that buyers shall place the same relevance on social standard compliance as on price, quality and delivery in purchasing decisions, instead of regarding the demand for adequate labor conditions as lip service. Policy makers and social standard setters can enforce the upholding of labor conditions at the production sites in emerging markets by leveraging their influence on buyers to alter purchasing practices towards consistent attention to social issues.

This research further focuses on the effect of supplier management practices on supplier compliance with the three most often violated social issues: working hours, compensation, and health and safety. The results may lead buyers to place more emphasis on socially responsible supplier selection but the implications are more nuanced. On the one hand, the buyer long-term orientation influences socially responsible supplier management practices as well as supplier social standard compliance with working hours and pay requirements. On the other hand, the limited influence of socially responsible supplier development on the upholding of social issues at the production sites in emerging markets challenges the existing development approaches. This is further supported by the limited progress reported by remediation programs (e.g., the Accord on Fire and Building Safety in Bangladesh, 2016). Accordingly, buyers, social standard setters and policy makers may build on these observations to review their development approaches aiming to improve the upholding of labor issues at production sites in emerging markets.

4.2 Theoretical contributions

This thesis seeks to illuminate the determinants of supplier social standard (non-)compliance by adopting the suppliers' and buyers' perspectives and it aims to provide three contributions to advance the limited knowledge on social issues in sustainable supply chain management research.

Previous research on social issues in supply chains has mainly concentrated on the buyer as the unit of analysis, paying limited attention to the supplier (Müller, Stölzle, 2015). As a result, this thesis utilizes the aspiration-driven behavior, as a notion of the behavioral theory of the firm, to study emerging economy producers' compliance adjustments with an externally imposed social standard attributed to historical and social aspirations over time. The results suggest that the behavioral theory of the firm is not only applicable to economic objectives of developed country firms but also to social aims of emerging economy producers. In addition, the findings confute the long-standing assumption of the behavioral theory of the firm that organizational aspirations parallel each other in influencing performance amendments by indicating that historical and social aspirations rather work in sequence to influence compliance adjustments with a social standard.

Sustainable supply chain management research takes congruence between the sustainability dimensions for granted (Carter, Easton, 2011; Pagell, Shevchenko, 2014) although the sustainability management literature emphasizes the tensions between the dimensions of sustainability (Hahn, Pinkse, Preuss, Figge, 2015). Following Matthews, Power, Touboulic and Marques (2016) who suggest to focus on the tensions to advance sustainable supply chain management research, this thesis builds on the institutional logics perspective and assesses how emerging market suppliers respond to conflicting objectives of the commercial and the social logic. The results indicate that with growing exposure to a social standard, producers follow decoupling and compromising strategies, and that the intensity of the tension as well as the extent of exposure to the social standard define the strategic response. These findings deepen the understanding of the institutional logics' perspective by providing evidence for the compromising strategy, by outlining the conditions under which decoupling and compromising strategies are pursued, and by illustrating the hybridization process of emerging economy producers.

Previous research recommends to investigate the social performance of suppliers along with the influence of buyers by collecting data at multiple levels (Beske-Janssen et al., 2015; Müller, Stölzle, 2015). Hence, this thesis draws on the resource-based view to examine the effective influence of socially responsible supplier selection and development on supplier social standard compliance with the three most often violated social aspects by analyzing buyer and supplier data. The findings validate socially responsible supplier selection as a key capability to ensure suppliers' compliance with working time and compensation obligations, and to prohibit suppliers' from violating health and safety requirements, reinforcing earlier propositions for the growing importance of supplier selection to ensure suppliers' compliance with social issues (e.g., Carter, Easton, 2011; Parmigiani et al., 2011). The results also fuel the debate on the influence of supplier development on the upholding of social aspects in supply chains (e.g., Klassen, Vereecke, 2012; Yawar, Seuring, 2017), indicating that the direct influence of socially responsible supplier development may be lesser than expected, and that its influence depends on the long-term orientation of a buyer in a supply relationship.

4.3 Selected limitations and directions for future research

This thesis focuses on working conditions as process-related labor issues that appear to be the main social issues in supply chains (Yawar, Seuring, 2017). Thereby, it excludes philanthropic (e.g., community development) and other business-related aspects (e.g., product safety) that also fall under a broader definition of social issues in supply chains (Homburg, Stierl, Bornemann, 2013). Hence, future studies may investigate how labor issues and product safety aspects relate to each other, and how advances to the upholding of one of these social issues spills over to the other.

Social audit reports provide the basis to assess social standard (non-)compliance of emerging economy producers but audits are subject to various criticism (e.g., Egels-Zandén, 2007; Egels-Zandén, 2014; Egels-Zandén, Lindholm, 2015; Short et al., 2016). Despite the criticism, social standards have become a widely applied vehicle to address social issues at production sites (Anner, 2012; Müller, Stölzle, 2015). This research ends with the assessment of compliance with an internationally recognized labor standard and the results challenge the observations made by Jayasinghe (2016) for a different labor standard. Hence, future research may explore how the configuration of different social standards shape the tension between commercial objectives and social obligations for emerging economy producers across countries.

This research focuses on the buyer-supplier dyad since buyers draw their attention and resources to address social issues at direct suppliers' sites, and these suppliers often do not live up to the social requirements (Jiang, 2009). Since social standards have started to extend the focus beyond direct suppliers (BSCI, 2014), the growing number of studies that focus on sustainability in multi-tier supply chains (e.g., Grimm, Hofstetter; Sarkis, 2014; Grimm, Hofstetter, Sarkis, 2016; Wilhelm, Blome, Bhakoo, Paulraj, 2016) may build on the results of this thesis to investigate the upholding of social issues in supply chains beyond first-tier suppliers.

Since study A and study B focus solely on the garment industry, and 85% of the sample of study C relates to clothing and textile producers, this research is biased towards the garment industry, in which production is largely located in emerging economies. While this is resonates with other studies that build on social audit data (e.g., Jayasinghe, 2016; Short et al., 2016; Young, Makhija, 2014), it limits the generalizability of the findings. Accordingly, future examinations may investigate the particularities of social standard (non-)compliance in more balanced multiple-industry studies.

References

Andersen, M.; Skjoett-Larsen, T. (2009): Corporate social responsibility in global supply chains, in: Supply Chain Management: An International Journal, 14, 75–86.

Anner, M. (2012): Corporate social responsibility and freedom of association rights: The precarious quest for legitimacy and control in global supply chains, in: Politics & Society, 40, 609–644.

Aravind, D.; Christmann, P. (2011): Decoupling of standard implementation from certification: Does quality of ISO 14001 implementation affect facilities' environmental performance?, in: Business Ethics Quarterly, 21, 73–102.

Awaysheh, A.; Klassen, R. D. (2010): The impact of supply chain structure on the use of supplier socially responsible practices, in: International Journal of Operations and Production Management, 30, 1246–1268.

Bartley, T. (2007): Institutional emergence in an era of globalization: The rise of transnational private regulation of labor and environmental conditions, in: American Journal of Sociology, 113, 297–351.

Baum, J. A. C.; Dahlin, K. B. (2007): Aspiration performance and railroads' patterns of learning from train wrecks and crashes, in: Organization Science, 18, 368–285.

Beske-Janssen, P.; Johnson, M. P.; Schaltegger, S. (2015): 20 years of performance measurement in sustainable supply chain management – what has been achieved?, in: Supply Chain Management: An International Journal, 20, 664–680.

Beske, P.; Seuring, S. (2014): Putting sustainability into supply chain management, in: Supply Chain Management: An International Journal, 19, 322–331.

Bloom, N.; Kretschmer, T.; Reenen, J. van (2011): Are family-friendly workplace practices a valuable firm resource. in: Strategic Management Journal, 32, 343–367.

Buckley, P. J.; Strange, R. (2015): The governance of the global factory: Location and control of world economic activity, in: Academy of Management Perspectives, 29, 237–249.

Business Social Compliance Initiative (2009): Code of conduct. Available at: http://www.bsci-intl.org/resources/code-of-conduct (accessed: 5 January 2014).

Business Social Compliance Initiative (2014): Annual report 2013. Available at: http://www.fta-intl.org/sites/default/files/bsci-2014-05-26-annual_report_2013-uk-a4-mai_2014-def-internet.pdf (accessed: 19 June 2016).

Carter, C. R.; Easton, P. L. (2011): Sustainable supply chain management: Evolution and future directions, in: International Journal of Physical Distribution & Logistics Management, 41, 46–62

Christmann, P.; Taylor, G. (2006): Firm self-regulation through international certifiable standards: Determinants of symbolic versus substantive implementation, in: Journal of International Business Studies, 6, 863–878.

Darnall, N.; Sides, S. (2008): Assessing the performance of voluntary environmental programs: Does certification matter?, in: The Policy Studies Journal, 36, 95–117.

Distelhorst, G.; Locke, R. M.; Pal, T.; Samel, H. (2015): Production goes global, compliance stays local: Private regulation in the global electronics industry, in: Regulation & Governance, 9, 224–242.

Dyllick, T.; Hockerts, K. (2002): Beyond the business case for corporate sustainability, in: Business Strategy and the Environment, 11, 130–141.

Egels-Zandén, N. (2014): Revisiting supplier compliance with MNC codes of conduct: Recoupling policy and practice at Chinese toy suppliers, in: Journal of Business Ethics, 119, 59–75.

Egels-Zandén, N.; Lindholm, H. (2015): Do codes of conduct improve worker rights in supply chains? A study of Fair Wear Foundation, in: Journal of Cleaner Production, 107, 31–40.

Ehrgott, M.; Reimann, F.; Kaufmann, L.; Carter, C. R. (2011): Social sustainability in selecting emerging economy suppliers, in: Journal of Business Ethics, 98, 99–119.

Elkington, J. (1998) Cannibals with forks: The triple bottom line of the 21st century. Stoney Creek: New Society Publishers.

Foerstl, K.; Reuter, C.; Hartmann, E.; Blome, C. (2010): Managing supplier sustainability risks in a dynamically changing environment – Sustainable supplier management in the chemical industry, in: Journal of Purchasing & Supply Management, 16, 118–130.

Fransen, L. (2011): Why do private governance organizations not converge? A political-institutional analysis of transnational labor standards regulation, in: Governance: An International Journal of Policy, Administration, and Institutions, 24, 359–387.

Gereffi G.; Lee, J. (2012): Why the world suddenly cares about global supply chains, in: Journal of Supply Chain Management, 48, 24–32.

Greve H. R. (2003): A behavioral theory of R&D expenditures and innovations: Evidence from shipbuilding, in: Academy of Management Journal, 46, 685–702.

Grimm, J. H.; Hofstetter, J. S.; Sarkis, J. (2014): Critical success factors for sub-supplier management: A sustainable food supply chain perspective, in: International Journal of Production Economics, 152, 159–173.

Grimm, J. H.; Hofstetter, J. S.; Sarkis, J. (2016): Exploring sub-suppliers' compliance with corporate sustainability standards, in: Journal of Cleaner Production, 112, 1971–1984.

Gualandris, J.; Klassen, R. D.; Vachon, S.; Kalchschmidt, M. (2015): Sustainable evaluation and verification in supply chains: Aligning and leveraging accountability to stakeholders, in: Journal of Operations Management, 38, 1–13.

Guler, I.; Guillén, M. F.; Macpherson, J. M. (2002): Global competition, institutions, and the diffusion of organizational practice: The international spread of ISO 9000 quality certificates, in: Administrative Science Quarterly, 47, 207–232.

Hahn, T.; Pinkse, J.; Preuss, L.; Figge, F. (2015): Tensions in corporate sustainability. Towards an integrative framework, in: Journal of Business Ethics, 127, 297–316.

Harms, D.; Hansen, E. G.; Schaltegger, S. (2013): Strategies in sustainable supply chain management: An empirical investigation of large German companies, in: Corporate Social Responsibility and Environmental Management, 20, 205–218.

Helms, W. S.; Oliver, C.; Webb, K. (2012): Antecedents of settlement on a new institutional practice: Negotiation of the ISO 26000 standard on social responsibility. Academy of Management Journal, 55, 1120–1145.

Harris J.; Bromiley P. (2007): Incentives to cheat: The influence of executive compensation and firm performance on financial misrepresentation, in: Organization Science, 18, 350–367.

Hofmann, E. (2011): Risk management in international supply chains: The case of natural hedging, in: Die Unternehmung, 65, 155–192.

Homburg, C.; Stierl, M.; Bornemann, T. (2013): Corporate social responsibility in business-to-business markets: How organizational customers account for supplier corporate social responsibility engagement, in: Journal of Marketing, 77, 54–72.

Jayasinghe, M. (2016): The operational and signaling benefits of voluntary labor code adoption: Reconceptualizing the scope of human resource management in emerging economies, in: Academy of Management Journal, 59, 658–677.

Jiang, B. (2009): Implementing supplier codes of conduct in global supply chains: Process explanations from theoretic and empirical perspectives, in: Journal of Business Ethics, 85, 77–92.

Jiang, B.; Baker, R. C.; Frazier, G. V. (2009): An analysis of job dissatisfaction and turnover to reduce global supply chain risk. Evidence from China, in: Journal of Operations Management, 27, 169–84.

King A. A.; Lenox, M. J. (2001): Lean and green? An empirical examination of the relationship between lean production and environmental performance, in: Production and Operations Management, 10, 244–256.

King A. A.; Lenox, M. J.; Terlaak, A. (2005): The strategic use of decentralized institutions: Exploring certification with the ISO 14001 management standard, in: Academy of Management Journal, 48, 1091–1106.

Klassen, R. D.; Vereecke, A. (2012): Social issues in supply chains: Capabilities link responsibility, risk (opportunity), and performance, in: International Journal of Production Economics, 140, 103–115.

Kortelainen, K. (2008): Global supply chains and social requirements: Case studies of labour condition auditing in the People's Republic of China, in: Business Strategy and the Environment, 17, 431–443

Kudla, N. L.; Klaas-Wissing, T. (2012): Sustainability in shipper-logistics service provider relationships. A tentative taxonomy based on agency theory and stimulus-response analysis, in: Journal of Purchasing & Supply Management, 18, 218–231.

Kudla, N.; Stölzle, W. (2011): Sustainability supply chain management research: A structured literature review, in: Die Unternehmung, 65, 261–300.

Lee, K. H.; Kim, J. W. (2009): Current status of CSR in the realm of supply management: The case of the Korean electronics industry, in: Supply Chain Management: An International Journal, 14, 138–148.

Locke, R.; Amengual, M.; Mangela, A. (2009): Virtue out of necessity? Compliance, commitment, and the improvement of labor conditions in global supply chains, in: Politics & Society, 37, 319–351.

Locke, R. M.; Qin, F.; Brause, A. (2007): Does monitoring improve labor standards? Lessons from Nike, in: Industrial and Labor Relations Review, 61, 3–31.

Locke, R. M.; Rissing, B. A.; Pal, T. (2013): Complements or substitutes? Private codes, state regulation and the enforcement of labour standards in global supply chains, in: British Journal of Industrial Relations, 51, 519–552.

Mamic, I. (2005): Managing global supply chain: The sports footwear, apparel and retail sectors, in: Journal of Business Ethics, 59, 81–100.

Matthews, L.; Power, D.; Touboulic, A.; Marques, L. (2016): Building bridges: Toward alternative theory of sustainable supply chain management, in: Journal of Supply Chain Management, 52, 82–94.

Mishina, Y.; Dykes, B. J.; Block, E. S.; Pollock, T. G. (2010): Why "good" firms do bad things: The effects of high aspirations, high expectation, and prominence on the incidence of corporate illegality, in: Academy of Management Journal, 53, 701–722.

Muller, C.; Vermeulen, W. J. V.; Glasbergen, P. (2012): Pushing or sharing as value-driven strategies for societal change in global supply chains: Two case studies in the British-South African fresh fruit supply chain, in: Business Strategy and the Environment, 21, 127–140.

Müller, M. (2016): Supplier Social Standard (Non-)Compliance: A Multi-Perspective Approach Focusing on Emerging Economies. Nürnberg: KDD Kompetenzzentrum Digital Druck.

Müller, M.; Stölzle, W. (2015): Socially responsible supply chains: A distinct avenue for future research. In: Bogaschewsky, R.; Essig, M.; Lasch, R.; Stölzle, W. (Eds.), Supply Management Research: Aktuelle Forschungsergebnisse 2015, 121–151, Wiesbaden: Springer Gabler.

O'Rourke, D. (2003): Outsourcing regulation. Analyzing nongovernmental systems of labor standards and monitoring, in: The Policy Studies Journal, 31, 1–29.

O'Rourke, D. (2006): Multi-stakeholder regulation: Privatizing or socializing global labor standards, in: World Development, 34, 899–918.

Pagell, M.; Shevchenko, A. (2014): Why research in sustainable supply chain management should have no future, in: Journal of Supply Chain Management, 50, 44–55.

Pagell, M.; Wu, Z. (2009): Building a more complete theory of sustainable supply chain management using case studies of 10 exemplars, in: Journal of Supply Chain Management, 45, 37–56.

Parmigiani, A.; Klassen, R. D.; Russo, M. V. (2011): Efficiency meets accountability: Performance implications of supply chain configuration, control and capabilities, in: Journal of Operations Management, 29, 212–223.

Pedersen, E. R.; Andersen, M. (2006): Safeguarding corporate social responsibility (CSR) in global supply chains: how codes of conduct are managed in buyer-supplier relationships, in: Journal of Public Affairs, 6, 228–240.

Perry, P.; Towers, N. (2013): Conceptual framework development: CSR implementation in fashion supply chains, in: International Journal of Physical Distribution and Logistics Management, 43, 478–500.

Peters, N. J.; Hofstetter, J. S.; Hoffmann, V. (2011): Institutional entrepreneurship capabilities for interorganizational sustainable supply chain strategies, in: International Journal of Logistics Management, 22, 52–86.

Reinecke, J.; Ansari, S. (2015): When times collide: Temporal brokerage at the intersection of markets and developments, in: Academy of Management Journal, 58, 618–648.

Reinecke, J.; Manning, S.; Hagen, O. von (2012): The emergence of a standards market: Multiplicity of sustainability standards in the global coffee industry, in: Organization Science, 33, 791–814.

Reuter, C.; Foerstl, K.; Hartmann, E.; Blome, C. (2010): Sustainable global supplier management: The role of dynamic capabilities in achieving competitive advantage, in: Journal of Supply Chain Management, 46, 45–63.

Schaltegger, S.; Beckmann, M.; Hansen, E. G. (2013): Transdisciplinarity in corporate sustainability: Mapping the field, in: Business Strategy and the Environment, 22, 219–229.

Short, J. L.; Toffel, M. W.; Hugill, A. R. (2016): Monitoring global supply chains, in: Strategic Management Journal, 37, 1878–1897.

Smith, W. K.; Lewis, M. W. (2011): Toward a theory of paradox: A dynamic equilibrium model of organizing, in: Academy of Management Review, 36, 381–403.

Terlaak, A. (2007): Order without law: The role of certified management standards in shaping socially desired firm behaviors, in: Academy of Management Review, 32, 968–985.

The Accord on Fire and Building Safety in Bangladesh (2016): Update April 2016. Available at: http://bangladeshaccord.org/wp-content/uploads/Accord-Progress-Factsheet-April-2016.pdf (accessed: 10 May 2016).

Toffel, M. W.; Short, J. L.; Ouellet, M. (2015): Codes in context: How states, markets, and civil society shape adherence to global labor standards, in: Regulation & Governance, 9, 205–223.

Touboulic, A.; Walker, H. (2015): Theories in sustainable supply chain management: A structured literature review, in: International Journal of Physical Distribution and Logistics Management, 45, 16–42.

Vogel, D. (2010): The private regulation of global corporate conduct, in: Business & Society, 49, 68–87.

Walker, H.; Seuring, S.; Sarkis, J.; Klassen, R. D. (2014): Sustainable operations management: Recent trends and future directions, in: International Journal of Operations & Production Management. 34, guest editorial.

Wilhelm, M.; Blome, C.; Bhakoo V.; Paulraj, A. (2016): Sustainability in multi-tier supply chains: Understanding the double agency role of the first-tier supplier, in: Journal of Operations Management, 41, 42–60.

Yawar, S. A.; Seuring, S. (2017): Management of social issues in supply chains: A literature review exploring social issues, actions and performance outcomes, in: Journal of Business Ethics, 141, 621–643.

Young, S. L.; Makhika, M. V. (2014): Firms corporate social responsibility behavior: An integration of institutional and profit maximization approaches, in: Journal of International Business Studies, 45, 670–698.

Zadek, S. (2004): The path to corporate social responsibility, in: Harvard Business Review, 82, 125–132.

Qualitätsmanagement mit Lieferanten in Schwellenländern - Zusammenspiel aus Einkaufspraktiken und „kognitiven Karten"

Tobias Kosmol

Abstract

Ein Großteil der bestehenden Managementforschung zu dem Zusammenhang zwischen Einkaufspraktiken und Unternehmenserfolg basiert auf der Nettoeffekt-Annahme, dass spezifische Praktiken unabhängig voneinander Ergebnisse beeinflussen. Die vorliegende Studie stellt diese Kernannahme infrage, indem sie eine *neo-konfigurative Perspektive* einnimmt und untersucht, wie verschiedene Kombinationen von Faktoren (sogenannte Konfigurationen) Ergebnisse bewirken. Eine weitere Limitation bestehender Studien zu dem Zusammenhang zwischen Einkaufspraktiken und Unternehmenserfolg ist der enge Fokus auf Einkaufspraktiken. Neuere verhaltenswissenschaftliche Beschaffungsmanagement-Forschung hat herausgefunden, dass das Verhalten von Managern entscheidend durch *kognitive Karten* beeinflusst wird, d.h. Filter, durch die Manager Informationen aus ihrer Umwelt wahrnehmen, vereinfachen und interpretieren. Mit Fokus auf die Lieferqualität untersucht diese Studie, wie *Konfigurationen* verschiedener Lieferantenqualitätsmanagement(LQM)-Praktiken und LQM-bezogener kognitiver Karten Unternehmen helfen, ihre Lieferqualität zu managen. Methodisch nutzt diese Studie *fuzzy-set qualitative comparative analysis (fsQCA)*, um LQM-Konfigurationen zu identifizieren, und einen *kognitiv-linguistischen Ansatz* für die computergestützte Textanalyse der kognitiven Karten von Einkaufsmanagern. Im Kontext der Beschaffung westlicher Unternehmen von chinesischen Lieferanten identifiziert die konfigurative fsQCA Analyse vier verschiedene Konfigurationen beim Überwinden von Barrieren für das LQM in Schwellenländern. LQM-bezogene kognitive Karten erweisen sich als ein Kernelement in diesen vier Konfigurationen. Diese Zusammenfassung basiert auf einem Artikel, der im *Journal of Purchasing and Supply Management* erschienen ist (Kosmol et al., 2017), und ist sowohl für die Wissenschaft wie auch für die Praxis bestimmt.

Wissenschaftliche Forschungsbeiträge

1 Einleitung

Die empirische Beschaffungsmanagement-Forschung zeigt positive Zusammenhänge zwischen spezifischen Einkaufspraktiken und dem Erfolg einkaufender Unternehmen (Foerstl et al., 2016; Zimmermann, Foerstl, 2014). Obwohl diese Forschung zu einem besseren Verständnis des Zusammenhangs zwischen Einkaufspraktiken und Unternehmenserfolg beigetragen hat, ist das Verständnis vom *Zusammenspiel* verschiedener Einkaufspraktiken aktuell begrenzt. Ein Grund hierfür ist, dass ein Großteil der bestehenden Forschung auf der Annahme von *Nettoeffekten* basiert (Misangyi et al., 2017), d.h., dass spezifische Einkaufspraktiken *unabhängig voneinander* Ergebnisse beeinflussen. Die vorliegende Studie stellt diese Kernannahme infrage, indem sie eine *neo-konfigurative Perspektive* (Misangyi et al., 2017) einnimmt. Die *neo-konfigurative Perspektive* wurde kürzlich in der Managementliteratur als eine effektive theoretische Perspektive eingeführt, um bis dahin mehrdeutige Ergebnisse in Situationen mit komplexen Kausalzusammenhänge zu erklären (Greckhamer et al., 2008). Indem sie das Zusammenspiel („*co-alignment*") oder die Passung („fit") zwischen mehreren Faktoren berücksichtigt, untersucht eine *neo-konfigurative Perspektive*, wie verschiedene Kombinationen von Faktoren (sogenannte Konfigurationen) Ergebnisse bewirken. Diese Perspektive legt nahe, dass verschiedene Kombinationen von Einkaufspraktiken – anstatt der Summe der Nettoeffekte einzelner Einkaufspraktiken – die Gesamtwirksamkeit von Beschaffungsstrategien beeinflussen.

Eine zweite Limitation bestehender Forschung zum Zusammenhang zwischen Einkaufspraktiken und Unternehmenserfolg ist der alleinige Fokus auf die Einkaufspraktiken selbst (Schorsch et al., 2017). Als wesentliche erklärende Variablen für den unterschiedlichen Erfolg von Lieferketten werden die beobachtbaren und handlungsorientierten Einkaufspraktiken angenommen, jedoch haben Forscher andere Faktoren vernachlässigt, die zusammen mit Einkaufspraktiken den Erfolg von Lieferketten beeinflussen könnten. Immer mehr Forschungsergebnisse des verhaltenswissenschaftlichen Beschaffungsmanagements (z.B. Eckerd et al., 2016; Kaufmann et al., 2017; Stanczyk et al., 2015) verweisen auf die Notwendigkeit, die traditionelle Perspektive (mit Fokus auf Handlungen und Praktiken) zu ergänzen durch eine Betrachtung der Kognition von Managern – wie Manager denken, ihre Umwelt verstehen und Entscheidungen treffen (Maitland, Sammartino, 2015b). Neuere Erkenntnisse über die Kognition von Managern zeigen, dass das Verhalten von Managern insbesondere von sogenannten *kognitiven Karten* beeinflusst wird, d.h. Filtern, durch die Manager Informationen aus ihrer Umwelt wahrnehmen, vereinfachen und interpretieren (Maitland, Sammartino, 2015a). In Anbetracht aktueller Forschungserkenntnisse ist daher die Ausgangsvermutung dieser Arbeit, dass kognitive Karten – zusammen mit Einkaufspraktiken – einen entscheidenden Faktor in den Konfigurationen für erfolgreiche Lieferketten darstellen.

Dieser Beitrag fokussiert speziell auf *Qualität* als eine kritische Erfolgskomponente. Der Qualitätsaspekt bietet sich für empirische Untersuchungen an, weil er gut und unmittelbar beobachtbar ist, z.B. in der Form von Qualitätsproblemen. Empirische Studien haben gezeigt, dass *individuelle* Lieferantenqualitätsmanagement(LQM)-Praktiken, wie z.B. Lieferantenentwicklung oder Lieferantenintegration, einen positiven Nettoeffekt auf die Lieferqualität haben können (Kaynak, Hartley, 2008; Soares et al., 2017). LQM-Praktiken werden hier definiert als „verschiedene Beschaffungsmanagement-Prozesse für die Reduktion des Auftretens und der Auswirkungen von Lieferausfällen aufgrund von Qualitätsproblemen" (Zsidisin et al., 2016, S. 909). Bestehende Forschung zum Zusammenhang zwischen LQM-Praktiken und Lieferqualität unterliegt den gleichen einschränkenden Annahmen, wie oben für den Zusammenhang zwischen Einkaufspraktiken und Unternehmenserfolg beschrieben: Die gemeinsame Wirkung verschiedener Praktiken wurde selten untersucht und es ist wenig über das Zusammenspiel zwischen Einkaufspraktiken und kognitiven Faktoren bekannt.

In Anbetracht dieser Limitationen sucht die vorliegende Studie Antworten auf folgende Forschungsfrage: *Wie helfen Konfigurationen verschiedener LQM-Praktiken und LQM-bezogener kognitiver Karten einkaufenden Unternehmen, ihre Lieferqualität zu managen?* Um diese Frage zu beantworten, wurde eine umfassende qualitative Studie zum LQM von 17 westlichen Produktionsunternehmen und ihren chinesischen Lieferanten durchgeführt. Die resultierende dyadische Datenbasis besteht aus 89 ausführlichen Interviews, ergänzt durch Dokumente und Beobachtungen. Um Konfigurationen von LQM-Praktiken und LQM-bezogenen kognitiven Karten zu untersuchen, wird *fuzzy-set qualitative comparative analysis (fsQCA)* (Ragin, 2008) angewandt. FsQCA ist eine konfigurative Methode, die analysiert, wie verschiedene Kombinationen von Faktoren (d.h. Konfigurationen) zu einem Ergebnis führen (Karatzas et al., 2016; Ragin, 2008) – sehr vereinfachend kann man sie als Clusteranalyse-ähnlich bezeichnen. Dieser methodische Ansatz ist folglich besonders geeignet für die vorliegende Studie, weil er hilft, besser zu verstehen, wie LQM-Praktiken und LQM-bezogene kognitive Karten als Konfigurationen zusammenarbeiten. Weil die empirische Untersuchung der Kognition von Managern herausfordernd ist (Maitland, Sammartino, 2015b), nutzt diese Studie ferner einen *kognitiv-linguistischen Ansatz* mittels computergestützter Textanalyse, um Erkenntnisse über die kognitiven Karten von Einkaufsmanagern zu gewinnen. Ein *kognitiv-linguistischer Ansatz* basiert darauf, dass subtile Unterschiede in der Sprache Unterschiede in der Kognition widerspiegeln (Pennebaker et al., 2001). In Summe will diese Studie drei theoretische Beiträge leisten:

- Sie fördert eine *neo-konfigurative Perspektive* (Misangyi et al., 2017) für die Beschaffungsmanagement-Forschung, welche die Aufmerksamkeit weg von einem Fokus auf Nettoeffekte individueller Faktoren und hin zu *kombinierten Effekten* mehrerer Faktoren lenkt. Die neuartige fsQCA-Methode erlaubt es, dieses konfigurative Denken in dem Forschungsdesign umzusetzen.

- Die Studie leistet einen Betrag zu der verhaltenswissenschaftlichen Beschaffungsmanagement-Forschung (Eckerd et al., 2016; Kaufmann et al., 2017; Stanczyk et al., 2015), indem sie zeigt, dass Forscher Einkaufspraktiken in Kombination mit kognitiven Faktoren betrachten sollten, wenn sie deren Erfolgseffekte untersuchen.

Wissenschaftliche Forschungsbeiträge

- Die Studie entwickelt eine *„Theorie mittlerer Reichweite"* (*„middle-range theory"*) (Craighead et al., 2016) für das LQM in Schwellenländern, die praxisrelevante Erkenntnisse für ein Phänomen mit hoher empirischer Relevanz liefert (Stanczyk et al., 2017). Theorien mittlerer Reichweite sind mehr kontextbezogen als „große Theorien", wie z.B. der Resource-Based View (Barney, 2012), und können auf spezifische Kontexte praktisch angewandt werden (Craighead et al., 2016). Die hier identifizierten LQM-Konfigurationen geben eine kontextspezifische, aber dennoch kompakte Erklärung für alternative Strategien, die Unternehmen implementieren können, um die Lieferqualität in Schwellenländern erfolgreich zu managen.

Die folgenden Abschnitte präsentieren den theoretischen Hintergrund, die Forschungsmethodik und Ergebnisse. Der Beitrag endet mit einem Fazit und Implikationen für Manager.

2 Theoretischer Hintergrund

2.1 Neo-konfigurative Perspektive

Diese Studie nimmt eine *neo-konfigurative Perspektive* (Misangyi et al., 2017) als theoretische Basis ein, um Konfigurationen von LQM-Praktiken und LQM-bezogenen kognitiven Karten zu identifizieren, die einkaufenden Unternehmen dabei helfen, die Lieferqualität zu managen. Konfiguratives Denken erlangt in der Managementliteratur vermehrt Aufmerksamkeit (z.B. Greckhamer, 2016; Misangyi, Acharya, 2014) und wurde kürzlich in das Forschungsfeld des Beschaffungsmanagements eingeführt (z.B. Timmer, Kaufmann, 2017). Im Kern unterscheidet sich eine neo-konfigurative Perspektive von konventionellen korrelationsbasierten Ansätzen (z.B. multiple Regressionsanalyse) dadurch, dass sie die *kausale Komplexität* berücksichtigt, die durch drei Merkmale gekennzeichnet ist: 1) konjunkte Kausalität, 2) Equifinalität und 3) kausale Asymmetrie (Misangyi et al., 2017).

- *Konjunkte Kausalität* bedeutet, dass Kombinationen voneinander abhängiger Faktoren (anstelle von Nettoeffekten individueller Variablen, wie in korrelationsbasierten Ansätzen) Ergebnisse bewirken (Misangyi et al., 2017). Diese Sichtweise auf Kausalität impliziert, dass Ergebnisse selten eine einzige Ursache haben, sondern die Folge *mehrerer, voneinander abhängiger erklärender Faktoren* sind.

- *Equifinalität* bedeutet, dass mehrere alternative Konfigurationen zu demselben Ergebnis führen können (Ragin, 2008). Während konventionelle korrelationsbasierte Ansätze (z.B. multiple Regressionsanalyse) Equifinalität nicht berücksichtigen (Vis, 2012), erlaubt eine neo-konfigurative Perspektive explizit *mehrere Weg zu einem bestimmten Ergebnis*.

- *Kausale Asymmetrie* bedeutet, dass Faktoren, die in einer Konfiguration einen positiven Effekt auf das Ergebnis haben, in einer anderen Konfiguration keinen oder einen umgekehrten Effekt haben können (Misangyi et al., 2017). Daher *kann sowohl die Anwesenheit als auch die Abwesenheit eines erklärenden Faktors dasselbe Ergebnis hervorbringen*, je nachdem, in welcher Kombination mit anderen Faktoren er auftritt.

Eine neo-konfigurative Perspektive (Misangyi et al., 2017) einnehmend, entwickelt dieser Beitrag ein konzeptionelles Modell, das wesentliche Faktoren des LQM beinhaltet, die einen Effekt auf die Lieferqualität bei der Beschaffung in Schwellenländern vermuten lassen (siehe **Abbildung 1**). Weil die fsQCA-Methode die Anzahl erklärender Faktoren begrenzt, die in die Analyse einbezogen werden können, muss sich dieses konzeptionelle Modell auf die wesentlichsten erklärenden Faktoren beschränken (Greckhamer, 2016). Folglich kombiniert das Modell drei LQM-Praktiken und zwei LQM-bezogene kognitive Karten als erklärende Faktoren. Das zu untersuchende Ergebnis ist der Grad, zu dem Unternehmen drei verschiedene Barrieren für erfolgreiches LQM in Schwellenländern überwunden haben. Die Auswahl dieser Faktoren fasst theoretische und empirische Literatur aus den Bereichen LQM, verhaltenswissenschaftliches Beschaffungsmanagement und der Beschaffung in Schwellenländern zusammen. Obwohl vorherige Literatur die Aufnahme jedes einzelnen Faktors in das Modell unterstützt (Busse et al., 2016; Zsidisin et al., 2016), sind ihre Effekte als Teil von Konfigurationen bisher noch nicht erforscht.

Abbildung 1: Konzeptionelles Modell für LQM in Schwellenländern

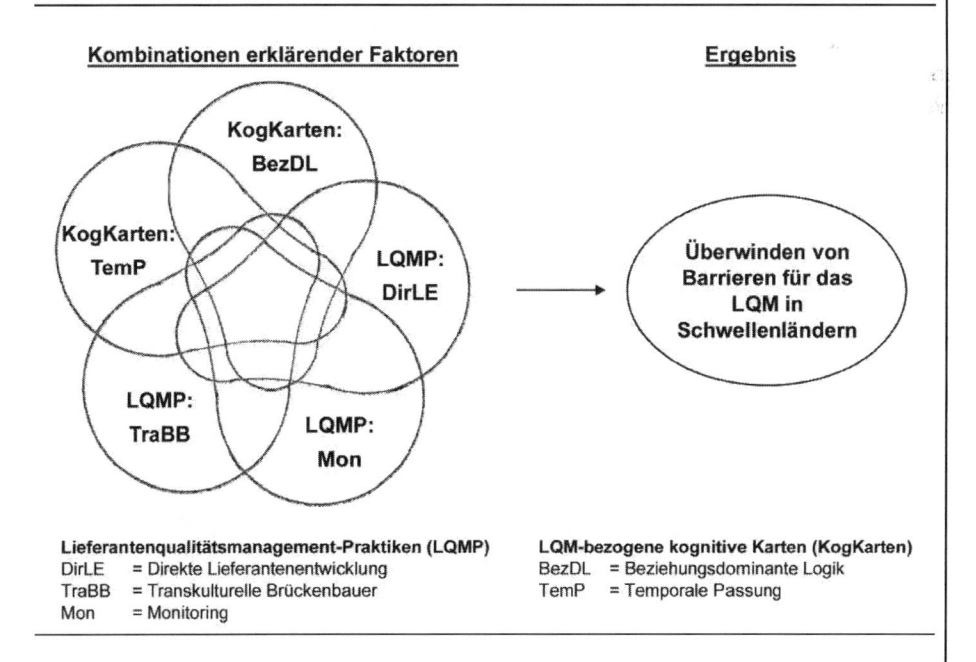

Lieferantenqualitätsmanagement-Praktiken (LQMP)
DirLE = Direkte Lieferantenentwicklung
TraBB = Transkultureller Brückenbauer
Mon = Monitoring

LQM-bezogene kognitive Karten (KogKarten)
BezDL = Beziehungsdominante Logik
TemP = Temporale Passung

2.2 Barrieren für das LQM in Schwellenländern

Beschaffung in Schwellenländern bezeichnet den Prozess des Einkaufs von Produkten, Teilen und Dienstleistungen durch einkaufende Unternehmen aus entwickelten Märkten, z.B. USA, Europäische Union, von Lieferanten in Schwellenländern, z.B. Brasilien, China oder Indien (Busse et al., 2016). Empirische Studien zeigen, dass westliche Unternehmen bei der Beschaffung in Schwellenländern auf verschiedene *Barrieren* treffen (Busse et al., 2016; Stanczyk et al., 2017). Barrieren werden hier definiert als kontextuelle Faktoren, die das einkaufende Unternehmen daran hindern, seine Leistungsziele zu erreichen. Die bestehende Forschung hat zahlreiche Barrieren für das LQM in Schwellenländern aufgezeigt, insbesondere wenn westliche Firmen von Lieferanten in Asien einkaufen (Busse et al., 2016; Stanczyk et al., 2017). Dieser Beitrag erfasst wesentliche Barrieren für das LQM in Schwellenländern, die sich in der vorherigen Forschung als wichtig herausgestellt haben:

- Die *psychische Distanz* wird definiert als die Summe der Faktoren, welche die Kommunikation zwischen Individuen aus verschiedenen Ländern behindern – in unserem Fall die Mitarbeiter des westlichen einkaufenden Unternehmens und des chinesischen Lieferanten (Busse et al., 2016; Johanson, Vahlne, 2009). Das Konstrukt der psychischen Distanz beinhaltet z.B. Faktoren wie kulturelle Distanz, sprachliche Unterschiede oder unterschiedliche Geschäftspraktiken.

- *Fähigkeitslücken* bezeichnen Defizite im technischen, betriebswirtschaftlichen und produktbezogenen Wissen des Lieferanten, die seine Fähigkeit beeinträchtigen, ein bestimmtes Produkt zuverlässig und mit mindestens zufriedenstellender Qualität zu liefern. Ungenügende Fähigkeiten des Lieferanten wurden in früheren Studien als eine wesentliche Ursache für das Scheitern der Beschaffung in Schwellenländern identifiziert (Horn et al., 2013; Lockström et al., 2011).

- Die *Dynamik des Beschaffungsmarktes* ist ein zentrales Merkmal, das Aktivitäten in entwickelten Märkten von denen in Schwellenländern unterscheidet, wobei Letztere durch Unsicherheit und ein hohes Veränderungstempo gekennzeichnet sind (Xu, Meyer, 2013). Die *Dynamik des Beschaffungsmarktes* wird definiert als der Grad der Veränderung in dem Beschaffungsmarkt eines Unternehmens und umfasst die zwei Dimensionen Unvorhersehbarkeit (d.h. mangelnde Regelmäßigkeit der Veränderungen) und Instabilität (d.h. das Ausmaß der Veränderungen) (Kovach et al., 2015).

2.3 LQM-Praktiken

Sowohl das Forschungsfeld des Lieferantenqualitätsmanagements als auch die Literatur zur Beschaffung in Schwellenländern unterstreichen die Bedeutung von LQM-Praktiken (Carter et al., 2017; Zsidisin et al., 2016). Basierend auf den Meta-Analysen von Foerstl et al. (2016) sowie Zimmermann und Foerstl (2014) zum Zusammenhang zwischen Einkaufspraktiken und Unternehmenserfolg werden LQM-Praktiken hier grob in zwei Kategorien eingeteilt: 1) externe, lieferantenseitige LQM-Praktiken und 2) interne, befähigende LQM-Praktiken.

Externe, lieferantenseitige LQM-Praktiken können unterschieden werden in relationale und transaktionale LQM-Praktiken, abhängig von dem Grad der Zusammenarbeit mit dem Lieferanten (Foerstl et al., 2016; Zimmermann, Foerstl, 2014).

- *Relationale LQM-Praktiken* (z.B. organisationsübergreifender Wissensaustausch) sind kooperativer Natur und benötigen die gemeinsame Beteiligung von einkaufendem Unternehmen und dem Lieferanten, um wirksam zu sein. Dieser Beitrag fokussiert sich auf die *direkte Lieferantenentwicklung* (Krause et al., 2007) als relationale LQM-Praktik, weil vorherige Studien dies als entscheidend für eine Verbesserung der Qualität von Lieferanten aus Schwellenländern identifiziert haben (Noshad, Awasthi, 2015). Basierend auf Krause et al. (2007) bezieht sich das Konstrukt der *direkten Lieferantenentwicklung* in dieser Studie darauf, inwieweit das einkaufende Unternehmen dezidierte Lieferantenentwicklungsteams nutzt, Personal zur Verbesserung der technischen Fähigkeiten des Lieferanten zur Verfügung stellt und regelmäßige Lieferantenbesuche durchführt.

- Im Gegensatz dazu werden *transaktionale LQM-Praktiken* (z.B. Lieferantenbeurteilung) mit Arm's-Length-Beziehungen assoziiert und benötigen nur die einseitige Beteiligung des einkaufenden Unternehmens. Diese Studie fokussiert sich auf *Monitoring* als eine wesentliche transaktionale LQM-Praktik. Monitoring wird definiert als der Versuch einer Partei, die Leistung einer anderen Partei zu messen (Heide et al., 2007). In dieser Studie beinhaltet Monitoring die beiden Dimensionen des *Ergebnis-Monitorings* (d.h. die Überprüfung der Produktqualität des Lieferanten) und des *Verhaltens-Monitorings* (d.h. die Bewertung der Prozesse, die zu Produktqualität führen sollen) (Heide et al., 2007).

Interne, befähigende LQM-Praktiken (z.B. Kompetenzentwicklung) bezeichnen Praktiken, die das einkaufende Unternehmen dabei unterstützen, seine externen, lieferantenseitigen LQM-Praktiken durchzuführen (Foerstl et al., 2016).

- Mehrere Studien haben die Bedeutung von *transkulturellen Brückenbauern* („*transcultural boundary spanners*") in Beschaffungsorganisationen hervorgehoben, um die kulturelle Anpassung zwischen westlichen Einkäufern und Lieferanten in Schwellenländern zu erleichtern (Jia et al., 2016). *Transkulturelle Brückenbauer* werden hier definiert als Individuen, die an der Peripherie oder Grenze des einkaufenden Unternehmens operieren und die kulturellen und sprachlichen Fähigkeiten haben, um signifikante Interaktionen zwischen Einkäufern und Lieferanten verschiedener Heimatländer zu ermöglichen (z.B. langfristige Expatriates, die sich an ihre Gastumgebung angepasst haben) (Jia et al., 2016).

Bestehende Forschung weist darauf hin, dass LQM-Praktiken Firmen dabei helfen können, Lieferqualität in Schwellenländern zu managen. Dennoch deutet das Fortbestehen der Herausforderungen – wie durch Samsungs Rückruf der Smartphones Galaxy Note 7 im Jahr 2016 illustriert (Martin, Jeong, 2017) – darauf hin, dass andere Faktoren jenseits der angewandten Praktiken das LQM in Schwellenländern beeinflussen könnten. Der nächste Abschnitt befasst sich daher mit LQM-bezogenen kognitiven Karten als einem möglicherweise fehlenden Puzzleteil in Studien zum LQM in Schwellenländern.

2.4 LQM-bezogene kognitive Karten

Verhaltenswissenschaftliche Beschaffungsmanagement-Forschung untersucht, wie das Verhalten von Einkaufsmanagern von den Annahmen des Homo oeconomicus abweicht (Carter et al., 2007; Schorsch et al., 2017). Ihre Ergebnisse deuten darauf hin, dass die Kognition von Managern ein entscheidender Faktor für die Erklärung des Entscheidungsverhaltens in der Einkaufsfunktion ist (Eckerd et al., 2016; Stanczyk et al., 2015). Die Forschung zur Kognition von Führungskräften lenkt besonderes Augenmerk auf die kognitiven Strukturen, die Manager für ihre Entscheidungsfindung nutzen (Maitland, Sammartino, 2015b; Martignoni et al., 2016). Diese kognitiven Strukturen werden durch persönliche und berufliche Erfahrungen von Managern geformt und in der Beschaffungsmanagement-Literatur als mentale Modelle (z.B. Schoenherr et al., 2014), Schemata (z.B., Kim et al., 2015) oder kognitive Karten (z.B. Kaufmann et al., 2016) bezeichnet. In dieser Studie werden *kognitive Karten* definiert als die vereinfachten mentalen Repräsentationen der Umwelt, die Manager in ihren Köpfen schaffen (Maitland, Sammartino, 2015a). Kognitive Karten funktionieren als Informationsfilter oder kognitive Brille, durch die Manager ihre komplexe Umwelt wahrnehmen, vereinfachen und interpretieren (Kor, Mesko, 2013).

Im Folgenden werden zwei Arten kognitiver Karten kurz vorgestellt, die besonders relevant sind für das Beschaffungsmanagement im Allgemeinen und die Beschaffung in Schwellenländern im Besonderen:

- *Beziehungsdominante Logik (BDL)* bezeichnet die Orientierung des Einkaufsteams in Bezug auf die Koordination und Integration mit der Lieferantenbasis (Kaufmann et al., 2016). Diese Studie untersucht unternehmenszentrierte BDLs und dyadisch-zentrierte BDL, die sich nach dem Grad ihrer Kooperationsbereitschaft unterscheiden. Ein Einkaufsteam mit einer *unternehmenszentrierten BDL* sieht seinen Beschaffungskontext als einen, der einseitige Anstrengungen erfordert, um den gewünschten Nutzen zu erreichen. Im Gegensatz dazu sieht ein Einkaufsteam mit einer *dyadisch-zentrierten BDL* seinen Beschaffungskontext als einen, der gemeinsame oder bilaterale Anstrengungen mit Lieferanten erfordert.

- *Temporale Passung* bezeichnet den Grad der Übereinstimmung zwischen den zeitlichen Orientierungen des Einkäufer- und des Lieferantenteams. Zeitliche Orientierungen „prägen, worauf wir achten, wie wir uns Problemen zuwenden und wie wir Phänomene interpretieren" (Reinecke, Ansari, 2015, S. 619). Frühere Studien zeigen, dass divergierende zeitliche Orientierungen Beziehungen zwischen westlichen Einkäufern und chinesischen Lieferanten belasten können (Lockström et al., 2011). Um einen differenzierten Blick auf die zeitlichen Orientierungen der Supply-Chain-Partner zu erhalten, werden diese als verschiedene Dimensionen mit Fokus auf Vergangenheit, Gegenwart und Zukunft konzipiert. *Temporaler Fokus* wird verstanden als „das Ausmaß, zu dem Menschen charakteristischerweise ihre Aufmerksamkeit auf Vergangenheit, Gegenwart und Zukunft richten" (Shipp et al., 2009, S. 1). Ein Vergangenheits-Fokus ist verbunden mit einer wiederholten Nutzung früherer Erfahrungen bei der Entscheidungsfindung (d.h. Lerner), ein Gegenwarts-Fokus ist verbunden mit dem Ergreifen von Chancen und spontanen Verhaltensweisen (d.h. Improvisatoren), und ein Zukunfts-Fokus ist in erster Linie verbunden mit der Vorstellung zukünftiger Ereignisse und Zielsetzungen (d.h. Planer) (Nadkarni, Chen, 2014; Shipp et al., 2009).

Im Folgenden wird die Methodik dieser qualitativen Studie vorgestellt.

3 Methodik

Um die Forschungsfrage zu beantworten, wie Konfigurationen verschiedener LQM-Praktiken und LQM-bezogener kognitiver Karten Unternehmen dabei helfen, die Lieferqualität zu managen, wurde eine umfassende qualitative Studie über das LQM von 17 westlichen Produktionsunternehmen und ihren chinesischen Lieferanten durchgeführt. Die Analyseeinheit ist die Einkäufer-Lieferanten-Beziehung zwischen einem westlichen einkaufenden Unternehmen und einem seiner chinesischen Schlüssellieferanten, wobei die Studie 17 dyadische Fälle umfasst. Der Begriff „westliche Unternehmen" bezeichnet in dieser Studie Firmen, deren Zentrale in Nordamerika oder Westeuropa liegt.

3.1 Sampling und Datenerhebung

LQM in Schwellenländern wie China stellt aus mehreren Gründen einen besonders aufschlussreichen Forschungskontext für diese Studie dar:

- LQM in China ist ein Phänomen mit hoher empirischer Relevanz. Westliche Unternehmen beschaffen einen erheblichen Teil ihres Einkaufsvolumens von Lieferanten in Schwellenländern (Najafi et al., 2013). Dadurch sind sie möglicherweise erhöhten Risiken in der Lieferqualität ausgesetzt (Reimann et al., 2017; Steven, Britto, 2016; Zsidisin et al., 2016). 2016 wurden in der Europäischen Union tatsächlich 53% der von Rückrufen betroffenen Non-Food-Produkte in China produziert oder eingekauft (RAPEX, 2017).

- Empirische Ergebnisse deuten darauf hin, dass die Wirksamkeit von LQM-Praktiken in Schwellenländern geringer ausfällt als in entwickelten Märkten (Kull, Wacker, 2010; Wiengarten, Ambrose, 2017).

- Die kulturellen Unterschiede zwischen westlichen einkaufenden Unternehmen und chinesischen Lieferanten bringen höchstwahrscheinlich Unterschiede in der „mentalen Programmierung" (Hofstede, 1984, p. 13) der Supply-Chain-Partner mit sich.

LQM in Schwellenländern ist daher ein kognitiv und verhaltenswissenschaftlich komplexes Phänomen (Busse et al., 2016; Stanczyk et al., 2017), das eine tiefergehende Untersuchung der Wechselwirkungen zwischen Kognition und Verhalten ermöglicht.

Die theoretische Sampling-Strategie für die westlichen einkaufenden Unternehmen konzentrierte sich auf sogenannte Exemplare/Leuchtturm-Unternehmen im Qualitätsmanagement (Pagell, Wu, 2009). In jedem dieser einkaufenden Unternehmen wurde ein hochrangiger Einkaufsmanager gebeten, eine Beziehung zu einem chinesischen Schlüssellieferanten zu identifizieren.

Daten wurden durch 89 semistrukturierte Tiefeninterviews mit mehreren Schlüsselinformanten innerhalb jeder Einkäufer-Lieferanten-Dyade gesammelt, ergänzt durch Dokumente und Vor-Ort-Beobachtungen. In jedem einkaufenden Unternehmen unterstützte ein hochrangiger Einkaufsmanager bei der Identifikation von Experten, die an der Schnittstelle zum Lieferanten arbeiten. Der Interviewleitfaden beinhaltete Fragen zu den wichtigsten Hindernissen und Erfolgsfaktoren von LQM in China. Um die Diskussion über Hindernisse und Erfolgsfaktoren konkreter zu gestalten, wurde eine von der Critical-Incident-Technik (Flanagan, 1954) inspirierte Datenerfassungstechnik verwendet, um spezifische Qualitätsvorfälle in der ausgewählten Lieferbeziehung zu diskutieren. Um das Vertrauen in die Genauigkeit der Befunde zu stärken, wurden die Interviewdaten mit umfangreichen Feldbeobachtungen und Dokumenten trianguliert (Eisenhardt, 1989). Kumuliert wurden mehr als zwölf Tage an Feldbeobachtungen bei zehn Lieferanten durchgeführt sowie Besichtigungen von Produktionsstätten bei den übrigen sieben Lieferanten. Außerdem wurden öffentlich zugängliche Dokumente (z.B. Branchenberichte, Geschäftsberichte) und firmeninterne Dokumente (z.B. Qualitätsberichte, E-Mail-Konversationen) von Einkäufern und Lieferanten zum Zwecke der Datentriangulation gesammelt und ausgewertet (Gibbert et al., 2008).

3.2 Fallstudienanalyse

Die Analyse erfolgte in zwei Schritten. In der ersten Phase wurden 17 Fallstudienberichte der Einkäufer-Lieferanten-Dyaden verfasst, um ein umfassendes Bild der spezifischen Barrieren, LQM-Praktiken und LQM-bezogenen kognitiven Karten zu zeichnen. In den Fallstudienberichten wurden Zitate aus den Interviews, Fotos und andere gesammelte Dokumenten verwendet, um eine hohe Genauigkeit zu erreichen. Durch diesen Prozess wurden die Daten quellenübergreifend trianguliert, verglichen und kontrastiert (Eisenhardt, 1989). Um die Reliabilität der Daten zu gewährleisten, wurden die Entwürfe der Fallstudienberichte von den Interviewpartnern überprüft.

3.3 Fuzzy-set qualitative comparative analysis

In der zweiten Phase wurde die fsQCA-Methode (Ragin, 2008) verwendet, um Muster über Fälle hinweg zu identifizieren. Der fsQCA-Ansatz schlägt eine Brücke zwischen konventionellen qualitativen und quantitativen Analysen, indem er die Komplexität der Fallstudienanalyse mit einem gewissen Grad an Verallgemeinerbarkeit durch set-theoretische Analysen kombiniert (Crilly, 2011). FsQCA hat in der Managementforschung wachsende Aufmerksamkeit erhalten (Misangyi et al., 2017) und wurde kürzlich in die Beschaffungsmanagement-Forschung eingeführt (Timmer, Kaufmann, 2017). Da eine detaillierte Erläuterung der fsQCA-Methode über den Rahmen dieses Beitrags hinausgeht, wird für eine ausführlichere Erläuterung auf den Primer zu fsQCA in dem im *Journal of Purchasing and Supply Management* erschienenen Artikel verwiesen[7].

Kurz gesagt, verwendet fsQCA eine set-theoretische Logik, um Konfigurationen von erklärenden Variablen (d.h. kausale Bedingungen, in der fsQCA-Terminologie) zu identifizieren, die mit einem zu untersuchenden Ergebnis assoziiert sind (hier: das Überwinden von Barrieren für das LQM in Schwellenländern). FsQCA ist die Methodik der Wahl für einen konfigurativen Ansatz, da fsQCA sowohl konzeptionell als auch analytisch kausale Komplexität adressiert (Misangyi et al., 2017).

3.4 Kognitiv-linguistische Analyse

Um Erkenntnisse über die kognitiven Karten von Einkaufsmanagern zu bekommen, nutzt diese Studie einen *kognitiv-linguistischen Ansatz* mittels computergestützter Textanalyse. Ein *kognitiv-linguistischer Ansatz* basiert darauf, dass subtile Unterschiede in der Sprache Unterschiede in der Kognition widerspiegeln (Pennebaker et al., 2001).

Zur Analyse der beiden kognitiven Karten zu *beziehungsdominanter Logik (BDL)* und zur *temporalen Passung* wurde die Software *Linguistic Inquiry and Word Count (LIWC)* (Pennebaker et al., 2001) eingesetzt. Diese Software analysiert Texte, indem sie die enthaltenen Wörter mit wissenschaftlich vordefinierten Wörterbüchern abgleicht. LIWC berechnet dann den prozentualen Anteil jener Wörter in den Interviewprotokollen, die eine bestimmte Kategorie in den vordefinierten LIWC-Wörterbüchern repräsentieren (Tausczik, Pennebaker, 2010).

---

[7] Co-Alignment of Supplier Quality Management Practices and Cognitive Maps – A Neo-Configurational Perspective. Journal of Purchasing & Supply Management. Forthcoming 2017. doi: 10.1016/j.pursup.2017.11.002 (zusammen mit F. Reimann und L. Kaufmann)

Wissenschaftliche Forschungsbeiträge

Um die *BDL* für jedes einkaufende Unternehmen zu operationalisieren, wurden die LIWC-Kategorien „inklusive Sprache" und „Andere" verwendet, um zu analysieren, inwieweit die dyadisch-zentrierte BDL des Einkaufsteams gegenüber der unternehmenszentrierten BDL überwiegt. Die Differenz zwischen den Werten für diese beiden Kategorien dient als Indikator für die Stärke der dyadisch-zentrierten BDL des Unternehmens. Die LIWC-Kategorie „inklusive Sprache" zählt Wörter, die Menschen benutzen, um Kategorien zu verbinden (hauptsächlich Konjunktionen, Präpositionen und einige Adverbien, z.B. „zusammen", „gemeinsam" und „mit"), während die LIWC-Kategorie „Andere" solche Wörter misst, die Menschen benutzen um auf andere zu verweisen (hauptsächlich Pronomen in der dritten Person, z.B. „ihre", „sein" und „seine").

Die Übereinstimmung der *temporalen Foki* der Supply-Chain-Partner wurde anhand der LIWC-Kategorien „Vergangenheit", „Gegenwart" und „Zukunft" analysiert. Diese Kategorien berechnen den prozentualen Anteil von Wörtern in den Interviewprotokollen, welche den Vergangenheits-Fokus einer Person widerspiegeln (z.B. „hat", „tat" und „war"), den Gegenwarts-Fokus (z.B. „ist", „tut" und „sind") und den Zukunfts-Fokus (z.B. „wird", „kann" und „soll") (Nadkarni, Chen, 2014). Das Ausmaß der kognitiven Verschiedenheit in den temporalen Fokusprofilen der Supply-Chain-Partner wurde berechnet, indem die normierten absoluten Differenzen in den LIWC-Werten zwischen Einkäufer und Lieferant für jede Dimension aufsummiert wurden.

4 Ergebnisse

Die Konfigurationstabelle (siehe **Tabelle 1**) zeigt die Ergebnisse der Suffizienz-Analyse („*sufficiency analysis*"); jede Spalte stellt eine eindeutige Konfiguration dar. Die Suffizienz-Analyse zeigt vier Konfigurationen, um Barrieren für LQM in Schwellenländern zu überwinden. Jede Konfiguration repräsentiert einen von vier alternativen Wegen für das LQM in Schwellenländern.

Tabelle zeigt auch zwei Fit-Werte: Konsistenz und Reichweite. *Konsistenz* misst, wie gut die Lösung den Daten entspricht und wird sowohl für die Gesamtlösung als auch für jede Konfiguration berechnet (Ragin, 2008). Die Gesamtlösung weist eine sehr gute set theoretische Konsistenz auf – der Wert von 0,95 liegt deutlich über der empfohlenen Schwelle von 0,80 (Misangyi, Acharya, 2014). Die *Reichweite* misst die empirische Relevanz der Gesamtlösung und ist vergleichbar mit einem R-Quadrat in der Regressionsanalyse (Ragin, 2008). Die Ergebnisse deuten darauf hin, dass die vier Konfigurationen, die mit dem Überwinden von Barrieren für das LQM in Schwellenländern assoziiert sind, etwa 89% des Ergebnisses erklären. Für jede einzelne Konfiguration werden zudem die *Konsistenz*, die *Roh-Reichweite* und die *eindeutige Reichweite* in **Tabelle** angegeben.

Qualitätsmanagement mit Lieferanten in Schwellenländern

Tabelle 1: Konfigurationstabelle

Konfiguration	Konfigurationen für das Überwinden von Barrieren für das LQM in Schwellenländern			
	Team Coaches	Hands-off-Lokalisierer	Synchronisierte Kontrolleure	Skeptische Aufseher
Kausale Bedingungen	1	2	3	4
LQM-bezogene kognitive Karten				
Dyadisch-zentrierte beziehungsdominante Logik	●	⊗		⊗
Temporale Passung		●	●	
LQM-Praktiken				
Direkte Lieferantenentwicklung	●			
Transkulturelle Brückenbauer	●	●		
Monitoring			●	●
Konsistenz	0.99	0.93	0.98	0.97
Roh-Reichweite	0.49	0.32	0.57	0.48
Eindeutige Reichweite	0.18	0.04	0.03	0.08
	Gesamtlösungs-Konsistenz		0.95	
	Gesamtlösungs-Reichweite:		0.89	

● Zentrale kausale Bedingung (vorhanden)
⊗ Zentrale kausale Bedingung (abwesend)
● Periphere kausale Bedingung (vorhanden)
⊗ Periphere kausale Bedingung (abwesend)

Leere Zellen in einer Konfiguration weisen auf eine Situation hin, in der die kausale Bedingung entweder vorhanden oder abwesend sein kann.

Um die Wirkungsmechanismen in jeder Konfiguration zu beleuchten, werden in den folgenden Abschnitten die vier ermittelten Konfigurationen beschrieben.

4.1 Team Coaches (Konfiguration 1)

Die erste Konfiguration für das Überwinden von Barrieren für das LQM in Schwellenländern („Team Coaches") kombiniert eine dyadisch-zentrierte BDL mit einem hohen

Einsatz von direkter Lieferantenentwicklung und transkulturellen Brückenbauern. Die meisten Firmen in dieser Konfiguration sind bekannte Business-to-Consumer(B2C)-Unternehmen mit viel China-Erfahrung, die sich in Familienbesitz und/oder -kontrolle befinden. Diese Konfiguration impliziert, dass die Einkaufsteams ihre Lieferantenbeziehungen durch eine teamorientierte kognitive Brille betrachten und gleichzeitig signifikant in die direkte Lieferantenentwicklung investieren.

4.2   Hands-off-Lokalisierer (Konfiguration 2)

Die zweite Konfiguration („Hands-off-Lokalisierer") zeigt das Fehlen einer dyadisch-zentrierten BDL und das Vorhandensein transkultureller Brückenbauer, begleitet von einer temporalen Passung zwischen dem westlichen einkaufenden Unternehmen und dem chinesischen Lieferanten. Die meisten Firmen in dieser Konfiguration sind mittelgroße Nischenanbieter, für die der chinesische Markt keine hohe Priorität hat. Diese Konfiguration legt nahe, dass ein unternehmenszentriertes einkaufendes Unternehmen erfolgreich Barrieren für das LQM in Schwellenländern überwinden kann, wenn es transkulturelle Brückenbauer einsetzt.

4.3   Synchronisierte Kontrolleure (Konfiguration 3)

Die dritte und empirisch relevanteste Konfiguration („Synchronisierte Kontrolleure") zeigt das Vorhandensein von Monitoring in Kombination mit temporaler Passung. Diese Konfiguration deutet darauf hin, dass ein einkaufendes Unternehmen erfolgreich Barrieren für das LQM in Schwellenländern überwinden kann, wenn die Monitoring-Aktivitäten mit einer ähnlichen zeitlichen Programmierung zwischen den Supply-Chain-Partnern zusammenfallen. Dies lässt sich dadurch erklären, dass die temporale Passung ein wichtiger zugrundeliegender Faktor für die Lieferbeziehung sein könnte. Die meisten Firmen in dieser Konfiguration sind große Business-to-Business(B2B)-Unternehmen.

4.4   Skeptische Aufseher (Konfiguration 4)

Die vierte Konfiguration („Skeptische Aufseher") kombiniert das Fehlen einer dyadisch-zentrierten BDL mit dem Einsatz von Monitoring. Die meisten Firmen in dieser Konstellation sind mittelgroße „Hidden Champions". Die Daten deuten darauf hin, dass die unternehmenszentrierte Denkweise zu einem kontrollorientierten Verhalten führen könnte. Dies wiederum reduziert Möglichkeiten zu gemeinsamen Verbesserungen mit dem Lieferanten und verstärkt im Laufe der Zeit die unternehmenszentrierte Denkweise des einkaufenden Unternehmens.

5 Fazit und Praxisimplikationen

Ziel dieser Studie war es, zu verstehen, wie Konfigurationen verschiedener LQM-Praktiken und LQM-bezogener kognitiver Karten Unternehmen helfen, ihre Lieferqualität zu managen. Aufbauend auf dem konzeptionellen Modell wurde eine konfigurative fsQCA-Analyse durchgeführt. Diese zeigt vier alternative Konfigurationen auf, wie Unternehmen erfolgreich Barrieren für das LQM in Schwellenländern überwinden können. Obwohl die Ergebnisse eine Reihe von Implikationen für jeden einzelnen der untersuchten Faktoren bieten, liegt der Schwerpunkt des neo-konfigurativen Ansatzes vor allem darauf zu verstehen, wie die Mechanismen als Konfigurationen effektiv zusammenarbeiten. Im Folgenden werden wichtige Implikationen für die Theorieentwicklung im Beschaffungsmanagement diskutiert, die sich aus der vorliegenden Studie ergeben.

5.1 Neo-konfigurative Perspektive für das Beschaffungsmanagement

Die Ergebnisse zeigen empirisch den Wert eines neo-konfigurativen Ansatzes für die Untersuchung kausal komplexer Beschaffungsmanagement-Phänomene, wie z.B. das LQM in Schwellenländern. Eine neo-konfigurative Perspektive verlagert die Aufmerksamkeit sowohl theoretisch als auch empirisch auf drei Merkmale kausaler Komplexität: 1) konjunkte Kausalität, 2) Equifinalität und 3) kausale Asymmetrie.

Erstens zeigen die Ergebnisse, dass bei kausal komplexen Beschaffungsmanagement-Phänomenen mehrere erklärende Faktoren in spezifischer Weise zusammenspielen, um ein Ergebnis zu bewirken (d.h. konjunkte Kausalität). Insbesondere bedeuten die Ergebnisse, dass das Zusammenspiel (*„co-alignment"*) zwischen den LQM-bezogenen kognitiven Karten des Einkaufsteams und den angewandten LQM-Praktiken den einkaufenden Unternehmen helfen kann, die Lieferqualität effektiv zu managen. Während Konfiguration 1 (*„Team Coaches"*) darauf hindeutet, dass relationale LQM-Praktiken (z.B. direkte Lieferantenentwicklung) in Kombination mit einer dyadisch-zentrierten BDL effektiver sind, deutet Konfiguration 4 (*„Skeptische Aufseher"*) darauf hin, dass transaktionale LQM-Praktiken (z.B. Monitoring) in Kombination mit einer unternehmenszentrierten BDL effektiver sind – und dass beide zum Erfolg führen (können). Die Berücksichtigung konjunkter Kausalität in der vorliegenden Studie zeigt daher, dass Ergebnisse nicht durch den Nettoeffekt relationaler oder transaktionaler LQM-Praktiken *per se* bewirkt werden, sondern durch die richtigen *Konfigurationen* von LQM-Praktiken und LQM-bezogenen kognitiven Karten.

Zweitens zeigen die Ergebnisse, dass bei kausal komplexen Beschaffungsmanagement-Phänomenen mehrere alternative Wege zu dem gleichen Ergebnis führen können (d.h. Equifinalität). Mit dem neo-konfigurativen Ansatz wurden vier alternati-

Wissenschaftliche Forschungsbeiträge

ve/gleichwertige Strategien identifiziert, die Unternehmen anwenden können, um die Lieferqualität in Schwellenländern erfolgreich zu managen.

Drittens zeigen die Ergebnisse, dass bei kausal komplexen Beschaffungsmanagement-Phänomenen sowohl das Vorhandensein als auch das Fehlen eines Faktors zu demselben Ergebnis führen kann, abhängig von seiner Kombination mit anderen Faktoren (d.h. kausale Asymmetrie). Die Ergebnisse deuten darauf hin, dass in Konfiguration 1 („*Team Coaches*") das Vorhandensein einer dyadisch-zentrierten BDL mit dem Ergebnis assoziiert ist, während in Konfiguration 4 („*Skeptische Aufseher*") gerade eben das Fehlen einer dyadisch-zentrierten BDL mit diesem assoziiert wird. Ebenso erweist sich ein Faktor, der in einer Konfiguration eine Schlüsselrolle spielt, wie z.B. die direkte Lieferantenentwicklung in Konfiguration 1, in anderen Konfigurationen als unabhängig vom zu untersuchenden Ergebnis.

Als erster theoretischer Beitrag der Studie wird daher für eine neo-konfigurative Perspektive (Misangyi et al., 2017) in der Beschaffungsmanagement-Forschung plädiert, weil diese das wissenschaftliche Denken über und das Verstehen von wichtigen Beschaffungsmanagement-Phänomenen verändern kann.

▪ *Schlussfolgerung 1:* Für kausal komplexe Beschaffungsmanagement-Phänomene liefern konfigurative Forschungsmethoden ein umfassenderes und realitätsgetreueres Verständnis von Ursache-Wirkungs-Beziehungen als Nettoeffekt-Analysen der betrachteten Einzelfaktoren.

5.2 LQM-bezogene kognitive Karten als wichtige Elemente in Konfigurationen

Während der erste theoretische Beitrag die Aufmerksamkeit auf Konfigurationen (d.h. Kombinationen von Faktoren) als solches lenkt, bezieht sich der zweite theoretische Beitrag auf die Arten von Faktoren, die als Teil solcher Konfigurationen betrachtet werden sollten. Die Ergebnisse zeigen, dass LQM-bezogene kognitive Karten ein wichtiger Bestandteil aller vier Konfigurationen sind. Dies deutet darauf hin, dass Beschaffungsmanagement-Forscher generell die Untersuchung von Einkaufspraktiken *in Kombination mit* kognitiven Faktoren verfolgen sollten, wenn sie deren Erfolgswirkung untersuchen – auch dies führt zu realitätsnäherer Forschung. Indem die vorliegende Studie das Zusammenspiel von Einkaufspraktiken und kognitiven Karten beleuchtet, leistet sie einen Beitrag zum entstehenden Feld des *verhaltenswissenschaftlichen Beschaffungsmanagements* (Eckerd et al., 2016; Kaufmann et al., 2017; Stanczyk et al., 2015).

Konkret weisen die Erkenntnisse über das Zusammenspiel zwischen der BDL des Einkaufsteams (dyadisch- vs. unternehmenszentriert) und den angewandten LQM-Praktiken (relational vs. transaktional) auf das theoretische Konstrukt der „*kognitiven Passung*" („cognitive fit") (Martignoni et al., 2016) zwischen den kognitiven Karten der Einkaufsmanager und ihrem Verhalten hin. Das Konzept der kognitiven Passung legt nahe, dass die Leistung verbessert wird, wenn spezifische kognitive Faktoren der Manager gut zu den Eigenschaften ihrer Umgebung passen (Martignoni et al., 2016). Kognitiver Fit ist daher ein potenziell nützliches Konzept, um zukünftige verhaltenswissenschaftliche Beschaffungsmanagement-Forschung zu leiten.

▪ *Schlussfolgerung 2:* Beide, sowohl Einkaufspraktiken als auch kognitive Aspekte, sind Schlüsselelemente in den Konfigurationen, die Beschaffungserfolge bewirken; ihre simultane Berücksichtigung führt zu realitätsnäherer Managementforschung.

5.3 Theorie mittlerer Reichweite für das LQM in Schwellenländern

Durch die Entwicklung einer *„Theorie mittlerer Reichweite"* (Craighead et al., 2016) für das LQM in Schwellenländern reagiert unsere Studie auf entsprechende Forschungsaufrufe (Wiengarten, Ambrose, 2017). Die vier identifizierten LQM-Konfigurationen liefern einen kontextspezifischen, aber dennoch kompakten Überblick über alternative, gleichwertige Strategien für Unternehmen, um die Lieferqualität in Schwellenländern erfolgreich zu managen. Die Studie identifiziert insbesondere die *temporale Passung*, die als Übereinstimmung in den Vergangenheits-, Gegenwarts- und Zukunfts-Fokus zwischen dem Einkäufer- und Lieferantenteam konzeptualisiert wird, als wichtigen aber bisher weitgehend vernachlässigten Erfolgsfaktor in globalen Lieferbeziehungen. Die Berücksichtigung der temporalen Passung in der Beschaffungsmanagement-Forschung erscheint besonders wichtig, da Zeitfaktoren vielen Konzepten im Supply Chain Management zugrunde liegen, wie z.B. partnerspezifischen Investitionen und Supply-Chain-Agilität. Eine fehlende zeitliche Passung zwischen Supply-Chain-Partnern kann die Umsetzung solcher Ansätze erschweren.

▪ *Schlussfolgerung 3:* Kognitive Karten sind besonders wichtige kognitive Elemente in Konfigurationen, die Beschaffungserfolge bewirken – insbesondere der Grad der temporalen Passung zwischen Einkäufer und Lieferant. Die Berücksichtigung von Zeitaspekten führt zu realitätsnäherer Beschaffungsmanagement-Forschung.

5.4 Praxisimplikationen

Die vorliegende Studie liefert mehrere Implikationen für die Praxis. Erstens deuten die Ergebnisse darauf hin, dass der Qualitätserfolg bei der Beschaffung in Schwellenländern weitgehend eine Frage der Übereinstimmung zwischen der „Denkweise" (d.h. LQM-bezogene kognitive Karten/Weltanschauungen) des Unternehmens, den angewandten LQM-Praktiken und zusätzlichen Faktoren wie Unternehmensgröße und verfügbaren Ressourcen ist. Manager in Unternehmen, die über ausreichende Ressourcen verfügen, könnten sich für einen *„Team Coach"*-Ansatz entscheiden (Konfiguration 1) und selektiv in direkte Lieferantenentwicklung investieren. Diese Strategie setzt voraus, dass das Einkaufsteam wirklich hinter der Idee steht, partnerschaftlich mit dem Lieferanten zusammenzuarbeiten, und bereit ist, gemeinsame Projekte in vollem Umfang zu unterstützen. Die Daten zeigen jedoch auch, dass Manager ähnliche Ergebnisse erzielen können, wenn sie sich auf den Einsatz von transkulturellen Brückenbauern (Konfiguration 2) oder Monitoring (Konfiguration 3) konzentrieren, vorausgesetzt, das zeitliche Fokusprofil des einkaufenden Unternehmens stimmt gut mit dem Zeithorizont des Lieferanten überein. In den Fällen, in denen das Einkaufsteam seine Lieferantenbeziehungen mehr als Arm's-Length-Beziehungen versteht, kann Managern auf Grundlage der Erkenntnisse vorsichtig geraten werden, stark in Monitoring-Aktivitäten zu investieren (Konfiguration 4).

Zweitens bieten die identifizierten Konfigurationen Praktikern Hilfestellung bei der Analyse ihrer LQM-Strategien in Schwellenländern und bei der Prüfung alternativer Optionen. Die LQM-Strategien können sich mit Veränderungen auf dem Beschaffungsmarkt weiterentwickeln, wie z.B. Chinas derzeitige Entwicklung von einem kostengünstigen Beschaffungsland zu einem innovationsgetriebenen Beschaffungsmarkt. Unternehmen, die feststellen, dass ihr derzeitiger Ansatz für LQM in einem bestimmten Beschaffungsmarkt nicht mehr mit ihrer angestrebten Strategie übereinstimmt, können einen Wechsel zu einer anderen der identifizierten Konfigurationen in Erwägung ziehen. Beispielsweise kann ein Wechsel von einem kontrollorientierten Ansatz (Konfiguration 4) zu einem kollaborativeren „*Team Coach*"-Ansatz (Konfiguration 1) eingeleitet werden. Dabei müssen sich die Manager jedoch darüber im Klaren sein, dass eine gleichzeitige Änderung *sowohl des Verhaltens als auch der Denkweise* ihrer Global-Sourcing-Teams erforderlich ist, um das richtige Zusammenspiel zu erreichen. Einfach neue LQM-Praktiken einzuführen, ohne gleichzeitig und in gleichem Maße die Einstellungen der involvierten Akteure zu adressieren, scheint wenig erfolgversprechend zu sein.

Drittens, basierend auf den empirischen Erkenntnissen aus der fsQCA-Analyse kann den für die Beschaffung in Schwellenländern verantwortlichen Managern geraten werden, das zeitliche Fokusprofil ihrer Einkaufsteams und ihrer Lieferanten explizit bei Entscheidungen über Einkaufsstrategien zu berücksichtigen. Wenn sie in dynamischen und schnelllebigen Beschaffungsmärkten wie China operieren, sollten westliche Manager mehr Aufmerksamkeit auf die Gegenwart lenken, indem sie spontan reagieren, auf eine höhere Taktfrequenz umschalten und Chancen ergreifen, um in einem sich dynamisch verändernden Markt Mehrwert mit Lieferanten zu generieren. Lieferantenmanagement in Schwellenländern ist – metaphorisch gesprochen – eher wie eine auf Improvisation basierende Jazz-Performance, während Lieferantenmanagement in stabilen Märkten eher ein Orchesterkonzert darstellt, in dem jedes Instrument seine Rolle kennt, plant und ausführt. Um die oft impliziten zeitlichen Brillen der beiden Parteien besser aufeinander abzustimmen, könnten Manager Prozesse entwickeln, um explizit Zeithorizonte mit ihren Supply-Chain-Partnern zu diskutieren.

Literatur

Barney, J. (2012): Purchasing, supply chain management and sustained competitive advantage: The relevance of resource-based theory, in: Journal of Supply Chain Management, 48(2), 3–6.

Busse, C.; Schleper, M.; Niu, M.; Wagner, S. M. (2016): Supplier development for sustainability: Contextual barriers in global supply chains, in: International Journal of Physical Distribution & Logistics Management, 46(5), 442–468.

Carter, C. R.; Kaufmann, L.; Michel, A. (2007): Behavioral supply management: A taxonomy of judgment and decision-making biases, in: International Journal of Physical Distribution & Logistics Management, 37(8), 631–669.

Carter, C. R.; Kosmol, T.; Kaufmann, L. (2017): Toward a supply chain practice view, in: Journal of Supply Chain Management, 53(1), 114–122.

Craighead, C. W.; Ketchen Jr., D. J.; Cheng, L. (2016): "Goldilocks" theorizing in supply chain research: Balancing scientific and practical utility via middle-range theory, in: Transportation Journal, 55(3), 241–257.

Crilly, D. (2011): Predicting stakeholder orientation in the multinational enterprise: A mid-range theory, in: Journal of International Business Studies, 42(5), 694–717.

Eckerd, S.; Boyer, K. K.; Qi, Y.; Eckerd, A.; Hill, J. A. (2016): Supply chain psychological contract breach: An experimental study across national cultures, in: Journal of Supply Chain Management, 52(3), 68–82.

Eisenhardt, K. M. (1989): Building theories from case study research, in: Academy of Management Review, 14(4), 532–550.

Flanagan, J. C. (1954): The critical incident technique, in: Psychological Bulletin, 51(4), 327–358.

Foerstl, K.; Franke, H.; Zimmermann, F. (2016): Mediation effects in the 'purchasing and supply management (PSM) practice–performance link': Findings from a meta-analytical structural equation model, in: Journal of Purchasing and Supply Management, 22(4), 351–366.

Gibbert, M.; Ruigrok, W.; Wicki, B. (2008): What passes as a rigorous case study?, in: Strategic Management Journal, 29(13), 1465–1474.

Greckhamer, T. (2016): CEO compensation in relation to worker compensation across countries: The configurational impact of country-level institutions, in: Strategic Management Journal, 37(4), 793–815.

Greckhamer, T.; Misangyi, V. F.; Elms, H.; Lacey, R. (2008): Using qualitative comparative analysis in strategic management research: An examination of combinations of industry, corporate, and business-unit effects, in: Organizational Research Methods, 11(4), 695–726.

Heide, J. B.; Wathne, K. H.; Rokkan, A. I. (2007): Interfirm monitoring, social contracts, and relationship outcomes, in: Journal of Marketing Research, 44(3), 425–433.

Hofstede, G. (1984): Culture's consequences: International differences in work-related values, 5th edition, Beverly Hills, CA: SAGE Publications, Inc.

Horn, P.; Schiele, H.; Werner, W. (2013): The 'ugly twins': Failed low-wage-country sourcing projects and their expensive replacements, in: Journal of Purchasing and Supply Management, 19(1), 27–38.

Jia, F.; Rutherford, C.; Lamming, R. (2016): Cultural adaptation and socialisation between Western buyers and Chinese suppliers: The formation of a hybrid culture, in: International Business Review, 25(6), 1246–1261.

Johanson, J.; Vahlne, J.-E. (2009): The Uppsala internationalization process model revisited: From liability of foreignness to liability of outsidership, in: Journal of International Business Studies, 40(9), 1411–1431.

Karatzas, A.; Johnson, M.; Bastl, M. (2016): Relationship determinants of performance in service triads: A configurational approach, in: Journal of Supply Chain Management, 52(3), 28–47.

Kaufmann, L.; Carter, C. R.; Rauer, J. (2016): The coevolution of relationship dominant logic and supply risk mitigation strategies, in: Journal of Business Logistics, 37(2), 87–106.

Kaufmann, L.; Wagner, C. M.; Carter, C. R. (2017): Individual modes and patterns of rational and intuitive decision-making by purchasing managers, in: Journal of Purchasing and Supply Management, 23(2), 82–93.

Kaynak, H.; Hartley, J. L. (2008): A replication and extension of quality management into the supply chain, in: Journal of Operations Management, 26(4), 468–489.

Kim, H.; Hur, D.; Schoenherr, T. (2015): When buyer-driven knowledge transfer activities really work: A motivation–opportunity–ability perspective, in: Journal of Supply Chain Management, 51(3), 33–60.

Kor, Y. Y.; Mesko, A. (2013): Dynamic managerial capabilities: Configuration and orchestration of top executives' capabilities and the firm's dominant logic, in: Strategic Management Journal, 34(2), 233–244.

Kosmol, T.; Reimann, F.; Kaufmann, L. (2017): Co-alignment of supplier quality management practices and cognitive maps – A neo-configurational perspective, in: Journal of Purchasing and Supply Management, 24(1), 1–20, doi: 10.1016/j.pursup.2017.11.002.

Kovach, J. J.; Hora, M.; Manikas, A.; Patel, P. C. (2015): Firm performance in dynamic environments: The role of operational slack and operational scope, in: Journal of Operations Management, 37, 1–12.

Krause, D. R.; Handfield, R. B.; Tyler, B. B. (2007): The relationships between supplier development, commitment, social capital accumulation and performance improvement, in: Journal of Operations Management, 25(2), 528–545.

Kull, T. J.; Wacker, J. G. (2010): Quality management effectiveness in Asia: The influence of culture, in: Journal of Operations Management, 28(3), 223–239.

Lockström, M.; Schadel, J.; Moser, R.; Harrison, N. (2011): Domestic supplier integration in the Chinese automotive industry: The buyer's perspective, in: Journal of Supply Chain Management, 47(4), 44–63.

Maitland, E.; Sammartino, A. (2015a): Decision making and uncertainty: The role of heuristics and experience in assessing a politically hazardous environment, in: Strategic Management Journal, 36(10), 1554–1578.

Maitland, E.; Sammartino, A. (2015b): Managerial cognition and internationalization, in: Journal of International Business Studies, 46(7), 733–760.

Martignoni, D.; Menon, A.; Siggelkow, N. (2016): Consequences of misspecified mental models: Contrasting effects and the role of cognitive fit, in: Strategic Management Journal, 37(13), 2545–2568.

Martin, T. W.; Jeong, E.-Y. (2017): Samsung blames Galaxy Note 7 overheating on problems at suppliers, in: The Wall Street Journal, January 22, 2017.

Misangyi, V. F.; Acharya, A. G. (2014): Substitutes or complements? A configurational examination of corporate governance mechanisms, in: Academy of Management Journal, 57(6), 1681–1705.

Misangyi, V. F.; Greckhamer, T.; Furnari, S.; Fiss, P. C.; Crilly, D.; Aguilera, R. (2017): Embracing causal complexity: The emergence of a neo-configurational perspective, in: Journal of Management, 43(1), 255–282.

Nadkarni, S.; Chen, J. (2014): Bridging yesterday, today, and tomorrow: CEO temporal focus, environmental dynamism, and rate of new product introduction, in: Academy of Management Journal, 57(6), 1810–1833.

Najafi, N.; Dubois, A.; Hulthén, K. (2013): Opportunism or strategic opportunity seeking? Three approaches to emerging country sourcing, in: Journal of Purchasing and Supply Management, 19(1), 49–57.

Noshad, K.; Awasthi, A. (2015): Supplier quality development: A review of literature and industry practices, in: International Journal of Production Research, 53(2), 466–487.

Pagell, M.; Wu, Z. (2009): Building a more complete theory of sustainable supply chain management using case studies of 10 exemplars, in: Journal of Supply Chain Management, 45(2), 37–56.

Pennebaker, J. W.; Francis, M. E.; Booth, R. J. (2001): Linguistic Inquiry and Word Count: LIWC 2001, Mahwah, NJ: Lawrence Erlbaum Associates.

Ragin, C. C. (2008): Redesigning social inquiry: Fuzzy sets and beyond, Chicago: University of Chicago Press.

RAPEX. (2017): Rapid alert system for dangerous products: 2016 annual report. Retrieved from https://ec.europa.eu/consumers/consumers_safety/safety_products/rapex/alerts/repository/content/pages/rapex/reports/docs/rapex_annual_report_2016_en.pdf.

Reimann, F.; Kosmol, T.; Kaufmann, L. (2017): Responses to supplier-induced disruptions: A fuzzy-set analysis, in: Journal of Supply Chain Management, 53(4), 37–66.

Reinecke, J.; Ansari, S. (2015): When times collide: Temporal brokerage at the intersection of markets and developments, in: Academy of Management Journal, 58(2), 618–648.

Schoenherr, T.; Griffith, D. A.; Chandra, A. (2014): Knowledge management in supply chains: The role of explicit and tacit knowledge, in: Journal of Business Logistics, 35(2), 121–135.

Schorsch, T.; Wallenburg, C. M.; Wieland, A. (2017): The human factor in SCM, in: International Journal of Physical Distribution & Logistics Management, 47(4), 238–262.

Shipp, A. J.; Edwards, J. R.; Lambert, L. S. (2009): Conceptualization and measurement of temporal focus: The subjective experience of the past, present, and future, in: Organizational Behavior and Human Decision Processes, 110(1), 1–22.

Soares, A.; Soltani, E.; Liao, Y.-Y. (2017): The influence of supply chain quality management practices on quality performance: an empirical investigation, in: Supply Chain Management: An International Journal, 22(2).

Stanczyk, A.; Cataldo, Z.; Blome, C.; Busse, C. (2017): The dark side of global sourcing: A systematic literature review and research agenda, in: International Journal of Physical Distribution & Logistics Management, 47(1), 41–67.

Stanczyk, A.; Foerstl, K.; Busse, C.; Blome, C. (2015): Global sourcing decision-making processes: Politics, intuition, and procedural rationality, in: Journal of Business Logistics, 36(2), 160–181.

Steven, A. B.; Britto, R. A. (2016): Emerging market presence, inventory, and product recall linkages, in: Journal of Operations Management, 46, 55–68.

Tausczik, Y. R.; Pennebaker, J. W. (2010): The psychological meaning of words: LIWC and computerized text analysis methods, in: Journal of Language and Social Psychology, 29(1), 24–54.

Timmer, S.; Kaufmann, L. (2017): Conflict minerals traceability – a fuzzy set analysis, in: International Journal of Physical Distribution & Logistics Management, 47(5), 344–367.

Vis, B. (2012): The comparative advantages of fsQCA and regression analysis for moderately large-N analyses, in: Sociological Methods & Research, 41(1), 168–198.

Wiengarten, F.; Ambrose, E. (2017): The role of geographical distance and its efficacy on global purchasing practices, in: International Journal of Operations & Production Management, 37(7), 1141.

Xu, D.; Meyer, K. E. (2013): Linking theory and context: 'Strategy research in emerging economies' after Wright et al. (2005), in: Journal of Management Studies, 50(7), 1322–1346.

Zimmermann, F.; Foerstl, K. (2014): A meta-analysis of the 'purchasing and supply management practice–performance link', in: Journal of Supply Chain Management, 50(3), 37–54.

Zsidisin, G. A.; Petkova, B.; Saunders, L. W.; Bisseling, M. (2016): Identifying and managing supply quality risk, in: The International Journal of Logistics Management, 27(3), 908–930.

Collaborative recovery from supply chain disruptions

Marie Katharina Brüning

Abstract

Today's supply chains are increasingly global and highly interconnected while aiming at the same time to lower inventory levels and shorten lead times. This combination leaves companies in supply chains more vulnerable to disruptions. The sharing of resources among supply chain actors is introduced as a method to recover quickly from disruptions. This research draws insights from relational view theory and adopts a multi-methodological approach. Case studies and expert interviews are used to develop a framework of promoting factors and effects of collaborative resource sharing in the context of supply chain risk management. The framework is tested empirically through a survey among 216 supply chain managers. We use a structural equation model to show that sharing both human and production resources increases the supply chain resilience. Trust and commitment are identified as main promoting factors. These empirical findings have implications for supply risk chain managers considering the implementation of joint risk management activities. The research also provides impulses for further empirical research in the fields of supply chain risk management and industrial relationships.

1 Introduction

This research examines the effect of collaborative resource sharing on supply chain resilience (SCRES) as a novel reactive risk management method. Consider the following motivating case study that has found ample discussion in literature: In 2011, Renesas' plant in Naka (Japan), a leading supplier for the electronics and automotive industry, was severely damaged by the Great East Japan Earthquake. The plant had to be shut down since its most relevant production resources (machines and equipment) were damaged. In particular, the cleanrooms to fabricate microcontrollers were destroyed (Clark, 2012; Renesas, 2011; Sheffi, 2005). Before the incident, Renesas had a worldwide market share of approximately 40% (Blanding, 2012; Endo, 2011; Park et al. 2013; Pollack, Lohr 2011). The product's criticality, the high level of product customization and Renesas' dominant market position made many global automotive manufacturers depend on Renesas (AFP, 2011). Compared to Renesas' losses of about 156 million USD, the financial consequences along the SC were even more severe: Nissan lost about 434 million USD, Honda about 550 million USD and Toyota about 1.2 billion USD due to the idle waiting times for crucial components (Blanding, 2012; Courtland, 2011). However, the close collaboration among different SC members, including Renesas's customers, suppliers, competitors and governmental organizations enabled limiting the damage. More than 2,500 employees from SC partners were actively involved in Renesas' recovery (Renesas 2011). Employees of partners companies were assigned to recovery activity teams by Renesas' emergency response taskforce. Production volumes were shifted to unaffected factories. Through this collaboration, the production infrastructure and capacity was quickly rebuild and the ramp-up of production could take place three months earlier than initially anticipated (Clark, 2012; Courtland, 2011; Pollack, Lohr, 2011; Renesas, 2011). The case study demonstrates the potential of SC collaboration (SCC) in the context of reactive SC risk management to improve SCRES.

Developing reactive risk management methods is of high practical relevance. This is because the severity and quantity of supply chain (SC) disruptions are increasing. SC disruptions are "unplanned and unanticipated events that disrupt the normal flow of goods and materials within a supply chain" (Craighead et al., 2007, p. 132). SC nowadays are more globalized, carry less inventory, and connect a reduced supplier bases (Brandon-Jones, 2014; Tukamuhabwa et al., 2015). Thus eliminating established mitigating factors, modern SC are increasingly vulnerable. SC risk management (SCRM) methods of many companies have not been adapted to these new framework conditions. Companies still focus on rather preventive and company-focused approaches (Marchese, Paramasivam, 2013; Thun, Hoenig, 2011).

Several authors have reported a deficiency of analyzing reactive risk management methods compared to preventive risk management methods in the SCRM literature (Natarajarathinam et al., 2009; Sodhi et al., 2012; Tukamuhabwa et al., 2015). Preventive measures focus on minimizing the likelihood of disruptions, e.g. through carrying buffer inventories and diversifying suppliers (Bode et al., 2011; Bovell, 2012). Reactive measures on the other hand, focus on limiting the severity of disruptions (Simchi-Levi et al. 2014). Existing SC risk methods also primarily focus on efforts of individual companies instead of looking at SC networks (Jüttner, Maklan, 2011; Stock et al., 2010). Ambulkar et al. (2015) and Li et al. (2015) hence suggest that risk management has to be extended to inter-organizational approaches in order to increase SCRES. We define SCRES here as a SC's ability to recover from a disruption and restore to normal operations in a timely manner (Christopher, Peck, 2004; Ponomarov, 2012; Tukamuhabwa et al. 2015; Wieland, Wallenburg, 2012).

This research advances our understanding of SC-wide, reactive SC risk approaches by transferring the concepts of SCC to the collaborative recovery from SC disruptions. To better understand the potential of collaborative resource sharing, the following research question is discussed in this contribution: "How does collaborative resource sharing affect the resilience of a supply network?" To answer the research question, this paper will 1) identify the promoting factors of collaborative recovery, 2) identify the types of shared resources, and 3) empirically test the effect of resource sharing on SCRES. Notably, the SC (not the individual company) is the unit of analysis for this research. **Table 1** depicts the research design, including the two steps of conceptual framework development and framework testing.

Table 1:   Research Design

Steps	Methods
1: Conceptual framework development (Section 2)	Literature review Case studies Expert interviews
2: Framework testing (Sections 3 and 4)	Survey: Large-scale questionnaire Statistical analysis: Structural equation modelling

To answer the research question, we draw inspiration from the relational view theory (RVT). Initially developed by Dyer and Singh (1998), it is an extension of the resource-based view theory. RVT is used as a basis to understand the role of resource sharing among SC partners as part of a SCC and in the special case of a SC disruption. The theory picks up the trend that networks of collaborating companies, instead of individual companies, compete against each other. Dyer and Singh (1998) state that inter-firm linkages and inter-organizational resources may be a source of relational rents and collaborative advantage. According to RVT, long-term SC relationships create value that neither partner would have been able to create independently (Nyaga et al., 2010). Companies seek to build collaborative relationships to access complementary resources (Cao et al., 2010; Park et al., 2004) and therefore improve collaborative advantage (Cao, Zhang, 2013; De Leeuw, Fransoo, 2009; Mentzer et al., 2000; Mohr, Spekman, 1994; Nyaga et al., 2010).

The remainder of the article is structured as follows: Section 2 presents the multi-methodological approach of hypothesis development, based on the RVT, a profound literature review, eight expert interviews and six case studies. Section 3 outlines the testing of the theoretical framework through an online survey. Section 4 covers the results of the hypothesis testing. Section 5 discusses the results and contrasts them with existing literature. Section 6 concludes with theoretical and managerial implications as well as suggestions for further research.

2 Conceptual framework development

2.1 Multi-methods framework development

In order to answer the research question, an empirical research approach was chosen. As pointed out by several researchers, there is a lack of empirical research in the field of SC risk management and SCRES (Sodhi et al., 2012; Thun, Hoenig, 2011; Tukamuhabwa et al., 2015; Scholten, Schilder, 2015). Developing a theoretical framework is understood as an iterative process (Kubicek, 1976). Accordingly, with a multi-methodological approach, the theoretical framework was continually modified with experience and information obtained from (1) six case studies, (2) eight expert interviews and an (3) extensive literature review (**Figure 1**).

Figure 1: Iterative framework development process

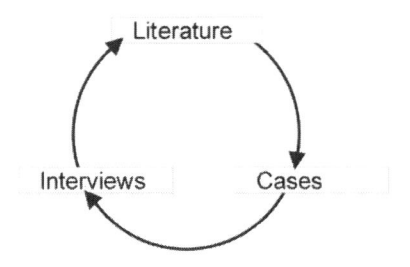

According to Boyer and Swink (2008), only the combination of multiple methods allows the development of an accurate picture of a research topic. Six case studies were conducted based on secondary data (Brüning et al., 2014). To ensure validity and reliability, established structured procedures were employed, such as case selection criteria and case study protocols. Then, eight semi-structured expert interviews were executed, providing the ability to extract a great variety of data due to interviewer's flexibility (Cooper, Schindler 2006). As suggested by Flick (2006), an interview guideline was developed and the interviewees reviewed their protocols. The developed theoretical framework is described in the following paragraphs.

2.2 Collaborative recovery

The aim of this research is to analyze the relation between collaborative resource sharing and SCRES. This relation describes a reactive risk management method that is called *collaborative recovery* in this contribution. Several researchers highlight the necessity to further investigate the interplay of SCC and SCRES. Bovell (2012) and Camarinha-Matos (2014) highlight the value of collaborative resource sharing with respect to SCRES. Company networks can dynamically combine the best fitting set of competencies and resources in order to deal with disruptions (Camarinha-Matos, 2014). Ambulkar et al. (2015) find that in order to be resilient, companies need to be able to reconfigure resources. Accordingly, they state that resources by themselves are not sufficient for achieving resilience; the ability to reconfigure them is decisive. Bode et al. (2011) present the reactive methods 'bridging' which focuses on collaborative actions, like establishing relationships with influential individuals in partner companies. Furthermore, they find that the levels of trust and dependency are crucial in choosing a reactive method. Bello and Bovell (2012) state that there is a lack in disruption recovery literature regarding the attention paid to relational resources that enable collaboration. Furthermore, existing research in this field focuses mainly on continuously existing intangible relational resources in SC instead of tangible and intangible resources actually shared during disruption recoveries. In addition, Cao and Zhang (2013) describe the lack of studies on collaborative advantage in the context of SC. The developed framework of collaborative recovery is depicted in **Figure 2**. It captures the types of resources shared, the promoting factors and the effect of resource sharing on SCRES.

Figure 2: Hypothesized framework of collaborative recovery

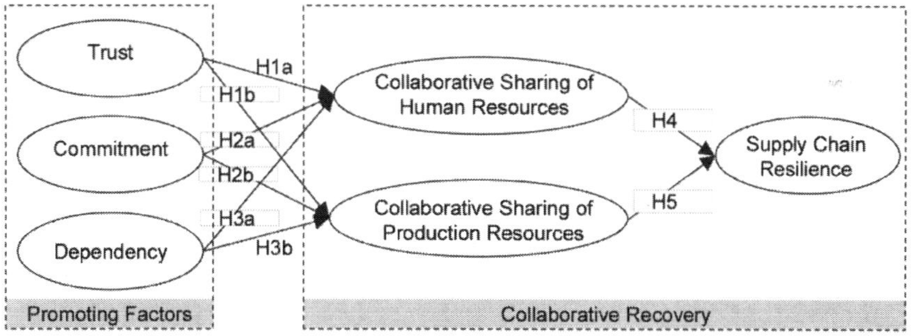

Types of resources shared

From a RVT perspective, resources are the key to collaborative advantage (Dyer, Singh 1998). Accordingly, Lavie (2006) argues that companies can obtain value from resources which are not controlled or fully owned by their internal organization. Cao et al. (2010) state that resource sharing is one element of SCC and is defined as "[…] *the process of leveraging capabilities and assets and investing in capabilities and assets with supply chain partners*" (Cao et al. 2010, p. 6621). Bovell (2012) and Bello and Bovell (2010) argue that collaboration mobilizes actors and gives companies greater access to resources. This is because mobilized actors are more willing to share and combine resources interorganizationally for joint activities, such as mutual risk resolution. During disruption recoveries, resources can be shared by various different actors, such as customers, suppliers, competitors, logistics service providers, governmental agencies or other sites of the affected company.

Resources are hence the central constructs of the developed framework. In particular, two types of resources are considered: human resources (HR) and production resources (PR). The term *HR* encompasses employees, managers or engineers as well as their know-how and skills. The term *PR* covers equipment, tools, facilities, machine capacities and warehouse capacities as well as information and know-how (for instance about production processes). An in-depth analysis of the conducted interviews and case-studies reveals that capacity adaptability, mobility, and availability are the main abilities that enable resources to be shared (Brüning et al., 2014).

Promoting factors

Three relational resources that promote collaborative recoveries are identified, namely *trust*, *commitment*, and *dependency*. From the RVT perspective, relational resources are highly relevant: According to Dyer and Singh (1998), the ability to generate relational rents increases with the companies' prior alliance experience, thus with the degree of compatibility in the companies' organizational systems, processes, and cultures.

Several studies found strong associations between SC partners' trust and relationship success (Kwon, Suh, 2005; Li et al., 2015; Mishra et al., 2016; Mohr, Spekman, 1994; Sheu et al., 2006). Trust is defined by Rousseau et al. (1998, p. 395) as *"the intention to accept vulnerability based upon positive expectations of the intentions or behavior of another"*. The concept of trust is composed of two main dimensions: *credibility* and *benevolence* (Doney, Cannon, 1997).

A large amount of studies likewise stress the relevance of commitment in collaborative relationships (Fawcett et al., 2006; Mohr, Spekman, 1994; Nyaga et al., 2010; Ryu et al., 2009; Sheu et al., 2006). Morgan and Hunt (1994, p. 23) define commitment as *"an exchange partner believing that an ongoing relationship with another is so important as to warrant maximum efforts at maintaining it; that is, the committed party believes the relationship is worth working on to ensure that it endures indefinitely"*. Commitment generally encompasses three dimensions, namely affective commitment, expectation of continuity, and willingness to invest in the relationship (Kumar et al., 1995).

According to the RVT, trust and commitment are relational network resources that can be leveraged to achieve collaborative advantage. Zhang and Huo (2013) argue that in relationships with a high level of trust, parties can access and share external resources faster and easier which facilitates SC cooperation and coordination. According to McEvily et al. (2003), trust can be a mobilizer that motivates companies to contribute and combine their resources in joint activities to achieve their goals and to resolve problems. Similarly, committed companies are motivated to make relationship-specific investments to realize their shared long-term goals (Mentzer et al., 2000; Sheu et al.,

2006; Vijayasarathy, 2010). Accordingly, Monczka et al. (1998, p. 557) explain that *"commitment to a relationship is most frequently demonstrated by committing resources to the relationship, which may occur in the form of an organization's time, money, facilities, etc."*. Dwyer et al. (1987, p. 19) state that committed parties *"purposefully engage resources to maintain relationships"*. The described arguments based on existing literature, case studies and expert interviews lead to the following hypotheses:

- *Hypotheses 1a and 1b:* A high level of trust between SC network partners leads to a high level of collaborative sharing of (a) HR (b) PR during disruption recoveries.

- *Hypotheses 2a and 2b:* A high level of commitment between SC network partners leads to a high level of collaborative sharing of (a) HR (b) PR during disruption recoveries.

According to the analyzed literature, cases and expert interviews, *dependency* seems to motivate SC members to share resources during SC disruption recoveries. Dependence exists *"when one party does not entirely control all of the conditions necessary for achievement of an action or a desired outcome"* (Handfield, Bechtel, 2002, p. 371; Monczka et al., 1998, p. 558). Thus, a company needs to maintain a relationship with a partner in order to achieve its goals (Hudnurkar et al., 2014; Sheu et al., 2006). Several authors suggest a positive effect of dependency on SCC (Bode et al., 2011; Ferrer et al., 2010; Hudnurkar et al., 2014; Mishra et al., 2016; Monczka et al., 1998; Scholten, Schilder, 2015; Sheu et al., 2006). High interdependence motivates to share key information and participate in joint efforts (Sheu et al., 2006).

The level of dependency is often related to the criticality of a product (De Leeuw, Fransoo, 2009; Ferrer et al., 2010; Whitney et al., 2014). The analyzed cases offer several examples of high product criticality which increases dependency and motivates network members to collaborate during SC disruption recoveries. For example, Renesas' microcontrollers are custom-made which makes switching to another supplier difficult (Endo, 2011; Pollack, Lohr, 2011).

From a RVT perspective, dependency is a relational resource which enables SC to collaboratively achieve advantages over competing SCs, by means of collaborative resource sharing. The importance of dependency with regard to collaborative recovery was stressed by all interviewed experts. With dependency, companies are intrinsically motivated to collaborate during SC disruption recoveries. Based on these findings, the following hypotheses are derived:

- *Hypotheses 3a/3b:* A high level of dependency between SC network partners leads to a high level of collaborative resource sharing of (a) HR (b) PR during disruption recoveries.

Effect on supply chain resilience

Based on an extensive literature review, Tukamuhabwa et al. (2015) conclude that companies that respond to a disruption faster and in a more cost-effective way than their competitors can improve their market position. Rice and Caniato (2003) state that in case of disruptions, companies can compete on their resilience capabilities. Following the RVT line of argumentation, a higher level SCRES is achieved if a SC recovers better than its competing SCs, thus if it holds a collaborative advantage with regard to SCRES. The success of a recovery often refers to the so-called *time to recover* (Simchi-Levi et al., 2014). The *time to recover* is defined as the time period between the occurrence of the disruption and the complete restoring of the SC.

Several researchers point out that there is a positive relation between the concepts SCC and SCRES (Bello, Bovell, 2012; Bovell, 2012; Blackhurst et al., 2011; Brüning, Bendul, 2015; Wieland, Wallenburg, 2012). For example, Christopher and Peck (2004, p. 9) state that *"building resilience to supply chain risks requires a high degree of collaboration"*. With regard to HR, Blackhurst et al. (2011) state that human capital factors, such as education and training of employees in the SC, can increase SCRES. With regard to PR, Blackhurst et al. (2011) argue that tangible PR can quickly be redesigned in case of a disruption in order to positively contribute to SCRES. Also, Scholten and Schilder (2015) find that collaborative resource sharing can increase SCRES. They give explicit examples, such as sharing transportation capacities and personnel, establishing site visits or adapting processes. According to RVT, network resources are leveraged in order to gain collaborative advantage, e.g. SCRES. Thus, SCs that use and share available resources during disruption recoveries may recover better, i.e. faster, than competing SCs. Based on the RVT line of argumentation and the described analysis results, the following hypotheses are derived:

- *Hypothesis 4:* A high level of collaborative sharing of HR during disruption recoveries leads to a high level of SC resilience.

- *Hypothesis 5:* A high level of collaborative sharing of PR during disruption recoveries leads to a high level of SC resilience.

3 Framework testing

In order to test the developed framework, we conducted a large scale online survey. The methodology and used items are further elaborated in this Section.

3.1 Data collection and sample

The online survey was conducted within six weeks in February and March of 2016. The survey was sent to 7,861 contacts. They received an invitation email including the link to the online survey, an incentive to participate (suggested by Dillman, 2014 and Frohlich, 2002), and information regarding confidentiality which reduces socially desirable responses (Podsakoff et al., 2003). After subtracting the mailing errors, there were 5,909 valid contacts. 1st reminders and 2nd reminders were sent via email to the contacts that had not yet responded (suggested by Dillman, 2014, and Frohlich, 2002). With 321 people participating in the survey, the resulting response rate is 5.4%. Several cases had to be eliminated mainly because they were incomplete in large parts, leaving a usable data set of 216 cases. The sample is a good representation of key informants. 56.3% of the participants work in the logistics / supply chain management sector and 50.7% have work experience of more than ten years with their current employer. In addition, 76.2% of the participants state that they have high or very high degree of knowledge about the survey topic. To test for non-response bias, Chi-square tests were applied to compare early to late respondents' answers in terms of participant's experience in company and company size (Armstrong, Overton, 1977; Wagner, Kemmerling, 2010). With no significant difference between the two groups at the level of 0.25, the absence of non-response biases is assumed.

3.2 Measures

We developed the survey using both existing and new items. An overview of the constructs and the associated literature can be found in **Table 2**. All items were measured on a seven-point Likert scale (1 = strongly disagree, 7 = strongly agree). Existing items were adjusted in two ways. First, the items for collaborative resource sharing (HR and PR) as well as for SCRES were rephrased in past tense, since they aimed at asking for circumstances during past disruption recoveries. Second, the items were adjusted to reflect this study's unit of analysis, the SC (Wieland, Wallenburg, 2013). An overview of all items can be found in the Appendix.

Table 2:   Overview of constructs

Construct	References (adapted from)
Trust	Doney, Cannon, 1997
Commitment	Wilson, Vlosky, 1997; Kumar et al., 1995
Dependency	Ganesan, 1994; Wagner, Bode, 2006
Collaborative Sharing of Human Resources	Cao et al., 2010; Park, 2011
Collaborative Sharing of Production Resources	Cao et al., 2010; Park, 2011
Supply Chain Resilience	Ponomarov, 2012; Park, 2011; Swafford et al., 2006

The construct *collaborative sharing of HR* is measured by four items. Item *HR1* (adapted from Cao et al., 2010; Cao, Zhang, 2013) assesses the sharing of know-how/expertise within SCs. Items *HR2*, *HR3* and *HR4* assess the abilities of the resources shared. HR2 (adapted from Park, 2011) measures the quick reorganization of HR in SC. *HR3* and *HR4* were newly developed based on the results of the case studies and expert interviews. They capture the adaptability to new tasks and mobility to exchange know-how and expertise in the SC. The 'availability of capacity' is not explicitly measured but it is inherent in *HR2* and *HR4*. The construct *collaborative sharing of PR* is represented by four items which are similar to the HR items (*PR5 to* PR8).

To measure the construct *trust*, the measurement developed by Doney and Cannon (1997) was selected. It covers the two dimensions of trust and consists of four items. The dimension *benevolence* is represented by two items. They capture the extent to which kept each other's best interests in mind and the extent to which they were concerned about each other's business success. The two other items reflect the dimension *credibility*. These items assess the degree of honesty between SC members and the extent to which they SC members keep each other's promises.

The construct *commitment* was operationalized based on the work of Wilson and Vlosky (1997) and Kumar et al. (1995). The items cover the three dimensions of commitment. The dimension *expectation of continuity* (adapted from Wilson, Vlosky, 1997) captures the members' desire to defend the relationships with each other for a long time. Also *willingness to invest* was measured by a scale developed by Wilson and Vlosky (1997). *Affective commitment* (adapted from Kumar et al., 1995) is composed of two items that assess to what extent the members like being associated with each other and the positive feeling towards each other.

Dependency was measured using five items. *DEPEND13* to *DEPEND16* (adapted from Ganesan, 1994) assess the SC partners' inability to find good alternatives, to replace a member, to achieve goals if a relationship was discontinued as well as a general dependency on each other. *DEPEND17* (adapted from Wagner, Bode, 2006) assesses the usage of single sourcing strategies.

To measure *supply chain resilience*, six existing items were adapted. Item *SCRES18* (adapted from Brandon-Jones et al., 2014; Ponomarov, 2012) captures the basic idea of *SCRES* from a RVT perspective, namely the rapid recovery compared to competing SC. *SCRES19* (adapted from Park, 2011) assesses the SC's ability to mitigate the disruption's severity. *SCRES20* to *SCRES23* (adapted from Ambulkar et al., 2015; Park, 2011) cover more detailed the responses to the disruption with regard to specific key performance measures.

3.3   The measurement model

To evaluate the measurement model's fit, the constructs' reliability as well as discriminant and convergent validity are assessed (Shah, Goldstein, 2006). For all analyzed constructs, the values for Cronbach's alpha are ≥ 0.7 (threshold suggested by Nunnally

1978, Swafford et al., 2006). A more detailed overview is given in the Appendix. We hence consider the constructs' reliability established.

Discriminant validity is demonstrated with the correlations among all items being < 1.0 (Anderson, Gerbing, 1988; Ramanathan, Gunasekaran, 2014). Convergent validity is demonstrated as all standardized factor loadings are ≥ 0.5 and significant at a 1% significance level (Anderson, Gerbing, 1988; Ramanathan, Gunasekaran, 2014; Swafford et al. 2006). All factor loadings can be found in the Appendix.

For confirmatory factor analysis (CFA), Chi-square, Normed Fit Index (NFI), Relative Fit Index (RFI), Incremental Fit Index (IFI), Trucker-Lewis Index (TLI), Comparative Fit Index (CFI), Root Mean Square Error of Approximation (RMSEA), and Standardized Root Mean Square Residual (SRMR) were used to evaluate the measurement model. **Table 3** provides an overview of the measures and thresholds used in the CFA. Based on them, all six measurement models were modified until all measures were judged to be satisfactory. Several correlations between measurement errors were made.

Table 3: Confirmatory factor analysis: measures, thresholds and results

Measures (Thresholds)	Chi-square $(x^2)^a$ $p \geq .05$	df	CMIN/DF $\leq 3.0^a$	NFI > $.90^{b,c,d}$	RFI > $.90^{b,c,d}$	IFI > $.90^{b,c,d}$	TLI > $.90^{b,c,d}$	CFI > $.90^{b,c,d}$	RMSEA $\leq .08^{e,f}$	SRMR $\leq .08^b$
Constructs (final measurement model)										
Trust_ Commitment	4.743; p: .093	2	2.371	.989	.966	.993	.980	.993	.080	.0184
Dependency	3.178; p: .365	3	1.059	.994	.980	1.000	.999	1.000	.017	.0168
Collaborative Sharing of Human Resources	1.902; p: .168	1	1.902	.995	.972	.998	.987	.998	.065	.0098
Collaborative Sharing of Production Resources	Measures cannot be calculated because the final model has only three items and, therefore, no degrees of freedom.									
Supply Chain Resilience	12.660; p: .081	7	1.809	.987	.973	.994	.988	.994	.061	.0186

[a] Segars, Grover, 1993; [b] Hu, Bentler, 1998; [c] Jöreskog, 1969; [d] Swafford et al., 2006; [e] Backhaus, 2011; [f] Byrne, 2010

The survey data shows that especially *PR8* and *PR5* show similar distributions. *PR8* focuses on the mobility of resources, thus a prerequisite of resource sharing which is covered by the more general item *PR5*. Furthermore, *PR8* displays the lowest standardized factor loading (0.713) and, consequently, was eliminated from the measurement model. After dropping it, the construct *collaborative sharing of PR* has only three remaining items. Most CFA measures cannot be calculated because a model with three items has no degrees of freedom. Therefore, consulting the remaining criteria, namely constructs' reliability, discriminant and convergent validity, is sufficient (Deepen, 2007). For the construct *collaborative sharing of PR* these criteria are satisfactory.

There is a high correlation value between the variables *trust* and *commitment* (0.758, p-value < 0.001). The significant correlation value is only slightly below the suggested threshold of multicollinearity (> 0.8, Field, 2009). An exploratory factor analysis (EFA) is conducted to understand the structure of item sets and to deal with the identified multicollinearity (Field, 2009). The eigenvalue (5.002, 62.52% of variance) as well as the scree plot indicate that it is sensible to treat *trust* and *commitment* as one construct (Cattell, 1966; Field, 2009; Kaiser, 1960). For the new construct *trust_commitment*, the four items with the highest loading are chosen, namely *TRUST9*, *TRUST10*, *COMM11* and *COMM12*. In **Table 4** the results of all measurement models are shown.

4 Analysis and results

Structural equation modeling (SEM) is performed using AMOS to test the structural model and the developed hypotheses. Several fit measures are used to assess whether the hypothesized model fits the data. Then, the standardized regression weights are evaluated to test the developed hypotheses. All hypotheses are directional (positively formulated) and the tests are therefore one-tailed (Field, 2009). Standardized regression weights with p-values < 0.05 are considered to be significant.

The results of the SEM show that the fit measures do not exceed the suggested thresholds and therefore indicate a good fit. Four of the six hypothesized relationships are significantly supported (**Table 4**). The standardized regression weight between the constructs *trust_commitment* and *collaborative sharing of HR* (0.383; p-value < 0.001) as well as *PR* (0.387; p-value < 0.001) have significant positive values. This shows that trust and commitment have a positive impact on both forms of collaborative resource sharing, thus supporting H1a/2a and H1b/2b. The relationships between *dependency* and *collaborative sharing of HR* (0.084, p-value: 0.259) as well as *PR* (0.015; p-value: 0.843) are relatively low and not significant. Hence, hypotheses 3a and 3b which state that there is a positive relation between dependency and collaborative resource sharing are not supported. The analysis confirms a positive, significant relationship between *collaborative resource sharing: HR* and *SCRES* (0.275; p-value: 0.002) as well as between the constructs *collaborative sharing of PR* and *SCRES* (0.292; p-value < 0.001). These results support hypotheses 4 and 5, stating that a high level of collaborative resource sharing (HR / PR) during SC disruption recoveries leads to a high level of SCRES.

Table 4: Hypothesis testing

Hypothesis		Standardized regression weight, p-value	Decision
H1a/2a:	Trust_Commitment → Collaborative Sharing of Human Resources	0.383, p-value: < 0.001	Supported
H1b/2b:	Trust_Commitment → Collaborative Sharing of Production Resources	0.387, p-value: < 0.001	Supported
H3a:	Dependency → Collaborative Sharing of Human Resources	0.084, p-value: 0.259	Not supported
H3b:	Dependency → Collaborative Sharing of Production Resources	0.015, p-value: 0.843	Not supported
H4:	Collaborative Sharing of Human Resources → Supply Chain Resilience	0.275, p-value: 0.002	Supported
H5:	Collaborative Sharing of Production Resources → Supply Chain Resilience	0.291, p-value < 0.001	Supported

In the tested model, the relationships between *dependency* and *collaborative resource sharing (HR and PR)* are not significant. However, the findings of the conducted case studies and expert interviews lead to the conclusion that dependency plays an important role in collaborative recoveries. *Dependency* was often described as the initial trigger that motivates companies to collaborate. It should be highlighted that all interviewed experts stressed the relevance of dependency in this context. Based on these findings, the role of dependency in the model was further analyzed. There is a significant correlation between *dependency* and *trust_commitment* (0.183, p-value: 0.026). The position of the construct *dependency* in the model was rearranged. The variable *dependency* is moved to be the only independent variable, positively influencing *trust_commitment*. In the modified model, there is a positive significant relationship between *dependency* and *trust_commitment* (0.187, p-value: 0.019). The results in **Table 5** and **Figure 3** show that all relationships are significant and the fit measures indicate a good fit. The modified model indicates that *dependency* plays indeed an important role in these collaboration activities but with a different line of argumentation. Dependency indirectly influences *collaborative resource sharing (HR and PR)* via *trust* and *commitment*.

Table 5: Structural equation modelling (modified model)

Measures (Thresholds)	Chi-square (x^2) [a] $p \geq .05$	df	CMIN/DF ≤ 3.0 [a]	TLI > $.90$ [b,c,d]	CFI > $.90$ [b,c,d]	IFI > $.90$ [b,c,d]	RMSEA $\leq .08$ [e,f]	SRMR $\leq .08$ [b]
Modified model	264.263	189	1.335	.972	.976	.977	.039	.0621

[a] Segars, Grover, 1993; [b] Hu, Bentler, 1998; [c] Jöreskog, 1969; [d] Swafford et al., 2006; [e] Backhaus, 2011; [f] Byrne, 2010

Figure 3: Structural equation modelling: hypothesis testing (modified model)

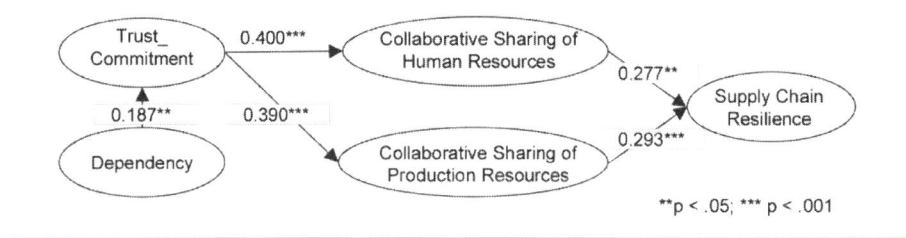

- Trust_Commitment → Collaborative Sharing of Human Resources: 0.400^{***}
- Trust_Commitment ↔ Dependency: 0.187^{**}
- Dependency → Collaborative Sharing of Human Resources / Production Resources: 0.390^{***}
- Collaborative Sharing of Human Resources → Supply Chain Resilience: 0.277^{**}
- Collaborative Sharing of Production Resources → Supply Chain Resilience: 0.293^{***}

$^{**}p < .05;\ ^{***}p < .001$

5 Discussion

The support of the hypothesis that both types of collaborative resource sharing have significant positive impacts on SCRES reflects the basic idea of the RVT: SC can gain collaborative advantage by leveraging interorganizational resources available in the network (Dyer, Singh, 1998). The resources available in the network and especially their potentials resemble the so-called complementary resource endowments. They are defined by Dyer and Singh (1998, p. 666) as *"distinctive resources of alliance partners that collectively generate greater rents than the sum of those obtained from the individual endowments of each partner"*. The findings are consistent with Lavie's (2006) argument that companies can obtain value from resources which are not controlled or fully owned by their internal organization. These survey results are also in line with previous studies. For example, Bovell (2012; Bello, Bovell, 2010) state that collaboration mobilizes actors and gives companies greater access to resources. This is because mobilized actors are more willing to share and combine resources interorganizationally for joint activities, such as mutual risk resolution. According to Camarinha-Matos (2014), company networks can dynamically combine the best fitting set of competencies and resources in order to deal with disruptions. Ambulkar et al. (2015), Bode et al. (2011) and Whitney et al. (2014) also discuss that resources are relevant for achieving SCRES.

The research results show that the concepts *trust* and *commitment* are very closely related. Existing literature in the field of SCC also emphasizes this close connection. Most researchers argue that trust is a determinant of commitment (Morgan, Hunt, 1994; Ryu et al., 2009). Kwon and Suh (2005) found that there is a positive relationship between the level of commitment and the level of trust, and that high levels of both are the basis for successful SC performance. Commitment is only consummated when partners feel that trust has been established between them (Kwon, Suh, 2005). Vijayasarathy (2010) examines relational antecedents of supply integration. According to his line of argumentation, companies value trustful relationships and have the expectation that trusted partners are interested in joint actions for mutual long-term benefits. Therefore, companies are willing and motivated to commit time, energy and resources to these partnerships. Similarly, Nyaga et al. (2010) argue that companies commit resources to relationships which they perceive as being trustful and a long-term investment.

According to the survey results, *dependency* indirectly influences collaborative resource sharing (HR and PR) trough *trust* and *commitment*. In most research projects in the field of SCC, dependency is understood as a concept having a direct positive effect on SCC (Corsten, Felde, 2005; Ferrer et al., 2010; Monczka et al., 1998; Sheu et al., 2006). Their frameworks and studies all analyze the joint impact of dependency and trust (and commitment) on SCC and regard the concepts as being on the same framework level. These framework assumptions are challenged by the results obtained in our study.

The resource dependency theory provides arguments for the influence of *dependency* on *trust* and *commitment*. Similar to the RVT (Dyer, Singh, 1998), the resource dependency theory (Pfeffer, Salancik, 1978) is closely connected to the resource-based view theory (Barney, 1991). From a resource dependency perspective, companies have to acquire resources from their environment in order to survive (Barringer, Harrison, 2000; Cao, Zhang, 2013). This need for external resources creates dependency among parties (Barringer, Harrison, 2000; Cao, Zhang, 2013; Pfeffer, Salancik, 1978; Zhang, Huo, 2013). To manage these interdependencies, companies want to gain power over the resources. One way to achieve this is to establish interorganizational relationships with the corresponding external parties (Barringer, Harrison, 2000; Cao, Zhang, 2013). Thus, with high interdependence, there is a greater willingness to participate in and commit to sustained long-term SC relationships (Vijayasarathy, 2010; Zhang, Huo, 2013). There are several research projects explicitly based on the resource dependency theory that support the positive relationship between the constructs dependency and trust and commitment (Mishra et al., 2016; Zhang, Huo, 2013).

6 Conclusion and implications

The aim of this research was to analyze the relation between collaborative resource sharing and SCRES. A framework that captures promoting factors, types and effects of collaborative resource sharing was developed and tested. The research results contribute in a number of ways to theory and practice.

The first theoretical contribution is that the study extends extant research regarding the joint impact of dependence and trust/commitment on SCC. The finding that dependency only indirectly influences collaborative resource sharing (being one element of SCC) trough trust and commitment is opposed to most existing research results in this area. The second contribution refers to the appropriateness of the employed items. Most items were adapted from existing scales according to this research's purpose. As all of the adapted items for the constructs trust, commitment, dependency and SCRES had satisfactory factor loadings, it can be assumed that the adaptations were appropriate and may also be employed in future surveys. The third contribution is related to the RVT. As most existing research in the field of SCRES and SCC that take the RVT perspective chose single companies or dyadic relations as unit of analysis (Ambulkar et al., 2015M; Bello, Bovell, 2012; Whitney et al., 2014). For this research, the unit of analysis is the SC and the employed items were adapted accordingly. To our knowledge it is until today the only research in the fields of SCRES and SCC that applies the RVT in this manner in a questionnaire. The fourth contribution also refers to the RVT. Commomly, the RVT deals with resources of closely related actors. Based on the survey results, it can be stated that it is sensible to apply a broader understanding of SC. Only when indirect and/or inactive SC partners are also incorporated, a more holistic and realistic network of SC can be analysed.

Due to its low redundancy requirements, collaborative recovery is in accordance with current SC characteristics, such as single sourcing and just-in-time inventory systems. This research has several important contributions for the management of collaborative recoveries. The first managerial contribution refers to the equipping of resources with the identified abilities. Leveraging and reconfiguring resources (HR and PR) is the main mechanism of collaborative recoveries. Adaptability, mobility and availability of capacity are the identified abilities which enable HR and PR to be shared during SC disruption recoveries. SC managers can prepare for quick recoveries by taking care that their resources are equipped with the identified abilities. This can be achieved in different ways. Owing to their mobility and high adaptability, HR are the key to a successful collaboration in the event of a disruption. With interorganizational trainings, a constant flow of employees within the SC ensures a high degree of mobility and facilitates the transfer of employees to different tasks if required. Co-locating employees among SC partners as a way to accomplish joint problem solving is also emphasized by Min et al. (2005). It could be useful to dedicate engineers to key partners to get to know their systems, procedures and processes (Corsten, Felde, 2005). Scholten and Schilder (2015) highlight the option of establishing boundary-spanning personnel that collect intelligence, provide contacts and enable coordination if required. In order to achieve this role and boundary-spanning knowledge and experience, personnel needs to be informed and educated. Mutual knowledge creation and joint learning within the SC can be encouraged. To facilitate the adaptability of PR, standardized parts and production processes can be established. Information and knowledge about PR have to be accessible to all involved SC members (Scholten et al., 2014). The second managerial contribution focuses on the SC actors involved in collaborative recoveries. Based on the survey results, collaboration during SC disruption recoveries is possible across all categories of SC partners. It mainly takes place between intraorganizational subsidiaries, first-tier customers and first-tier supplies. However, indirect and/or inactive SC members, such as competitors, governmental agencies, and logistics service providers can also be crucial partners. Thus, when planning for collaborative recovery actions, SC managers may consider engaging with multiple actors, including indirect and/or inactive SC partners. Especially collaborating with competitors is counterintuitive for many SC managers. However, these partnerships can also be valuable during SC disruption recoveries. The third managerial contribution refers to the management of SC relationships. Commitment and trust were identified as the relational resources that promote collaborative recoveries. To establish and maintain committed and trusting SC relationships, companies need to make SC partner perceive them as trustworthy and demonstrate their commitment to the relationship. It also requires actions that benefit the relationship and not primary the individual company (Faisal et al., 2006). For SC managers, it is important to pay attention to this interplay of dependency and trust (and commitment) and their joint effects (Zhang, Huo, 2013). Dependency and trust (and commitment) need to be managed simultaneously. In SC relationships with a high level of dependency, it is advisable to invest in resources to develop and maintain trust with these SC partners (Zhang, Huo, 2013).

This research has some limitations which lead to further research opportunities. First, as most of the survey respondents' companies are headquartered in Germany (76 %) and predominantly belong to three different industries, there are limitations concerning the SEM results' generalizability. Replications of the study in other countries and/or industries would increase generalizability. Second, more research on the relation between trust, commitment and dependency could lead to additional findings and valuable conclusions in the field of SCC. The close relationship between trust and commitment could induce researchers to combine both already in the conceptualization phase. By refining the construct dependency and/or specifying the hypotheses, other findings regarding the role of dependency in collaborative recovery may reveal. Third, some conclusions on the appropriateness of the employed items can be drawn. The newly developed items should be applied in other studies to further test and validate them. Fourth, further research could explore how collaborative recovery can be compared and/or combined with other existing risk management methods.

Appendix: Construct items

Construct	Items
Collaborative Sharing of Human Resources Cronbach's alpha: 0.851	HR1: The members of our supply network shared know-how/expertise.
	HR2: Our supply network quickly reorganized supply network human resources (employees).
	HR3: In our supply network, employees were able to adapt to new tasks.
	HR4: In our supply network, employees were mobile enough to exchange know-how/expertise.[a]
Collaborative Sharing of Production Resources Cronbach's alpha: 0.828	PR5: The members of our supply network shared production resources (e.g. tools, facilities, machine or warehouse capacity).
	PR6: Our supply network quickly reorganized supply network production resources (e.g. tools, facilities, machine or warehouse capacity).
	PR7: In our supply network, it was possible to adapt production resources (e.g. tool, facilities, machines or warehouses) to new tasks.[a]
	PR8: In our supply network, production resources (e.g. machines, tools) were mobile enough to be shared by the members.
Trust_Commitment Cronbach's alpha: 0.867	TRUST9: The members were genuinely concerned that each other's business succeeds. (Dimension: Benevolence)
	TRUST10: The members were always honest with each other. (Dimension: Credibility)
	COMM11: The members intended to maintain the relationships with each other for a long time. (Dimension: Expectation of continuity)
	COMM12: The members had positive feelings towards each other which is a major reason they continued working with each other. (Dimension: Affective commitment)[a]
Dependency Cronbach's alpha: 0.831	DEPEND13: The members did not have good alternatives to each other.
	DEPEND14: It would have been difficult for the members to replace members.
	DEPEND15: The members were quite dependent on each other.
	DEPEND16: The members would have had difficulties achieving their goals, if the relationships with these members were discontinued.
	DEPEND17: The members frequently pursued single sourcing strategies.[a]
Supply Chain Resilience Cronbach's alpha: 0.924	SCRES18: Our supply chain recovered* more rapidly than our competitors' supply chains would have been able to.
	SCRES19: Our supply network was able to mitigate the severity of the supply network disruption's effect better than our competitors' supply chains would have been able to.

	SCRES20: Our supply chain was able to provide a quicker response to the disruption than our competitors' supply chains would have been able to in terms of: Recovering manufacturing lead times
	SCRES21: ... Recovering level of customer service
	SCRES22: ... Recovering delivery reliability
	SCRES23: ... Recovering sales volumes[a]

[a] The corresponding parameter is set to 1 to fix the scale of measurement.

References

AFP (2011): Japan cars: Aftershocks to Japan Automakers "to Last Months", in: Nikkei, 15 April 2011.

Ambulkar, S.; Blackhurst, J.; Grawe, S. (2015): Firm's resilience to supply chain disruptions: Scale development and empirical examination, in: Journal of Operations Management, 33, 111–122.

Anderson, J. C.; Gerbing, D. W. (1988): Structural equation modeling in practice: A review and recommended two-step approach, in: Psychological bulletin, 103(3), 411–423.

Armstrong, J. S.; Overton, T. S. (1977): Estimating nonresponse bias in mail surveys, in: Journal of Marketing Research, 14(3), 396–402.

Backhaus, K.; Erichson, B.; Weiber, R. (2011): Fortgeschrittene Multivariate Analysemethoden, Heidelberg: Springer-Verlag.

Barney, J. (1991): Firm resources and sustained competitive advantage, in: Journal of Management, 17(1), 99–120.

Barringer, B. R.; Harrison, J. S. (2000): Walking a tightrope: creating value through interorganizational relationships, in: Journal of Management, 26(3), 367–403.

Bello, D.; Bovell, L. (2012): Collaboration analysis: Joint resolution of problems in global supply networks, in: Information Knowledge Systems Management, 11(1/2), 77–99.

Blackhurst, J.; Dunn, K. S.; Craighead, C. W. (2011): An empirically derived framework of global supply resiliency, in: Journal of Business Logistics, 32(4), 374–391.

Blanding, M. (2012): Operations' Intricate Science, Tuck, 29 November 2012. Available at: http://www.tuck.dartmouth.edu/news/articles/operations-intricate-science.

Bode, C.; Wagner, S. M.; Petersen, K. J.; Ellram, L. M. (2011): Understanding Responses to Supply Chain Disruptions: Insights from Information Processing and Resource Dependence Perspectives, in: Academy of Management Journal, 54(4), 833–856.

Bovell, L. J. (2012): Joint Resolution of Supply Chain Risks: The Role of Risk Characteristics and Problem Solving Approach. Unpublished, Georgia State University.

Boyer, K. K.; Swink, M. L. (2008): Empirical elephants—why multiple methods are essential to quality research in operations and supply chain management, in: Journal of Operations Management, 26, 337–348.

Brandon-Jones, E.; Squire, B.; Autry, C.; Petersen, K. J. (2014): A Contingent Resource-Based Perspective of Supply Chain Resilience and Robustness, in: Journal of Supply Chain Management, 50, 55–73.

Brüning, M.; Bendul, J. (2015): Self-Healing Supply Networks – Collaborative Recovery from Supply Network Disruptions by Sharing Network Resources, in: Association, I. P. a. S. E. a. R. (ed.): Proceedings of 24th IPSERA Conference, Amsterdam.

Brüning, M.; Hartono, N. T.; Bendul, J. (2014): Collaborative Recovery from Supply Network Disruption: A Multiple Case Study. Proceedings of the 12th International Logistics and Supply Chain Congress, Istanbul.

Byrne, B. M. (2010): Structural equation modeling with AMOS: Basic concepts, applications, and programming.

Camarinha-Matos, L. M. (2014): Collaborative networks: A mechanism for enterprise agility and resilience, in: Mertins, K. et al. (ed.): Enterprise Interoperability VI – Interoperability for Agility, Resilience, and Plasticity of Collaborations: Springer International Publishing, 3–11.

Cao, M.; Vonderembse, M. A.; Zhang, Q.; Ragu-Nathan, T. S. (2010): Supply chain collaboration: conceptualisation and instrument development, in: International Journal of Production Research, 48(22), 6613–6635.

Cao, M.; Zhang, Q. (2013): Supply Chain Collaboration, London: Springer Verlag.

Cattell, R. B. (1966): The scree test for the number of factors, in: Multivariate Behavioral Research, 1, 245–276.

Christopher, M.; Peck, H. (2004): Building the Resilient Supply Chain. International Journal of Logistics Management, 15(2), 1–14.

Clark, D. (2012): Quake-Rocked Renesas Feels Renewed, More Relevant, in: The Wall Street Journal, 23 February 2012

Corsten, D.; Felde, J. (2005): Exploring the performance effects of key-supplier collaboration: an empirical investigation into Swiss buyer-supplier relationships, in: International Journal of Physical Distribution & Logistics Management, 35(6), 445–461.

Courtland, R. (2011): How Japanese Chipmaker Renesas Recovered from the Earthquake, in: IEEE Spectrum, 23 August 2011.

Craighead, C. W.; Blackhurst, J.; Rungtusanatham, M. J.; Handfield, R. B. (2007): The Severity of Supply Chain Disruptions: Design Characteristics and Mitigation Capabilities, in: Decision Sciences, 38(1), 131–156.

De Leeuw, S.; Fransoo, J. (2009): Drivers of close supply chain collaboration: one size fits all?, in: International Journal of Operations & Production Management, 29(7), 720–739.

Dillman, D. A.; Smyth, J. D.; Christian, L. M. (2014): Internet, Phone, Mail and Mixed-Mode Surveys: The Tailored Design Method, Hoboken, NJ: John Wiley.

Doney, P. M.; Cannon, J. P. (1997): An examination of the nature of trust in buyer-seller relationships, in: Journal of Marketing, 61(2), 35–51.

Dwyer, F. R.; Schurr, P. H., & Oh, S. (1987): Developing buyer-seller relationships, in: The Journal of Marketing, 11(27).

Dyer, J. H.; Singh, H. (1998): The relational view: Cooperative strategy and sources of interorganizational competitive advantage, in: Academy of Management Review, 23, 660–679.

Endo, K. (2011): Viewpoint: How Japan's car industry almost shut down, British Broadcasting Corporation.

Fawcett, S. E.; Ogden, J. A.; Magnan, G. M.; Bixby Cooper, M. (2006): Organizational commitment and governance for supply chain success, in: International Journal of Physical Distribution & Logistics Management, 36(1), 22–35.

Ferrer, M.; Santa, R.; Hyland, P. W.; Bretherton, P. (2010): Relational factors that explain supply chain relationships, in: Asia Pacific Journal of Marketing and Logistics, 22(3), 419–440.

Field, A. (2009): Discovering statistics using SPSS, Sage.

Flick, U. (2006): An Introduction to Qualitative Research, London: Sage Publications.

Ganesan, S. (1994): Determinants of long-term orientation in buyer-seller relationships, in: The Journal of Marketing, 58(2), 1–19.

Handfield, R. B.; Bechtel, C. (2002): The role of trust and relationship structure in improving supply chain responsiveness, in: Industrial Marketing Management, 31(4), 367–382.

Hu, L. T.; Bentler, P. M. (1998): Fit indices in covariance structure modeling: Sensitivity to underparameterized model misspecification, in: Psychological methods, 3(4), 424–453.

Hudnurkar, M.; Jakhar, S.; Rathod, U. (2014): Factors affecting collaboration in supply chain: a literature review, in: Procedia-Social and Behavioral Sciences, 133, 189–202.

Jöreskog, K. G. (1969): A general approach to confirmatory maximum likelihood factor analysis, in: Psychometrika, 34(2 Part 1), 183–202.

Jüttner, U.; Maklan, S. (2011): Supply chain resilience in the global financial crisis: an empirical study, in: Supply Chain Management: An International Journal, 16(4), 246–259.

Kaiser, H. F. (1960): The application of electronic computers to factor analysis, in: Educational and Psychological Measurement, 20, 141–151.

Kubicek, H. (1976): Heuristische Bezugsrahmen und heuristisch angelegte Forschungsdesigns als Elemente einer Konstruktionsstrategie empirischer Forschung, in: Köhler, R. (ed.): Empirische und handlungstheoretische Forschungskonzeptionen in der Betriebswirtschaftslehre, Stuttgart: J. B. Metzlersche Verlagsbuchhandlung und Carl Ernst Poeschel Verlag GmbH.

Kumar, N.; Scheer, L. K.; Steenkamp, J.-B. E. M. (1995): The effects of perceived interdependence on dealer attitudes, in: Journal of Marketing Research, 32(August), 348–358.

Kwon, I. W. G.; Suh, T. (2005): Trust, commitment and relationships in supply chain management: a path analysis, in: Supply Chain Management: An International Journal, 10(1), 26–33.

Lavie, D. (2006): The competitive advantage of interconnected firms: An extension of the resource-based view, in: Academy of Management Review, 31(3), 638–658.

Li, G.; Fan, H.; Lee, P. K.; Cheng, T. C. E. (2015): Joint supply chain risk management: An agency and collaboration perspective, in: International Journal of Production Economics, 164, 83–94.

Marchese, K.; Paramasivam, S. (2013): Deloitte: The Ripple Effect: How manufacturing and retail executives view the growing challenge of supply chain risk.

McEvily, B.; Perrone, V.; Zaheer, A. (2003): Trust as an organizing principle, in: Organization Science, 14(1), 91–103.

Mentzer, J. T.; Min, S.; Zacharia, Z. G. (2000): The nature of interfirm partnering in supply chain management, in: Journal of Retailing, 76(4), 549–568.

Min, S.; Roath, A. S.; Daugherty, P. J.; Genchev, S. E.; Chen, H.; Arndt, A. D.; Glenn, R. G. (2005): Supply chain collaboration: what's happening?, in: The International Journal of Logistics Management, 16(2), 237–258.

Mishra, D.; Sharma, R. R. K.; Kumar, S.; Dubey, R. (2016): Bridging and buffering: Strategies for mitigating supply risk and improving supply chain performance, in: International Journal of Production Economics, 180, 183–197.

Mohr, J.; Spekman, R. (1994): Characteristics of partnership success: partnership attributes, communication behavior, and conflict resolution techniques, in: Strategic Management Journal, 15(2), 135–152.

Monczka, R. M.; Petersen, K. J.; Handfield, R. B.; Ragatz, G. L. (1998): Success Factors in Strategic Supplier Alliances: The Buying Company Perspective, in: Decision Sciences, 29(3), 553–577.

Morgan, R. M.; Hunt, S. D. (1994): The commitment-trust theory of relationship marketing, in: The Journal of Marketing, 20–38.

Natarajarathinam, M.; Capar, I.; Narayanan, A. (2009): Managing supply chains in times of crisis: a review of literature and insights, in: International Journal of Physical Distribution & Logistics Management, 39(7), 535.

Nishiguchi, T.; Beaudet, A. (1998): The Toyota Group and the Aisin Fire, in: MIT Sloan Management Review, 40(1), 49–59.

Nunnally, J. C. (1978): Psychometric Theory, New York: McGraw-Hill.

Nyaga, G. N.; Whipple, J. M.; Lynch, D. F. (2010): Examining supply chain relationships: do buyer and supplier perspectives on collaborative relationships differ?, in: Journal of Operations Management, 28(2), 101–114.

Park, K. (2011): Flexible and Redundant Supply Chain Practices to Build Strategic Supply Chain Resilience: Contingent and Resource-based Perspectives. Unpublished Doctoral dissertation, University of Toledo.

Park, N. K.; Mezias, J. M.; Song, J. (2004): A resource-based view of strategic alliances and firm value in the electronic marketplace, in: Journal of Management, 30(1), 7–27.

Pfeffer, J.; Salancik, G. R. (1978): The external control of organizations: A resource dependence perspective, New York: Harper & Row.

Podsakoff, P. M.; MacKenzie, S. B.; Lee, J.-Y.; Podsakoff, N. P. (2003): Common Method Biases in Behavioral Research: A Critical Review of the Literature and Recommended Remedies, in: Journal of Applied Psychology, 88(5), 879–903.

Pollack, A.; Lohr, S. (2011): Renesas in Japan Scrambles to Make a Critical Car Chip. NYTimes.com.

Ponomarov, S. (2012): Antecedents and consequences of supply chain resilience: a dynamic capabilities perspective. Unpublished Doctoral Dissertation, University of Tennessee.

Ramanathan, U.; Gunasekaran, A. (2014): Supply chain collaboration: Impact of success in long-term partnerships, in: International Journal of Production Economics, 147(Part B), 252–259.

Renesas (2011): CSR and Environmental Report: Renesas Electronics Corporation.

Rice, J. B.; Caniato, F. (2003): Building a secure and resilient supply network, in: Supply Chain Management Review, 7(5), 22–30.

Rousseau, D. M.; Sitkin, S. B.; Burt, R. S.; Camerer, C. (1998): Not so different after all: A cross-discipline view of trust, in: Academy of Management Review, 23(3), 393–404.

Ryu, I.; So, S.; Koo, C. (2009): The role of partnership in supply chain performance, in: Industrial Management & Data Systems, 109(4), 496–514.

Scholten, K.; Schilder, S. (2015): The role of collaboration in supply chain resilience, in: Supply Chain Management: An International Journal, 20(4), 471–484.

Segars, A. H.; Grover, V. (1993): Re-examining perceived ease of use and usefulness: A confirmatory factor analysis, in: MIS Quarterly, 17(4), 517–525.

Shah, R.; Goldstein, S. M. (2006): Use of structural equation modeling in operations management research: looking back and forward, in: Journal of Operations Management, 24(2), 148–169.

Sheffi, Y. (2005): The Resilient Enterprise: Overcoming Vulnerability for Competitive Advantage, Cambridge, Massachusetts: MIT Press.

Sheu, C.; Yen, H.; Chae, D. (2006): Determinants of supplier-retailer collaboration: evidence from an international study, in: International Journal of Operations and Production Management, 26(1), 24–49.

Simchi-Levi, D.; Schmidt, W.; Wei, Y. (2014): From Superstorms to Factory Fires, in: Harvard Business Review, 92(1/2), 97–101.

Sodhi, M.; Son, B.-G.; Tang, C. S. (2012): Researchers' perspectives on supply chain risk management, in: Production and Operations Management, 21(1).

Stock, J. R.; Boyer, S. L.; Harmon, T. (2010): Research opportunities in supply chain management, in: Journal of the Academy of Marketing Science, 38, 32–41.

Swafford, P. M.; Ghosh, S.; Murthy, N. (2006): The antecedents of supply chain agility of a firm: scale development and model testing, in: Journal of Operations Management, 24(2), 170–188.

Thun, J. H.; Hoenig, D. (2011): An empirical analysis of supply chain risk management in the German automotive industry, in: International Journal of Production Economics, 131(1), 242–249.

Tukamuhabwa, B. R.; Stevenson, M.; Busby, J.; Zorzini, M. (2015): Supply chain resilience: definition, review and theoretical foundations for further study, in: International Journal of Production Research.

Vijayasarathy, L. R. (2010): Supply integration: an investigation of its multidimensionality and relational antecedents, in: International Journal of Production Economics, 124(2), 489–505.

Wagner, S. M.; Bode, C. (2006): An empirical investigation into supply chain vulnerability, in: Journal of purchasing and supply management, 12(6), 301–312.

Wagner, S. M.; Kemmerling, R. (2010): Handling nonresponse in logistics research, in: Journal of Business Logistics, 31(2), 357–381.

Whitney, D. E.; Luo, J.; Heller, D. A. (2014): The benefits and constraints of temporary sourcing diversification in supply chain disruption and recovery, in: Journal of purchasing and supply management, 20(4), 238–250.

Wieland, A.; Wallenburg, C. M. (2012): Dealing with supply chain risks: linking risk management practices and strategies to performance, in: International Journal of Physical Distribution & Logistics Management, 42(10), 887–905.

Wieland, A.; Wallenburg, C. M. (2013): The influence of relational competencies on supply chain resilience: a relational view, in: International Journal of Physical Distribution & Logistics Management, 43(4), 300–320.

Wilson, E. J.; Vlosky, R. P. (1997): Partnering relationship activities: building theory from case study research, in: Journal of Business Research, 39(1), 59–70.

Wu, L.; Chuang, C. H.; Hsu, C. H. (2014): Information sharing and collaborative behaviors in enabling supply chain performance: A social exchange perspective, in: International Journal of Production Economics, 148 (122–132).

Zhang, M.; Huo, B. (2013): The impact of dependence and trust on supply chain integration, in: International Journal of Physical Distribution & Logistics Management, 43(7), 544–563.

Optimal framing of scores in procurement auctions

Nicolas Fugger, Christian Paul, Achim Wambach

Abstract

In many procurement projects buyers face suppliers who differ with regard to the non-price attributes of the goods and services they offer. In order to make the offers of different suppliers comparable to each other, buyers can use so called scores that assign a monetary value to the non-price attributes. These scores are often framed as bonuses or handicaps and are part of most procurement auctions. In this paper, we examine how the framing of these scores as bonuses or handicaps influences suppliers' beliefs about the strength of their competitors and thereby affects their bidding behavior in first-price reverse auctions. Our main finding is that suppliers who receive a bonus (handicap) underestimate (overestimate) the strength of their competitors. As a consequence, procurement auctions with non-price differences framed as handicaps result in lower prices than auctions in which scores are expressed as bonuses.

1 Introduction

Over the last decades the use of reverse auctions to procure goods and services has been steadily growing (Elmaghraby, 2007). Carter et al. (2004) provide a conservative estimate of the annual volume of reverse auctions in the US of 400 billion USD and report that 85% of firms surveyed in a large scale study consider using procurement auctions. One reason for the popularity of reverse auctions is that nowadays the internet enables buyers to communicate easily with suppliers independent of their location. The closely connected expansion of the supply base makes it attractive for buyers to employ competitive procurement mechanisms like reverse auctions (Beall et al., 2003). The competition between suppliers drives down prices. For example, Verespej (2002) reports realized cost savings attributed to reverse auctions between 20–40% in a diverse set of industries. Furthermore, reverse auctions can reduce transaction times (Shugan, 2005).

In contrast to selling auctions in which revenue maximization is equivalent to maximizing the (expected) price, the considerations of a buyer in a procurement auction are more complex. The reason is that most of the times suppliers do not offer completely homogeneous goods or services and the buyer has to incorporate this heterogeneity into the design of the procurement auction. Consider, for example, a car manufacturer that needs to procure seats for a new series of models. This manufacturer is not only interested in the price it has to pay per seat but also in non-price attributes. Such attributes can be characteristics of the product like the availability of options like seat heating or the touch and feel of the product but also characteristics of the contract offered like time of delivery, warranty, or the option to adjust the quantity. Obviously, all these attributes can be important for the manufacturer and hence need to be considered when selecting an offer. A purely price-based procurement auction that does not take into account supplier specific differences would yield inefficient outcomes by selecting the wrong supplier and more importantly for the buyer purely price-based auctions do not maximize her expected revenue (Naegelen, 2002).

The existence of such heterogeneity among suppliers does not rule out the use of procurement auctions. To take into account non-price attributes, buyers often conduct so called scoring auctions. In a scoring auction the buyer[8] determines a scoring rule which assigns monetary values to non-price attributes before the auction starts. This score in combination with a supplier's bid provides a one-dimensional measure, the quality-adjusted bid, which takes into account both price and non-price attributes. Thereby, it allows the buyer to set up a binding procurement auction in which suppliers compete on quality-adjusted bids. Similar to a standard procurement auction the bidder who places the lowest quality-adjusted bid wins the scoring auction. One commonly used way to set up a scoring auction is to express a supplier's score as a bonus or as a handicap. In this case a positive score is called a bonus and a negative score is denoted as a handicap.

Consider the following example in which a buyer wants to procure a good and faces two potential suppliers, A and B. The good provided by supplier A is of higher quality than the good provided by supplier B. The buyer assigns a monetary value of 5,000 USD to the quality difference. In this case, the buyer wants to procure the good of supplier A if this is less than 5,000 USD more expensive than the good of supplier B and, vice versa, the good of supplier B if it is more than 5,000 USD cheaper than the good of supplier A. The buyer can express her preferences using various different scores. She can assign bonuses to both suppliers, e.g. a bonus of 8,000 USD to supplier A and a bonus of 3,000 USD to supplier B. She can assign handicaps to both suppliers, e.g. a handicap of 2,000 USD to supplier A and a handicap of 7,000 USD to suppli-

---

[8] In practice, the actual buyer is often a representative of the procuring company who aggregates the preferences of the company's different departments. Throughout the paper the term buyer's preferences denotes the aggregated preferences of the different departments of the procuring company.

er B. And she can also assign a bonus to supplier A and a handicap to supplier B, e.g. a bonus of 1,000 USD to supplier A and a handicap of 4,000 USD to supplier B.

For given bids, all three – and many more – pairs of scores induce the same allocation and the same price.[9] Supplier A wins the auction if his bid is at most 5,000 USD higher than the bid of supplier B and supplier B wins the auction if his bid is more than 5,000 USD lower than that of supplier A. In any case, the price is equal to the winner's bid. Only the difference between a supplier's own score and his competitor's score, i.e. a relative measure, is important but not its absolute value. This means the framing of the scores as bonuses or handicaps should not affect outcomes. However, this requires that suppliers do not only observe their own scores but also have precise information about their competitors' scores. Even though it is the relative score which is crucial for a supplier to interpret his own position and to place his bid, suppliers are often only informed about their own score in practice. As a consequence, bidding behavior depends crucially on the interpretation of the position associated with the own score.

In this paper, we investigate if the framing of the score as a bonus or a handicap influences suppliers' bidding behavior in first-price procurement auctions. In order to do so we set up an experiment which captures two key aspects of procurement practice. First, the buyer can express her preferences either as bonuses or as handicaps. Second, suppliers only learn their own score and have uncertainty about their competitors' scores. Our results show that the buyer's framing decision has substantial influence on suppliers' bidding behavior. In auctions in which scores are framed as handicaps suppliers place lower bids than in auctions in which scores are framed as bonuses. Furthermore, our observations indicate that this is due to a systematically biased perception of their own position. Suppliers who receive a bonus overestimate their own position and assume to be stronger than their competitors whereas suppliers who receive a handicap assume to be in a weaker position than their competitors.

In the next Section we review the literature. Section 3 presents our experimental design and our hypotheses. In Section 4 we report our results. Finally, Section 5 concludes.

2 Literature review

In contrast to procurement practice, the academic literature on scoring auctions has so far concentrated on settings in which suppliers are also informed about their competitors' scores. The focus of this research is to identify the optimal scoring auction. An optimal scoring auction balances the consideration of price and non-price attributes. On the one hand, non-price attributes have to be considered in order to increase effi-

---

[9] We assume that the winning supplier is paid his bid. If he were paid his quality-adjusted bid, he would change his bidding strategy accordingly.

ciency. On the other hand, the consideration of non-price attributes can induce an asymmetry between suppliers, which reduces price competition and might therefore have a negative influence on the buyer's profit.

Economic literature about scoring auctions distinguishes between situations in which suppliers' non-price attributes are fixed and those in which suppliers can adjust them. A general result in this literature is that the ability to commit herself to a certain scoring rule is important for the buyer. This commitment, however, requires that scores are public, which is not the case in the setting we focus on.

Asker and Cantillon (2008) analyze a procurement situation with multiple non-price attributes. They first prove that these attributes can be represented by a single score and then they show that scoring auctions dominate alternatives like buyer-determined auctions and menu auctions, in which suppliers place various offers.

Naegelen (2002) analyzes the design of optimal scoring rules in a setting in which suppliers' non-price attributes are fixed. She shows that a buyer who can commit herself to a scoring rule before the auction starts maximizes her expected profit by under-rewarding non-price attributes in her scoring rule. This way she reduces the asymmetry between suppliers and thereby intensifies price-competition. One drawback from a welfare perspective is that such a scoring auction can lead to inefficient allocations. Furthermore, the buyer needs commitment power when designing the auction, because she might be forced to select an offer that is not ex-post optimal for her.

Che (1993) shows that a scoring auction which under-rewards non-price attributes is also optimal in a setting in which suppliers can adjust their non-price attributes prior to the auction. Putting less weight on non-price attributes reduces suppliers' incentives to provide high quality. Consequently, it decreases the information rent the buyer has to pay suppliers due to their private information about their quality improvement costs, but also leads to inefficiently low quality provision. Branco (1997) generalizes the model of Che (1993) by allowing for correlated costs. He shows that in this case the optimal procurement mechanism can be implemented as a two-stage mechanism in which suppliers first take part in a scoring auction and the winner then negotiates with the buyer about the adjustment of non-price attributes based on all the bids, i.e. the information elicited in the scoring auction.

In practice buyer's exact preferences are (ex-ante) not public information and suppliers are often able to adjust the characteristics of the good to be provided. This is taken up by Dini et al. (2006) who provide an overview of important aspects of scoring rules from a practitioner's perspective. They focus on situations in which suppliers can adjust their non-price attributes to the scoring rule and recommend simple and predictable scoring rules, which set the right incentives for suppliers to make efficient offers. Here, efficiency means that suppliers invest in non-price attributes as long as the marginal costs are smaller than the buyer's marginal valuation for the quality improvement. In this context Strecker (2010) argues that the buyer faces a trade-off with regard to the revelation of her preferences towards suppliers. On the one hand, suppliers need information about the buyer's preferences to make efficient offers, but on the other hand they might exploit this additional information later on. In contrast to that, we focus on a procurement situation in which the suppliers' qualities are already determined and the scores can only affect the suppliers' bidding behavior but not their quality choice.

As mentioned by Asker and Cantillon (2008), there are also other competitive procurement mechanisms that can be employed to consider heterogeneity among suppliers. One way to take non-price attributes into account is to conduct a buyer-determined procurement auction in which the buyer assesses the different attributes after suppliers made their offers. In buyer-determined procurement auctions, which are also known as beauty contests, suppliers make offers specifying price and non-price attributes. When all offers are placed the buyer selects the offer that maximizes her utility, which need not be the lowest bid. This way she has the last say in a buyer-determined procurement auction. One advantage of a buyer-determined auction is that it is easy to conduct. The buyer does not need to screen all suppliers and does not have to specify her exact preferences beforehand, which might be very complex. However, Fugger et al. (2016) show that buyer-determined procurement auctions are prone to collusion, i.e. they are likely to result in high prices. The reasoning is as follows: If suppliers are not aware of the buyer's exact preferences, i.e. her decision rule, they all face a positive winning probability if their bids are similar. As a consequence, they can share profits in expectation and might have no incentive to compete. Engelbrecht-Wiggans et al. (2007) compared buyer-determined procurement auctions with price-based reverse auctions and purely price-based mechanisms and found that buyer-determined procurement auctions are more profitable for the buyer only if the number of suppliers is large. Similar to Fugger et al. (2016) they observed that price competition is less pronounced in buyer-determined procurement auctions. These results suggest that scoring auctions outperform buyer-determined procurement auctions if non-price attributes can easily be evaluated before the procurement starts.

3 Experimental design and hypotheses

We analyze a procurement setting in which one buyer faces two potential suppliers that compete in a first-price sealed-bid scoring auction. One of the two suppliers provides better quality than the other supplier. In the following we denote the buyer's preferred supplier, i.e. the supplier who provides higher quality, as supplier A and the other supplier as supplier B. The suppliers neither know if they are the preferred supplier nor do they know the exact size of the quality difference. In our experiment the buyer's valuation for the good provided by B is $v_B = 100$, whereas she assigns a value of $v_A = 104$ to the good provided by A. In order to take this into account, the buyer employs a naive scoring rule that perfectly reflects her preferences. She assigns scores

$(s_A, s_B) = (s + 4, s)$, which can either be framed as bonuses or handicaps. Scores are called bonuses if $s > 0$ and handicaps if $s < -4$.

In each auction the buyer can determine whether the scores are framed as bonuses or handicaps. To do so she chooses between two pairs of scores that express her preferences. One of the pairs consists of positive scores (bonuses) and the other pair consists of negative scores (handicaps). Bonuses are integers between 2 and 16 and handicaps integers between –2 and –16. There is a total of 11 bonus and handicap pairs that are all equally likely to be presented to the buyer. The two pairs of scores that the buyer can choose from before the auction starts are symmetric in the sense that if the buyer can assign the k-th highest bonus she can also choose to assign the k-th highest handicap. For example, the buyer might choose between the bonus pair (2,6) and the handicap pair (–16, –12). Here 2 is the smallest possible bonus and –16 the smallest possible handicap.

Suppliers know that their ex-ante probability of being the buyer's preferred supplier is one half. After the buyer decides whether she wants to frame the scores as bonuses or handicaps, suppliers observe their own costs and their own score. Suppliers' costs are independently and identically distributed between 0 and 100 and each integer is equally likely. They know that their competitor also receives a bonus (handicap) in case they receive a bonus (handicap). After both suppliers place their bids b_i the supplier who offers the lower score-adjusted bid $b_i + s_i$ wins the auction and earns the difference between his bid b_i and his cost c_i. In case of a tie the supplier with the higher score is selected. This means for a given bid the own score affects the winning probability but not the profit in case of winning. After the bidding suppliers only observe whether they won the auction or not but receive no further information about their competitor's bid or score.

As it is common in procurement practice, suppliers have limited information about their competitor's score in our experiment. They only know that their competitor also receives a bonus (handicap) if they receive a bonus (handicap). This means that receiving a bonus or handicap per se reveals no information about their relative standing and therefore the framing of the score as a bonus or a handicap should have no or only little influence on bidding behavior. Only the size of the score might affect bidding behavior. Since bonuses (handicaps) are always positive (negative) a bonus (handicap) close to zero implies that it is likely to be in the weaker (stronger) position compared to the competitor. In this case, a supplier with a handicap close to zero should place a higher bid than a supplier with a bonus close to zero. However, this is not what we observe.

The bidding behavior of a supplier given his score strongly depends on his beliefs about his competitor's score. For a supplier a focal anchoring point for estimating his competitor's score might be a score of zero. If the estimate of the competitor's score is biased towards this anchoring point, suppliers will, on the one hand, interpret a positive score, i.e. a bonus, as good news and will, on the other hand, perceive a negative score, i.e. a handicap, as bad news.

> **Hypothesis 1: Perception bias**
> Suppliers expect to be preferred if they receive a positive score (bonus) and to have a disadvantage if they receive a negative score (handicap).

Based on the assumption that estimates of the competitors' scores are biased towards zero, suppliers who receive a bonus (handicap) believe to be in a stronger (weaker) position than their competitor. We denote a supplier as stronger (weaker) if his score-adjusted costs $c_i + s_i$ are drawn from a more (less) favorable distribution than his competitor's score-adjusted cost $c_j + s_j$. A well known result in auction theory is that such weakness (strength) leads to more (less) aggressive bidding behavior, i.e. a bidder that is weaker (stronger) than his competitor places a lower (higher) bid given the same cost realization (Krishna, 2010, pp. 46-51). Given that Hypothesis 1 holds it follows that suppliers bid more aggressively if they receive a handicap than when they receive a bonus.

> **Hypothesis 2: Asymmetry effect**
> Suppliers who receive a bonus bid less aggressively, i.e. place higher bids, than suppliers who receive a handicap.

A concern regularly raised by practitioners is that buyers should use handicaps carefully as suppliers perceive them as unkind and try to reciprocate such unkind actions with another unkind action. The basic idea behind this advice is that people like to be kind to those who are kind to them and unkind to those who are unkind to them. See, for example, Rabin (1993) or Dufwenberg and Kirchsteiger (2004). As we assume that suppliers believe to be in a better position when they receive a bonus than when they receive a handicap, suppliers could interpret the buyer's decision to assign a negative score to them as unkind. Vice versa, they should perceive the assignment of a bonus as a kind action. Reciprocity then implies that suppliers should place higher bids if they receive a handicap in order to punish the buyer who assigned it. Similarly, a supplier who receives a bonus reciprocates it by bidding more aggressively. This reciprocity effect is opposed to the asymmetry effect.

> **Hypothesis 3: Reciprocity effect**
> Suppliers will bid less aggressively when the handicap was assigned by the buyer and more aggressively when the bonus was assigned by the buyer.

To be able to identify a possible reciprocity effect we have two treatments. In the buyer's choice treatment the buyer actively determines the framing of the scores. In the random choice treatment the buyer is inactive and the framing is randomly determined. As a consequence, there is nothing to reciprocate in the second treatment and no reciprocity effect should be observed. This is depicted in **Figure 1**.

Figure 1: Observability of the asymmetry and the reciprocity effect in our treatments

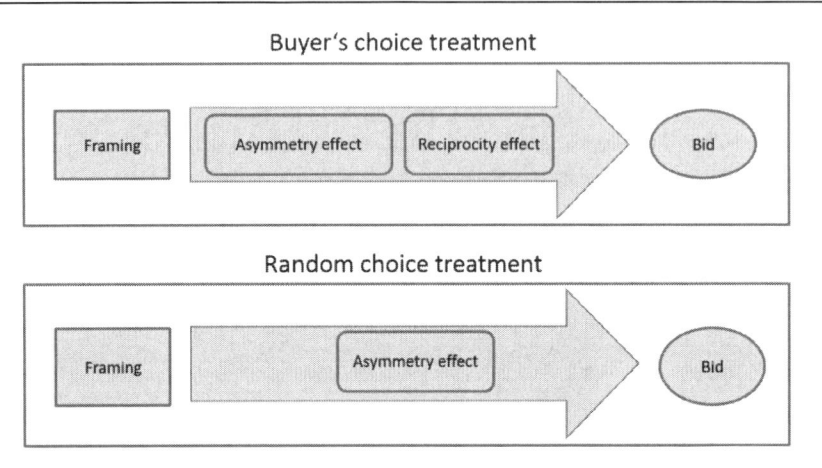

Buyer's choice treatment

Framing → Asymmetry effect → Reciprocity effect → Bid

Random choice treatment

Framing → Asymmetry effect → Bid

Notes: Displayed is the observability of the asymmetry and a reciprocity effect. In the random choice treatment we rule out a reciprocity effect by randomizing the framing. Hence, we can directly measure the asymmetry effect. In the buyer's choice treatment the observed effect is an aggregate of the asymmetry and a reciprocity effect.

Organization

The experiment was conducted in the Cologne Laboratory for Economic Research (CLER). A random sample of the CLER subject pool was invited using the recruitment software ORSEE (Greiner, 2015). Each subject participated only one time and earning money was the only incentive offered. The experiment was programmed using zTree (Fischbacher, 2007). 120 subjects divided into four cohorts of 30 subjects participated in the experiment. In each cohort 10 subjects were in the role of buyers and 20 in the role of suppliers. Roles were fixed during the experiment. Each subject participated in a total of 50 reverse auctions: 10 standard reverse auctions and 40 scoring auctions. In each auction one buyer faced two suppliers.

To make sure that participants fully understood the instructions they had to answer control questions privately on their computers. The experiment only proceeded when all subjects answered all questions correctly. Before the main part of the experiment started, subjects participated in a sequence of ten purely price-based procurement auctions, i.e. procurement auctions without a scoring rule. This way, suppliers got used to the auction environment and could acquire bidding experience before the actual experiment started. In the main part of the experiment participants first took part in a sequence of 20 scoring auctions in which the buyer actively determined the framing of the scores as bonuses and handicaps followed by a sequence of 20 scoring auctions in which the buyer was passive and the framing of the scores was randomly determined by the computer. To control for order effects we employed a counter-balanced design and the order was reversed in half of our sessions. As mentioned above, our control treatment in which the framing is randomly determined allows us to examine if suppliers try to reciprocate the buyer's framing decision as depicted in **Figure 1**.

At the end of the experiment all suppliers estimated their opponent's expected score for the case that their own bonus was 9 ECU and for the case that their own handicap was –9 ECU. These scores were the average bonus score and handicap score, respectively. Both estimates were incentivized and half of the suppliers were asked in reverse order to control for order effects. A participant who correctly estimated the competitor's expected score earned 4 EUR. For each integer the estimate differed from the correct value 30 Cent were deducted. This incentivized belief elicitation at the very end of the experiment provides a conservative estimate of the suppliers' perception bias, because suppliers had the opportunity to learn during the experiment.

4 Experimental results

4.1 Beliefs

The interpretation of a bonus as an advantage and of a handicap as a disadvantage relies strongly on the beliefs about the competitor's score. For that reason we will first analyze if the experimental findings support **Hypothesis 1**, which states that beliefs are biased towards zero. In order to examine if a supplier has biased beliefs we compare each supplier's estimate of his competitor's score to his own median score during the experiment. We do this separately for bonuses and handicaps.

Our results show systematic differences between beliefs about the competitor's bonus score and the own median bonus score, as well as between beliefs about the competitor's handicap score and the own median handicap score. The same holds true if we consider the average instead of the median. On the one hand, 76% of the suppliers underestimated their competitor's expected bonus, i.e. believed that they had an advantage when they received a bonus. On the other hand, 70% overestimated their competitor's expected handicap, i.e. believed that they were disadvantaged when they received a handicap. This indicates that most suppliers interpreted the assignment of a bonus as good news and vice versa the assignment of a handicap as bad news. Furthermore, we find that for most subjects the perception bias was symmetric in the sense that the sum of the individual bonus and the individual handicap estimates was zero.

Wissenschaftliche Forschungsbeiträge

Figure 2 illustrates the suppliers' beliefs about their competitor's score and the median of the actual scores. The black bars on the left represent the distribution of the suppliers' belief about the competitor's score given that the supplier himself received a handicap of −SeECU and the grey bars for the case that their own bonus was 9 ECU. The median of actual bonuses was 9 (average 8.6) ECU and the median of the actual handicaps was −9 ECU (average 9.5 ECU). In contrast to that, the median estimate of the competitor's score in case of a bonus was 5 (average 6.4) ECU and −5 (average −6.9) ECU in case of a handicap.

> **Result 1:**
> Suppliers underestimated their competitors' bonuses (Wilcoxon signed rank test and *t*-test, $p<0.001$) and overestimated their competitors' handicaps (Wilcoxon signed rank test and *t*-test, $p<0.001$).

Figure 2: Distribution of suppliers' estimates about competitors' quality scores

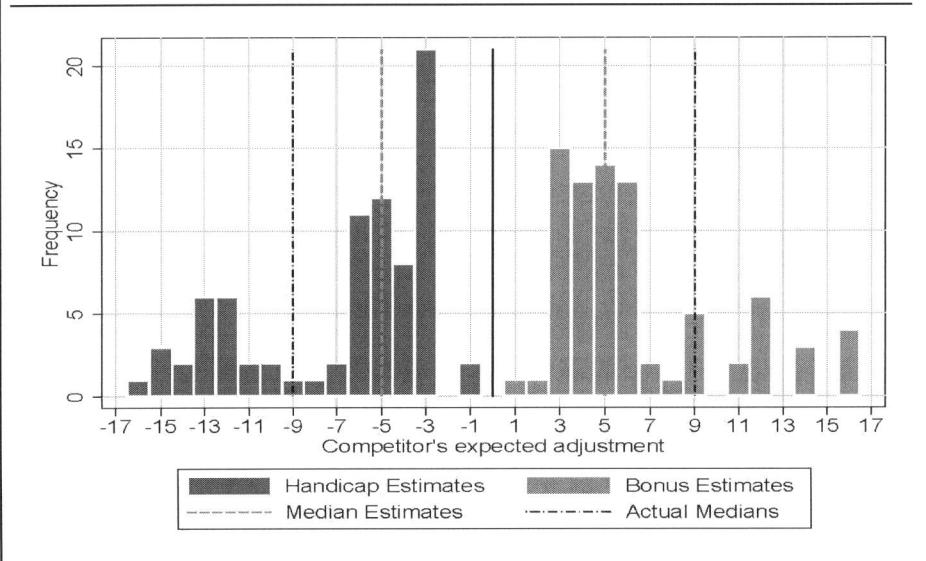

Notes: Displayed are the distributions of suppliers' estimates about their competitors' scores in case their own bonus was 9 ECU (grey bars) and in case their own handicap was −9 ECU (black bars). The dashed/dotted lines illustrate that the median actual scores of competitors' are −9 ECU in case of a handicap and 9 ECU in case of a bonus.

4.2 Bidding

In this Section we analyze the suppliers' bidding behavior. In particular, we investigate if the framing of the score as a bonus or handicap influenced bidding. In line with the significant perception bias indicated by suppliers' stated beliefs, we find that suppliers placed substantially lower bids when they received a handicap compared to the case in which they received a bonus. Controlling for suppliers' costs the average bid in case of a handicap was 4.5 ECU smaller than the average bid in case of a bonus. Taking into account that the average bid was 67.7 ECU the influence of the framing was substantial. **Figure 3** illustrates the bidding behavior.

Figure 3: Bids in auctions with score framed as bonus or handicap

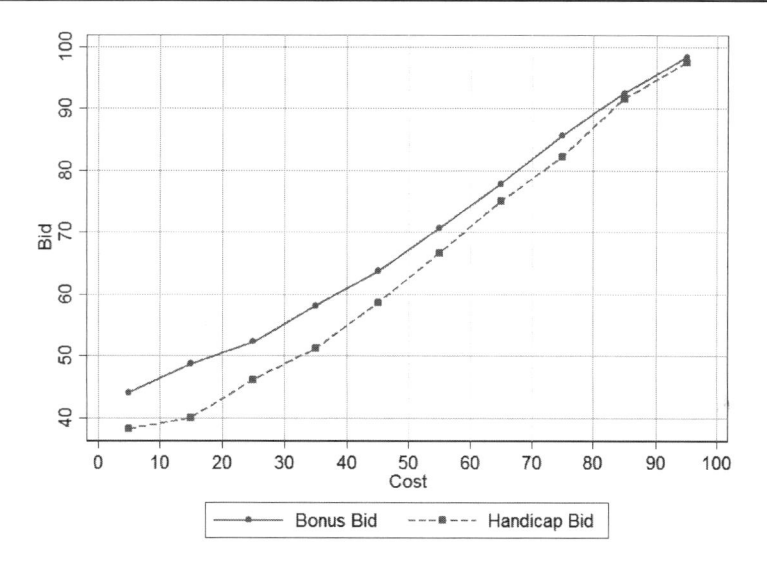

Notes: Displayed are bidding functions for bonus and handicap auctions. Markers illustrate the average bids given that the costs are between 0 and 10, 11 and 20, 21 and 30, etc.

Running individual regressions for each supplier we find that 90% of the suppliers placed lower bids when they were assigned a handicap compared to the case in which they were assigned a bonus. For 75% of the suppliers this difference is significant on a 10% level. **Table 1** presents a random-effects panel regression of the suppliers' bidding behavior. Here the variable Handicap represents a dummy variable that is one if the score was framed as a handicap and zero in case of framing as a bonus. The variable Buyer is a treatment dummy that is one if the buyer actively determined the framing of the scores and is zero if the buyer was passive and the framing was randomly determined by the computer. One feature of our within-subject design is that it inherently provides a between-subject design which we use to check for consistency. In a within-subjects design a subject participates in more than one treatment. In our case subjects participated both in the buyer's choice treatment and the random choice treatment, which allows us to analyze this treatment effect on an individual level. The results of the between-subjects analysis, which only considers bids in the first sequence of scoring auctions, are presented in the first two columns and those of the within-subjects analysis, which takes into account all bids placed in stages two and three, in the last two columns.

Table 1: Random-effects panel regression of bidding behavior

	Bid			
	Between-subjects design (Stage 2)		Within-subjects design (Stage 2+3)	
	(1)	(2)	(3)	(4)
Costs	0.653***	0.653***	0.662***	0.662***
	(0.0176)	(0.0172)	(0.0172)	(0.0172)
Handicap	-4.543***	-4.192***	-4.767***	-4.516***
	(0.450)	(0.654)	(0.392)	(0.496)
Period	-0.119**	-0.119**	-0.0498**	-0.0501**
	(0.0463)	(0.0463)	(0.0163)	(0.0162)
Buyer		0.0462		-0.242
		(1.133)		(0.396)
Buyer x Handicap		-0.706		-0.509
		(0.920)		(0.572)
Constant	39.25***	39.26***	37.50***	37.63***
	(1.845)	(2.009)	(1.448)	(1.448)
Observations	1600	1600	3200	3200
Suppliers	80	80	80	80
R2	0.7995	0.7996	0.8075	0.8076

Robust standard errors in parentheses

* $p<0.05$, ** $p<0.01$, *** $p<0.001$

Notes: Reported are random-effects panel regressions. Handicap is a dummy variable that is equal to zero in case of a positive score and equal to one in case of a negative score. Buyer is a dummy variable that is equal to one if the buyer determines the framing of the scores and equal to zero if it is randomly determined.

The regressions reported in **Table 1** confirm the substantial influence of the framing decision. We further observe that bids became more aggressive over time and find no indication for a reciprocity effect. Even though the framing of scores as handicaps was more profitable for buyers than the framing as bonuses buyers used bonuses roughly as frequently as handicaps (48.6% vs. 51.4%) and did not change their behavior over time.

> **Result 2:**
> Suppliers bid more aggressively when they had a handicap than when they had a bonus (**Table 1**, $p<0.001$).

While our data provides strong evidence for a perception bias and an asymmetry effect, which both indicates sufficient statistical power, we do not observe evidence for a reciprocity effect. Our data shows no difference between suppliers' bidding behavior in the buyer's choice treatment and in the random choice treatment.

> **Result 3:**
> There is no evidence for a reciprocity effect.

An important question especially for practitioners is whether the effect that handicaps made suppliers bid more aggressively wore off over time. While **Table 1** shows that bidding in general became more aggressive over time, we analyze if the time trends depend on the framing as bonuses or handicaps in **Table 2**. When taking into account all 80 rounds of scoring auctions we find a weakly significant time trend towards lower bids when scores were framed as bonuses ($p=0.0954$) and a highly significant time trend towards lower bids when scores were framed as handicaps ($p=0.002$). However, we find no indication that these time trends differed significantly. This implies that the effect of the framing was stable over time and especially that the effect of the framing as handicaps does not wear off over time.

Table 2: Random-effects panel regressions of bidding behavior over time

	Bid	
	Between-subjects design (Stage 2) (1)	Within-subjects design (Stage 2+3) (2)
Costs	0.653***	0.662***
	(0.0176)	(0.0172)
Handicap	-3.403***	-4.151***
	(0.941)	(0.635)
Period	-0.0658	-0.0348
	(0.0600)	(0.0209)
Handicap x Period	-0.109	-0.0300
	(0.0797)	(0.0262)
Constant	37.50***	36.69***
	(1.620)	(1.393)
Observations	1600	3200
Participants	80	80
R2	0.7999	0.8075

Robust standard errors in parentheses

*** $p<0.001$

Notes: Reported are random-effects panel regressions. Handicap is a dummy variable that is equal to zero in case of a positive score and equal to one in case of a negative score.

5 Conclusion

Reverse auctions play an important role in procurement practice and in many situations buyers face suppliers whose goods or services differ with regard to non-price attributes. To consider this heterogeneity buyers employ scoring auctions in which they assign a monetary value, a so called score, to suppliers' non-price attributes. As a consequence, quality scores are an essential part of most procurement auctions and procurement managers have long been asking if and how the framing of these scores influences suppliers' bidding behavior. We analyze these questions in a controlled laboratory experiment and find that the framing of the quality scores as bonuses or handicaps has a strong impact. First, the framing influences suppliers' beliefs about their relative position. A supplier who receives a handicap (bonus) expects to be in a weaker (stronger) position than his competitor, i.e. he believes that his competitor had a score closer to zero. Second and in line with the former observation, the framing has a strong influence on suppliers' bidding behavior. Suppliers who receive a handicap bid more aggressive than suppliers who received a bonus in order to compensate their disadvantage. Our data indicates that buyers can increase their profits by framing quality scores as handicaps.

We find no evidence that the profitability of the framing as handicaps wears off over time nor that suppliers receiving a handicap feel treated unfairly and hence increase their bids. However, when interpreting our results one has to take into account that in our setting participation in the auction was costless for suppliers. In settings in which participation comes at a cost, however, a supplier who receives a handicap might be less likely to participate. The reason is that he expects lower profits from the participation, because he assumes to be in a weak position and hence bids more aggressively. Hence, there might be a trade-off between attracting more bidders and making them bid more aggressively in some situations.

References

Asker, J.; Cantillon, E. (2008): Properties of Scoring Auctions, in: RAND Journal of Economics, 39(1), 69–85.

Beall, S. et al. (2003): The Role of Reverse Auctions in Strategic Sourcing. CAPS Research.

Branco, F. (1997): The Design of Multidimensional Auctions, in: RAND Journal of Economics, 28(1), 63–81.

Carter, C. R. et al. (2004): Reverse Auctions – Grounded Theory From the Buyer and Supplier Perspective, in: Transportation Research Part E: Logistics and Transportation Review, 40(3), 229–254.

Che, Y.-K. (1993): Design Competition Through Multidimensional Auctions, in: RAND Journal of Economics, 24(4), 668–680.

Dini, F.; Pacini, R.; Valletti, T. (2006): Scoring Rules, in: Dimitri, N.; Piga, G.; Spagnolo, G. (eds.): Handbook of Procurement, New York: Cambridge University Press, 293–321.

Dufwenberg, M.; Kirchsteiger, G. (2004): A Theory of Sequential Reciprocity, in: Games and Economic Behavior, 47(2), 268–298.

Elmaghraby, W. J. (2007): Auctions within E-Sourcing Events, in: Production and Operations Management, 16(4), 409–422.

Engelbrecht-Wiggans, R.; Haruvy, E.; Katok, E. (2007): A Comparison of Buyer-Determined and Price-Based Multiattribute Mechanisms, in: Marketing Science, 26(5), 629–641.

Fischbacher, U. (2007): Z-Tree: Zurich Toolbox for Ready-Made Economic Experiments, in: Experimental Economics, 10(2), 171–178.

Fugger, N.; Katok, E.; Wambach, A. (2016): Collusion in Dynamic Buyer-Determined Reverse Auctions, in: Management Science, 62(2), 518–533.

Greiner, B. (2015): Subject Pool Recruitment Procedures: Organizing Experiments with ORSEE, in: Journal of the Economic Science Association, 1(1), 114–125.

Krishna, V. (2010): Auction Theory, 2nd edition, San Diego: Academic Press.

Naegelen, F. (2002): Implementing Optimal Procurement Auctions with Exogenous Quality, in: Review of Economic Design, 7(2), 135–153.

Rabin, M. (1993): Incorporating Fairness into Game Theory and Economics, in: American Economic Review, 83(5), 1281–1302.

Shugan, S. M. (2005) Marketing and Designing Transaction Games, in: Marketing Science, 24(4), 525–530.

Strecker, S. (2010): Information Revelation in Multiattribute English Auctions, in: Decision Support Systems, 49(3), 272–280.

Verespej, M. A. (2002): E-Procurement Explosion, in: Industry Week, 24–26.

Integrated segmentation of supply and demand with service differentiation (Extended abstract)

Benedikt Schulte

Abstract

The presented research studies the integrated segmentation of supply and demand with service differentiation by means of service-level menus. A service-level menu is a self-selection mechanism that allows customers to choose among several offerings, each with its own cost and guaranteed level of service. The provision of different levels of service can be achieved by use of inventory rationing, in particular, by use of critical-level policies. The presented research takes an integrated perspective on the inventory management policy on one hand and the joint setting of prices and service levels on the other hand. This integrated perspective comprises an answer to the question when the introduction of a service-level menu is likely to significantly increase profits.

1 Introduction

This article presents an overview of the key findings of the author's PhD thesis (Schulte, 2015), which studies the integrated segmentation of supply and demand with service differentiation by means of service-level menus. Parts and overviews of the presented research have also been published in Schulte and Pibernik (2016), Schulte and Pibernik (2017), and Schulte (2018).

The remainder of this article is structured as follows: Section 2 provides an introduction to the topic of service differentiation and Section 3 summarizes the main findings of the aforementioned PhD thesis including some notes on implementation.

Wissenschaftliche Forschungsbeiträge

2 Motivation and introduction to service differentiation

In today's complex supply chains contractually stipulated service levels constitute an important tool for customers to manage the risk that suppliers might not be able to deliver requested items on time and in full. However, different customers have varying preferences in terms of delivery service. While some customers demand high levels of product availability and immediate delivery, this may not be as critical to others. From the supplier's point of view, the customers who demand better service are often the most profitable ones and are often willing to pay a premium for a higher level of service. How suppliers, that is, manufacturers and retailers, deal with this form of customer heterogeneity can have a substantial performance impact in terms of both costs and revenues. It stands to reason that the differentiation strategies that have successfully been employed to exploit other forms of customer heterogeneity (e.g., willingness to pay, preferences for certain tangible product features) can – or should – also be applied to deal with heterogeneous preferences in terms of delivery service. An undifferentiated fulfillment strategy, that is, one with only a single level of service, will inevitably lead to some customers being unsatisfied, high costs in conjunction with customers who are „over-serviced," or a combination of both.

One intuitive approach to service-level differentiation could be a self-selection mechanism where the supplier offers several types of service contracts, each with its own cost and guaranteed level of service. For example, a „gold contract" might guarantee a 99% fill rate within twenty-four hours, while a „silver contract" promises 90% fill rate within forty-eight hours, and so on (cf. Arslan et al., 2007). Naturally, the supplier would charge a higher price for the gold contract vs. the silver contract. Although this form of service differentiation is frequently associated with spare/service parts operations, it does not have to be restricted to this domain. Suppliers may not always be able to charge higher prices for higher levels of service, but they may want to implement a discount program to incentivize a customer to accept a lower level of service relative to the standard service (e.g., the gold contract). In this case, differentiation does not necessarily generate additional revenues, but it creates some flexibility/slack that can be used to lower operational costs (e.g., for inventory and/or capacity).

Introducing service-level menus changes how suppliers interact with their customers, by allowing the latter to choose among several offerings. However, such a change in the customer interaction model also requires a change in the operating model as the following example shows: A technology company introduced differentiated service levels for certain products, but its production and distribution network could only provide a single level of service. Accordingly, the company offered different service levels and charged different prices but all customers received the best possible service. This not only led to higher-than-necessary costs for the company but also upset those customers who paid higher prices while receiving the same level of service.

As shown by the aforementioned example the introduction of service-level menus requires a new operating approach that allows to provide multiple levels of service. This can be achieved by use of inventory rationing, in particular, by use of critical-level policies that protect parts of the inventory for orders/customers requiring a higher level of service. Such critical-level policies are not only intuitive but also easy-to-implement: One can, for instance, think about inventory being kept in two separate bins. Initially, all demands are filled from the first bin. Once the first bin is exhausted, high-priority orders are served from the second bin, while low-priority orders are rejected or backordered. In this example, the critical level is equal to the content of the second bin. Clearly, this model can be extended to more than two customer classes (or bins).

While inventory rationing and critical-level policies have already been studied extensively (see Samii et al., 2012, for an example in a single-period setting and Arslan et al., 2007, for an example in a multi-period setting), previous research focussed on the operational aspects of service differentiation, that is, which inventory-rationing policies to use and how to determine the parameters of these policies in order to obtain the desired service levels. In contrast, the author's PhD thesis addresses service-level differentiation in an integrated fashion. It includes the question of price-setting into the discussion and also sheds light on the question when such a service-differentiation strategy is likely to significantly increase profits.

3   Summary of findings

The presented research consists of three consecutive parts, with the first two being largely independent and the third one building on the previous two. The following paragraphs summarize the contribution of these three parts and discuss which elements are necessary for successful implementation of a service-differentiation strategy.

Throughout the discussion one analytical setting is maintained: A profit-maximizing, monopolistic firm supplies a single product from a single warehouse over a finite period of time to a set of heterogeneous customers. Prior to the selling period the firm purchases a number of units of the product. During the selling period, customer demands follow a Poisson process. Whether a given customer demand is fulfilled depends on the current pricing policy and the current inventory. Any remaining units of stock at the end of the selling period are either salvaged or held for future sale such that either a salvage value or holding costs are incurred.

The first part, which has been published in Schulte and Pibernik (2016), provides explicit service-level expressions for a single-period critical-level policy with an arbitrary number of customer classes; structural insights into critical-level policies, including a characterization of the service levels in terms of when the critical levels are hit; and an algorithm with which to compute the design parameters of such a policy. These results contribute to the theoretical body of knowledge for single-period critical-level policies, as similar results had previously only been available for situations in which there are no more than two customer classes. Additionally, the first part contains an extensive numerical study that provides insights into the behavior of n-class critical-level policies.

The second part examines the simultaneous optimization of price and service level, that is, it studies the price-setting newsvendor with Poisson demand. It provides a solution approach that covers a broad class of price-demand functions, including linear and iso-elastic demand functions; an approximate solution approach for arbitrary price-demand relationships; and analytical and numerical insights. The corresponding results make a valuable contribution to the existing research, as the price-setting newsvendor had previously only been studied for continuous demand distributions.

To the best of our knowledge, the third part (published in Schulte and Pibernik, 2017) presents the first study of the combination of service-level differentiation and pricing. It not only presents an analytical model for service-level-based price differentiation but also includes an equivalent dynamic pricing model and a characterization of situations in which service-level based price differentiation is profitable. It also provides a solution approach for either of these situations. Thus, the presented research has immediate relevance for companies that consider to use service-level menus. Decision-makers from such companies learn that the relationship between their current price and the price-setting newsvendor price is an important indicator for the potential profitability of service-level-based price differentiation. If the current price is not significantly less than the price-setting newsvendor price, then service-differentiation should not further be pursued. In contrast, if (e.g., due to regulation, competition, customer expectations, or other influences) the current price is significantly less than the price-setting newsvendor price, then a particular form of service-level based price differentiation, which we term service-level-based upselling, has the potential to increase profits significantly.

Clearly, a successful implementation of a service-differentiation strategy requires more than the analytical and conceptual results described so far – for instance, the analytical approaches must be adapted to each specific situation. In addition, four elements seem to be critical for successful implementation of a service differentiation strategy. First, the company must ensure that stable inventory-management processes, including a common ERP system, standard processes, and reliable inventory records, are in place. This prerequisite might seem irrelevant, but companies that may have accumulated multiple warehouses of varying sizes in several locations often have neither a unified ERP system nor established standard processes (and when it comes to incorrect inventory records any supply manager will have his or her own stories). Second, in order to manage service-level guarantees and ensure effective customer communication, a service differentiation strategy requires an appropriate ERP system that provides service-level reporting on the product level and the customer level and that ensures a high level of transparency and data quality. Third, the company must ensure sufficient capabilities among its employees, including the advanced analytical capabilities required to set up and manage the ERP system and a high level of discipline (including the warehouse personnel because service differentiation sometimes requires employees not to fulfill an order even when the items are in stock). Fourth, these companies need to foster a culture of innovation because further significant innovation will be required to adapt the existing research to the requirements of real-life companies.

Acknowledgement: During the time of this dissertation, the author was supported by a fellowship granted by the Foundation of German Business (sdw).

References

Arslan, H.; Graves, S. C.; Roemer, T. A. (2007): A single-product inventory model for multiple demand classes, in: Management Science, 53(9), 1486–1500.

Samii, A. B.; Pibernik, R.; Yadav, P.; Vereecke, A. (2012): Reservation and allocation policies for influenza vaccines, in: European Journal of Operational Research, 222(3), 495–507.

Schulte, B. (2015): Integrated Segmentation of Supply and Demand with Service Differentiation, PhD Thesis, Würzburg University.

Schulte, B. (2018): Integrated Segmentation of Supply and Demand with Service Differentiation, in: Fink A.; Fügenschuh A.; Geiger M. (eds): Operations Research Proceedings 2016. Operations Research Proceedings (GOR (Gesellschaft für Operations Research e.V.)), Springer, Cham.

Schulte, B.; Pibernik, R. (2016): Service differentiation in a single-period inventory model with numerous customer classes, in: OR Spectrum, 38(4), 921–948.

Schulte, B.; Pibernik, R. (2017): Profitability of Service-Level-Based Price Differentiation with Inventory Rationing, in: Production and Operations Management, 26(5), 903–923.

Supplier development considering interdependencies in the inbound logistics of the automotive industry

Sönke Wieczorrek, Martin Grunewald, Thomas S. Spengler

Abstract

Besides product quality and costs, the logistics performance is increasingly focused on supplier development activities in the automotive industry. This is because inbound logistics networks in the automotive industry are very large and many process disruptions occur. These disruptions lead to additional handling efforts and should be avoided. Existing approaches of supplier development concentrate on the development of single suppliers. Interdependencies between suppliers are not considered. However, especially in the inbound logistics there are network effects. For instance, a delay at one supplier affects the timeliness of all other suppliers on the same route. Therefore, it could be beneficial to develop a supplier with a relatively small importance for the automotive manufacturer (OEM) but with strong impact on the other suppliers. Accordingly, we introduce an approach that assigns improvement measures to suppliers, taking into account the interdependencies in the automotive inbound logistics. We introduce a two-stage approach to evaluate the effect of improvement measures in the first step and to assign these measures to suppliers optimally under the OEM's budget constraints in the second step, using Monte Carlo Simulation and a knapsack model. A first numerical example shows great potential compared to an approach with a state-of-the-art decision rule for supplier development.

1   Introduction

Automotive manufacturers (OEMs) aim to provide customer-specific products and services. Consequently, new challenges in purchasing and inbound logistics occur. In particular, the increasing number of parts in combination with decreasing order sizes raises the cost of parts transport from the suppliers to the OEMs' production sites. This is why OEMs operate large transport networks in inbound logistics. BMW, for instance, works with 13,000 suppliers in 70 countries (BMW Group, 2017). Volkswagen

Wissenschaftliche Forschungsbeiträge

Group provides a transport network for 27 of its European production sites with more than 5,800 suppliers (Wieczorrek et al., 2017, p. 54).

Currently, a rethinking of the collaboration with the suppliers takes place in the automotive industry. The automotive industry, particularly in Europe, was known for having very strict contracts with their suppliers, enforcing contractual penalties for process disruptions. In recent years, this way of working has been altered to a more collaborative approach, in which OEMs work on improvement measures together with their suppliers, seeing them as process partners (Wieczorrek et al., 2017). Although this approach has high potential, OEMs only have limited personnel and monetary resources for improving the performance of their supply base this way. Therefore, it is crucial for OEMs to decide which supplier should be developed first and which improvement measure should be used.

Supplier management offers a wide range of instruments to evaluate and develop the processes between suppliers, OEMs, and logistics service providers (LSPs) in this context. Specifically, supplier evaluation and supplier development provide a vast array of approaches for identifying low-performance suppliers and improving their (logistics) capabilities by applying supplier-specific measures (Glock et al., 2016). In practical settings in inbound logistics, OEMs often base their decisions upon common criteria, such as the supplier's shipping volume and failure rate, to decide whether a supplier should be developed or not.

Although this approach has been proven effective regarding product quality and costs, it is problematic to use such common criteria regarding supplier development in logistics. The isolated look on the performance of one single supplier without considering the network structure is insufficient regarding supplier development in logistics. Due to the small order sizes, parts are collected from several suppliers on one route. If a delay occurs at one supplier, it will also affect the other suppliers of the route. Therefore, relatively small suppliers are able to affect the timeliness of larger suppliers and vice versa. Accordingly, the following research question needs to be answered:

"How can interdependencies within the transport network be taken into account regarding decisions concerning supplier development?"

Against this background, we analyze a problem setting from the inbound logistics of the automotive industry. To this end, we develop a two-stage approach. In the first stage, we use Monte Carlo Simulation to examine the effects of measures that reduce delays at single suppliers. Based on these results, we choose the most effective measures by solving a knapsack problem in the second stage. We compare our approach to a state-of-the-art decision rule for supplier development. The remainder of the paper is organized as follows. In Section 2 we provide a short literature review on interdependencies in supply networks, supplier evaluation, and supplier development. This is followed by a description of the problem setting in a more detailed way in Section 3. The two-staged solution approach is introduced in Section 4. A first numerical example of the approach is given in Section 5. In Section 6, we will provide a conclusion and an outlook to future research.

2 Literature review

In this Section, we briefly regard interdependencies in supply networks and existing approaches of supplier evaluation and supplier development in scientific literature. We depict the interdependencies in Section 2.1. In Section 2.2, we review supplier evaluation methods, before we focus on literature for supplier development in Section 2.3. In this context, it is important to keep in mind that the differentiation between approaches of supplier evaluation and supplier development is not very clear (Wieczorrek et al., 2017, p. 59). Approaches for supplier development usually imply methods to evaluate which suppliers need to be developed. Some authors integrate this evaluation step into their models for supplier development.

2.1 Interdependencies in supply networks

To understand interdependencies in supply networks, we first define a (supply) network as a set of interrelated actors, in which each actor influences other actors by interacting through flows among them (Borgatti/Li, 2009, pp. 6–9). In context of supply networks, interdependencies result from interactions in different areas of inter-firm collaboration, such as the collection and transport of the goods from several suppliers to the OEM by an LSP. Hedvall et al. (2017) provide case studies about interdependencies within transport networks. They emphasize on the relations between OEM, supplier, and LSP. In this setting they describe interdependencies among the involved activities, resources, and actors (Hedvall et al., 2017). Interdependencies in supply networks receive attention in both Supply Chain Design and Supply Chain Risk Management. By assessing the structure of networks, the efficiency of network configurations can be evaluated in Supply Chain Design settings (Kim et al., 2011, p. 209). In Supply Chain Risk Management settings, the spreading of risks within a network is investigated. Risks, such as operational failures, may quickly propagate through the entire supply chain, affecting its overall performance (Basole/Bellamy 2014, p. 109). That is why it is important to identify the most influential actors within a network (Basole/Bellamy, 2014, p. 116). With knowledge about the influence of the actors and the underlying network structure, risk propagation can be predicted and avoided (e.g. by applying specific measures).

There are different approaches to analyze supply network structures to obtain the abovementioned information about its structure and the most influential actors within. Borgatti and Li (2009) propose Social Network Analysis (SNA) (Borgatti/Li, 2009). SNA has been adopted to supply networks to analyze the pattern of ties between suppliers and OEM (Kim et al., 2011, pp. 195–196). Several characteristic parameters can be analytically calculated to quantify the properties of networks or to identify influential suppliers (Borgatti/Li, 2009, pp. 11–18; Kim et al., 2011, pp. 195-196). Besides the SNA approach, Garvey et al. (2015) use a Baysean Network to model risk propagation in supply networks (Garvey et al., 2015). However, in both approaches the decision maker needs complete information about the network structure. Since in transport networks the material flow may also depend on decisions of the LSP (such as vehicle routing), the network structure emerges over the time (Pathak et al., 2010, p. 123). Because of this, we need to find a different approach to consider interdependencies for our problem setting.

2.2 Supplier evaluation

Supplier evaluation is an important method for analyzing supplier data in a systematic way. It enables decision makers to find "weak" suppliers in the set of their company's suppliers (supply base) and supports transparency of suppliers' performances (Janker, 2008, p. 80; Irlinger, 2012, p. 34). The results of supplier evaluation are heavily dependent on the selected evaluation approach and evaluation criteria. Most common evaluation criteria are quality, delivery, price/cost, manufacturing capability, and service (Ho et al., 2010, p. 21). In this context the term "delivery" is quite unspecific. Janker collected different key performance indicators (KPI) for logistics purpose, such as delivery failure rate, delayed delivery rate, adherence to delivery dates, service level, lead time, and delivery fulfilment (Janker, 2008, p. 111). On one hand, all of these KPIs are based on time, which is necessary to model delays in transport networks. On the other hand, these KPIs solely focus on a single supplier without taking its network relations into consideration.

Regarding the evaluation approaches, there are big differences between theoretical models and practical applications. In scientific literature, there is a distinction between many complex approaches, such as Data Envelopment Analysis (DEA), linear optimization, and Analytic Hierarchy Process (AHP) (Ho et al., 2010, pp. 16–21; Chai et al, 2012, pp. 3876–3881). Moreover, Wu and Olsen point out the influence of uncertain input parameters on supplier evaluation decisions using Monte Carlo Simulation (Wu/Olson, 2008, pp. 650–652). Nevertheless, due to their complexity, these approaches often do not find their way into practical application. Schmitz and Platts study the logistics performance measurement of suppliers in logistics, comparing supplier evaluation efforts of four OEMs. It turns out that all of them use common logistics KPI approaches (Schmitz/Platts, 2004, pp. 237–240), but none of them takes network considerations into account. Overall, there are no approaches that consider network interdependencies in a supplier evaluation context – neither by the design of the approaches, nor by the selected evaluation criteria. This aggravates the ability of decision makers to take a closer look on logistics processes in terms of supplier evaluation, hence to find and to assign appropriate improvement measures during supplier development.

2.3 Supplier development

In addition to the abovementioned evaluation methods, supplier development can be described as "any effort of a buying firm with its supplier to increase the performance and/or capabilities of the supplier and meet the buying firm's supply needs" (Krause/Ellram, 1997, p. 21). Furthermore, most authors conclude that there is a majority of positive effects triggered by supplier development, e.g. increased supplier satisfaction as well as the performance and the performance abilities (see e.g. Humphreys et al., 2004, pp. 136–137; Wagner, 2006, pp. 691–693).

Based on an empirical study, Krause et al. (1998) describe the process of supplier development. At first, suppliers need to be identified for development. Next, the manufacturing company builds up a cross-functional team, initiates communication with the supplier, and identifies critical performance areas as well as improvement opportunities. Both the manufacturer and the supplier then agree on improvement measures and simultaneously work on them with joint resources. Afterwards, the supplier is rewarded for its efforts and a continuous improvement process is implemented (Krause et al., 1998, p. 44). In scientific literature, supplier development efforts are described from different perspectives. For instance, there are optimization approaches calculating optimal investments for supplier development measures subject to budget constraints of the OEM (Bhattacharyya/Guiffrida, 2015, pp. 3778–3779), or focusing on investment in green supplier development measures (Bai et al., 2016, pp. 511–517).

Nevertheless, two approaches dealing with the automotive industry (Dölle, 2013) and particularly automotive logistics (Pauli, 2012) can be identified. Dölle describes supplier evaluation from a more strategic standpoint, aiming to find a theoretical understanding for the development of the relationship between manufacturers and their suppliers. He depicts the change from a supplier-centered view to a network-based understanding of manufacturer-supplier-relationships (Dölle, 2013, pp. 195–199). Even though in Dölle's work logistics is seen as an important process between the manufacturer and the supplier, the strategic point of view is insufficient to describe interdependencies between the OEM and its suppliers on an operational level. Transport processes cannot be captured this way.

Pauli's model describes supplier development in automotive inbound logistics. For this purpose, he sets up a process and corresponding methods for supplier development in logistics. The process consists of three stages. At first stage, the suppliers to be developed will be identified. The second stage is to create measures for the identified suppliers. Finally, these measures will be assigned to the suppliers in the third stage (Pauli, 2012, pp. 53–150). Taking a more detailed view on the evaluation in the first stage, it becomes evident that the decision of whether to pick a supplier for supplier development is split into two parts: The first part consists of a KPI approach (see Section 2.2), whereas the second part is about evaluating the "strategic importance" of a supplier. There is no approach of evaluating the network relationships between the suppliers; hence it is not possible to consider interdependencies within the transport network.

Therefore, we develop a new approach that takes interdependencies between suppliers as well as the assignment of measures into account to improve the overall performance of the network. As a result, our approach consists of two stages. In the first stage, we examine the effects of measures to reduce delays at single suppliers within the transport network. Having considered complex network structures, we apply Monte Carlo Simulation. In the second stage, formulate a knapsack problem to assign measures to suppliers that are most beneficial for the OEM and the performance of the transport network, respectively.

3 Problem setting

Our problem setting is motivated by the inbound logistics of the automotive industry, which is characterized by geographically dispersed suppliers and demanding facilities as well as small shipping volumes. Due to this reason, the most common transport concept in the (German) automotive industry is area forwarding using less-than-truckloads (LTL) (Schöneberg et al., 2013). The process is initiated by the facilities of the OEM sending call-offs to their suppliers. As a second step, the suppliers produce their quantities according to the delivery dates stated in the call-offs. To ship its parts to the OEM, a supplier sends a delivery note to the LSP. In the third step, the LSP plans vehicle routes according to the delivery notes from the suppliers in its area of responsibility. The actual collection and the transport of the parts are performed in the fourth step. The sink of the routes can be the facilities of the manufacturer or a consolidation center (CC). In the second case, there is a joint material collection for different destinations (OEM facilities) at the suppliers. The material will then be reordered at the CC and will be transported to the destinations on a direct link. Furthermore, the LSP is allowed to collect goods for other customers as well. Therefore, the routes change daily and are not known in advance to the OEM. However, the likelihoods for the routes can be derived from historical data.

As a matter of fact, transport processes are subject to disruptions. While large disruptive events like earthquakes and flooding receive great media attention, small disruptive events occur a lot more frequently and have a huge impact on logistic processes as well. For instance, sometimes suppliers use non-palletized small load carriers for packaging. This increases handling operations and impedes the tie-down of the containers. That often leads to delays at the collection of the goods. Furthermore, sometimes incorrect labels have been printed or wrong documents have been filed, leading to higher administrative efforts for both LSP and OEM. These are just examples for all kinds of disruptions which happen on a daily basis. We concentrate on disruptions that lead to a delay in the transport process. We assume that the occurrence probability and the distribution of the length of a delay are known for each supplier. Every delay at a supplier leads to the same delay at the next supplier on the route in addition to the delay that may occur at the next supplier. As a result, delays of suppliers add up within a route. Because delays are usual in practice, time buffers are scheduled. Due to this reason, we assume that a delay on a route is only considered if a certain time limit is exceeded.

If a delay occurs, there will be contingency plans. First, the manufacturer would check its stock and calculate if the production can be maintained at no extra route. If this is not the case, the supplier needs to organize an extra route to get its parts transported to the OEM. This is usually operated by an express parcel service. In some cases, when there is no time for an extra route, the OEM could shift its sequence on the production line to build other models first. Unfortunately, there are many restrictions. For a sequence shift, parts that are planned for later production need to be available earlier. This often leads to consecutive shortages. In worst case, the production line stops.

Instead of looking at the aforementioned reactive measures, we focus in our setting on proactive measures to avoid the negative effects of the disruptions and to minimize the costly reactive measures. Penalty payments are well known common measures to encourage the suppliers to comply with the contracts, but the effects of penalties are limited. On the contrary, recent studies point out that there are positive links between collaborative measures in combination with trust and the supplier performance (Nagati/Rebolledo, 2013, pp. 184–186). A typical procedure is to analyze the problem in detail with the involved partners first and to organize trainings afterwards. The improvement measure may vary depending on disruption type, objective (reducing or eliminating the disruption), the length, effect and costs. In our problem setting, we assume that the costs and the effect on the disruption are known in advance. In particular, a reduction of the disruption can be interpreted as a reduction of the occurrence probability of a delay at a supplier. In contrast, the impact of an improvement measure on the overall network is not known in advance because the interdependencies between suppliers on the same route are not known in advance.

Due to limited personnel and monetary resources, the OEM has to assign the right measure to the right supplier of a transport network under its own budget constraint. An example of the decision situation is depicted in **Figure 1**. We assume that the network consists of five suppliers and one LSP, and routes may vary in all three periods. Even though the OEM knows its own shipping volume, it has no information about the quantities for other customers of the LSP, which is why it can only assume the likelihood of certain routes. Supposing delays at supplier 2 and supplier 4, which affect all other suppliers on their routes as well, the OEM has to decide on the improvement measures which should be assigned to supplier 2, supplier 4, or both under its own budget restrictions. Taking into account that measures can be customized to the suppliers, and that the routes are subject to changes, the OEM cannot predict whether the assignment of a measure to a supplier is beneficial for the overall net-

Wissenschaftliche Forschungsbeiträge

work. The OEM can hardly decide which supplier to develop. In Section 4 we will provide a solution approach for this problem setting.

Figure 1: Example of the decision situation

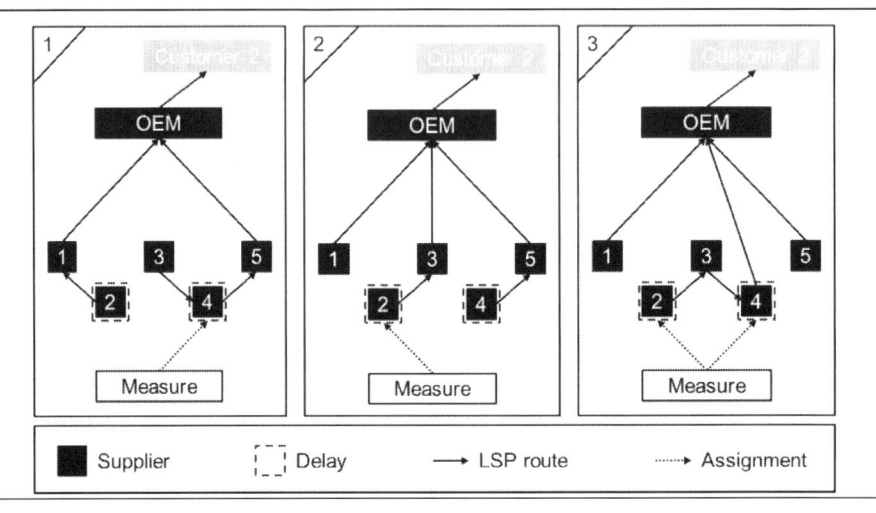

4 Solution approach

We introduce a solution approach considering effects from interdependencies between suppliers in the inbound logistics network in context of supplier development decisions. The approach consists of two stages. In the first stage, we examine the effects of applying measures reducing delays at single suppliers on the overall network. This enables the decision maker to gather information about the influence of the network structure and about potential interdependencies between suppliers within the transport network. The model considers many random events, such as the failure rate of each supplier and the lengths of delays. Furthermore, the vehicle routes are not known in advance and may vary in each period. Due to this complex network structure, we choose Monte Carlo Simulation to include the abovementioned random events and the interdependencies between the suppliers into our model. This complies with Pathak et al.'s proposal of using simulation approaches for network modelling to capture its variable structures (Pathak et al., 2010, p. 123). Moreover, a Monte Carlo Simulation approach is faster in terms of computing time and easier to apply in comparison to analytical approaches, such as SNA. These advantages may increase with increasing network size. The application of discrete event simulation models, however, is not advantageous either since it is too complex and not necessary for homogeneous experiments. In the second stage, improvement measures are assigned to the suppliers. This is modeled as a knapsack problem, considering the effects of measures from first stage, the costs for each measure, and the budget restriction of the OEM.

4.1 Stage 1: Effects of measures

To make reasonable supplier development decisions, we first need to find out to what extent an improvement measure at a particular supplier influences the overall performance of the network. To do so, we introduce a new KPI to quantify the overall performance of the network: the aggregated delayed shipping volume V^d of the network. It is the sum of the shipping volume V_i^d of a route i arriving late at the sink of the network:

$$V^d = \sum_{i \in Routes} V_i^d \qquad (1)$$

The shipping volume V_i^s of a route i is only delayed, if the delay on the route $delay_i$ exceeds a certain time limit T. Thus, the delayed shipping volume V_i^d is determined by

$$V_i^d = \begin{cases} 0, & delay_i < T \\ V_i^s, & delay_i \geq T \end{cases} \qquad (2)$$

The value of V_i^d is computed n times using Monte Carlo Simulation. In each simulation run, we first assign the suppliers to routes randomly according to their likelihood of being part of that particular route. Then, delays are assigned randomly to all suppliers according to their failure rate and their probability distribution of the length of the delay. Based on these randomly assigned input parameters, we obtain the aggregated delayed shipping volume V_r^d for each simulation run r. For high values of r, we gather valid information about the aggregated delayed shipping volume under the aforementioned stochastic circumstances. The mean aggregated delayed shipping volume $\bar{V}^d$ can be computed as

$$\bar{V}^d = \frac{\sum_{r=1}^{n} V_r^d}{n} \qquad (3)$$

Moreover, $\bar{V}^d$ can be interpreted as the upper boundary for the mean aggregated delayed volume in the transport network (assuming no improvement measures are in effect yet). Nevertheless, there are different measures at hand to improve the aggregated delayed shipping volume. The effect of a certain measure m on a single supplier's performance can be modeled as an improvement of the failure rate of the supplier. Considering this, we simulate the impact of a successful supplier development measure by lowering the failure rate for each supplier j, while all other suppliers keep their actual failure rate. Now, the simulation runs are computed again for each measure m at a supplier j. The resulting mean aggregated delayed shipping volume $\bar{V}_{mj}^d$ is lower than $\bar{V}^d$ to the extent of supplier j's influence on the overall network performance. The relative difference between these numbers is called network performance improvement $NWPI_{mj}$ and can be computed for each measure m and supplier j:

$$NWPI_{mj} = 1 - \frac{\bar{V}^d_{mj}}{\bar{V}^d} \qquad (4)$$

The bigger the value for $NWPI_{mj}$ is, the more the performance of the overall network can be improved by applying measure m at supplier j. Knowing the effects of a supplier development measure m at a supplier j on the overall network, we can use this information to assign measures to suppliers. This is demonstrated in the next Section.

4.2 Stage 2: Assignment of measures

The assignment of measures is based on a knapsack problem. First, we introduce all symbols and second we formulate and describe the used knapsack problem.

Every measure m at a supplier j can be characterized by the improvement of the network performance $NWPI_{mj}$ and the costs C_{mj}. A decision variable x_{mj} is introduced to describe the assignment of measures to suppliers. It takes on a value of 1, if measure m is assigned to supplier j, and 0 otherwise. The total available budget B for measures is known.

The objective is to maximize the sum of the network performance improvements (see (5)). In constraint set (6) the sum of all costs of the used measures is limited by the budget B. Furthermore, at most one measure can be assigned to a supplier (see (7)). Constraint set (8) defines the decision variable x_{mj}. The resulting problem can be described as a standard knapsack problem. Despite the fact that the knapsack problem is NP-hard, it can be solved to optimality in reasonable time for typical numbers of suppliers and measures.

$$\max Z = \sum_{m \in Measures} \sum_{j \in Suppliers} NWPI_{mj} \cdot x_{mj} \qquad (5)$$

s.t.

$$\sum_{m \in Measures} \sum_{j \in Suppliers} C_{mj} \cdot x_{mj} \leq B \qquad (6)$$

$$\sum_{m \in Measures} x_{mj} \leq 1 \, ; \, \forall j \in Suppliers \qquad (7)$$

$$x_{mj} \in \{0; 1\} \qquad (8)$$

5 Numerical example

In this Section, we provide a first numerical example for our solution approach. In Section 5.1, the model data and the benchmark are introduced. In Section 5.2, we present the results and compare them with a state-of-the-art decision rule for supplier development.

5.1 Data and benchmark

The considered transport network consists of 46 suppliers and one sink. One LSP picks up the parts from the suppliers. The numerical example is based on fixed shipping volumes, meaning the parts supply is constant. As an input parameter, we use the mean shipping volume of the suppliers from a month-long period. This data has been collected by the OEM. Based on the location and the shipping volume of the suppliers, we derive sets of feasible routes for each supplier. If there are multiple feasible routes for a supplier, the probability of each route is assumed to be equal. The initial failure rate for each supplier is assumed to be 5%. The duration of a delay follows a Gamma distribution with the parameter set $\alpha = 1.5$ and $\beta = 1.7$. Both parameters have been derived from the OEM's data. Furthermore, we assume that a delay on a route is only considered if a 30-minute time limit is exceeded. Each Monte Carlo Simulation is performed with 20,000 runs.

We assume that every measure causes the same cost for the OEM, regardless to which supplier a measure is applied to. The effect of a measure is that a failure at a supplier will be eliminated; hence its failure rate is 0 after supplier development. Given these assumptions, we base the supplier development decision directly on the results of the Monte Carlo Simulation without solving the knapsack problem. Since the effects at a single supplier and the costs are the same for each measure at each supplier, it is most beneficial for the OEM to develop its suppliers according to their network performance improvement KPI. The decision rule is as follows: If there are two suppliers (supplier 1 and supplier 2), then select supplier 1 for supplier development first, if its network performance improvement is greater than the network performance improvement of supplier 2 (see (9)).

$$Supplier\ 1 \succ Supplier\ 2 \Leftrightarrow NWPI_1 > NWPI_2 \qquad (9)$$

In practical applications, suppliers are often selected for supplier development measures according to their shipping volume V_j^s. This means that if supplier 1's shipping volume is higher than supplier 2's, supplier 1 will be developed first (see (10)). This ranking we use as benchmark for our approach.

$$Supplier\ 1 \succ Supplier\ 2 \Leftrightarrow V_1^s > V_2^s \qquad (10)$$

5.2 Results and implications for supplier development

In a first step we compare the ranking of the suppliers referring to our new defined network performance (NWPI) with the ranking referring to the shipping volume of the supplier (V_j^s). Second, we compare our approach with this benchmark for 3, 5 or 10 improvement measures that can be assigned.

Table 1:   Comparison of NWPI ranking to volume ranking

Rank ($NWPI_j$)	Rank (V_j^s)	j (+/-)	Rank ($NWPI_j$)	Rank (V_j^s)	j (+/-)	Rank ($NWPI_j$)	Rank (V_j^s)	j (+/-)
1 (4.2%)	2 (66.9%)	S36 (+1)	17 (2.7%)	19 (12.8%)	S37 (+2)	33 (1.1%)	13 (25.9%)	S6 (-20)
2 (4.1%)	1 (100.0%)	S46 (-1)	18 (2.6%)	45 (0.3%)	S19 (+27)	34 (0.9%)	17 (16.3%)	S23 (-17)
2 (4.1%)	44 (0.7%)	S18 (+42)	19 (2.3%)	29 (6.7%)	S43 (+10)	35 (0.9%)	32 (5%)	S10 (-3)
4 (3.6%)	3 (66.2%)	S14 (-1)	20 (2.3%)	31 (6.0%)	S12 (+11)	36 (0.9%)	15 (21.4%)	S30 (-21)
5 (3.4%)	11 (37.8%)	S16 (+6)	21 (2.3%)	4 (54.5%)	S34 (-17)	37 (0.8%)	40 (1.6%)	S33 (+3)
6 (3.2%)	6 (46.5%)	S42 (+0)	22 (2.3%)	41 (1.5%)	S27 (+19)	38 (0.5%)	22 (11%)	S41 (-16)
7 (3.2%)	12 (33.7%)	S1 (+5)	23 (2.2%)	5 (52.9%)	S11 (-18)	39 (0.5%)	43 (0.8%)	S22 (+4)
8 (2.9%)	37 (3.3%)	S38 (+29)	24 (2.0%)	33 (3.7%)	S32 (+9)	40 (0.5%)	21 (11.4%)	S24 (-19)
9 (2.9%)	14 (22.7%)	S4 (+5)	25 (2.0%)	30 (6.3%)	S45 (+5)	41 (0.5%)	42 (1%)	S7 (+1)
10 (2.9%)	20 (11.8%)	S39 (+10)	26 (2.0%)	39 (2.4%)	S8 (+13)	42 (0.4%)	27 (7.4%)	S13 (-15)
11 (2.9%)	7 (45.4%)	S29 (-4)	27 (1.9%)	35 (3.4%)	S2 (+8)	43 (0.4%)	38 (3%)	S35 (-5)
12 (2.8%)	46 (0.1%)	S40 (+34)	28 (1.9%)	10 (39.7%)	S20 (-18)	44 (0.3%)	24 (7.9%)	S17 (-20)
13 (2.8%)	9 (41.5%)	S5 (-4)	29 (1.9%)	23 (9.5%)	S21 (-6)	45 (0.3%)	28 (7%)	S28 (-17)
14 (2.8%)	34 (3.7%)	S44 (+20)	30 (1.9%)	8 (44.1%)	S15 (-22)	46 (0.1%)	36 (3.4%)	S9 (-10)
15 (2.8%)	18 (16.1%)	S26 (+3)	31 (1.7%)	25 (7.7%)	S25 (-6)			
16 (2.7%)	16 (18.4%)	S3 (0)	32 (1.6%)	26 (7.6%)	S31 (-6)			

The resulting NWPI ranking in comparison to the ranking based on shipping volumes is given in **Table 1**. In the column "Rank ($NWPI_j$)" the rank of each supplier according to the NWPI approach can be found. The parenthesized value corresponds to the improvement of the network performance of the supplier. The rank of the supplier according to its shipping volume is shown in column "Rank (V_j^s)". The parenthesized value corresponds to the relative shipping volume of the supplier. The largest shipping volume (supplier S46) is normalized to 1. In addition to that, column "j (+/-)" provides the name of the supplier and the difference between the two ranking methods.

The following example helps to interpret **Table 1**: If we consider supplier S14 (ranked fourth according to NWPI), we can see that supplier development measures performed with this supplier (its failure rate would drop to 0) would result in a drop of the mean aggregated delayed shipping volume by 3.6%. S14 has the third most shipping volume, which is 66.2% compared to the largest supplier within the network. It would be ranked third according to its shipping volume. The difference between both ranking approaches is -1, which means that S14 would be developed later when using the NWPI approach instead of the shipping volume criterion. There are three more suppliers (S36, S46, and S18) with a larger impact on the network performance than S14. It becomes evident that the results using NWPI approach deviate from the shipping volume ranking. While the NWPI approach reflects the network perspective, the volume ranking is based on a single criterion to describe a supplier. The mean rank difference between both methods is 11.6 ranks, the largest positive deviation is 42 ranks, and the largest negative deviation is 22 ranks. However, suppliers with a very high shipping volume (e.g. S14, S36 and S46) also have a very high rank using the NWPI approach. Because in the case of delay at such a supplier, the impact on the network performance would be even high without considering any interdependencies to other suppliers due to the high shipping volume of the supplier. In contrast, for suppliers with small or medium shipping volume the impact due to interdependencies can outweigh the impact of the shipping volume of the supplier.

In the following paragraph we compare our approach with the benchmark regarding a budget for 3, 5 or 10 improvement measures. Because of the assumption that the costs for all improvement measures are the same, the assignment of the measures corresponds to the ranking of the suppliers. In this case, solving the knapsack problem leads to the same result and therefore is not discussed in detail. **Figure 2** shows the different improvements of the mean aggregated shipping volume for the NWPI approach and the benchmark. The NWPI approach shows better results than the common supplier evaluation approach. The more suppliers are developed, the larger the positive effect of using NWPI approach will be. For the TOP 3 suppliers, the NWPI approach is 1% better than the benchmark, for the TOP 5 it is 4% better, and for the TOP 10 it is 6% better. This corresponds to the results of the ranking. Both rankings (according to shipping volume and according to NWPI) of the TOP 3 suppliers differ only by one supplier. For TOP 5 and TOP 10 suppliers the difference is three and seven suppliers, respectively. This is because with the decreasing difference of the shipping volumes of the suppliers, the impact of the interdependencies between the suppliers increases.

Overall, we can state that the NWPI approach leads to higher potential if the number of improvement measures increases (or the budget, respectively) and the difference between the shipping volumes of the suppliers decreases.

Wissenschaftliche Forschungsbeiträge

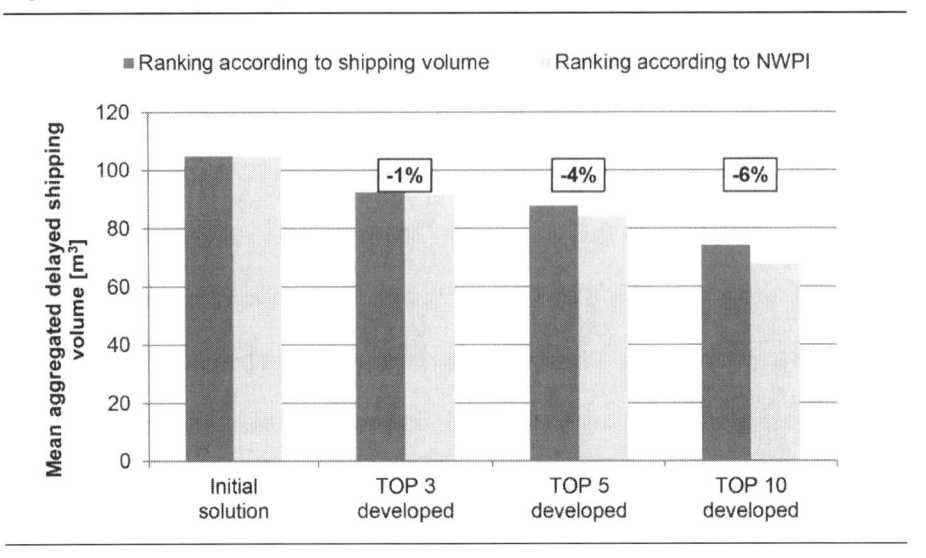

Figure 2: Comparison of the approaches

■ Ranking according to shipping volume   ■ Ranking according to NWPI

[Bar chart: Mean aggregated delayed shipping volume [m³] for Initial solution, TOP 3 developed (-1%), TOP 5 developed (-4%), TOP 10 developed (-6%)]

6 Conclusions

OEMs apply methods for supplier evaluation and supplier development to improve the performance of their supply base. An OEM needs to select suppliers for supplier development first. Afterwards, the OEM has to decide on which measures will be implemented. In this context, the OEM evaluates its suppliers according to certain criteria. Existing approaches, however, do not consider interdependencies resulting from the network structure between the suppliers. For instance, delays in transport process caused by one supplier can affect other suppliers on the same route of the LSP. Therefore, it is hard to predict the impact of an improvement measure at a particular supplier on the overall performance of the network. Based on the unknown impact of an improvement measure it is hard for the OEM to decide which supplier should be developed regarding a limited budget.

Against this background, we introduce a two-stage approach, which evaluates different improvement measures regarding interdependencies between suppliers in an inbound logistics network and decide about the assignment of improvement measures to suppliers. In the first stage, we provide a Monte Carlo Simulation to evaluate the influence of particular measures at particular suppliers on the overall performance of the network. We incorporated stochastic events from the OEM's point of view, such as vehicle routes and delays at the suppliers. Knowing the effects of the measures from Monte Carlo Simulation and the cost for each measure from the OEM, we formulate a knapsack problem in the second stage. The goal is to assign measures to the suppliers optimally in a way that the overall network performance improvement is maximized, considering a restricted budget of the OEM. In a first numerical example, we compare our new approach to a common decision rule for supplier development from a practical application. For this setting, we show that our approach can reduce the delayed shipping volume in the transport network by up to 6% through a more efficient assignment of measures.

The key finding of this paper is that the consideration of interdependencies between suppliers in inbound logistics leads to better results concerning the application of measures in supplier development. As an implication for the industry, our results encourage decision makers to take interdependencies between the suppliers in the automotive inbound logistics into account to improve the overall network performance. This leads to cost reduction due to more stable transport processes. Because of the formulation as a knapsack model, decision makers could optimally assign measures according to their budget or personnel resources, respectively. When managing large inbound networks, our model formulation helps to keep track of a huge amount of information. Particularly in the case of similar suppliers regarding their shipping volumes and their failure rates, applying our model leads to better development plans compared to the state-of-the arte decision rule. Neglecting interdependencies is insufficient in practical settings. Even though our case is motivated by the automotive industry, it is applicable to companies in other industries, provided that they have a substantially large set of suppliers and a restricted budget for supplier development measures. In this paper, we focus on the purchase and transport of production material for supplying the production of an OEM. Other potential procurement scenarios are the purchase of spare parts and the purchase of logistics services. It is certainly possible to extend this view to spare parts logistics, although the structure of the network and the order lot sizes are fairly different, which might lead to different network characteristics and interdependencies. For the purchase of services, specifically in rebuy situations, our model could be used to compare and to analyze the performances of sub-networks with different LSPs.

Our new approach for supplier development in logistics is limited in three main points. First, it focuses only on delays. Even though many process disruptions at suppliers result in delays, there are still other important KPIs describing supplier performance. Second, we take interdependencies between suppliers into account, but we have not yet evaluated interdependencies between measures and interdependencies between suppliers and their suppliers (upstream suppliers). Third, our numerical example is limited regarding all possible constellations. For further research, our goal is to address these abovementioned limitations. By integrating fluctuating demands, we will implement the adherence to quantities as a second KPI to evaluate the suppliers. Moreover, it will be necessary to decide about the assignment of bundles of measures, so that interdependencies between measures could be considered as well. Since process disruptions could also be caused by upstream suppliers of the OEM, we need to make sure, if and how the application of a specific measure works in practice. However, the analysis of interdependencies between upstream suppliers is subject of e.g. Supply Chain Risk Management (Ivanov et al., 2015) or "Tier-n Management" (Träger et al., 2017). Finally, we will extend our numerical study by the assumption of different failure rates as well as different costs and impacts of measures.

References

Bai, C.; Dhavale, D.; Sarkis, J. (2016): Complex investment decisions using rough set and fuzzy c-means: An example of investment in green supply chains, in: European Journal of Operational Research 248, 507–521.

Basole, R. C.; Bellamy, M. A. (2014): Visual analysis of supply network risks: Insights from the electronics industry, in: Decision Support Systems 67, 109–120.

Bhattacharyya, K.; Guiffrida, A. L. (2015): An optimization framework for improving supplier delivery performance, in: Applied Mathematical Modelling 39(13), 3771–3783.

BMW Group (2017): Lieferantenmanagement. Available at: https://www.bmwgroup.com/de/verantwortung/lieferanten-management.html, (accessed: 06 January 2017).

Borgatti, S. P.; Li, X. (2009): On social network analysis in a supply chain context, in: Journal of Supply Chain Management 45(2), 5–21.

Chai, J.; Liu, J. N. K.; Ngai, E. W. T. (2013): Application of decision-making techniques in supplier selection: A systematic review of literature, in: Expert Systems with Applications 40(10), 3872–3885.

Dölle, J. E. (2013): Lieferantenmanagement in der Automobilindustrie. Struktur und Entwicklung der Lieferantenbeziehungen von Automobilherstellern, Wiesbaden.

Garvey, M. D.; Carnovale, S.; Yeniyurt, S. (2015): An analytical framework for supply network risk propagation: A Bayesian network approach, in: European Journal of Operational Research 243, 618–627.

Glock, C.; Grosse, E. H.; Ries, J. M. (2016): Decision Support Models for Supplier Development. Systematic Literature Review and Research Agenda, in: Grubbström, R. W.; Hinterhuber, H. H. (Eds.): PrePrints. 19th International Working Seminar on Production Economics, Innsbruck, Austria, 22.–26.02.2016 (Vol. 1), 159–170.

Hedvall, K.; Dubois, A.; Lind, F. (2017): Variety in freight transport service procurement approaches, in: Transportation Research Proceida 25, 806–823.

Ho, W.; Xu, X.; Dey, P. K. (2010): Multi-criteria decision making approaches for supplier evaluation and selection: A literature review, in: European Journal of Operational Research 202(1), 16–24.

Humphreys, P. K.; Li, W.; Chan, L. Y. (2004): The impact of supplier development on buyer–supplier performance, in: Omega 32(2), 131–143.

Irlinger, W. (2012): Kausalmodelle zur Lieferantenbewertung, Wiesbaden.

Ivanov, D.; Dolgui, A.; Sokolov, B. (2015): Supply Chain Design With Disruption Considerations: Review of Research Streams on the Ripple Effect in the Supply Chain, in: IFAC-PapersOnLine 48(3), 1700–1707.

Janker, C. G. (2008): Multivariate Lieferantenbewertung. Empirisch gestützte Konzeption eines anforderungsgerechten Bewertungssystems, 2. Auflage, Wiesbaden.

Kim, Y.; Choi, T. Y.; Yan, T.; Dooley, K. (2011): Structural investigation of supply networks: A social network analysis approach, in: Journal of Operations Management 29(3), 194–211.

Krause, D. R.; Ellram, L. M. (1997): Critical elements of supplier development. The buying-firm perspective, in: European Journal of Purchasing & Supply Management 3(1), 21–31.

Krause, D. R.; Handfield, R. B.; Scannell, T. V. (1998): An empirical investigation of supplier development: reactive and strategic processes, in: Journal of Operations Management 17(1), 39–58.

Nagati, H.; Rebolledo, C. (2013): Supplier development efforts: The suppliers point of view, in: Industrial Marketing Management 42(2), 180–188.

Pathak, S.; McDonald, M.; Mahadevan, S. (2010): A framework for designing policies for networked systems with uncertainty, in: Decision Support Systems 49, 121–131.

Pauli, M. (2012): Logistische Lieferantenentwicklung in der Automobilindustrie. Methodische Verbesserung der logistischen Leistungsfähigkeit von Lieferanten bei variantenreicher Serienproduktion. Dortmund.

Schmitz, J.; Platts, K. W. (2004): Supplier logistics performance measurement: Indications from a study in the automotive industry, in: International Journal of Production Economics 89(2), 231–243.

Schöneberg, T.; Koberstein, A.; Suhl, L. (2013): A stochastic programming approach to determine robust delivery profiles in area forwarding inbound logistics networks, in: OR Spectrum 35(4), 807–834.

Träger, D.; Wellbrock, W.; Kanowski, K.-D. (2017): Tier-n Management – Innovatives Supply Chain Management bei der Daimler AG, in: Göpfert, I.; Braun, D.; Schulz, M. (Eds.): Automobillogistik. Stand und Zukunftstrends, Wiesbaden, 103–126.

Wagner, S. M. (2006): A firm's responses to deficient suppliers and competitive advantage, in: Journal of Business Research 59 (6), 686–695.

Wieczorrek, S.; Hermes, A.; Grunewald, M.; Spengler, T. S.; Braun, M. (2017): Logistisches Prozesspartnermanagement in der Beschaffungslogistik bei der Volkswagen AG, in: Göpfert, I.; Braun, D.; Schulz, M. (Eds.): Automobillogistik. Stand und Zukunftstrends, Wiesbaden, 53–75.

Wu, D.; Olson, D. L. (2008): Supply chain risk, simulation, and vendor selection, in: International Journal of Production Economics 114(2), 646–655.

How do buyers respond to corporate social irresponsibility of suppliers? (Extended abstract)

Maximilian Merath, Christoph Bode

Abstract

Often, corporate social responsibility (CSR) is solely associated with "doing good", although firms also have the responsibility to prevent corporate social irresponsibility (CSI) (i.e., "avoiding bad"). Many firms engage in CSR in the hopes that a reputation for CSR mitigates negative stakeholder reactions in case the firm suddenly gets involved in a CSI incident. However, research on the effects of CSR reputation on stakeholder reactions to CSI is equivocal and has mainly focused on consumers and investors. Some studies theorize insurance-like effects of ex ante CSR in case of misconduct mitigating subsequent stakeholder reactions, whereas other studies suggest that a reputation for CSR may also aggravate negative reactions to CSI. Moreover, some firms might engage in shallowly symbolic CSR while stakeholders often demand substantive actions. The present study is innovative in that it focusses on the business-to-business (B2B) context from a purchasing perspective and proposes a model which explains the conditions under which CSR acts like an insurance or like a liability subsequent to CSI. The predictions are tested by means of a vignette experiment with supply chain managers. The empirical insights add to the understanding of how CSR activities affect negative stakeholder reactions to CSI and provide important theoretical and practical implications.

1 Introduction

Although the concept of corporate social responsibility (CSR) has received considerable attention in business practice and research, there is still no general agreement on its definition. In the academic literature, there is a strong focus on linking CSR to the idea of "doing good", although "avoiding bad" also constitutes an important aspect in order for a firm to be perceived as socially responsible (Lin-Hi and Müller, 2013). Despite the growing attention that stakeholders devote to environmental and social misconduct (Fiaschi et al., 2017), the increased pressure they can exert on firms to behave in socially responsible ways (Campbell, 2007), and the circumstance that firms are increasingly held accountable for irresponsible behavior in their supply chains (Kim and Davis, 2016; Hartmann and Moeller, 2014), the issue of corporate social irresponsibility (CSI) has received scant attention in the CSR literature.

CSI incidents are frequent among all industries and can take various forms ranging from environmental disasters (e.g., the BP Deepwater Horizon oil spill in 2010) to workplace disasters and poor occupational safety and health standards (e.g., the Rana Plaza building collapse in 2013) all the way to corruption and collusion scandals (e.g., the price-fixing cartel of the truck makers DAF, Daimler, Iveco, and Volvo-Renault between 1997 and 2011). These incidents and the frequency of their occurrence highlight that the prevention of CSI is a challenging task for managers and that firms often fail to "avoid bad". Subsequent negative stakeholder reactions pose substantial risks, which need to be addressed (Lin-Hi and Blumberg, 2016).

Against this backdrop, we investigate whether the effect of a CSR reputation on negative stakeholder reactions to CSI in B2B contexts depend on CSI severity and the reputation's nature (substantive vs. symbolic). The results of a randomized vignette experiment suggest that CSR reputations mitigate negative reactions to non-severe CSI but that CSR reputations driven by symbolic actions can pose a burden for firms in case of severe incidents. Thereby, this study focusses on the role of the purchasing function as gatekeeper to CSI in the supply chain of the focal firm and contributes to a better understanding of negative stakeholder reactions to CSI. Moreover, the results provide important and innovative insights for managers that are concerned with stakeholder management and the allocation of resources to CSR activities while facing the risk of CSI incidents.

2 Conceptual background

2.1 Corporate social responsibility (CSR)

CSR is often understood as the activities of a firm which contribute to "further some social good, beyond the interests of the firm and what is required by the law" (McWilliams and Siegel, 2001). This means that CSR requires firms to do more than what is legally necessary. Furthermore, CSR definitions often emphasize the concept's multidimensionality. Typically, environmental, social, and governance (ESG) activities are captured to determine the degree to which a firm behaves socially responsible (Arvidsson, 2010; Cheng et al., 2014). Examples of such activities include the use of renewable raw materials (Ketola, 2010), the establishment of corporate foundations (Westhues and Einwiller, 2006), and the presence of an external auditor to examine, verify, and validate a CSR report (Lynes and Andrachuk, 2008). By engaging in CSR-related activities, firms may establish and maintain a positive reputation for CSR (Vanhamme and Grobben, 2009; McWilliams and Siegel, 2001).

2.2 Substantive and symbolic management of CSR

Firms face increasing pressures to uphold high standards of ethical, social and environmental conduct and perceive a need to engage in CSR-related activities (Campbell, 2007). According to institutional theory, there are two strategies of how firms can respond to these pressures: They can either pursue a *substantive* or a *symbolic* adaptation approach (Ashforth and Gibbs, 1990). The former comprises considerable changes in core procedures or long-term investments that entail certain risks but ensure compliance with the expectations imposed by the external environment (Eccles et al., 2012). In contrast, the latter encompasses activities that seek to decouple the firm's actual practices from the external demands by superficial actions that merely show *ceremonial conformity* but do not necessarily have any substance (Ashforth and Gibbs, 1990; Meyer and Rowan, 1977).

Although symbolic activities do not involve concrete changes in organizational procedures, they may suffice to promote a firm's legitimacy, because the "appearance rather than the fact of conformity is often presumed to be sufficient for the attainment of legitimacy" (Oliver, 1991). Hence, it is not surprising that, all else equal, managers tend to prefer to pursue the less time-consuming and resource-intensive stakeholder management via symbolic assurances (Ashforth and Gibbs, 1990). However, this preference for symbolic assurances carries a risk. A dilemma results from the circumstance that stakeholders typically demand substantive action. If symbolic CSR actions are interpreted as "green-washing" for the sake of being granted legitimacy, firms may be perceived as untrustworthy and manipulative (Walker and Wan, 2012).

2.3 Corporate social irresponsibility (CSI)

CSR is often merely linked to the idea of "doing good", but also entails the necessity of "avoiding bad". The latter is considered a precondition for a firm to be perceived as a responsible actor (Lin-Hi and Müller, 2013). In line with Lin-Hi and Müller (2013, p. 1932), we define CSI as firm-induced incidents "that result in (potential) disadvantages and/or harm to other actors" and are related to at least one of the three key dimensions of CSR (environment, society, and governance). The examination of CSI in the academic literature started with Armstrong (1977) and the topic has since only been rarely addressed. Nevertheless, examples of irresponsible behavior are frequent and widespread across industries. They include diverse incidents, such as, for instance, the release of toxic chemicals into waterways (Greenpeace, 2014), corruption scandals (Clark, 2010), and labor law violations (Reuters, 2014).

The probability of the occurrence of CSI is a function of the complexity of a firm's business (Vanessa et al., 2006). The globalization of markets and increasing interconnectedness of supply networks have recently added to the complexity that firms face and make it an even more challenging task for managers to prevent CSI. In the light of this development, it is essential to be aware of the fact that consumers not only blame firms for CSI that occurs inside their own barriers but also hold buying firms responsible for their suppliers' environmental and social misconduct (Hartmann and Moeller, 2014). This so-called "chain liability effect" amplifies the need for globalized firms to enhance the transparency within and control over their supply chains, because a lack of one or both of these aspects makes it even more complicated for firms to prevent CSI.

2.4 The fragility of insurance-like effects of ex ante CSR

Many firms pursue CSR-related actions in the belief that this protects them from future reputational damage (Vanhamme et al., 2015, Janssen et al., 2015). Nevertheless, several industry examples of CSI give rise to the assumption that the effects of a reputation for CSR on stakeholder reactions to irresponsible behavior are more complex than the "insurance mechanism" would suggest. The German car manufacturer Volkswagen (VW) was highly praised for its strong commitment to CSR until it became publicly known in fall 2015 that the firm cheated on the pollution tests of their diesel vehicles by using an illegally manipulating software. This scandal already cost VW several billions of U.S. dollars, but the corresponding negative consequences might still not be discernible to the full extent. The firm has been heavily criticized in public although other car manufacturers were and still are exposed to similar accusations (McGee, 2016). Another example concerns the "Deepwater Horizon" oil spill of British Petroleum (BP). For years prior to the disaster, BP has spent lots of resources on its "Beyond Petroleum" campaign in order to be perceived as a socially responsible firm. Nevertheless, the firm has suffered tremendously from the disaster in 2010. It is argued that a driver of the stakeholder criticism was the firm's CSR engagement prior to the event (Janssen et al., 2015).

2.5 Contrast and assimilation effects subsequent to CSI

CSR-related activities do not necessarily need to translate into positive effects for a firm, especially if this involvement is perceived as insincere (Sen and Bhattacharya, 2001). When a firm with a reputation for CSR is involved in CSI, consumers can lose their more positive perception and trust this firm less than if it would have not been promoted as socially responsible (Swaen and Vanhamme, 2003). Kang et al. (2016) argue that, in a similar fashion as brand commitment in case of product recalls (Germann et al., 2014), a reputation for CSR might attenuate negative stakeholder reactions to non-severe CSI, but augment negative responses to severe CSI. Based on insights from research on contrast and assimilation effects (Anderson, 1973; Hovland et al., 1957), it has been suggested that CSI of low severity could result in assimilation effects if a firm has a reputation for CSR prior to the incident (Janssen et al., 2015). In this case, the disparity between a stakeholder's expectations and the firm's true CSR performance might be small enough to be tolerated and assimilated towards a more positive perception by stakeholders. However, there exist not only thresholds for acceptance but also for rejection and neutrality. A further increase in disparity will not be accepted beyond the threshold of acceptance and, therefore, severe CSI that considerably fails to meet a stakeholder's expectations based on a firm's ex ante CSR reputation might result in contrast effects. Hence, stakeholders will respond more negatively than if they would not have perceived this firm as socially responsible.

3 Method

We used a vignette-based experimental approach to investigate the effects of a firm's CSR reputation in the aftermath of CSI in B2B contexts. This approach is relatively novel in the purchasing context, although a number of researchers (e.g., Hawn and Ioannou, 2012; Lin-Hi and Müller, 2013; Aguinis and Bradley, 2014; Eckerd, 2016; Kang, Germann, and Grewal, 2016) recommended it to study behavioral aspects of CSR and supply chain disruptions.

A key aspect of vignette experiments is the design and validation of the vignettes. We carefully constructed vignettes that assigned the participants to the role of a professional buyer who is considering to buy a specific product from a potential supplier. Thereby, a projective technique – a form of indirect questioning from the perspective of another person or group – was utilized, to limit potential demand characteristics and effects of social desirability (Fisher, 1993; Thomas et al., 2013). In line with the principle of form postponement, all vignettes contained the same introductory paragraph (*common module*). This is recommended in order to ensure that all participants are provided with a similar contextual background (Rungtusanatham et al., 2011). Our factors of interest, CSR reputation and CSI severity, were manipulated in a subsequent *experimental cues module*. All other factors of the vignettes were held constant. In total, using a 3 (CSR reputation: *none, symbolic,* or *substantive*) x 2 (CSI severity: *low* or *high*) full factorial design, six vignettes were created. After reading a vignette, participants were asked to answer questions regarding their intentions and perception of the situation.

Between March and June 2017, data were collected by means of a self-administered online experiment. Contact addresses were obtained from a commercial business data provider. The participants of our experiment were full-time working professionals with direct experience in supply chain management working for firms of 15 different industries from Germany, Austria, and Switzerland. The subjects received an invitation via e-mail to participate online and were randomly assigned to one of the six treatment conditions. In total, out of the 1064 managers which have been invited, 153 managers completed the experiment resulting in an effective response rate of 14.4%. Five observations were dropped because of irregular participation duration and 13 observations were dropped due to outlier analysis, resulting in a full sample of 135 usable scenarios. On average, participants had almost 17 years of experience in supply chain management ($SD = 10.62$) and 16.3% of the participants were female.

To be able to capture stakeholder reactions in a B2B context, we focused on two distinct customer outcomes as dependent variables: *Purchase intention* (*PI*) and *intention to engage in negative word-of-mouth* (*nWOM*). The measures described in the following subsection use seven-point rating scales (anchored at 1 := "not at all" to 7 := "totally").

4 Results

Parametric tests (e.g., ANOVA) are appropriate and robust for Likert-type data and can be used with "small sample sizes, with unequal variances, and with non-normal distributions, with no fear of 'coming to the wrong conclusion'" (Norman, 2010). We conducted two two-way ANOVAs with CSR reputation (none, symbolic, or substantive) and CSI severity (low or high) as between-subjects factors.

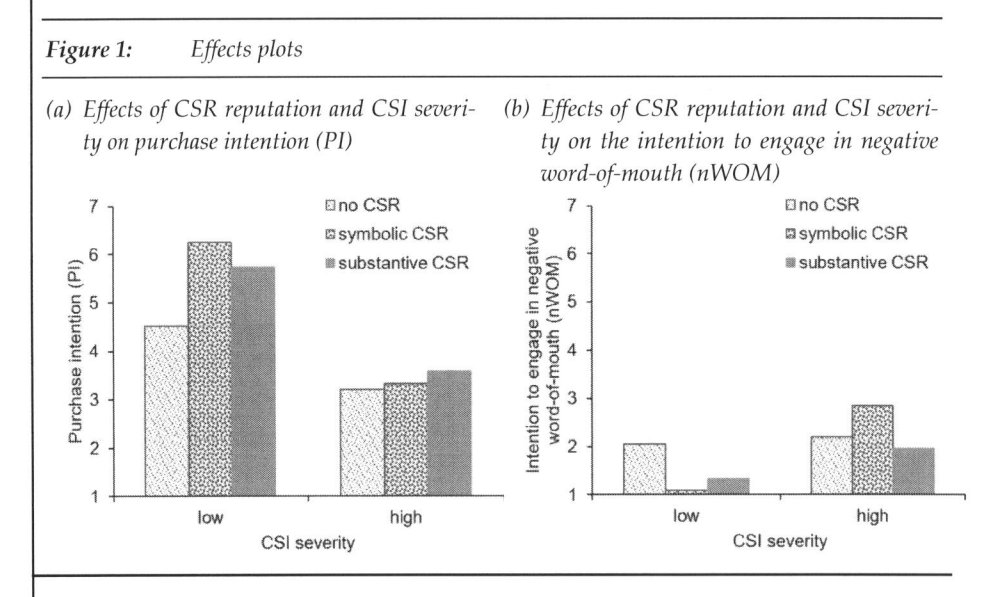

Figure 1: *Effects plots*

(a) *Effects of CSR reputation and CSI severity on purchase intention (PI)*

(b) *Effects of CSR reputation and CSI severity on the intention to engage in negative word-of-mouth (nWOM)*

PI was the dependent variable for the first ANOVA. The results revealed a marginally significant interaction effect between CSR reputation and CSI severity ($p = 0.06$). In addition, there were significant main effects of CSR reputation ($p < 0.05$) and CSI severity ($p < 0.001$). These main effects were qualified by the significant interaction, hence, we do not dwell on them. Planned contrast analysis revealed that when CSI severity was low, PI was higher for substantive and symbolic CSR reputations than for no CSR reputation (all statistically significant at the $p < 0.05$ level). Furthermore, when CSI severity was high, PI was not significantly different for different CSR reputation types.

The second ANOVA used nWOM as dependent variable. Similarly, the results revealed a statistically significant interaction between CSR reputation and CSI severity ($p < 0.01$). There was also a significant main effect of CSI severity ($p < 0.001$) which was qualified by the mentioned interaction effect. Planned contrasts were used to analyze which groups exactly differed. When CSI severity was low, nWOM was significantly lower for substantive and symbolic CSR than for no CSR (all statistically significant at the $p < 0.05$ level). When CSI severity was high, nWOM was not significantly different between the substantive and no CSR conditions ($p = 0.45$). Finally, nWOM was significantly higher for symbolic CSR than for no CSR ($p < 0.05$). **Figure 1** (a and b) depicts the two interaction effects.

5 Discussion

In the academic literature, the topic of CSI has only rarely been addressed although "avoiding bad" is considered a precondition for firms to be perceived as socially responsible. Furthermore, the recurrent examples of firms that are involved in CSI underline that it is a challenging task to prevent environmental and social misconduct. Subsequent negative stakeholder reactions have the potential to severely damage a firm's performance and reputation and need to be addressed by the responsible managers. Many firms believe that their ex ante CSR engagement may provide insurance-like effects which attenuate negative effects from CSI. A number of research efforts support this idea. However, we demonstrate that the role that a firm's reputation for CSR plays in managing stakeholder reactions to CSI is more complex. Thereby, we contribute to the literature on CSR, CSI, and disruption management by (1) providing insights into the moderating effects of ex ante CSR reputations in case of CSI, (2) demonstrating that the insurance-like or aggravating effects of prior CSR reputations are determined by the reputation's nature (substantive/ symbolic) and the severity of CSI, and (3) improving our understanding of B2B relationships.

We provide empirical support for the circumstance that insurance-like or risk-mitigating effects of CSR do not always hold and contribute to specifying the relevant boundary conditions. Whether a firm benefits from "doing good" or not when it is involved in CSI depends on the nature of a firm's CSR reputation (substantive/ symbolic) and CSI severity. Based on our results, we conclude that both substantive and symbolic CSR reputations mitigate negative stakeholder reactions to corporate environmental and social misconduct if the severity of a specific CSI incident is low. However, when firms are involved in severe CSI, these insurance-like effects do not hold.

Our findings entail several implications for managerial practice. A key finding of our study is that CSR engagement is worthwhile not just in B2C but also in B2B contexts. Both substantive and symbolic CSR reputations are able to provide insurance-like effects in case of non-severe CSI in industrial buying situations. This provides a strong justification for an intensified involvement in CSR. However, another important finding is that engaging in CSR without considering the nature of the specific actions can backfire in times of crisis. Customers may be able to distinguish between substantive and symbolic actions, which has important repercussions on their behavior. CSR reputations based on symbolic actions do not suffice to fully avoid more intense negative stakeholder reactions when a firm is involved in severe CSI. Thus, managers should be aware of the nature of their firm's own CSR engagement and avoid investments in symbolic CSR actions if the expected probability of severe environmental or social misconduct is considerably high.

References

Aguinis, H.; Bradley, K. J. (2014): Best practice recommendations for designing and implementing experimental vignette methodology studies, in: Organizational Research Methods, 17, 351–371.

Anderson, R. E. (1973): Consumer dissatisfaction: The effect of disconfirmed expectancy on perceived product performance, in: Journal of Marketing Research, 10, 38–44.

Armstrong, J. S. (1977): Social irresponsibility in management. Journal of Business Research, 5, 185–213.

Arvidsson, S. (2010): Communication of corporate social responsibility: A study of the views of management teams in large companies, in: Journal of Business Ethics, 96, 339–354.

Ashforth, B. E.; Gibbs, B. W. (1990): The double-edge of organizational legitimation, in: Organization Science, 1, 177–194.

Campbell, J. L. (2007): Why would corporations behave in socially responsible ways? An institutional theory of corporate social responsibility. in: Academy of Management Review, 32, 946–967.

Cheng, B.; Ioannou, I.; Serafeim, G. (2014): Corporate social responsibility and access to finance, in: Strategic Management Journal, 35, 1–23.

Clark, A. (2010): Daimler settles US bribery charges. Available at: https://www.theguardian.com/business/2010/mar/24/daimler-settles-us-bribery-charges (accessed: 02 October 2017).

Eccles, R. G.; Ioannou, I.; Serafeim, G. (2012): The impact of a corporate culture of sustainability on corporate behavior and performance. National Bureau of Economic Research Working Paper No. 17950.

Eckerd, S. (2016): Experiments in purchasing and supply management research, in: Journal of Purchasing and Supply Management, 22, 258–261.

Fiaschi, D.; Giuliani, E.; Nieri, F. (2017): Overcoming the liability of origin by doing no-harm: Emerging country firms' social irresponsibility as they go global, in: Journal of World Business, 52, 546–563.

Fisher, R. J. (1993): Social desirability bias and the validity of indirect questioning, in: Journal of Consumer Research, 20, 303–315.

Germann, F.; Grewal, R.; Ross Jr., W. T.; Srivastava, R. K. (2014): Product recalls and the moderating role of brand commitment, in: Marketing Letters, 25, 179–191.

Greenpeace (2014): A monstrous mess: Toxic water pollution in China.

Hartmann, J.; Moeller, S. (2014): Chain liability in multitier supply chains? Responsibility attributions for unsustainable supplier behavior, in: Journal of Operations Management, 32, 281–294.

Hawn, O. V.; Ioannou, I. (2012): Do actions speak louder than words? The case of corporate social responsibility (CSR), Academy of Management Proceedings.

Hovland, C. I.; Harvey, O.; Sherif, M. (1957): Assimilation and contrast effects in reactions to communication and attitude change, in: The Journal of Abnormal and Social Psychology, 55, 244.

Janssen, C.; Sen, S.; Bhattacharya, C. (2015): Corporate crises in the age of corporate social responsibility, in: Business Horizons, 58, 183–192.

Kang, C.; Germann, F.; Grewal, R. (2016): Washing away your sins? Corporate social responsibility, corporate social irresponsibility, and firm performance, in: Journal of Marketing, 80, 59–79.

Ketola, T. (2010): Five leaps to corporate sustainability through a corporate responsibility portfolio matrix, in: Corporate Social Responsibility and Environmental Management, 17, 320–336.

Kim, S.; Choi, S. M. (2016): Congruence effects in post-crisis CSR communication: The mediating role of attribution of corporate motives, in: Journal of Business Ethics (https://doi.org/10.1007/s10551-016-3425-y).

Kim, Y. H.; Davis, G. F. (2016): Challenges for global supply chain sustainability: Evidence from conflict minerals reports. Academy of Management Journal, 59, 1896-1916.

Lin-Hi, N.; Blumberg, I. (2016): The link between (not) practicing CSR and corporate reputation: Psychological foundations and managerial implications, in: Journal of Business Ethics, 1–14.

Lin-Hi, N.; Müller, K. (2013). The CSR bottom line: Preventing corporate social irresponsibility, in: Journal of Business Research, 66, 1928–1936.

Lynes, J. K.; Andrachuk, M. (2008): Motivations for corporate social and environmental responsibility: A case study of Scandinavian Airlines, in: Journal of International Management, 14, 377–390.

McGee, P. (2016): Volkswagen pledges to regain consumer trust. Available at: https://www.ft.com/content/eadc3150-0d17-11e6-ad80-67655613c2d6 (accessed 02 October 2017).

McWilliams, A.; Siegel, D. (2001): Corporate social responsibility: A theory of the firm perspective, in: Academy of Management Review, 26, 117–127.

Meyer, J. W.; Rowan, B. (1977): Institutionalized organizations: Formal structure as myth and ceremony, in: American Journal of Sociology, 83, 340–363.

Norman, G. (2010): Likert scales, levels of measurement and the "laws" of statistics, in: Advances in Health Sciences Education, 15, 625–632.

Oliver, C. (1991): Strategic responses to institutional processes, in: Academy of Management Review, 16, 145–179.

Reuters (2014): Wal-Mart must pay $188 million in workers' class action. Available at: http://www.reuters.com/article/us-walmart-lawsuit-idUSKBN0JU1XJ20141216 (accessed 02 October 2017).

Rungtusanatham, M. J.; Wallin, C.; Eckerd, S. (2011): The vignette in a scenario-based role-playing experiment, in: Journal of Supply Chain Management, 47, 9–16.

Sen, S.; Bhattacharya, C. B. (2001): Does doing good always lead to doing better? Consumer reactions to corporate social responsibility, in: Journal of Marketing Research, 38, 225–243.

Swaen, V.; Vanhamme, J. (2003): Do accusations of irresponsible acts hurts companies more when they promote themselves as socially responsible?, in: Laurent, G. D.; Merunka, D.; Zaichowsky, J. (eds.): Marketing Communications and Consumer Behavior Proceedings.

Thomas, S. P.; Thomas, R. W.; Manrodt, K. B.; Rutner, S. M. (2013): An experimental test of negotiation strategy effects on knowledge sharing intentions in buyer–supplier relationships, in: Journal of Supply Chain Management, 49, 96–113.

Vanessa, M. S.; Jijun, G.; Bansal, P. (2006): Being good while being bad: Social responsibility and the international diversification of US firms, in: Journal of International Business Studies, 37, 850–862.

Vanhamme, J.; Grobben, B. (2009): "Too good to be true!". The effectiveness of CSR history in countering negative publicity, in: Journal of Business Ethics, 85, 273–283.

Vanhamme, J.; Swaen, V.; Berens, G.; Janssen, C. (2015): Playing with fire: Aggravating and buffering effects of ex ante CSR communication campaigns for companies facing allegations of social irresponsibility, in: Marketing Letters, 26, 565–578.

Walker, K.; Wan, F. (2012): The harm of symbolic actions and green-washing: Corporate actions and communications on environmental performance and their financial implications, in: Journal of Business Ethics, 109, 227–242.

Westhues, M.; Einwiller, S. (2006): Corporate foundations: Their role for corporate social responsibility, in: Corporate Reputation Review, 9, 144–153.

Specific investments in the supply chain – a literature review on the state-of-the-art knowledge with an outlook on safeguarding mechanisms and avenues for future research

Julia Burkhardt

Abstract

Increased outsourcing activities and the shift of value creation along the supply chain led to various supply chain management approaches, with the aim to increase efficiency and decrease risks in the supply chain that are associated with product quality, production costs or product availability. A common tool to achieve those goals are specific investments executed in the supply chain context. The literature review captures the state-of-the-art knowledge on specific investments in the supply chain context and discloses definitions, opportunities, risks, characteristics, motivation and categories of tangible and intangible specific investments. Furthermore, the paper sheds light on safeguarding mechanisms and reveals the need for further research on executing specific investments beyond the dyad.

1 Introduction

The world today is dominated by increased outsourcing activities and a shift of value creation along the supply chain. Outsourcing is one factor that enables firms to generate cost savings along the supply chain (Trent, Monczka, 2003). The supply chain can be understood as a global network of interlinked multiple buyer-supplier-relationships. Resulting from this perception of the supply chain, stakeholders increasingly put pressure on buying firms holding them accountable for their behavior, the availability and quality of the products along the supply chain (Mena et al., 2013; Mentzer et al., 2008). Consequently, buyers started to implement supply chain management approaches to increase efficiency and decrease risks that are associated with quality, availability and social or environmental behavior along the supply chain. One of the commonly used buyer-supplier management tools, which has emerged as a core concept of the transaction cost theory from Williamson (1985), are specific investments. They are one of the key components to improve the relationship with business partners, networks or strategic alliances, resulting in improved business performance (Kwon, 2009). Hence, they can be used to generate a competitive advantage in the supply chain with one specific partner or in one specific context, as specific investments can not be reassigned to an alternative use (Williamson, 1985) . They are "necessary to support a particular transaction, but are not readily re-deployable or useful to any other transaction" (Morrill, Morrill, 2003). Specific investments from the buyer to the supplier, the supplier into the buyer or intra specific investments (buyer or supplier invests in themselves with the aim to generate use for the buyer-supplier relationship) are common in practice. The aim is to contribute to value adding of produced goods or increase of the core competencies along the supply chain (de Vita et al., 2011). Wagner and Bode (2014) state that specific investments encourage suppliers to share their innovations with the buyer. Furthermore, bilateral specific investments help reducing uncertainties in regards to further transaction or cooperation between partners (Chen et al., 2017). Hence, specific investments strengthen inter-firm relationships (Lothia et al., 1994). However, specific investments are also associated with risk. Specific investments create a hold-up and lock-in situation for business partners as they are specific to one transaction only. In case a supplier changes its behavior or acts opportunistically, the investments are quickly lost. This requires safeguards, e.g. contracts or governance mechanisms between supply chain partners.

Specific investments play an incremental role in strengthening the buyer-supplier relationship, adding value to the supply chain and reducing uncertainties. Nevertheless, apart from de Vita et al. (2011), literature lacks a structured overview of the existing body of knowledge regarding specific investments. De Vita et al. (2011) gave a comprehensive overview on specific investments as well as on their expected influence on firms' performances. This paper provides an updated overview of the body of knowledge and in contrary to de Vita et al. (2011) includes according safeguarding mechanisms in the review instead of the performance aspect. It includes definitions, background and the characteristics of specific investments, the various categories of specific investments as well as the motivation and antecedents for specific investments that buyers or suppliers can execute and the according safeguarding mechanisms to safeguard the investments. This state-of-the-art research on specific investments adds knowledge to the current body of literature. Furthermore, the literature review aims to identify relevant research topics and derives future research opportunities.

2 Methodology

To get an overview of the state-of-the-art research on specific investments in the supply chain context, this paper wants to identify the existing knowledge on the topic and transfer it into useable format (Denyer, Tranfield, 2009). The review and especially the data collection orientates itself on requirements established by Denyer and Tranfield (2009) and vom Brocke et al. (2009). According to both guidelines, every literature review requires the guarantee of rigor and validity throughout the research process and of the review. Rigor refers to the reliability and validity of the research process. The reliability of a research describes the replicability of the research process. Reliability is given when the process of choosing articles is transparent, clearly reported and all decisions taken are justified and documented for the reader. Validity of the research is affected by the degree to which the chosen literature from the research uncovers the sources the researcher wants to collect. The validity answers the question "Does the researcher search right?" (vom Brocke et al., 2009). The search for the "right" literature includes decisions on the selection of databases, publications, keywords, covered periods, considered articles, backward and forward search as well as ongoing evaluation of sources. Backward search refers to reviewing older literature cited in articles extracted from keyword search, whereas forward search refers to reviewing articles that have been cited in the articles (Webster, Watson, 2002).

2.1 Data collection

The goal of the review is to collect all relevant papers on specific investments in the context of supply chain management that explain why specific investments are applied in the management of supply chains and what kind of specific investments are existent. To follow the guidelines of vom Brocke et al. (2009), the research should prevent systematic errors, minimize bias and maximize validity to guarantee rigor and validity of the research. A checklist was used to identify relevant papers. Only f English-speaking, peer-reviewed journals in the field of SCM within the period between 1980 and 2017 were included. Although the idea of specific investments dates back to the 1930s, the concept of "supply chain management" dates back as late as the 1990s by Lisa Ellram. As the research wants to focus on specific investments in the supply chain context only the narrowing of the period was chosen. The research was run through a database search that inter alia included all EBSCOhost databases, Jstor-Journal Storage, ScienceDirect and Wiley Online Library. As predicted and often stated in literature before, the usage of different databases is revealed in different articles. This underlines the importance of running research through more than one database. For the execution of the literature research, a set of keywords was generated. This set is composed of the following terms: "invest", "fund", "specific", "idiosyncratic", "dedicated", "relational", "supplier", "supply chain", "focal firm", "focal company", "supply chain management", "supply management", "supplier", "buyer". This intentionally leaves out various keywords that are also linked to the topic; to name a few: "unilateral", "relationship-specific, "dedicated", "asset". After the first keyword search, the outcome generated 23.2016 hits. After narrowing the scope to title, keyword or abstract the results were limited to 12.328 hits. The results were further narrowed down to title and keywords to allow further limitation of the results to 403. As the author only required results from academic journals and peer reviewed academic journals this filter was applied as well. Additionally, by adding the filter for fully accessible texts in English and setting the filter to publications after 1980, the outcome of the literature research came down to 83 articles on the searched topic. By manually and automatically removing duplicates from the list 45 hits were left. The 45 articles in question were then further evaluated, the abstracts were scanned and after a relevance check the list was reduced to 33 papers that focus on specific investments between buyer and supplier in the supply chain. These 33 papers further proceeded into the bibliometric analysis and the content analysis.

Table 1: Scope of the literature review

Step	Filter Type	Specification	Number of results in database
1	Keyword Search	((invest* OR fund)) AND ((*specific OR idiosyncratic OR dedicated OR relational)) AND ((supplier* OR "supply chain" OR OEM OR "focal firm" OR "focal compan*" OR buyer OR manufacturer))	23,016
2	Scope 1	Title OR Keywords OR Abstract	12,328
3	Scope 2	Title OR Keywords	403
4	Type of Publication 1	Academic journals	169
5	Type of Publication 2	Academic journals (peer review)	138
6	Availability	Full text only	125
7	Language	English only	83
8	Publication date	Since 1980	83
9	Removing duplicates	Manually and automatically	45
10	**Abstract screening (manually)**	**Focus on specific investments between buyer and supplier**	33

2.2 Bibliometric analysis

The outcome of the research identified 33 relevant articles that proceeded into the bibliometric analysis. The bibliometric analysis helps to understand the academic debate on a certain topic by disclosing existing clusters such as year of publications or journal of publication (Müller, Stölzle, 2012). De Vita et al. (2011) published an overview of categories of asset specificity in 2011 and provided a good overview of the existing literature. This could lead to the thought that yet another review of specific investments is not necessary in the given field. However, the bibliometric analysis revealed that during the last ten years and especially during the last six years, research on the topic of specific investments in the supply chain has intensified and had a peak in 2014 with five publications, illustrating that the literature has evolved further since 2011. The topic is constantly relevant in research over a period of ten years. **Figure 1** illustrates the distribution of articles over the years.

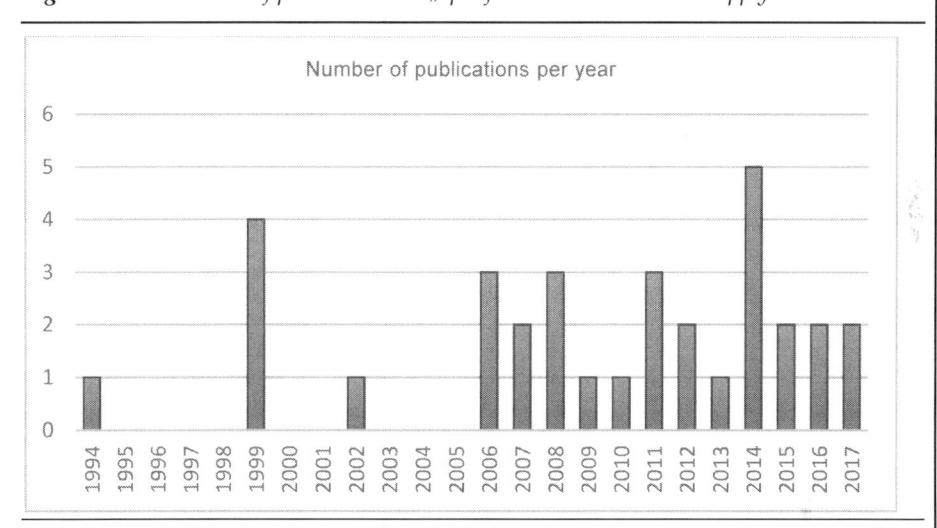

Figure 1: Number of publications on „specific investments" in the supply chain

Number of publications per year

The 33 articles were published in 25 different journals between 1994 and 2017. **Table 2** gives an overview of the various journals, their rankings at VHB and ABS and the number of articles that were published in the given journal. VHB is the German Academic Association for Business Research. They offer a rating of academic journals online. The ABS is the chartered association of business schools and business research and also publishes an academic journal guide online. The Journal of Business and Industrial Marketing holds the lead in publishing articles (4) on specific investments, followed by the Industrial Marketing Management (3) and the Journal of Operations Management (3).

The bibliometric analysis illustrates that specific investments in the supply chain have been of interest in research over a course of ten years.

Table 2: Journals, ranking and number of articles per journal in question

Name of journal	VHB	ABS	Number of articles
Journal of Business & Industrial Marketing	C	2	4
Industrial Marketing Management	B	3	3
Journal of Operations Management	A	4	3
Journal of Business-to-Business Marketing	C	2	2
Asia Pacific Journal of Management	C	3	1
Organization Science	A+	4	1
The Accounting Review	A+	4	1
Journal of the Academy of Marketing Science	A	4	1
Manufacturing & Service Operations Management	A	3	1
Strategic Management Journal	A	4	1
British Journal of Management	B	4	1
Decision Sciences Journal	B	3	1
Financial Management	B	3	1
International Journal of Production Economics	B	3	1
Journal of Business Research	B	3	1
Management International Review	B	3	1
Supply Chain Management: An International Journal	B	3	1
European Journal of Marketing	C	3	1
International Journal of Retail & Distribution Management	C	2	1
Journal of Marketing Management	C	2	1
Frontiers of Business Research in China	-	-	1
Journal of Marketing Development and Competitiveness	-	-	1
Journal of Marketing Thought	-	-	1
Management	-	-	1
Periodica Polytechnica Social and Management Sciences	-	-	1

3 Content analysis

The content analysis clusters the body of knowledge retrieved from the 33 articles during the literature search. Derived from the literature research this article provides definitions, backgrounds and characteristics of specific investments. Additionally, the content analysis sheds light on the motivation and antecedents for carrying out specific investments in the supply chain. Furthermore, the various types of specific investments found in literature are categorized.

3.1 Definition, background and characteristics of specific investments

The definition of a topic is essential to generate a basic understanding. This is of importance, as most topics tend to have various definitions. De Vita et al. (2011) present various definitions of asset specificity in their paper. Since then, further definitions of the topic have evolved in the literature. The term "specific investments" originates back to Williamson in 1985. He defined specific investments as durable investments that are undertaken in support of particular transactions, the opportunity cost of which investments is much lower in best alternative uses or by alternative users should the original transaction be prematurely terminated (Williamson, 1985). Relationship specific investments are specific investments between the firm and its stakeholders, in this case a partner of his in the supply chain. De Vita et al. (2011) define specific investments as "non redeployable investments specifically dedicated to the relationship" (p. 337). They are used to generate value for the partners and outside the companies (Williamson, 1985).

Literature divides specific investments into tangible and intangible investments (Williamson, 1985). "By definition, a specific asset investment (SAI) is an intangible or tangible asset that is invested in by the buyer and seller for the sake of an established transactional relationship." (Chen et al., 2017).

Advantages of specific investments
Xie et al. (2010) analyzed the magnitude and asymmetry of these investments to investigate the effect on the extent of dependencies. Kim (2015) found out that "transaction specific investment made by the less dependent party are asymmetrically bigger than that made by the counterpart" One example that could be mentioned is Xerox and Whirlpool. They involved their suppliers in early phases of the product development which led to the need of specific design and engineering investments (Lohtia, Krapfel, 1994). This example indicates the strategic character of specific investments. They can act as "source of competitive advantage and a barrier to the exit of a relationship" (Bensaou, Anderson, 1999). Bensaou and Anderson (1999) empirically investigated that idiosyncratic investments into suppliers "are a mechanism to absorb unpredictability

stemming from a fast pace of technological change in the component market, as well as a means to cope with component complexity". They argue that the strategic character of specific investments can be used to lock in valuable suppliers through unique components or capabilities (long-term bonding mechanism). Furthermore, specific investments tend to reduce production costs and increase productivity.

Risks of specific investments

Buvik (2002) raises awareness that specific investments require formalized administrative structures to stabilize the relationship. Relationship-specific investments have highly customized character and cannot be redeployed or transferred without negative consequences for their value (Takashima, Kim, 2016). According to Grover and Malhotra (2003), supplier relation-specific investments can be seen as investments in a dedicated relationship that loose certain value when transferred to other relationships. A specific investment (seen as a resource) is considered to be dependent "when it would lose value if separated from the firm" (Alchian, Woodward, 1987, p. 113). Based on transaction cost analysis, many studies provided evidence for trust reducing opportunistic behavior and creating preferred conditions for specific investments (Carney, 1998; Husted, 1994). Klein et al. (1978) offer an example for that: "An OEM may make investments in production equipment, logistic systems and/or employee training that are idiosyncratic to a particular supplier in an attempt to lower its production costs. However, because of their low salvage value, these assets make it costly for the OEM to switch to a new supplier. The supplier, knowing that the OEM is somewhat 'locked-in' to the relationship, has an incentive to behave opportunistically. For example, a supplier could demand price increases and insist on renegotiating its contract after an OEM has irreversibly committed to the exchange. Thus, investments in specialized assets expose the OEM to potentially opportunistic behavior unless an appropriate mechanism can be designed to safeguard the OEM's investment". Hence specific investments come with high risk of opportunistic behavior (Kang et al. 2009), as relationship-specific investments cause dependencies between involved actors. The involved actors are often forced into a lock-in situation, in which the relationship cannot be redeployed without loss. Ebers and Semrau (2015) examined that the direction of investments (buyer to supplier or supplier to buyer) impacts the upcoming transaction costs. The more specific an investment into a supplier, the higher the transaction costs for the buyer. Considering the assumption that partners act opportunistically, safeguards for specific investments are highly important.

3.2 Types of specific investments

De Vita et al. (2011) review the different categories of specific assets, developed by Williamson (1985), Malone et al. (1987) and Zaheer and Venkatraman (1995). Derived from that they introduce the following seven categories of specific assets in their paper: human, physical, site, dedicated, brand, temporal and procedural investments.

Yeung et al. (2013) mention the following forms of specific investments; human specificity (e.g. trainings), physical specificity (e.g. equipment, tools, fixtures) or investments solely dedicated to the relationship with the partner. Drawn from the review of the 33 papers, the present paper uses the following categorization for specific investments: tangible and intangible investments as used by Chen (2017) and Williamson (1985) with according sub-categories (**Table 3**).

Tangible investments in the supply chain mostly require monetary investments. One category of tangible investments is the **IT-adaption** between business partners. Another common specific tangible form of investments are **specialized technologies** in the supply chain. This can include the development and provision of specialized tools or machinery that can only be utilized in the context of one buyer and one supplier and would be useless for any other business relationship (Mahapatra et al., 2012). The authors also emphasize the relationship between these investments and the stage of the product life cycle by hypothesizing that "the relationship between competitive intensity and supplier development investments is stronger in the maturity stage of the product life cycle" (Mahapatra et al., 2012). Specialized technology also includes transferring key-technology from one firm to the other. Literature also mentions **tangible specific relation-building** investments, like planning and building plants close to existent business partners to guarantee local exchange, reduce transportation time and enable close collaboration.

Intangible investments, on the other hand, are not as concrete. One part of intangible investments would be the creation of **specific organizational knowledge**. The creation of specific organizational knowledge includes the training of employees. The training aims to increase skill of workers regarding technical specifications, component performance requirements, information technology or design of specific business processes or setting up specific machines (Corsten et al., 2011; Buvik, 2002). The created knowledge is specific to the interaction or context between buyer and supplier. Specific organizational knowledge is also built through support with human resources between companies. Through the exchange of employees, specific knowledge about each company is shared between business partners. Apart from investments into the creation of knowledge, it is also common to execute specific R&D expenditures (Raman, Shahrur, 2008). Raman and Shahrur (2008) provide various examples for that: suppliers invest specifically to ensure their production is ready for highly specialized parts of the OEM. Another example are software companies that develop software solutions for certain operating systems for particular firms (e.g. Linux, Mac OS). A further category of intangible investments is **specific organizational information**, which is created through the information exchange between buyer and supplier. This includes best practice sharing between business partners, general information exchange and know-how exchange, including engineering know-how specific to the given context. Kwon (2009) built a research model that differs between investments for mutual understanding, investments for mutual adjustments and investments for joint work in terms of relationship specific investments. **Specific relational-building** investments are another category of intangible investment. These investments include soft factors like the promise to maintain the business partnership or efforts to generate positive reputation spill-over effects between firms.

Table 3: Types of specific investments derived from literature

Tangible Investments		Intangible Investments	
Type	Source	Type	Source
Specialized technology	Mahapatra, Narasimhan, 2012; Yeung et al., 2013	Specific organizational knowledge	Subramani, Venkatraman, 2003; Corsten et al., 2011; Buvik, 2002
IT-Adaption	Raman, Shahrur, 2008; Heide, John, 1990	Specific organizational information	Kwon, 2009
Specific relational building	Buvik, 2012	Specific relational building	Gelei, Kenesei, 2016

3.3 Motivation and antecedents for specific investments

One of the positive effects of specific investments according to Williamson (1985) is establishing a cooperative relationship that helps to reduce both, transaction costs and uncertainties (Chen et al., 2017). This is due to the fact that transaction cost economics and relational exchange theory see trust and specific investments as "antecedents of the joint efforts" (Claro et al., 2006). Next to the transaction cost theory of Williamson (1985), other theories are used to reason why firms tend to make specific investments. The literature review derived the following theories to explain the motivation for specific investments in inter-organizational relationship settings: agency theory, relational view (relational rent) and the already mentioned transactional theory.

Kang et al. (2009) address spillover effects (yielding future transactions with the same exchange partner) as positive outcome of specific investments. Kohtamäki and Bourlakis (2012) hypothesize that relationship-specific investments create relationship-oriented learning and capability effects due to a strong resource-base and deployment. According to the resource-based view, relationship-specific investments may strengthen the relationship between supplier and buyer resource-based (Kohtamäki, Bourlakis, 2012). The relational view deepens the insight from the resource-based view by including relational (inter-organizational) aspects of the company. Xie et al. (2010) also point out that the buyer-supplier relationship quality is significantly impacted by specific investments. Yu et al. (2006) focus on suppliers' investments dedicated to a specific buyer. They argue that transaction-specific investments can increase production efficiency of manufacturers. The main problem is the motivation of suppliers to make such investments (e.g. due to theoretical based problems like hazards). The aim of buyer specific investments into the sub-supplier is to achieve compliance along the supply chain, generate access to scarce resources, prevent bottlenecks and achieve the required quality. Kang et al. (2009) analyzed the conditions and motivations to make specific investments and claim that some unilateral investments can be useful even without any kind of safeguarding or reciprocal commitment.

4 Discussion of safeguards

One outcome of Section 3 is that some specific investments do not need safeguards e.g. when long-term relationships exist. However, the literature review also shed light on the various risks associated with specific investments. Hence, safeguards for specific investments are of importance when partners in the supply chain are assuming opportunistic behavior. In cases where specific investments have been placed by two partners, a "mutual hostage situation arises" that acts as safeguard for the specific investments (Williamson, 1985). However, the more specific the investment by one partner, the higher the transaction costs the more important are safeguarding mechanisms to protect the vulnerability of the actor who has placed the specific investments. The examined literature divides safeguards in formal and informal mechanisms. The degree of investment specificity influences the chosen safeguarding options. The more specific an investment, the more likely are formal safeguards, like contracts or vertical integration. Informal safeguarding mechanisms are broadly used when specific investments are placed. They include joint actions with partners, information sharing, supplier verification, joint planning, monitoring and quasi integration (Zaheer, Venkatraman, 1994; Wagner, Bode, 2013).

Research shows that formal safeguards often play a limited role in inter firm relationships (Yu et al., 2006). Informal, normative governance, however, can act as "self-enforcing mechanisms and presumes long-term repeated transactions with the partner" (Lee, Johnson, 2010, p. 278) as they are built over time next to the formal safeguards (Gulati, 1995). Informal safeguarding mechanisms intend to build closer ties with the exchange partners and foster trust building and long lasting cooperation rather than building complicated contracts (Bensaou, Anderson, 1999). Strengthening ties can be achieved through joint actions and expectations of continuity of the anticipated long-term business relationship (Heide, John, 1988). Additionally, literature points to relational norms as safeguards (flexibility, information exchange and solidarity) as they help to reduce the hazard of opportunism.

Wagner and Bode (2013) found out that the duration of the business relationship can act as safeguard. They found that the longer the relationship between two business partners, the more likely it is that the investments are safeguarded. This is true as long term relationships between partners generate trust. Trust and normative behavior, such as goodwill or reputation, act as self-enforcing safeguards (Dyer, 1996). They reduce transaction costs by "replacing contracts with handshakes" (Adler, 2001). Trust can also be created through information sharing between parties. According to the principal-agent-theory, information asymmetry is a significant reason for opportunistic behavior. The sharing of information reduces information asymmetry and the likelihood of opportunistic behavior in the supply chain (Noordewier et al., 1990, Wagner, Bode, 2013). Gulati et al. (2005) observed that cooperation between two business partners can also act as safeguard. Furthermore, the dependence of the supplier on the specific investments can serve as a safeguard (Bensaou, Anderson, 1999). Buyers tend to invest more in suppliers when they presume that the investment is of importance for the supplier. This can be seen as quasi integration, which describes the degree of linkage between buyer and supplier (Zaheer, Venkatraman, 1995). The more a supplier chooses to allocate significant portions of its output to one particular buyer, the more likely, that both will not act opportunistically (Subramani, Venkatraman, 2003). The more intensive buyer and supplier are working together, the less opportunistic a supplier will behave in the relationship. Relational governance, that emerges from values and agreed-upon processes found in social relationships, reduces transaction costs (Poppo, Zenger, 2002). The expectation of long-term continuity of the relationship protects firms of the pressure of immediate performance measurement. It rather gives firms the chance to develop long-term solutions. The transaction costs that emerge to develop this solutions, also act as safeguards against ending the relationship. Ghijsen et al. (2010) find one further safeguard. They discovered that the supplier is more committed in situations where he is exploited to power asymmetry compared to the buyer. Hence, power asymmetry between partners can act as safeguard.

4.1   Summary of the paper

The aim of the paper was to present the current body of knowledge about specific investments with a focus on definition, characteristics, background, motivation and antecedents. Furthermore, the various categories of specific investments as well as safeguards for investments were introduced, since specific investments are an incremental part of managing the supply chain.

This literature review generated a state-of-the-art knowledge status on the existing literature of specific investments in the supply chain. For this purpose, the review applied the literature search process of vom Brocke et al. (2009) which resulted in the in-depth scan of 33 articles contributing to the understanding of specific investments in the supply chain. The review showed that research on the topic of specific investments has constantly been executed over a period of at least 10 years by various academics, proofing the continuing relevance of the topic for the research community. Specific investments are "non redeployable investments specifically dedicated to a relationship" (de Vita et al., 2011, p. 337) with a "durable nature" (Stump, Joshi, 1999) that lose their value when they are transferred to another relationship. They are executed to strengthen the relationship between buyer and supplier, increase the efficiency in the long run, and aim to achieve compliance along the supply chain (Yu et al., 2006, Xie et al., 2010). Specific investments can be categorized in tangible and intangible investments with further sub-categories. Tangible investments can be further classified into specialized technology e.g. setting up special machinery needed for a transaction), IT-adaption between firms, e.g. adjustment to different IT-Systems and specific relational building, e.g. building plants close to your business partners to reduce barriers (Buvik, 2002). Next to the tangible investments, literature also provides a set of intangible investments. Drawn from literature, they are segmented into the categories: creation of specific organizational knowledge e.g., execution of joint R&D expenditures (Raman, Shahrur, 2008), specific organizational information, e.g. sharing best practices between companies and specific relational building, which includes the mutual promise to maintain business together. The mutual commitment to maintain business together can also serve as safeguard for specific investments. Literature usually divides safeguards into formal and informal safeguarding mechanisms. Formal safeguards include contracts, whereas informal safeguards are usually governance mechanisms like the promise to maintain business or trust between two business partners that help to safeguard the specific investments to avoid sunk costs.

4.2 Limitation of the research

The present literature review has intentionally hard limitations regarding the keyword search. This is one result of using the research framework of vom Brocke et al. (2009), and the attempt to search the "right" literature rather than all of the existing literature in the given field. Hence, the keyword search has rather been strictly limited and therefore articles loosely related to the topic of specific investments have not been included in the results of the research. As the purpose of the article was to provide the state-of-the-art knowledge on specific investments in the supply chain context, the given search terms were appropriate. While a less strict keyword search would have increased the quantity of articles, additional insights in regards to the topic are questionable.

4.3 Implications for practice

Specific investments are commonly used in practice and broadly used across industries in the buyer-supplier relationship. As mentioned in the beginning, consumers start holding buyers accountable for incidents in the supply chain. Hence the buyer needs to get into even more control of his supply chain than usually. The common concept of directing responsibility to the first-tier supplier is not sufficient anymore in many cases. First approaches in practice show that buyers occasionally started to invest in their sub-supplier, enhancing the supplier relationship to the sub-supplier level. One producer of premium orange juice, for example, started to place specific investments in their orange producer to improve the quality of the organic oranges and to guarantee that the process was strictly organic. Through the interaction between buyer and sub-supplier the quality of the oranges improved and the relationships between buyer and sub-supplier did tremendously improve. This is without question a good approach to get an improved relationship between buyer, supplier and sub-supplier. Furthermore, it helps the buyer to reach aspired quality of productsand secure the availability of products. One aspect that buyers also frequently mention is the potential access to innovation when directly interacting with the sub-supplier.

4.4 Further research

Keeping the shift of value creation along the supply chain towards lower tier suppliers in mind and the phenomena that focal firms are increasingly made responsible for the conditions in the entire supply chain, it was stumbling to realize that the literature and the described practices on applying specific investments in the supply chain have only been thought of in the context of the dyad between buyer and supplier although the actual idea of supply chain management is the interaction of all supply chain partners. The focus of the revised research lies on cases of dyadic relationships (Williamson, 1985), with rare exceptions like Gelei and Kenesei (2016) that investigated specific investments in the triad of supplier, buyer and customer. The usual approach of only concentrating on the buyer-supplier relationship, however, is often bound to fail. Due to an increasing amount of incidents along the supply chain stemming from suppliers beyond the first-tier, a shift of perception of the management of supply chains already occurred in the minds of several companies. Lately most violations against the buyers' requirements, incidents and failures in the supply chain became apparent further down in the supply chain. Lower tier suppliers have a high impact on the supply chain, especially regarding their growing number and their ramifications in the supply chain. The earthquake in Japan, followed by the Tsunami in 2011 revealed how the breakdown of one sub-supplier in the supply chain can affect several suppliers and buyers. This new gained awareness of the importance of lower tier suppliers requires an active management of sub-suppliers as Hofstetter (2016) pointed out correctly. Authors from the sustainability side did also claim the need of active sub-supplier management (Grimm et al., 2014, 2016; Wilhelm et al., 2016; Tachizawa, Wong, 2014).

One form of an active management of sub suppliers could be the use of specific investments. It is of interest whether the positive effects found in the dyadic relation like strengthening cooperative relationships (Chen et al., 2017) or fostering relationship-oriented learning (Kohtamäki, Bourlakis, 2012) and improving the compliance with buyers requirements would also exist in a triadic relationship.

Research should start to investigate the direct interaction between buyer and sub-supplier, focusing on the effect of specific investments for the triadic relationship. The first question of interest is under which conditions and purposes a buyer should consider investing into his sub-supplier and the second question is to examine the consequences of such a specific investment from the buyer into the sub-supplier. Resulting from the consideration to apply specific investments in the triad, the question arises whether the existing safeguarding mechanisms can be transferred into the setting of the triadic relationship. These considerations call for further research of antecedents of specific investments in the triad as well as categories and benefits of specific investments into the sub-supplier and finally safeguarding mechanisms for specific investments in the triad.

References

ABS Association of Business Schools (2015): Academic Journal Guide 2015. Available at: http://gsom.spbu.ru/files/abs-list-2015.pdf (accessed: 07 December 2017).

Adler, P. (2001): Market, hierarchy, and trust: the knowledge economy and the future of capitalism, in: Organization Science, 12(2), 214–234.

Alchian, A.; Woodward, S (1987): Reflections on the Theory of the Firm, in: Journal of Institutional and Theoretical Economics (JITE)/Zeitschrift für die gesamte Staatswissenschaft 143(1), 110–136.

Bensaou, M.; Anderson, E. (1999): Buyer-Supplier Relations in Industrial Markets: When Do Buyers Risk Making Idiosyncratic Investments?, in: Organization Science, 460–481.

Brocke, J. vom; Simons, A.; Niehaves, B.; Reimer, K.; Plattfaut, R.; Cleven, A. (2009): Reconstructing the giant: on the importance of rigour in documenting the literature search process.

Buvik, Arnt (2002): Manufacturer-Specific Asset Investments and Inter-Firm Governance Forms. An Empirical Test of the Contingent Effect of Exchange Frequency, in: Journal of Business-to-Business Marketing, 37–71.

Carney, M (1998): The Competitiveness of networked production. The Role of Trust and Asset Specificity, in: Journal of Management Studies, 35(4), 457–479.

Chen, P.-Y.; Chen, K.-Y.; Wu, L.-Y. (2017): The impact of trust and commitment on value creation in asymmetric buyer–seller relationships. The mediation effect of specific asset investments, in: Journal of Business & Industrial Marketing 32(3), 457–471. DOI: 10.1108/JBIM-09-2014-0171.

Corsten, D.; Gruen, T.; Peyinghaus, M. (2011): The effects of supplier-to-buyer identification on operational performance. An empirical investigation of inter-organizational identification in automotive relationships, in: Journal of Operations Management 29(6), 549–560. DOI: 10.1016/j.jom.2010.10.002.

Denyer, D.; Tranfield, D. (2009): Producing a systematic review (The sage handbook of organizational research methods).

Dyer, J. (1996): Specialized Supplier Networks as a Source of Competitive Advantage: Evidence from the Auto Industry, in: Strategic Management Journal, 17(4), 271–291.

Ebers, M.; Semrau, T. (2015): What drives the allocation of specific investments between buyer and supplier?, in: Journal of Business Research 68(2), 415–424. DOI: 10.1016/j.jbusres.2014.06.007.

Gelei, A.; Kenesei, Z. (2016): The Effect of Relation-Specific Investments in the Supply Chain Triad on Innovation Performance.

Husted, B (1993): Transaction costs, norms, and social networks: a preliminary study of cooperation in industrial buyer-seller relationships in the United States and Mexico, Centro de Estudios Estrategicos. Available at: https://repositorio.itesm.mx/ortec/handle/11285/574484.

German Academic Association for Business Research (2011): Gesamtübersicht JQ 2.1. Available at: http://vhbonline.org/uploads/media/Ranking_Gesamt_2.1.pdf (accessed: 17 December 2013).

Grimm, J. H.; Hofstetter, J. S.; Sarkis, J. (2014): Critical factors for sub-supplier management. A sustainable food supply chains perspective, in: International Journal of Production Economics 152, 159–173. DOI: 10.1016/j.ijpe.2013.12.011.

Grimm, J. H.; Hofstetter, J. S.; Sarkis, J. (2016): Exploring sub-suppliers' compliance with corporate sustainability standards, in: Journal of Cleaner Production 112, 1971–1984. DOI: 10.1016/j.jclepro.2014.11.036.

Grover, V.; Malhotra, M. K. (2003): Transaction cost framework in operations and supply chain management research. Theory and measurement, in: Journal of Operations Management 21(4), 457–473. DOI: 10.1016/S0272-6963(03)00040-8.

Heide, J.; John, G. (1988): The Role of Dependence Balancing in Safeguarding Transaction-Specific Assets in Conventional Channels, in: Journal of Marketing 52(1), 20–35.

Xie, Y. H.; Suh, T.; Kwon, I.-W. G. (2010): Do the magnitude and asymmetry of specific asset investments matter in the supplier–buyer relationship?, in: Journal of Marketing Management 26(9–10), 858–877. DOI: 10.1080/02672570903441488.

Hofstetter, J. (2016): Towards a framework for sub-supplier management. AOM Submission #15827 2016.

Kang, M.-P.; Mahoney, J. T.; Tan, D. (2009): Why firms make unilateral investments specific to other firms. The case of OEM suppliers, in: Strategic Management Journal 30(2), 117–135. DOI: 10.1002/smj.730.

Kim, S. D. (2015): Bureaucratic Structuring, Transaction Specific Investment, and Relationship Quality: Moderating Roles of Information Exchange between Manufacturer and Distributor, in: Journal of Marketing Thought 2(1), 1–13.

Klein, B.; Crawford, R.; Alchian, A. (1978): Vertical Integration, Appropriable rents, and the competitive contracting process, in: The Journal of Law and Economics, 297–326.

Kohtamäki, M.; Bourlakis, M. (2012): Antecedents of relationship learning in supplier partnerships from the perspective of an industrial customer. The direct effects model, in: Journal of Business & Industrial Marketing 27(4), 299–310. DOI: 10.1108/08858621211221670.

Kwon, Y.-C. (2011): Relationship-specific investments, social capital, and performance. The case of Korean exporter/foreign buyer relations, in: Asia Pacific Journal of Management 28(4), 761–773. DOI: 10.1007/s10490-009-9172-1.

Lohtia, R.; Krapfel, R. E. (1994): The Impact of Transaction-specific Investments on Buyer-Seller Relationships, in: Journal of Business & Industrial Marketing 9(1), 6–16. DOI: 10.1108/08858629410053434.

Lothia, R.; Brooks, C. M.; Krapfel, R. E. (1994): What Constitutes a Transaction-Specific Asset? An Examination of the Dimensions and Types, in: Journal of Business Research, 261–270.

Mahapatra, S. K.; Das, A.; Narasimhan, R. (2012): A contingent theory of supplier management initiatives. Effects of competitive intensity and product life cycle, in: Journal of Operations Management 30(5), 406–422. DOI: 10.1016/j.jom.2012.03.004.

Mena, C.; Humphries, A.; Choi, T. Y. (2013): Toward a Theory of Multi-Tier Supply Chain Management, in: Journal of Supply Chain Management 49(2), 58–77. DOI: 10.1111/jscm.12003.

Mentzer, J. T.; Stank, T. P.; Esper, T. L. (2008): Supply Chain Management and its relationship to logistics, marketing, production, and operations management, in: Journal of Business Logistics 29(1), 31–46. DOI: 10.1002/j.2158-1592.2008.tb00067.x.

Mueller, M.; Stoelzle, W. (2015): Socially responsible supply chains: A distinct avenue for future research?, in: Supply Management Research, 121–151.

Morrill, C.; Morrill, J. (2003): Internal auditors and the external audit. A transaction cost perspective, in: Managerial Auditing Journal 18(6/7), 490–504. DOI: 10.1108/02686900310482632.

Noordewier, G.; John, G.; Nevin, J. (1990): Performance Outcomes of Purchasing Arrangements in Industrial Buyer-Vendor Relationships, in: Journal of Marketing 54(4), 80-93.

Williamson, O. E. (1985): The Economic Institution of Capitalism: Firms, Markets, Relational Contracting, New York: Free Press.

Pimentel Claro, D.; Borin de Oliveira Claro, P.; Hagelaar, G. (2006): Coordinating collaborative joint efforts with suppliers. The effects of trust, transaction specific investment and information network in the Dutch flower industry, in: Supply Chain Management: An International Journal 11(3), 216–224. DOI: 10.1108/13598540610662112.

Poppo, L.; Zenger, T. (2002): Do Formal Contracts and Relational Governance Function as Substitutes or Complements?, in: Strategic Management Journal, 23(8), 707–725.

Raman, K.; Shahrur, H. (2008): Relationship-Specific Investments and Earnings Management. Evidence on Corporate Suppliers and Customers, in: The Accounting Review 83(4), 1041–1081. DOI: 10.2308/accr.2008.83.4.1041.

Stump, R. L.; Joshi, A. W. (1999): To Be or Not to Be [Locked in]. An Investigation of Buyers' Commitments of Dedicated Investments to Support New Transactions, in: Journal of Business-to-Business Marketing 5(3), 33–63. DOI: 10.1300/J033v05n03_03.

Subramani, M.; Venkatraman, N. (2003): Safeguarding Investments in Asymmetric Interorganizational Relationships: Theory and Evidence, in: The Academy of Management Journal, 46(1), 46–62.

Tachizawa, M.; Yew Wong, Chee (2014): Towards a theory of multi-tier sustainable supply chains. A systematic literature review, in: Supply Chain Management: An International Journal 19(5/6), pp. 643–663. DOI: 10.1108/SCM-02-2014-0070.

Takashima, K; Kim, C. (2016): The effectiveness of power-dependence management in retailing, in: International Journal of Retail & Distribution Management 44(1), pp. 71–88. DOI: 10.1108/IJRDM-03-2015-0039.

Trent, R. J.; Monczka, R. M. (2003): Understanding integrated global sourcing, in: International Journal of Physical Distribution & Logistics Management 33(7), 607–629. DOI: 10.1108/09600030310499286.

Vita, G. de; Tekaya, A.; Wang, C. L. (2011): The Many Faces of Asset Specificity. A Critical Review of Key Theoretical Perspectives, in: International Journal of Management Reviews 13(4), 329–348. DOI: 10.1111/j.1468-2370.2010.00294.x.

Wagner, S. M.; Bode, C. (2014): Supplier relationship-specific investments and the role of safeguards for supplier innovation sharing, in: Journal of Operations Management 32(3), 65–78. DOI: 10.1016/j.jom.2013.11.001.

Webster, J.; Watson, R. T. (2002): Analyzing the Past to Prepare for the Future: Writing a Literature Review, in: Management Information Systems 2002, 13–23. Available at: http://www.jstor.org/stable/4132319.

Wilhelm, M.; Blome, C.; Wieck, E.; Xiao, C. Y. (2016): Implementing sustainability in multi-tier supply chains. Strategies and contingencies in managing sub-suppliers, in: International Journal of Production Economics 182, 196–212. DOI: 10.1016/j.ijpe.2016.08.006.

Yeung, K.; Lee, P. K. C.; Yeung, A. C. L.; Cheng, T. C. E. (2013): Supplier partnership and cost performance. The moderating roles of specific investments and environmental uncertainty, in: International Journal of Production Economics 144(2), 546–559. DOI: 10.1016/j.ijpe.2013.04.008.

Yu, C.-M. J.; Liao, T.J.; Lin, Z.-D. (2006): Formal governance mechanisms, relational governance mechanisms, and transaction-specific investments in supplier–manufacturer relationships, in: Industrial Marketing Management 35 (2), 128–139. DOI: 10.1016/j.indmarman.2005.01.004.

Zaheer, A.; Venkatraman, N. (1995): Relational governance as an interorganizational strategy: An empirical test of the role of trust in economic exchange, in: Strategic Management Journal, 16(5), 373–392.

Teil B

Anwendungsorientierte Forschungsbeiträge

Single approaches for complexity management in product development: An empirical research

Wolfgang Vogel, Rainer Lasch

Abstract

Increasing complexity in product development has been one of the biggest issues during the last years. Companies in many different marketplaces are confronted with technology innovation, changing customer requirements, globalization of markets and competition as well as market uncertainty. In today's highly competitive environment, it is fundamental to bring new products quickly and with customers' individual settings to market. Product development is one of the most complex tasks and uncertain processes in the company and its complexity have the biggest influence on a company's complexity. Managing a company's complexity is a strategic issue to be competitive. In literature, a vast number of different single approaches for managing complexity are described. To compare literature findings with the practice, an empirical research was conducted in the German manufacturing industry. The data was collected through questionnaires between 2015 and 2016. An empirical research regarding specific approaches for managing complexity in product development does not exist yet. Covering this research gap is the purpose of this paper.

1 Introduction

Companies in high-technology marketplaces are confronted with technology innovation, dynamic market environment, market globalization, an increasing number of demanding customers and uncertainty. These are trends that manufacturing companies cannot escape (Voigt et al., 2011, p. 1; Miragliotta, Perona, Portioli-Staudacher, 2002, p. 382; Perona, Miragliotta, 2004, p. 103). According to ElMaraghy and ElMaraghy (2014, p. 1), "increasing global competition makes it necessary to generate wealth by being more competitive and offering goods and services that are differentiated by design and innovation". For a company's success, it is fundamental to design and manufacture new products quickly and bring them to market with customer's individual settings (Lübke, 2007, pp. 2–3, ElMaraghy, ElMaraghy, 2014, p. 1). Customers' individual needs and the increasing global competition are the reasons why many companies are present in the market with a diversified product (ElMaraghy, ElMaraghy, 2014, p. 1). In consequence, the companies cope with these trends by developing new product variants, which lead to an increased complexity in the company (Brosch, Krause, 2011, p. 1) and especially in product development (Kim, Wilemon, 2012, p. 1). For developing new product variants, resources are required (Wleklinski, 2001, p. 27; Bohne, 1998, pp. 9–10), which have to be procured (Vogel, 2017, p. 92). In product development, the amount of required resources is associated with the amount of product variants and product development complexity (Bohne, 1998, pp. 9-10). According to Wleklinksi (2001, p. 27), the success of development projects is connected with the amount of available resources. The objective of procurement is to provide all required objects which are not produced by the company itself (Arnold, 1997, p. 3). Procurement is connected with the amount of required resources (Franke, Firchau, 2001, p. 9). Thus, resources and their procurement play a central role for product development and a company's success (Vogel, 2017, p. 84, 92).

Increasing complexity is one of the biggest challenges that manufacturing companies have to face today (ElMaraghy et al., 2012, p. 793). In addition, increasing complexity is often related to increasing costs (Meyer, 2007, p. 94). Complexity is a phenomenon and evolutionary process, which presents a challenge especially for science and engineering. Complexity is characterized through change, choice and selection as well as perception and progress. Furthermore, complexity is intensified through innovations in products and processes (Warnecke, 2010, p. 639). Originally, the term "complexity" comes from the Latin word "complexus", which signifies "extensive, interrelated, confusing, entwined or twisted together" (ElMaraghy et al., 2012, p. 794; Grübner, 2007, pp. 40–41; Gießmann, 2010, p. 30). In literature, many different definitions for the term "complexity" are presented, because the meaning is vague and ambiguous. However, an explicit, universal and widely accepted definition does not exist (Brosch, Krause, 2011, p. 2; ElMaraghy et al., 2012, p. 794).

Product development is an important source to be competitive and to gain a competitive advantage over other business firms (Schaefer, 1999, p. 311). During the product development process, 80% of product costs are defined (Bayer, 2010, p. 89). Furthermore, the corresponding processes for production and procurement are determined (Dehnen, 2004, p. 26; Lübke, 2007, pp. 70–71; Bick, Drexl-Wittbecker, 2008, pp. 70–71). According to Schulte (1992, pp. 86–87), increasing complexity, especially in product development, leads to increasing costs in all parts along the value chain. Over the last years, the relevance of product development has changed significantly and become of central importance in a company's strategy (Davila, 2000, p. 383). According to Bick and Drexl-Wittbecker (2008, p. 20) and Davila (2000, p. 386), product development is one of the most complex tasks and uncertain processes in the company. The objective of product development is "to translate an idea into a tangible physical asset" (Davila, 2000, p. 385). Complexity in product development has continuously increased in the last years (Lübke, 2007, pp. 1–4; Krause, Franke, Gausemeier, 2007, pp. 3–4; ElMaraghy et al., 2012, pp. 793–797) and has the biggest influence on a company's complexity (Krause, Franke, Gausemeier, 2007, pp. 3–4, 23). Managing a company's complexity is a strategic issue to be competitive (Miragliotta, Perona, Portioli-Staudacher, 2002, p. 383). In literature, several objectives and strategies (Wildemann, 2012, p. 69) as well as a vast number of different single approaches for managing complexity are described (Gießmann, 2010, pp. 57–70).

For a target-oriented and effective complexity management, information is needed. In principle, the information needed can be gathered through scientific research, especially literature research, or empirical research. To compare literature results with the real world, empirical studies are conducted. During the last fifteen years, several empirical studies regarding complexity management were conducted in various fields of industries and regions/countries and are focused on different fields in the company and along the value chain. Previous empirical studies regarding complexity management in the field product development have been done by six different authors. However, none of the previous empirical studies regarding complexity management in product development concerns specific approaches for complexity management in product development. Furthermore, the previous empirical studies do not compare their results with the literature. As a result of this, we want to close this research gap by our empirical research to verify scientific findings and to compare the literature and the empirical results to identify similarities and differences.

This research paper is structured as follows: In Section 2, the paper gives an overview of the research methodology and presents a literature overview of the different single approaches which are applied for managing a company's complexity and their objectives. Furthermore, the existing empirical research in the field of complexity management is described and analyzed to identify gaps in the literature. Section 3 is focused on the empirical research and represents the research methodology and objectives, questionnaire design as well as the data collection methodology and sample description. In Section 4, the empirical findings are described. In the first part, the sample results and the data validation are presented. The second part gives an overview of the results regarding the single approaches for managing complexity and their targeted strategies. In the last part of Section 4, the empirical findings are compared with the existing literature results to identify communalities and differences. Section 5 concludes the paper by answering the research questions. Furthermore, the research gap is closed with implications for future research.

2 Literature review

2.1 Research methodology and boundary definition

The purpose of this paper is to compare literature findings regarding specific single approaches for complexity management with the real world to increase transparency and knowledge by identifying similarities and differences. For data collection, an empirical study in the manufacturing industry of Germany was conducted.

In literature, a vast number of different single approaches for managing variety and complexity are described (Gießmann, 2010, p. 56). Single approaches are methods or tools used for structuring or dealing with a task, situation or problem (Oxford Living Dictonaries, 2017a; Dictionary, 2017; Lindemann, Baumberger, 2006, p.7; Kieviet, 2014, p. 2, 44; Krause, Franke, Gausemeier, 2007, p. 9; Wildemann, 1998, p. 55). They are considered as single entities on their own and have no interrelationship with other approaches. Further, the approaches are focused on specific objectives and strategies (e.g. complexity reduction or avoidance) to solve a problem in the company and to achieve a long-term or overall aim (Lindemann, Baumberger, 2006, p. 9; Cambridge Dictionary, 2017; Oxford Living Dictonaries, 2017b).

In the first step before starting an empirical research, the existing literature and empirical studies must be reviewed. For the literature review, we used the methodology of Fink (2014, p. 3) and determined the following three research questions:

- RQ1: What different single approaches for complexity management currently exist in scientific literature?

- RQ2: What focus and objectives do the existing single approaches have?

- RQ3: What empirical studies in the field of complexity management in general and regarding specific complexity management single approaches currently exist in scientific literature?

In the next step, we defined the right search terms and databases. The search terms are formulated with a particular grammar and logic and are based on the research questions. In our literature research, we searched in English- and German-language literature and databases to extend the amount of relevant literature. The finalized search terms are created through an iterative process, starting with one key word and adding more, inclusive all potential synonyms of the particular key words in order to identify all important literature sources. According to Vogel and Lasch (2016, p. 5) and Vogel (2017, p. 95), the literature research was performed in the following eight English and German databases, which are specialized in science and economics: EBSCOhost, Emerald, GENIOS/WISO, Google Scholar, IEEE Xplore, JSTOR, ScienceDirect and SpringerLink. The time period was restricted between 1900/01/01 and 2015/12/31, because our empirical study was performed in the years 2015 and 2016 and we want to compare the empirical results with the existing literature in the same time period.

The literature search resulted in a certain amount of literature sources including research papers from journals, conference proceedings, books, essays and PhD theses. The specific amount of literature sources regarding the two issues are presented as follows: single approaches for complexity management (130,722 literature sources) and empirical studies in the field complexity management (26,699 literature sources). However, several literature sources were found multiple times.

To identify the relevant literature sources, the existing literature was analyzed, evaluated and synthesized based on the aforementioned research questions by using qualitative data analysis techniques. According to Fink (2014, p. 5), literature research always accumulates many publications, but only a few are relevant for scientific research. Thus, it is necessary to synthesize the results to identify the relevant literature sources. For the qualitative data analysis, we followed the methodology of Vogel and Lasch (2016, p. 6), which is described in detail in their publication. The results are described in the following Sections 2.2 and 2.3.

2.2 Single approaches for managing complexity

As already mentioned, the researched literature was analyzed and synthesized based on the qualitative content analysis techniques and the aforementioned research questions. The synthesizing process resulted in 288 relevant literature sources in the time period between 1962 and 2015 (see **Tables 6 and 7** in the appendix).

In literature, a vast number of different single approaches for managing complexity in the company and along the value chain (including the fields of product development, procurement, production, logistics, etc.) with specific purposes (e.g. complexity reduction or avoidance) are described. As already mentioned, a single approach is a method which is focused on a specific strategy and is used for structuring or dealing with a task or situation in a company to solve a problem or to achieve a particular objective.

Generally, the approaches can be divided into four overall categories, according to their focus: *product, product portfolio, process* and *organization* (Lasch, 2014, pp. 216–228; Gießmann, 2010, pp. 57–70; Gießmann, Lasch, 2011, pp. 11–20). According to literature, the most important approaches in each category are presented and discussed as follows:

Approaches focused on **product** can be differentiated into two purposes: product splitting or product bundling. However, the two types stand in no competition to each other. The optimal combination of both can help the company to achieve potentials (Wildemann, 2013, p. 148). Modular concept, modular system, standardization and differential construction are focused on product splitting. Approaches using the same parts, platform concepts and integral construction are focused on product bundling

(Wildemann, 2013, p. 148; Gießmann, 2010, p. 57). The objective of *modular concepts* is to separate the product into independent and standardized components, modules or assembly units, called subsystems (Göpfert, Steinbrecher, 2001, pp. 353–356; Piller, Waringer, 1999, pp. 37–40). The subsystems can be substituted at any time (Piller, Waringer, 1999, pp. 38–39). Baldwin and Clark (2000, p. 63) define a module as a "unit whose structural elements are powerfully connected among themselves and relatively weakly connected to elements in other units". The modular concept is the basis for other approaches, such as modular system and platform concept (Lindemann, Maurer, 2006, p. 43). A *modular system* is characterized by one or more base plates on which different mounting parts can be assembled (Rapp, 1999, p. 52). Modular system and the modular concept are similar, but the modular concept has no base plate (Zich, 1996, p. 40). *Standardization* is used to reduce the variety on the level of the product (Jeschke, 1997, p. 22). The objective is to standardize objects (Maune, 2001, pp. 25–26; Bohn, 2009, p. 232). Components that have optical or technological differences but the same function can be substituted by identical elements (Wildemann, 2013, pp. 143–146, 155–160). In *differential construction*, the components are separated into different component parts to increase the amount of same parts (Ehrlenspiel, 1995, p. 419; Schuh, Schwenk, 2001, p. 79). The opposite of differential construction is *integral construction*. The objective is to combine different parts into one component to reduce variety (Ehrlenspiel, 1995, p. 419; Schuh, Schwenk, 2001, p. 80). Further product bundling strategies are the platform concept and using the same parts. *Using same parts* is the overall use of standardized parts in the product (Stang, Hesse, Warnecke, 2002, p. 110). Contrary to standardization, the concept using same parts reduces functionally different parts or devices to one identical part or material basis (Bliss, 2000, p. 42). The objective of a *platform concept* is to use same parts in different product lines, brands or product life cycles. The platform concept is a special case of the modular concept (Ley and Hofer, 1999, p. 57). It consists of a summary of components, functions and interfaces which are standardized over the whole product family (Schuh, Schwenk 2001, p. 87; Schuh, 2005, p. 133).

Focused on **product portfolio**, three different approaches can be used for managing complexity in the company: packaging, reducing product range and reducing customer. The objective of *packaging* objective is to reduce the product portfolio complexity by limiting a product's configuration possibilities (Bliss, 2000, p. 40; Schuh, Schwenk, 2001, p. 83). For packaging, a fixed combination of layout properties is built from several functions or modules (Schuh, 1989, p. 59). Another approach for reducing the product portfolio and its complexity is to *reduce the product range*. Products with high complexity and low benefit are removed from the portfolio (Bliss, 2000, pp. 39–40; Kirchhof, 2003, p. 116). An alternative for reducing the product portfolio is to *reduce the number of customers*. Certain customers or groups of customers are not supplied in the future (Bliss, 2000, p. 41). In certain situations, the approaches reducing product range and reducing customers are directly correlated (Gießmann, 2010, p. 64).

Single approaches for complexity management in product development

In the category **process**, also three different approaches exist for complexity management: postponement concept, standardization of processes and modularity of processes. The *postponement concept* is based on shifting the order penetration point to the end of the value chain (Klug, 2010, pp. 55–56; Gießmann, 2010, p. 64; Köster, 1998, pp. 82–83). A company's performance process, especially the production process, is separated into two parts: order neutral and order related. Ideally, the order penetration point should be located at the transition point between order neutral and order related processes (Köster, 1998, pp. 82–83). The *standardization of processes* is an approach for coordinating future situations by providing a concrete solution (Dehnen, 2004, pp. 154–155). It is used in frequently recurring and less diversified processes. For reducing process complexity, the inputs and outputs, the work flow as well as the interfaces are fixed and standardized (Meyer, 2007, p. 63). *Process modularity* is based on dividing a large process into smaller sub-processes. They can be designed and operated independently, while the sub-processes ensure that the whole process fulfills its objectives (Blecker, Abdelkafi, 2006a, p. 77; Abdelkafi, 2008, pp. 152–154). In literature, further single approaches such as sourcing strategies, production segmentation or self-monitoring control cycles (kanban systems) exist in the category process. However, these single approaches are not in the focus of our empirical research, because we focused our research on approaches for complexity management in the field of product development. According to Wildemann (1998, pp. 60–61), Reiners and Sasse (1999, pp. 230–231), Bliss (2000, pp. 45–54), Klug (2010, pp. 67–68, 117-124), Gießmann and Lasch (2011, pp. 17-20), Reiss (2011, p. 78) and Wildemann (2012, pp. 223–229), these approaches are focused more on logistics, production and procurement than on product development.

The approaches focused on **organization** can be subdivided into delayering and empowerment. *Delayering* is characterized by reducing the levels of hierarchy in the company to increase the work and information flow. Espinosa, Harnden and Walker (2007, pp. 334–335, 340–344) argue that companies with strong hierarchical structures have problems with managing dynamic environmental complexity. Another approach focused on organization is *empowerment*. The objective is to delegate decision-making authority to subordinated hierarchies or operational levels to reduce coordination and organizational complexity (Bliss, 2000, pp. 49–50; Meffert, Burmann, Kirchgeorg, 2012, p. 314; Adam, Rollberg, 1995, pp. 667–669).

According to our literature research, the mentioned approaches are applied for six different purposes, called **complexity strategies**: complexity reduction, mastering, avoidance, outsourcing and increasing as well as in general for complexity management. *Complexity reduction* is based on a direct and short-term reduction of parts, products and processes (Wildemann, 2013, pp. 76–77). *Mastering complexity* is characterized by effectively handling unavoidable complexity along the value chain. It has a medium-term to long-term focus (Wildemann, 2005, p. 36; Wildemann, 2013, pp. 76, 78). The strategy with the longest horizon is *complexity avoidance*. The objective is to avoid and prevent the generation of complexity early (Wildemann, 2013, pp. 76, 79).

The idea of *complexity outsourcing* is to displace complexity to an external business partner to reduce a company's internal complexity, costs and risks (Rosenberg, 2002, pp. 225–227; Schönsleben, 2011, p. 72; Gabath, 2008, p. 67). To complement the complexity strategies, the target-oriented *increasing of complexity* is also referred to in the literature (Meyer, 2007, p. 35; Puhl, 1999, p. 23; Kirchhof, 2003, pp. 62–63). However, the complexity strategies outsourcing and increasing have less relevance in literature and practice (Schoeneberg, 2014a, p. 21; Meyer, 2007, p. 35). *Complexity acceptance* is also mentioned in literature as a complexity strategy (Hasenpusch, Moos, Schwellbach, 2004, p. 137). However, in this research, complexity acceptance is not considered, because in literature no specific procedure has been pointed out for science and practice.

To identify the main purpose (complexity strategy) of each approach, a literature analysis was performed based on the results of our literature research (see Section 2.1). **Table 1** presents the results of our literature analysis and gives an overview of the different approaches, the total amount of literature sources which are concerned with the specific single approaches and the main purpose (complexity strategy) of each approach. Since several literature sources assign more than one purpose or strategy for a certain complexity management approach, the total amount of literature occurrence (see **Table 1**, last column) is higher than the total amount of literature sources (see **Table 1**, third column). The complexity strategies used most often are color-marked.

For example, 158 authors describe modular concept as a complexity management approach. However, modular concept is assigned for the different complexity strategies 186 times. Modular concept is assigned in literature 121 times for complexity reduction (65%), thirty-six times (19%) for complexity mastering and twenty times (11%) for complexity avoidance. Furthermore, modular concept is already assigned in literature for general complexity management (N: 9; 5%).

As a result of this literature analysis, all approaches are mostly used for complexity reduction. Thus, this is the main complexity strategy regarding the single complexity approaches. An overview of the authors, the existing single approaches for complexity management in literature and the particular purposes are cited in the appendix (**Table 6** Part A–I and **Table 7** Part A–D).

Another result of our literature analysis is that literature focuses more and more on the different complexity management single approaches over time. Generally, the literature sources are published between the time period 1962 and 2015. However, the amount of publications regarding all single approaches has increased between 2005 and 2015. Thus, there is an increasing interest in science regarding the specific complexity management approaches in the last ten years. For example, 110 publications (70%) concerning the modular concept were published between 2005 and 2015. For the other approaches, the trends are similar (see **Table 6** Part A–I and **Table 7** Part A–D in the appendix).

Table 1: Overview on applied complexity management approaches, their purposes and occurrence in the literature

Focus	Single approaches for complexity management	Total amount of literature sources, which concern with a specific approach	Targeted complexity strategy (Purpose)						Total amount of literature occurrence
			Reduction	Mastering	Avoidance	Increasing	Outsourcing	General	
			N (%)	N (%)	N (%)	N (%)	N (%)	N (%)	N (%)
Product	Modular concept	158	121 (65%)	36 (19%)	20 (11%)	0 (0%)	0 (0%)	9 (5%)	186 (100%)
	Modular system	60	38 (57%)	16 (24%)	7 (10%)	0 (0%)	0 (0%)	6 (9%)	67 (100%)
	Standardization	90	72 (73%)	9 (9%)	12 (12%)	0 (0%)	0 (0%)	6 (6%)	99 (100%)
	Using same parts	56	38 (64%)	10 (17%)	8 (14%)	0 (0%)	0 (0%)	3 (5%)	59 (100%)
	Platform concept	87	68 (72%)	16 (17%)	6 (6%)	0 (0%)	0 (0%)	5 (5%)	95 (100%)
	Differential construction	19	12 (50%)	2 (8%)	1 (4%)	6 (25%)	2 (8%)	1 (4%)	24 (100%)
	Integral construction	29	19 (58%)	5 (15%)	3 (9%)	4 (12%)	0 (0%)	2 (6%)	33 (100%)
Product portfolio	Packaging	23	19 (83%)	2 (9%)	0 (0%)	0 (0%)	0 (0%)	2 (9%)	23 (100%)
	Reducing product range	25	22 (85%)	0 (0%)	1 (4%)	0 (0%)	0 (0%)	3 (12%)	26 (100%)
	Reducing of customers	11	10 (91%)	0 (0%)	0 (0%)	0 (0%)	0 (0%)	1 (9%)	11 (100%)
Process	Postponement concept	40	26 (60%)	11 (26%)	2 (5%)	0 (0%)	0 (0%)	4 (9%)	43 (100%)
	Standardization of processes	20	13 (57%)	1 (4%)	7 (30%)	0 (0%)	0 (0%)	2 (9%)	23 (100%)
	Modularity of processes	15	12 (60%)	2 (10%)	5 (25%)	0 (0%)	0 (0%)	1 (5%)	20 (100%)
Organization	Delayering	9	5 (56%)	3 (33%)	0 (0%)	0 (0%)	0 (0%)	1 (11%)	9 (100%)
	Empowerment	14	9 (64%)	2 (14%)	0 (0%)	0 (0%)	0 (0%)	3 (21%)	14 (100%)

■ Complexity strategy which is mostly used in literature for a specific complexity management single approach (more than 50%)

2.3 Existing empirical studies in the field of complexity management and identification of gaps in literature

Before starting an empirical research, it is important to review existing studies in the same or a similar scientific area to get an overview of their objectives, research methodologies and findings (Madu, 1998, pp. 354–355). According to Madu (1998), we performed a literature research to identify all existing empirical researches in the field of complexity management in manufacturing companies and especially regarding complexity management single approaches during the last years. The literature research was performed analogously to the literature research about the approaches for complexity management (see Section 2.1).

As a result of our literature research, we found 72 different empirical studies in the field of complexity management published in the time period between 1999 and 2015. The identified studies were analyzed and synthesized according to their content, research objectives, focus, field of industry, region/country, research period and applied data collection methodology. The empirical studies are focused on eight different fields: general in manufacturing companies (N: 32; 44%), product development (N: 6; 8%), production (N: 3; 4%), logistics (N: 5; 7%), order processing / distribution / sale (N: 4; 6%), internal supply chain (N: 16; 22%), remanufacturing (N: 2; 3%) and other fields (N: 4; 6%).

Previous empirical studies regarding product development have been done by six authors with different objectives between the time period 2005 and 2013: Li et al. (2005), Kim and Wilemon (2009, 2012), Newman (2009), Chronéer and Bergquist (2012) and Grussenmeyer and Blecker (2013). The empirical studies were conducted in different countries and fields of industries and the authors pursued different objectives as well.

As a result of the analysis of the existing empirical studies regarding complexity in product development as well as other fields (e.g. general in manufacturing companies, production, logistics, etc.), we come to the conclusion that empirical research regarding specific single approaches for managing complexity in product development and their main objectives does not yet exist. In this paper, we want to close this literature gap by presenting an empirical research in the field of product development in manufacturing companies in Germany.

3 Empirical research

3.1 Research methodology and objectives

For our empirical research, we followed the methodology of Flynn et al. (1990, pp. 253 255) based on social sciences. Flynn et al. (1990, pp. 253–255) describe a six stage systematic approach for conducting an empirical research, starting with the determination of the theoretical foundation (see **Figure 1**). This helps the researcher to describe what happens in the real world (Moody, 2002, p. 1). In stage II, the research design, which is applied to the research problem and the theoretical foundation, is selected (e.g. survey, single or multiple case study, etc.). Next, the data collection methods (e.g. questionnaires, interviews, historical archive analysis, etc.) and sample description for research implementation (e.g. sample industry and size, country, pilot testing, etc.) are selected in the stages III and IV. Several data collection methods are described in literature. In principle, the existing methods can be used alone or can be combined for better results. However, the mostly used data collection method is the questionnaire (Flynn et al., 1990, pp. 258–259). Before preparing the research report for publication (stage VI), the collected data is processed and analyzed in stage V (Flynn et al., 1990, pp. 264–268).

Figure 1: Six stage systematic approach for empirical research, developed by Flynn et al.

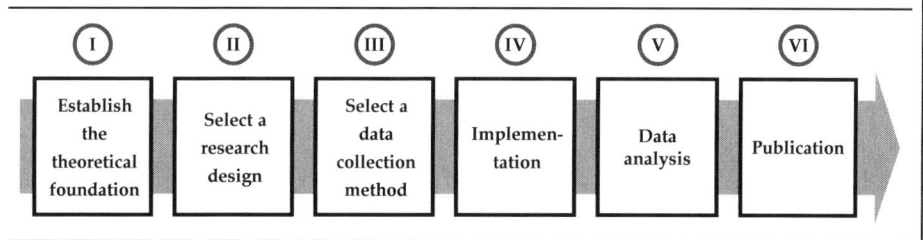

```
(I)           (II)          (III)         (IV)          (V)          (VI)
Establish   Select a      Select a    Implemen-     Data         Publication
the         research      data        tation        analysis
theoretical design        collection
foundation                method
```

To perform an empirical research, the research questions and objectives must be defined. In this case, we use an empirical research to document the current state in practice regarding the application of specific single approaches for complexity handling in the manufacturing industry of Germany. Furthermore, we compare the results from literature with the results from the real world to identify commonalities and differences. For our research, we determined two further research questions, focused on our empiricism (called empirical research question) to close the research gap:

- RQ4: What single approaches are applied for complexity management in product development and what specific complexity strategy are they focused on?

- RQ5: What are the significant differences and commonalities between literature and the practical (empirical) results?

3.2 Questionnaire design, data collection methodology, sample description and statistical analysis

The implementation of a research starts with the selection of the data collection method and the sample description (Flynn et al., 1990, pp. 256–263). In our research, we applied a standardized questionnaire with four questions and a fixed response possibility for data collection method. The data was collected from a stratified random sample out of a given population of 17,862 manufacturing companies with more than fifty employees, located in Germany. The population of 17,862 manufacturing companies was determined, based on the Amadeus database, where all manufacturing companies of Germany at the beginning of our empirical research in 2015 are documented. According to Gießmann (2010, p. 89), only companies with more than fifty employees were selected, because it is supposed that the complexity phenomenon primarily occurs in bigger companies rather than in smaller ones. The research was conducted in 2015 and 2016. A standardized questionnaire was sent in two stages by e-mail to 3,086 companies, exclusive of service and printing companies. In the cover letter, the companies were asked to send the questionnaire to an experienced employee from the product development department. The stratified random sample size (n = 1,565) is calculated based on the population (N = 17,862), a safety factor (t = 2) which depends on the respondents' level of significance, the proportion of the elements within the random sample which fulfills the feature characteristic (p = 0.5), and the sampling error (d = 0.05) (Mayer, 2013, p. 66; Raab, Poost, Eichhorn, 2009, p. 84). According to questionnaire's design, we structured the questionnaire in two main parts and started with general information regarding the respondents: company size, field of industry and respondent's position in the company. The second part concerns questions regarding the application of specific single approaches for complexity management in product development. The questions were formulated based on the research questions. The scale items were designed as statements and the interviewees were asked about their assessment. In our questionnaire, we used nominal scales and ordinal scales for measurement. Before starting our empirical research, the questionnaire was pretested in 2014 by forty experts from the potential target group to check and refine the wording, understanding, relevance as well as the measurement instrument, the questionnaire length and the time for responding. Based on the results and comments from the experts, the questionnaire was revised and checked again by a smaller group of experts.

A questionnaire belongs to the quantitative research methods and must be analyzed by using statistical methods to validate an existing theory (Flynn et al., 1990, pp. 264–267). For statistical analysis, several statistical tests or data analysis techniques exist that a researcher can use. However, there is no general rule to select a particular approach (Madu, 1998, p. 354). In our empirical research, we analyzed the empirical data by using descriptive parameters (means, frequencies and proportions). Some multivariate analysis techniques were applied as well. However, their results were not significant. Thus, these results are not described in detail in this paper.

4 Analysis of empirical research and findings

4.1 Sample results and data validation

As already mentioned, the questionnaire was sent by e-mail to 3,086 manufacturing companies with more than 50 employees, located in Germany. For response rate counting, the researcher has to determine the net sample size by reducing the total sample size based on the amount of e-mails that were undeliverable or rejected by the companies (Gießmann, 2010, p. 90). The final sample size was a total of 2,817 companies. In this research, 295 questionnaires were answered completely and resulted in a response rate of 10.5%. According to Meffert (1992, p. 202), this response rate is acceptable. The range comprised eleven different fields of industry, which were clustered in the following four industry clusters, according to their characteristics: technical industries, resource industries, consumer goods industry and others. About 60% of the respondents were from the technical industry such as engineering (30.5%), metal (10.5%), electrical and optics (9.8%), automotive (8.1%) (see **Figure 2**). Traditionally, the technical industry is Germany's major field of industry with a percentage of 63.5%, based on the Amadeus database. For validation of the results, the percentage of the empirical research was compared with the percentage of the database to identify differences and communalities. In all industry clusters, the percentages of empirical research and database are very close. Thus, distortions can be avoided and the empirical findings are representative for generalization.

Figure 2: Percentage of received questionnaires according to industry and comparison of results and database percentages

		N = 295 (100%)		% Amadeus Database	
Technical Industry N = 174 (59.0%)	Automotive	24	8.1%	16.9%	
	Engineering	90	30.5%	20.6%	63.5%
	Electrical & Optics	29	9.8%	12.0%	
	Metal	31	10.5%	14.1%	
Resource Industry N = 51 (17.3%)	Petroleum & Plastics	14	4.7%	6.7%	
	Chemical & Pharmaceutical	24	8.1%	7.9%	17.3%
	Glas, Ceramic, Pit & Quarry	13	4.4%	2.7%	
Consumer goods Industry N = 56 (19.0%)	Food, Forage & Tobacco	17	5.8%	8.8%	
	Lumber, Papers, Printing & Furniture	26	8.8%	6.4%	16.9%
	Clothing & Textile	13	4.4%	1.8%	
	Others	14	4.7%	2.2%	

Next, the number of employees and the position profiles of the respondents were analyzed (see **Figures 3** and **4**). Small and middle-sized companies between 50 and 250 employees are the biggest group in our empirical research, with 61.8% (see **Figure 3**). Larger companies with more than 250 employees represent 38.2%. These results show that small and middle-sized companies are highly interested in empirical studies regarding complexity management and especially in product development.

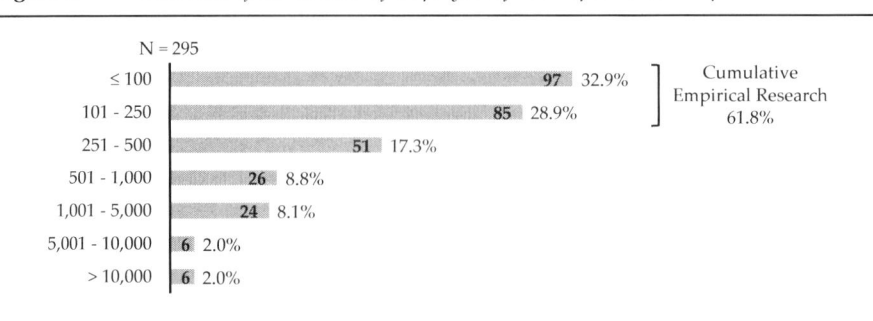

Figure 3: Overview of the number of employees of the respondents' companies

N = 295

Employees	Count	Percentage
≤ 100	97	32.9%
101 - 250	85	28.9%
251 - 500	51	17.3%
501 - 1,000	26	8.8%
1,001 - 5,000	24	8.1%
5,001 - 10,000	6	2.0%
> 10,000	6	2.0%

Cumulative Empirical Research 61.8% (≤ 100 and 101 - 250)

The analysis of the respondents' position profiles shows that complexity in product development is an important issue for management (**Figure 4**). 80% of the respondents can be allocated to the upper management, consisting of the following three groups: presidents, CEOs and COOs (18.0%); directors and division managers (26.1%); senior managers and department managers (35.9%).

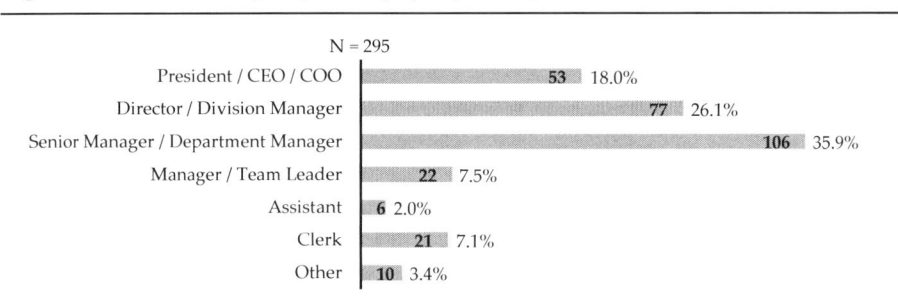

Figure 4: Overview of the position profile of the respondents

N = 295

Position	Count	Percentage
President / CEO / COO	53	18.0%
Director / Division Manager	77	26.1%
Senior Manager / Department Manager	106	35.9%
Manager / Team Leader	22	7.5%
Assistant	6	2.0%
Clerk	21	7.1%
Other	10	3.4%

4.2 Results regarding single approaches for managing complexity

The main research objective was to identify the approaches which are applied for complexity management in product development and the specific strategy they are focused on. In literature, fifteen approaches were listed, focused on six different complexity strategies (Section 2.2). The six complexity strategies comprise five specific strategies (reduction, mastering, avoidance, increasing and outsourcing) as well as a more general strategy (general complexity management). In our empirical research, we used only the five specific strategies in our questionnaire to reduce the amount of

Single approaches for complexity management in product development

response possibilities and get a precise answer from the respondents. The approaches were evaluated by the respondents according to their awareness level, application in the company and focused strategy. The questionnaire responses were analyzed by descriptive statistics. Based on the statistical analysis, the results were clustered into three groups:

- single approaches which are known *and* applied,
- single approaches which are known and *not* applied,
- single approaches which are *un*known.

We assumed that a specific approach that is not known cannot be applied by the company. **Figure 5** presents the principle which was applied for analyzing the empirical results according to familiarity with and application of the various approaches in the different branches.

Figure 5: Analysis of the results according to familiarity with and application of the various single approaches

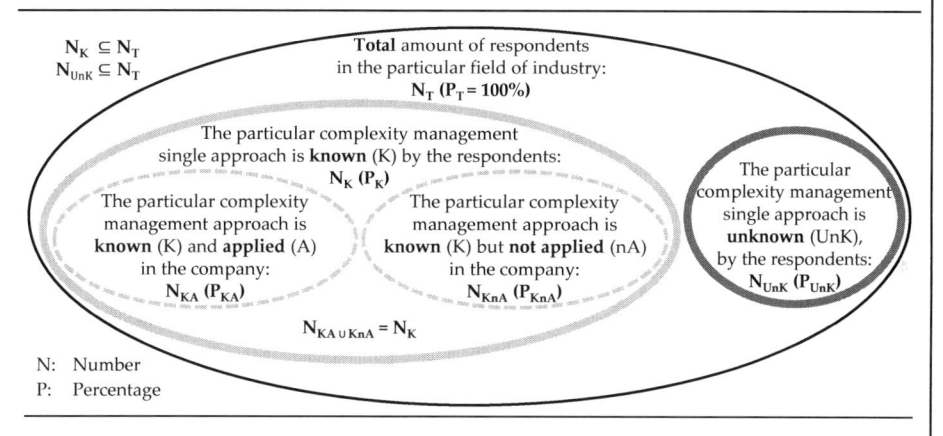

$N_K \subseteq N_T$
$N_{UnK} \subseteq N_T$

Total amount of respondents in the particular field of industry: N_T ($P_T = 100\%$)

The particular complexity management single approach is **known** (K) by the respondents: N_K (P_K)

The particular complexity management approach is **known** (K) and **applied** (A) in the company: N_{KA} (P_{KA})

The particular complexity management approach is **known** (K) but **not applied** (nA) in the company: N_{KnA} (P_{KnA})

The particular complexity management single approach is **unknown** (UnK), by the respondents: N_{UnK} (P_{UnK})

$N_{KA \cup KnA} = N_K$

N: Number
P: Percentage

Based on **Figure 5**, the empirical data is structured and analyzed. The analytical results are shown in **Table 2**, Part A–C. In **Table 2**, the different single approaches and the respondents' answers are presented. Furthermore, the empirical results are separated based on the respondents' fields of industry. For example, in the automotive industry, the approach modular concept is known by 23 respondents (N_K) and unknown by only one (N_{UnK}). Even though 23 respondents know the approach modular concept, only 17 (N_{KA}) apply this approach for complexity management in their company. Six respondents know this approach, but do not apply it (N_{KnA}). The reason for this should by analyzed in further research.

The approaches which are predominately known and used for complexity management in the company were color-marked. For our color marking, we defined three different levels according to the normal distribution and the standard deviation σ in which results could be found from the average: 100%–95% (±3σ), 94%–68% (±2σ) and less than 68% (±σ) (Hellwig, Sypli, 2014, p. 42).

Table 2 shows that nine single approaches are predominately known and applied for complexity management in product development by more than 68% of the respondents: *modular concept, modular system, standardization, using same parts, platform concept, reducing product range, standardization of processes, modularity of processes* and *empowerment*.

Further analysis of the results in **Table 2** shows that other approaches such as *differential* or *integral construction, packaging, reducing of customers* or *postponement concept* are not commonly known and applied in product development by the respondents. Furthermore, even though the approach delayering is commonly known in practice, it is not commonly applied in product development. These results lead to the conclusion that the application of specific approaches such as packaging, reducing of customers, postponement concept or delayering are not used for complexity management in product development by the respondents, because the application of these approaches cannot be influenced by the product development department itself. Reasons for this could be that these approaches originate in other fields along the value chain such as production or distribution and sale. Another surprising result is that the approaches *differential* or *integral construction* are not commonly known and applied for complexity management in product development, although these approaches can be assigned to product development. According to literature, integral and differential construction are used for product design during the product development process (Ehrlenspiel, 1995, pp. 414–422; Schuh, Schwenk, 2001, pp. 71–80). It would therefore be interesting to investigate the reasons for this discrepancy.

Single approaches for complexity management in product development

Table 2 - Part A: Empirical results according to familiarity and application

Explanation:
- ■ 100%–95%
- ▨ 94%–68%
- ☐ less than 68%

N_K (P_K) Known
N_{UnK} (P_{UnK}) Unknown
N_{KA} (P_{KA}) Known & Applied
N_{KnA} (P_{KnA}) Known & not Applied

Single approaches		Technical Industry				Resource Industry			Consumer goods Industry				Weighted Average
		Automotive	Engineering	Electrical & Optics	Metal	Petroleum & Plastics	Chemical & Pharmaceutical	Glass, Ceramic, Pit & Quarry	Food, Forage and Tobacco	Lumber, Papers, Printing & Furniture	Clothing & Textile	Others	
	N_T:	24	90	29	31	14	24	13	17	26	13	14	
Modular concept	N_K	23	86	28	26	10	18	11	13	25	11	13	
	P_K	96%	96%	97%	84%	71%	75%	85%	76%	96%	85%	93%	89%
	N_{UnK}	1	4	1	5	4	6	2	4	1	2	1	
	P_{UnK}	4%	4%	3%	16%	29%	25%	15%	24%	4%	15%	7%	11%
	N_{KA}	17	80	23	14	6	15	9	11	20	8	11	
	P_{KA}	74%	93%	82%	54%	60%	83%	82%	85%	80%	73%	85%	81%
	N_{KnA}	6	6	5	12	4	3	2	2	5	3	2	
	P_{KnA}	26%	7%	18%	46%	40%	17%	18%	15%	20%	27%	15%	19%
Modular system	N_K	23	86	26	26	10	19	12	12	25	11	13	
	P_K	96%	96%	90%	84%	71%	79%	92%	71%	96%	85%	93%	89%
	N_{UnK}	1	4	3	5	4	5	1	5	1	2	1	
	P_{UnK}	4%	4%	10%	16%	29%	21%	8%	29%	4%	15%	7%	11%
	N_{KA}	17	76	22	16	8	17	8	10	17	9	9	
	P_{KA}	74%	88%	85%	62%	80%	89%	67%	83%	68%	82%	69%	79%
	N_{KnA}	6	10	4	10	2	2	4	2	8	2	4	
	P_{KnA}	26%	12%	15%	38%	20%	11%	33%	17%	32%	18%	31%	21%
Standardization	N_K	23	85	26	28	11	20	13	16	25	12	14	
	P_K	96%	94%	90%	90%	79%	83%	100%	94%	96%	92%	100%	93%
	N_{UnK}	1	5	3	3	3	4	0	1	1	1	0	
	P_{UnK}	4%	6%	10%	10%	21%	17%	0%	6%	4%	8%	0%	7%
	N_{KA}	21	80	23	25	11	20	12	16	23	10	11	
	P_{KA}	91%	94%	88%	89%	100%	100%	92%	100%	92%	83%	79%	92%
	N_{KnA}	2	5	3	3	0	0	1	0	2	2	3	
	P_{KnA}	9%	6%	12%	11%	0%	0%	8%	0%	8%	17%	21%	8%
Using same parts	N_K	23	86	26	28	10	18	12	15	24	12	14	
	P_K	96%	96%	90%	90%	71%	75%	92%	88%	92%	92%	100%	91%
	N_{UnK}	1	4	3	3	4	6	1	2	2	1	0	
	P_{UnK}	4%	4%	10%	10%	29%	25%	8%	12%	8%	8%	0%	9%
	N_{KA}	22	82	24	22	9	17	10	13	19	12	11	
	P_{KA}	96%	95%	92%	79%	90%	94%	83%	87%	79%	100%	79%	90%
	N_{KnA}	1	4	2	6	1	1	2	2	5	0	3	
	P_{KnA}	4%	5%	8%	21%	10%	6%	17%	13%	21%	0%	21%	10%
Platform concept	N_K	23	76	26	26	11	16	10	12	25	10	12	
	P_K	96%	84%	90%	84%	79%	67%	77%	71%	96%	77%	86%	84%
	N_{UnK}	1	14	3	5	3	8	3	5	1	3	2	
	P_{UnK}	4%	16%	10%	16%	21%	33%	23%	29%	4%	23%	14%	16%
	N_{KA}	14	54	20	14	10	14	6	8	18	8	7	
	P_{KA}	61%	71%	77%	54%	91%	88%	60%	67%	72%	80%	58%	70%
	N_{KnA}	9	22	6	12	1	2	4	4	7	2	5	
	P_{KnA}	39%	29%	23%	46%	9%	12%	40%	33%	28%	20%	42%	30%
Differential construction	N_K	14	56	14	15	6	10	4	8	15	7	9	
	P_K	58%	62%	48%	48%	43%	42%	31%	47%	58%	54%	64%	54%
	N_{UnK}	10	34	15	16	8	14	9	9	11	6	5	
	P_{UnK}	42%	38%	52%	52%	57%	58%	69%	53%	42%	46%	36%	46%
	N_{KA}	8	39	8	9	2	3	1	6	6	4	4	
	P_{KA}	57%	70%	57%	60%	33%	30%	25%	75%	40%	57%	44%	57%
	N_{KnA}	6	17	6	6	4	7	3	2	9	3	5	
	P_{KnA}	43%	30%	43%	40%	67%	70%	75%	25%	60%	43%	56%	43%

Anwendungsorientierte Forschungsbeiträge

Table 2 - Part B: Empirical results according to familiarity and application

Explanation:			Technical Industry				Resource Industry			Consumer goods Industry				
■ 100% - 95% ▨ 94% - 68% ☐ less than 68% N_K (P_K) Known N_{UnK} (P_{UnK}) Unknown N_{KA} (P_{KA}) Known & Applied N_{KnA} (P_{KnA}) Known & not Applied			Automotive	Engineering	Electrical & Optics	Metal	Petroleum & Plastics	Chemical & Pharmaceutical	Glass, Ceramic, Pit & Quarry	Food, Forage and Tobacco	Lumber, Papers, Printing & Furniture	Clothing & Textile	Others	Weighted Average
Single approaches		N_T:	24	90	29	31	14	24	13	17	26	13	14	
Integral construction		N_K P_K	16 67%	63 70%	18 62%	24 77%	8 57%	13 54%	7 54%	8 47%	22 85%	7 54%	12 86%	67%
		N_{UnK} P_{UnK}	8 33%	27 30%	11 38%	7 23%	6 43%	11 46%	6 46%	9 53%	4 15%	6 46%	2 14%	33%
		N_{KA} P_{KA}	12 75%	49 78%	14 78%	16 67%	3 38%	8 62%	4 57%	4 50%	15 68%	4 57%	6 50%	68%
		N_{KnA} P_{KnA}	4 25%	14 22%	4 22%	8 33%	5 63%	5 38%	3 43%	4 50%	7 32%	3 43%	6 50%	32%
Packaging		N_K P_K	21 88%	61 68%	19 66%	17 55%	9 64%	13 54%	9 69%	9 53%	17 65%	7 54%	10 71%	65%
		N_{UnK} P_{UnK}	3 12%	29 32%	10 34%	14 45%	5 36%	11 46%	4 31%	8 47%	9 35%	6 46%	4 29%	35%
		N_{KA} P_{KA}	11 52%	41 67%	10 53%	7 41%	4 44%	8 62%	5 56%	6 67%	10 59%	5 71%	6 60%	59%
		N_{KnA} P_{KnA}	10 48%	20 33%	9 47%	10 59%	5 56%	5 38%	4 44%	3 33%	7 41%	2 29%	4 40%	41%
Reducing product range		N_K P_K	23 96%	81 90%	26 90%	26 84%	11 79%	20 83%	13 100%	15 88%	25 96%	10 77%	13 93%	89%
		N_{UnK} P_{UnK}	1 4%	9 10%	3 10%	5 16%	3 21%	4 17%	0 0%	2 12%	1 4%	3 23%	1 7%	11%
		N_{KA} P_{KA}	14 61%	47 58%	15 58%	18 69%	8 73%	17 85%	11 85%	11 73%	17 68%	9 90%	10 77%	67%
		N_{KnA} P_{KnA}	9 39%	34 42%	11 42%	8 31%	3 27%	3 15%	2 15%	4 27%	8 32%	1 10%	3 23%	33%
Reducing of customers		N_K P_K	20 83%	59 66%	22 76%	21 68%	9 64%	16 67%	11 85%	15 88%	18 69%	10 77%	13 93%	73%
		N_{UnK} P_{UnK}	4 17%	31 34%	7 24%	10 32%	5 36%	8 33%	2 15%	2 12%	8 33%	3 23%	1 7%	27%
		N_{KA} P_{KA}	6 30%	20 34%	3 14%	12 57%	0 0%	11 69%	5 45%	7 47%	8 44%	3 30%	6 46%	38%
		N_{KnA} P_{KnA}	14 70%	39 66%	19 86%	9 43%	9 100%	5 31%	6 55%	8 53%	10 56%	7 70%	7 54%	62%
Postponement concept		N_K P_K	14 58%	46 51%	15 52%	9 29%	5 36%	9 38%	5 38%	5 29%	15 58%	5 38%	8 57%	46%
		N_{UnK} P_{UnK}	10 42%	44 49%	14 48%	22 71%	9 64%	15 62%	8 62%	12 71%	11 42%	8 62%	6 43%	54%
		N_{KA} P_{KA}	5 36%	26 57%	9 60%	4 44%	4 80%	6 67%	2 40%	3 60%	7 47%	2 40%	1 13%	51%
		N_{KnA} P_{KnA}	9 64%	20 43%	6 40%	5 56%	1 20%	3 33%	3 60%	2 40%	8 53%	3 60%	7 88%	49%
Standardization of processes		N_K P_K	23 96%	85 94%	27 93%	28 90%	11 79%	23 96%	12 92%	15 88%	26 100%	11 85%	14 100%	93%
		N_{UnK} P_{UnK}	1 4%	5 6%	2 7%	3 10%	3 21%	1 4%	1 8%	2 12%	0 0%	2 15%	0 0%	7%
		N_{KA} P_{KA}	21 91%	74 87%	25 93%	26 93%	8 73%	22 96%	12 100%	15 100%	21 81%	11 100%	12 86%	90%
		N_{KnA} P_{KnA}	2 9%	11 13%	2 7%	2 7%	3 27%	1 4%	0 0%	0 0%	5 19%	0 0%	2 14%	10%

168

Single approaches for complexity management in product development

Table 2 - Part C: Empirical results according to familiarity and application

Explanation:		Technical Industry				Resource Industry			Consumer goods Industry				
		Automotive	Engineering	Electrical & Optics	Metal	Petroleum & Plastics	Chemical & Pharmaceutical	Glass, Ceramic, Pit & Quarry	Food, Forage and Tobacco	Lumber, Papers, Printing & Furniture	Clothing & Textile	Others	Weighted Average

Legend:
- ■ 100% - 95%
- ▨ 94% - 68%
- ☐ less than 68%

N_K (P_K) Known
N_{UnK} (P_{UnK}) Unknown
N_{KA} (P_{KA}) Known & Applied
N_{KnA} (P_{KnA}) Known & not Applied

		Auto	Eng	E&O	Metal	P&P	C&P	GCQ	FFT	LPF	C&T	Others	WAvg
Single approaches	N_T:	24	90	29	31	14	24	13	17	26	13	14	
Modularity of processes	N_K	21	68	22	26	9	14	11	12	22	7	11	
	P_K	88%	76%	76%	84%	64%	58%	85%	71%	85%	54%	79%	76%
	N_{UnK}	3	22	7	5	5	10	2	5	4	6	3	
	P_{UnK}	12%	24%	24%	16%	36%	42%	15%	29%	15%	46%	21%	24%
	N_{KA}	17	46	15	19	6	14	7	8	13	5	8	
	P_{KA}	81%	68%	68%	73%	67%	100%	64%	67%	59%	71%	73%	71%
	N_{KnA}	4	22	7	7	3	0	4	4	9	2	3	
	P_{KnA}	19%	32%	32%	27%	33%	0%	36%	33%	41%	29%	27%	29%
Delayering	N_K	23	74	25	24	12	19	12	14	24	9	14	
	P_K	96%	82%	86%	77%	86%	79%	92%	82%	92%	69%	100%	85%
	N_{UnK}	1	16	9	7	2	5	1	3	2	4	0	
	P_{UnK}	4%	18%	14%	23%	14%	21%	8%	18%	85	31%	0%	15%
	N_{KA}	14	47	14	12	8	13	6	6	11	6	8	
	P_{KA}	61%	64%	56%	50%	67%	68%	50%	43%	46%	67%	57%	58%
	N_{KnA}	9	27	11	12	4	6	6	8	13	3	6	
	P_{KnA}	39%	36%	44%	50%	33%	32%	50%	57%	54%	33%	43%	42%
Empowerment	N_K	22	70	26	27	12	17	9	13	21	11	14	
	P_K	92%	78%	90%	87%	86%	71%	69%	76%	81%	85%	100%	82%
	N_{UnK}	2	20	3	4	2	7	4	4	5	2	0	
	P_{UnK}	8%	22%	10%	13%	14%	29%	31%	24%	19%	15%	0%	18%
	N_{KA}	14	52	21	14	10	13	8	8	14	5	9	
	P_{KA}	64%	74%	81%	70%	83%	76%	89%	62%	67%	45%	64%	72%
	N_{KnA}	8	18	5	8	2	4	1	5	7	6	5	
	P_{KnA}	36%	26%	19%	30%	17%	24%	11%	38%	33%	55%	36%	29%

Comparing the results within the three industry clusters technical industry, resource industry and consumer goods industry regarding the nine single approaches that are predominately known and applied by more than 68% of the respondents, it can be seen that some fields of industry apply specific approaches more often than others. Within the technical industry, the field engineering is the benchmark for modular concept, modular system as well as standardization. The approaches using same parts and modularity of processes are applied most often by the automotive industry. Further, the approaches platform concept and empowerment are mainly applied in the electrical and optics industry and the approach reducing product range is mainly applied in the metal industry. The approach standardization of processes is applied in the same way in two fields of industries: electrical and optics as well as metal. Furthermore, our analysis shows that for most approaches, the percentage value for "approach is known and applied (P_{KA})" of the different fields of industries within the technical industry cluster does not vary much. For example, the percentage values within the approach standardization vary from 94% (engineering industry) to 89% (metal industry). However, there are some approaches with a great variation between the highest and lowest percentage value (e.g. modular concept: 93% – engineering industry vs. 54% – metal industry). Another surprising result is that the automotive industry has the second lowest value within the approach platform concept. In literature, platform concept is often described as an important strategy for complexity management and product development in the automotive industry. The objective is to reduce complexity by increasing the use of same parts (see Section 2.2). Furthermore, the platform concept has a direct influence on the product development strategy and costs as well as on logistics and production (Maune, 2001, p. 29–30; Adam, 1998, p. 60). Further research should analyze the reasons for this result. Regarding the resource industry cluster, the chemical and pharmaceutical industry is the leading industry for the approaches modular concept, modular system, standardization, using same parts, reducing product range and modularity of processes. The approach standardization is applied by the petroleum and plastics industry in the same way as by the chemical and pharmaceutical industry. The platform concept is also most often applied by the petroleum and plastics industry. Furthermore, the approaches standardization of processes and empowerment are mainly known and applied by the glass, ceramic, pit and quarry industry. Within the consumer goods industry cluster, the industry branches food, forage and tobacco as well as clothing and textile are the leading branches. The approaches modular concept, modular system, standardization as well as standardization of processes are mainly known and applied by the food, forage and tobacco industry. The approach standardization of processes is applied by the clothing and textile industry in the same way. Further, the approaches using same parts, platform concept, reducing product range and modularity of processes are applied most in the clothing and textile industry. In addition, the field of industry lumber, papers, printing and furniture is the leading industry regarding the approach empowerment. Analyzing the different percentage values for "approach is known and applied (P_{KA})" of the different fields of industry within the resource and the consumer goods industry, we identified approaches with low variation (e.g. resource industry: standardization: 100% vs. 92%, or consumer goods industry: standardization: 96% vs. 92%) as well as with high variation (e.g. resource industry: platform concept: 91% vs. 60%, or consumer goods industry: reducing product range: 90% vs. 73%).

Based on the analytical results presented in **Table 2** the different single approaches were analyzed in the next step according to their targeted strategy. For data analysis, only the approaches and strategies that are known and applied by the respondents were used. In our research, several respondents assigned more than one purpose or strategy for a certain complexity management approach. As already mentioned, the same occurs in literature (see Section 2.2).

Table 3 presents an overview of the applied approaches and their purposes for complexity management in product development. The complexity strategies with the highest values are color-marked. For example, in our research, 133 respondents use the

Single approaches for complexity management in product development

approach modular concept for complexity mastering (43.3%) and 96 respondents use it for complexity reduction (31.3%). The strategy with the highest value has priority 1 (black color-marked) and the strategy with the second highest value has priority 2 (grey color-marked). However, no explicit tendency towards a specific strategy could be identified in this case and for most other approaches. Only the approach "modularity of processes" is assigned with more than 50% to the strategy complexity mastering. Based on the results, the complexity approaches are mainly used for complexity reduction or mastering. However, as already mentioned, no explicit tendency towards one specific strategy can be identified. The strategy complexity avoidance is also used in practice but is not as important as complexity reduction or mastering. The strategies, which are used fewest in the manufacturing industry, are complexity increasing and outsourcing.

Table 3: Empirical results according to applied single approaches and their purpose

Complexity strategy with: priority 1 and the highest value / priority 2 and the second highest value		Complexity strategy								
		Reduction		Mastering		Avoidance		Increasing		Outsourcing	
Focus	Single approaches	N	%	N	%	N	%	N	%	N	%
Product	Modular concept	96	31.3%	133	43.3%	47	15.3%	18	5.9%	13	4.2%
	Modular system	99	30.8%	123	38.3%	64	19.9%	22	6.9%	13	4.0%
	Standardization	127	37.5%	100	29.5%	100	29.5%	6	1.8%	6	1.8%
	Using same parts	108	34.2%	100	31.6%	91	28.8%	13	4.1%	4	1.3%
	Platform concept	91	34.6%	84	31.9%	69	26.2%	14	5.3%	5	1.9%
	Differential construction	30	23.1%	53	40.8%	17	13.1%	18	13.8%	12	9.2%
	Integral construction	47	27.3%	69	40.1%	30	17.4%	19	11.0%	7	4.1%
Product portfolio	Packaging	41	24.6%	65	38.9%	35	21.0%	17	10.2%	9	5.4%
	Reducing product range	116	46.2%	53	21.1%	65	25.9%	6	2.4%	11	4.4%
	Reducing of customers	66	46.5%	28	19.7%	37	26.1%	6	4.2%	5	3.5%
Process	Postponement concept	28	24.6%	48	42.1%	21	18.4%	10	8.8%	7	6.1%
	Standardization of processes	92	29.6%	133	42.8%	69	22.2%	8	2.6%	9	2.9%
	Modularity of processes	54	24.5%	110	50.1%	35	15.8%	14	6.4%	7	3.2%
Organization	Delayering	52	28.6%	64	35.2%	55	30.2%	8	4.4%	3	1.6%
	Empowerment	62	29.5%	81	38.6%	48	22.9%	12	5.7%	7	3.3%

After analyzing the different single approaches according to their targeted strategy, the results from **Table 3** are separated regarding the different fields of industries and industry clusters. Only the complexity strategies with the highest values in each approach and field of industry are described in **Table 4**, whereas the strategies with the second, third, etc. highest value are not presented in the table.

For example, in the automotive industry, 38% of the respondents use the approach modular concept for complexity mastering (M). This is the highest value and is therefore presented in **Table 4**. Furthermore, 28% of the respondents also use this approach for complexity reduction (R), 24% use it for the strategy complexity avoidance (A) and 10% for complexity outsourcing (O). These values are not presented in **Table 4**. However, there is no explicit tendency in this case, because no complexity strategy is assigned by more than 50% of the respondents. Analyzing the other results, there is often also no explicit tendency towards a specific strategy for most approaches and within the different fields of industry and industry clusters. The complexity strategies which are assigned by more than 50% of the respondents are color-marked.

In **Tables 3 and 4** it is seen that the approaches modular concept, modular system, differential and integral construction, packaging, postponement concept, standardization and modularity of processes as well as delayering and empowerment are applied for complexity mastering in most fields of industry. However, some fields of industry apply these approaches also for complexity reduction, avoidance or increasing but not for outsourcing. For example, the approach modular concept is applied for complexity mastering by most fields of industry, but also for complexity reduction and avoidance in the industry branches petroleum and plastics; glass, ceramic, pit and quarry as well as food, forage and tobacco. The single approaches which are applied for complexity reduction in most fields of industry (e.g. standardization, using same parts, platform concept, etc.) are also used for mastering, avoidance and outsourcing but not for increasing.

When comparing the percentage values within the different industry clusters it can be seen that only in the technical industry cluster, the combination between the specific single approach and its targeted strategy are often equal. Within the other industry clusters, the results are mostly not consistent regarding the combination between approach and targeted strategy.

Furthermore, within the different fields of industry several single approaches with different targeted complexity strategies are applied for complexity management in product development. No industrial branch focusses only on one specific complexity strategy (see **Table 4**, last five rows). For example, in the automotive industry, six approaches are used for complexity reduction (standardization, platform concept, reducing product range, reducing of customers, standardization of processes, empowerment) and seven for complexity mastering (modular concept, modular system, integral construction, packaging, postponement concept, standardization of processes, modularity of processes). Furthermore, two approaches are used for complexity avoidance (using same parts, delayering) and one for a targeted complexity increasing (differential construction). Comparing these results between the different industry branches, the strategies complexity mastering (N: 7) and complexity reduction (N: 4) are mostly used in the different fields of industry for complexity management.

Single approaches for complexity management in product development

Table 4: Empirical results according to applied single approaches and their purpose in the different fields of industry

Explanation to complexity strategy with priority 1 and the highest value: R: Reduction / M: Mastering / A: Avoidance / I: Increasing / O: Outsourcing. Note: If there is more than one strategy listed, the percentage of the different strategies is equal		Technical Industry				Resource Industry			Consumer goods Industry			
Focus	Single approaches	Automotive	Engineering	Electrical & Optics	Metal	Petroleum & Plastics	Chemical & Pharmaceutical	Glass, Ceramic, Pit & Quarry	Food, Forage and Tobacco	Lumber, Papers, Printing & Furniture	Clothing & Textile	Others
Product	Modular concept	M 38%	M 48%	M 41%	M 55%	R,M 38%	M 41%	R,A 31%	R 40%	M 49%	M 56%	A 40%
	Modular system	M 31%	M 44%	M 39%	M 42%	A 33%	R 39%	R 31%	M 47%	M 41%	R 50%	R,A 36%
	Standardization	R 35%	R 40%	R 37%	R 35%	A 43%	R 39%	A 50%	M 39%	R 41%	R 43%	R 42%
	Using same parts	A 39%	R 36%	R 35%	M 39%	M,A 36%	A 35%	R 40%	M 47%	M 37%	R 50%	A 55%
	Platform concept	R 39%	R 38%	M 34%	R 44%	M 50%	R 35%	R,A 38%	R 55%	M 42%	R 44%	A 63%
	Differential construction	I 29%	M 53%	M 60%	M 31%	A 50%	R,M,A 33%	A 100%	R 33%	R,A 25%	R,M 40%	M 67%
	Integral construction	M 31%	M 44%	M 50%	R 32%	M,A 33%	R,M 44%	A 50%	R,A 40%	R,A 47%	R,A,I 33%	M 57%
Product portfolio	Packaging	M 40%	M 41%	M 40%	M 45%	A 44%	M 45%	R,M 38%	M 44%	M 29%	M,A 40%	R,M 33%
	Reducing product range	R 42%	R 45%	R 41%	A 32%	R 40%	R 56%	R 44%	R 57%	R 52%	R 44%	R 90%
	Reducing of customers	R 55%	R 38%	R 41%	R 58%	R,A 33%	R 38%	R,M,A,O 25%	R 54%	R 62%	R 67%	R 50%
Process	Postponement concept	M 36%	M 50%	M 47%	M 33%	R,M 50%	A,I 33%	M 50%	A 60%	M 44%	R 75%	A 67%
	Standardization of processes	R,M 36%	M 45%	M 47%	R,M 32%	M 54%	M 38%	M 50%	M 53%	M 41%	M 42%	R 45%
	Modularity of processes	M 42%	M 51%	M 55%	M 45%	M 67%	R,M 41%	M 50%	M 70%	M 57%	M 38%	R,M 38%
Organization	Delayering	A 43%	M 46%	R,M,A 31%	A 35%	M 56%	M,A 32%	A 43%	A 43%	M 50%	R 60%	R 44%
	Empowerment	R 31%	M 53%	M 42%	M 33%	M 44%	R,M 33%	R 42%	M 38%	M 41%	R 57%	A 42%
Total amount of applied complexity strategies in each field of industry	Reduction	6	5	5	5	4	9	8	6	4	11	8
	Mastering	7	10	11	9	9	8	5	7	11	5	4
	Avoidance	2		1	2	7	4	7	3	1	2	6
	Increasing	1					1				1	
	Outsourcing							1				

173

4.3 Comparison between empirical and literature results

A further research objective was to compare the empirical findings regarding specific complexity management single approaches and their focused strategy with the literature findings to identify differences and commonalities. The comparison gives the opportunity to refine existing scientific knowledge or theories and to identify further research gaps.

Table 5 presents a comparison between literature findings and empirical findings regarding the different complexity management single approaches and their targeted strategy. Literature findings are described in Section 2.2 (see **Table 1**) and empirical findings are described in Section 4.2 (see **Table 3**).

Table 5: Comparison of literature findings versus empirical findings

Complexity strategy with: ■ priority 1 and the highest value ▨ priority 2 and the second highest value		Literature's findings – Complexity strategy					Empirical findings – Complexity strategy				
Focus	Single approaches	Reduction	Mastering	Avoidance	Increasing	Outsourcing	Reduction	Mastering	Avoidance	Increasing	Outsourcing
Product	Modular concept	■●					▨	■●			
	Modular system	■●					▨	■●			
	Standardization	■●					■●	▨			
	Using same parts	■●					■●	▨			
	Platform concept	■●					■●	▨			
	Differential construction	■●					▨	■●			
	Integral construction	■●					▨	■●			
Product portfolio	Packaging	■●					▨	■●			
	Reducing product range	■●					■●		▨		
	Reducing of customers	■●					■●		▨		
Process	Postponement concept	■●					▨	■●			
	Standardization of processes	■●					▨	■●			
	Modularity of processes	■●					▨	■●			
Organization	Delayering	■●						■●			
	Empowerment	■●					▨	■●			

In the literature, the different complexity approaches are focused on one specific strategy with an explicit tendency with more than 50%. All approaches are mostly used for complexity reduction and have priority 1 with the highest value (black color-marked). However, in our empirical research we found that the different single approaches could not be assigned to a specific strategy, because no explicit tendency with more than 50% could be identified (see Section 4.2 and **Table 3**). The complexity strategy which is assigned most by the respondents has the highest value and priority 1 (black color-marked). The strategy with the second highest value has priority 2 (grey color-marked). According to our empirical research, the complexity management approaches are mainly used for complexity mastering and/or reduction. Analyzing the empirical data regarding the specific single approaches within the different fields of industry and industry clusters, the results are similar. No explicit tendency can be identified. Analyzing the empirical data regarding the most applied complexity strategies in the different industry branches, no branch focusses only on one specific strategy. However, complexity mastering and complexity reduction are the strategies that are mostly applied.

The reason for this is that the specific approaches are evaluated by the respondents based on different situations and perceptions. Furthermore, in the company, complexity cannot be handled with only one specific complexity strategy. For example, companies often cannot reduce complexity to a minimum level, because they need a certain amount of complexity to achieve an optimum complexity degree to be competitive. Thus, companies are often focused on mastering complexity rather than reducing it. Each new situation or complexity problem requires an individual evaluation with the selection of a specific approach and strategy.

From a scientific perspective, this comparison establishes a connection between scientific research and practice and allows the researcher an insight in the real world. This study gives the researcher an overview of what is already known in practice about this issue and practicioners' tendencies. It closes a currently existing gap in scientific literature by comparing literature findings and empirical findings to identify similarities and differences. Based on this comparison, the theoretical findings in literature can be confirmed, advanced or progressed. Furthermore, the empirical research shows that in practice the application of a specific complexity management single approach depends on the situation and complexity problem as well as the desired strategy. Thus, the approaches cannot be assigned to one specific strategy. Based on this research and comparison, researchers can build new ideas, theories and hypotheses for their own research.

From a practical perspective, this empirical study gives the practitioner an overview of the different approaches for complexity management and their focus and targeted strategy. Further, this study also answers the following questions: "What different approaches are used by other practitioners in other fields of industry?" and "What focus or strategy is pursued by other practitioners in other fields of industry by using a specific single approach?" by providing an overview of the complexity management single approaches and their main focus or strategy. However, a specific recommendation regarding the application of a specific single approach cannot be given, because the selection and application of a specific approach and strategy depends on a company's situation or complexity problem. However, this empirical research helps the practitioner to find the right approach for his specific situation or complexity problem.

5 Conclusion and outlook

This paper's objective is to provide an overview of the practical application of specific single approaches for complexity management in the manufacturing industry of Germany. Furthermore, the empirical results are compared with the literature findings to identify commonalities and differences for verifying proposed scientific knowledge and theories as well as to develop additional knowledge for science and practice.

Before starting our empirical study, we reviewed the literature regarding the specific complexity management single approaches and previously existing empirical studies in the field of complexity management (see Sections 2.2 and 2.3). Furthermore, we reviewed the existing studies especially regarding specific single approaches for managing complexity in the company and pointed out the gaps in literature.

As a result of our literature search, we identified 72 empirical studies regarding complexity management. However, only six studies are focused on product development. As a result of the analysis of the previous empirical studies regarding product development as well as other fields, we found that an empirical research in the field product development in manufacturing companies in Germany and focused on the application of specific single approaches for managing complexity in the company and especially in product development does not yet exist. In this paper, we want to close this gap.

To conduct this research, we used the methodology of Flynn et al. (1990, pp. 253–255). The research methodology, the objectives, the sample description and the methods for statistical analysis are described in Section 3. For data collection, a standardized questionnaire with four questions and a fixed response possibility was sent in two stages by e-mail to 3,086 companies with more than fifty employees located in Germany. In this research, which comprised eleven different fields of industry, 295 questionnaires were completed, which resulted in a response rate of 10.5%. For statistical analysis, we used methods of descriptive statistics. The results are described in Section 4. For this empirical research, we determined two empirical research questions, which were answered as follows.

For answering the first empirical research question (RQ 4), the data regarding the complexity management approaches, their objectives and practical application were analyzed and evaluated. For complexity management, fifteen different approaches focused on five different strategies were applied in practice. **Tables 2** and **3** present an overview of the different approaches, their awareness level and application as well as the focused strategy. We found that the following nine approaches are predominately known and used for complexity management in the manufacturing industry in Germany: *modular concept, modular system, standardization, using same parts, platform concept, reducing product range, standardization of processes, modularity of processes and empowerment*. Based on the respondents' answers, the approaches *differential* or *integral construction, packaging, reducing of customers* or *postponement concept* are not commonly known and applied in product development. Next, the results of **Table 3** are compared within the three industry clusters. According to this comparison, some industry branches apply specific approaches more often than other branches. Furthermore, the complexity management single approaches are mainly used for complexity reduction or mastering. However, no explicit tendency towards one specific strategy can be identified. Analyzing these results regarding the different fields of industries and industry clusters, the results are equal.

For answering the second empirical research question (RQ 5), the empirical findings regarding the approaches for complexity management were compared with the literature findings to identify the significant differences and commonalities (see Section 4.3). In literature, the approaches are focused mostly on complexity reduction. In our research, we come to the conclusion that the approaches could not be assigned to a specific complexity strategy. Regarding complexity strategy, no explicit tendency can be identified.

Further research should analyze the differences between theory and practice more in detail and the empirical findings should be used for further discussions und evaluations in literature. Furthermore, our research was focused on the manufacturing industry in Germany. Future research may also include other countries and sectors. It would be interesting to compare the empirical results from this study with the results from a further study, which is conducted in other fields of industry or countries/regions.

References

Abdelkafi, N. (2008): Variety-Induced Complexity in Mass Customization: Concepts and Management, Berlin.

Adam, D. (1998): Produktions-Management, 9th edition, Wiesbaden.

Adam, D. (2004): Controlling bei Komplexität, in: Bensberg, F.; vom Brocke, J.; Schultz, M. (Eds.): Trendberichte zum Controlling: Festschrift für Heinz Lothar Groß, Berlin.

Adam, D.; Rollberg, R. (1995): Komplexitätskosten, in: Die Betriebswirtschaft, 55 (5), 667–670.

Adrian, O. (2007): Platform Concept: A Breakthrough in Surface Radar Architecture, in: Proceedings of the International Conference on Radar Systems, Edinburgh.

Agrawalla, R. (2011): Systems Engineering To Conquer Complexity, in: Proceedings of the 3rd International Conference on Electronics Computer Technology, Kanyakumari.

AlGeddawy, T.; ElMaraghy, H. (2010): Assembly systems layout design model for delayed products differentiation, in: International Journal of Production Research, 48 (18), 5281–5305.

Anderson, B.; Hagen, C.; Reifel, J.; Stettler, E. (2006): Complexity: customization's evil twin, in: Strategy & Leadership, 34 (5), 19–27.

Armbruster, D.; Kieser, A. (2003): Jeder Mitarbeiter ein Unternehmer!? Wie Intrapreneurshipprogramme Mitarbeiter zwar nicht zu echten Unternehmern machen, aber doch zu höheren Leistungen anspornen können, in: Zeitschrift für Personalforschung, 17 (2), 151–175.

Arnold, U. (1997): Beschaffungsmanagement, 2nd edition, Stuttgart.

A.T. Kearney (2004): The Complexity Challenge: A Survey on Complexity Management Across the Supply Chain. Available at: http://atkearneyprocurementsolutions.com/knowledge/publications/2004/Complexity_Management_S.pdf (accessed: 20 May 2015).

Aurich, J.; Barbian, P.; Wagenknecht, C. (2003): Prozessmodule zur Gestaltung flexibilitätsgerechter Produktionssysteme, in: ZWF Zeitschrift für wirtschaftlichen Fabrikbetrieb, 98 (5), 214–218.

Aurich, J.; Wagenknecht, C. (2003): Bausteinbasierte Modellierung unternehmensübergreifender Produktionsprozesse, in: ZWF Zeitschrift für wirtschaftlichen Fabrikbetrieb, 98 (12), 661–665.

Aurich, J.; Grzegorski, A.; Lehmann, F. (2007): Management vielfaltsinduzierter Prozesskomplexität in globalen Netzwerken, in: Industrie Management, 23 (6), 13–16.

Aurich, J.; Grzegorski, A. (2008): Vielfaltsinduzierte Komplexität in Ingenieurprozessen: Gestaltung, Beherrschung und Verbesserung komplexer Ingenieurprozesse in Netzwerken global verteilter Entwicklungs- und Produktionsstandorte, in: ZWF Zeitschrift für wirtschaftlichen Fabrikbetrieb, 103 (5), 316–321.

Baldwin, C.; Clark, K. (2000): Design Rules: The Power of Modularity, Cambridge.

Battezzati, L.; Magnani, R. (2000): Supply chains for FMCG and industrial products in Italy: Practices and the advantages of postponement, in: International Journal of Physical Distribution & Logistics Management, 30 (5), 413–424.

Bauernhansl, T.; Schatz, A.; Jäger, J. (2014): Komplexität bewirtschaften – Industrie 4.0 und die Folgen: Neue Herausforderungen für sozio-technische Produktionssysteme, in: ZWF Zeitschrift für wirtschaftlichen Fabrikbetrieb, 109 (5), 347–350.

Baumberger, G. (2007): Methoden zur kundenspezifischen Produktdefinition bei individualisierten Produkten, München.

Bayer, T. (2010): Integriertes Variantenmanagement: Variantenkostenbewertung mit faktoranalytischen Komplexitätstreibern, München.

Beckmann, H. (2012): Prozessorientiertes Supply Chain Engineering: Strategien, Konzepte und Methoden zur modellbasierten Gestaltung, Wiesbaden.

Beetz, R.; Grimm, A.; Eickmeyer, T. (2008): Die Strategie der Integrierten Wertschöpfungskette zur Anlaufsteuerung bei der Vorserienlogistik der AUDI AG, in: Schuh, G.; Stölzle, W.; Straube, F. (Eds.): Anlaufmanagement in der Automobilindustrie erfolgreich umsetzen: Ein Leitfaden für die Praxis, Wiesbaden.

Beimborn, D.; Gleisner, F.; Joachim, N; Hackethal, A. (2009): The Role of Process Standardization in Achieving IT Business Value, in: Proceedings of the 42nd Hawaii International Conference on System Sciences, Waikoloa, Hawaii.

Benettm, S. (1999): Komplexitätsmanagement in der Investitionsgüterindustrie, Bamberg.

Bick, W.; Drexl-Wittbecker, S. (2008): Komplexität reduzieren: Konzept. Methoden. Praxis., Stuttgart.

Biedermann, W.; Lindemann, U. (2013): Structural Complexity Management in Sustainable Engineering, in: Kauffmann, J.; Lee, K.-M. (Eds.): Handbook of Sustainable Engineering, 2nd edition, Dordrecht.

Bittermann, H.-J. (2014): Kurz, aber effektiv, in: Automobil Industrie, 3, 58–59.

Blecker, T.; Friedrich, G.; Kaluza, B.; Abdelkafi, N.; Kreutler, G. (2005): Information and Management Systems for Product Customization, Boston.

Blecker, T.; Abdelkafi, N. (2006a): Complexity in Variety-Rich-Production Systems, in: Blecker, T.; Kesten, W. (Eds.): Complexity Management in Supply Chains: Concepts, Tools and Methods, Berlin.

Blecker, T.; Abdelkafi, N. (2006b): Complexity and variety in mass customization systems: analysis and recommendations, in: Management Decision, 44 (7), 908–929.

Blecker, T.; Abdelkafi, N. (2006c): Modularity and Delayed Product Differentiation in Assemble-To-Order Systems, in: Blecker, T.; Friedrich, G. (Eds.): Mass Customization: Challenges and Solutions, New-York.

Bliss, C. A. (1998): Komplexitätsreduktion und Komplexitätsbeherrschung bei der Schmitz-Anhänger Fahrzeugbau-Gesellschaft mbH, in: Adam, D. (Ed.): Komplexitätsmanagement, Wiesbaden.

Bliss, C. A. (2000): Management von Komplexität: Ein integrierter, systemtheoretischer Ansatz zur Komplexitätsreduktion, Wiesbaden.

Blockus, M.-O. (2010): Komplexität in Dienstleistungsunternehmen: Komplexitätsformen, Kosten- und Nutzenwirkungen, empirische Befunde und Managementimplikationen, Wiesbaden.

Böckle, G. (2005): Introduction to Software Product Line Engineering, in: Pohl, K.; Böckle, G.; van der Linden, F. (Eds.): Software Product Line Engineering: Foundations, Principles, and Techniques, Berlin.

Böhmann, T.; Krcmar, H. (2005): Einfach besser? Zur Anwendbarkeit des industriellen Komplexitätsmanagements auf variantenreiche IT-Dienstleistungen, in: Ferst, O.-K.; Sinz, E.-J.; Eckert, S.; Isselhorst, T. (Eds.): Wirtschaftsinformatik 2005: eEconomy, eGovernment, eSociety, Heidelberg.

Bohn, M. (2009): Logistik im Kontext des ausländischen Markteintritts: Entwicklung von Gestaltungsempfehlungen für den ausländischen Markteintritt unter besonderer Berücksichtigung der Erfolgskomponente Logistik, Berlin.

Bohne, F. (1998): Komplexitätskostenmanagement in der Automobilindustrie: Identifizierung und Gestaltung vielfaltsinduzierter Kosten, Wiesbaden.

Boyksen, M.; Kotlik, L. (2013): Komplexitätscontrolling: Komplexität erkennen, bewerten und optimieren, in: Controller Magazin, November/December, 48–52.

Braun, C. (2015): Komplexität interner Dienstleistungen: Konzeptualisierung, Messung und Integration in ein Wirkungsmodell, Wiesbaden.

Brosch, M.; Krause, D. (2011): Design for Supply Chain Requirements: An Approach to Detect the Capabilities to Postpone, in: Proceedings of the ASME 2011 International Design Engineering Technical Conferences & Computers and Information in Engineering Conference IDETC/CIE 2011, Washington, USA.

Buchholz, M. (2012): Theorie der Variantenvielfalt: Ein produktions- und absatzwirtschaftliches Erklärungsmodell, Wiesbaden.

Cambridge Dictionary (2017): Single. Available at: https://dictionary.cambridge.org/de/worterbuch/englisch/single (accessed: 26 November 2017).

Caniato, F.; Crippa, L.; Größler, A. (2010): Product Complexity and Modularity as Drivers of New Product Development and Supply Chain Management Integration?, in: GIC-Prodesc Proceedings of the German-Italian Conference on the Interdependencies between New Product Development and Supply Chain Management in Hamburg, Hamburg.

Cao, H.; Zhang, H.; Liu, M. (2011): Global Modular Production Network: from System Perspective, in: Procedia Engineering, 23, 786–791.

Child, P.; Dietrichs, R.; Sanders, F.-H.; Wisniowski, S. (1991a): SMR Forum: The Management of Complexity, in: Sloan Management Review, 33 (1), 73–80.

Child, P.; Dietrichs, R.; Sanders, F.-H.; Wisniowski, S. (1991b): The management of complexity, in: The McKinsey Quarterly, 28 (4), 52–69.

Chronéer, D.; Bergquist, B. (2012): Managerial Complexity in Process Industrial R&D Projects: A Swedish Study, in: Project Management Journal, 43 (2), 21–36.

Coenenberg, A.; Prillmann, M. (1995): Erfolgswirkungen der Variantenvielfalt und Variantenmanagement: Empirische Erkenntnisse aus der Elektronikindustrie, in: ZfB Zeitschrift für Betriebswirtschaft, 65 (11), 1231–1253.

Crichton, E.; Edgar, D. (1995): Managing complexity for competitive advantage: an IT perspective, in: International Journal of Contemporary Hospitality Management 7 (2/3), 12–18.

Dehnen, K. (2004): Strategisches Komplexitätsmanagement in der Produktentwicklung, Hamburg.

Dictionary (2017): Approach. Available at: http://www.dictionary.com/browse/approach (accessed: 26 November 2017).

Dombkins, D. (1997): PROJAM: The Management of Complex Projects and Programs, Deakin University.

Dombrowski, U.; Herrmann, C.; Lacker, T.; Sonnentag, S. (2009): Modernisierung kleiner und mittlerer Unternehmen: Ein ganzheitliches Konzept, Berlin.

Duerre, M.; Steger, U. (2010): Empirical study of industry complexity, in: Schwand, A.; Franklin, J. (Eds.): Logistics: The Backbone for Managing Complex Organizations, Bern.

Durst, M. (2007): Wertorientiertes Management von IT-Architekturen, Wiesbaden.

Ehrlenspiel, K. (1995): Integrierte Produktentwicklung: Methoden für Prozessorganisation, Produkterstellung und Konstruktion, München.

Ehrlenspiel, K.; Kiewert, A.; Lindemann, U.; Mörtl, M. (2014): Kostengünstig Entwickeln und Konstruieren: Kostenmanagement bei der integrierten Produktentwicklung, 7th edition, Berlin.

Eilmann, J.; Nyhuis, P. (2012): Modellierung von Prozesskosten in der Beschaffung: Integration von Logistikkosten in eine modellbasierte Methodik zur Bewertung und Gestaltung der Beschaffung, in: ZWF Zeitschrift für wirtschaftlichen Fabrikbetrieb, 107 (9), 657–661.

Eitelwein, O.; Malz, S.; Weber, J. (2012): Erfolg durch Modularisierung, in: Zeitschrift für Controlling & Management, Sonderheft 2, 79–84.

ElMaraghy, W.; ElMaraghy, H.; Tomiyama, T.; Monostori, L. (2012): Complexity in engineering design and manufacturing. CIRP Annals – Manufacturing Technology, 61, 793–814.

El Haouzi, H.; Thomas, A.; Pétin, J. (2008): Contribution to reusability and modularity of manufacturing systems simulation models: Application to distributed control simulation within DFT context, in: International Journal of Production Economics, 112, 48–61.

ElMaraghy, H.; ElMaraghy, W. (2014): Variety, Complexity and Value Creation, in: Zaeh, M. (Ed.): Enabling Manufacturing Competitiveness and Economic Sustainability: Proceedings of the 5th International Conference on Changeable, Agile, Reconfigurable and Virtual Production (CARV 2013) in Munich, October 6–9, Cham.

Espinosa, A.; Harnden, R.; Walker, J. (2007): Beyond hierarchy: a complexity management perspective, in: Kybernetes, 36 (3/4), 333–347.

Ethiraj, S.; Levinthal, D. (2004): Modularity and Innovation in Complex Systems, in: Management Science, 50 (2), 159–173.

Eversheim, W.; Schenke, F.-B.; Warnke, L. (1998): Komplexität im Unternehmen verringern und beherrschen – Optimale Gestaltung von Produkten und Produktionssystemen, in: Adam, D. (Ed.): Komplexitätsmanagement, Wiesbaden.

Fettke, P.; Loos, P. (2005): Der Beitrag der Referenzmodellierung zum Business Engineering, in: HMD – Praxis der Wirtschaftsinformatik, 241, 18–26.

Fink, A. (2014): Conducting Research Literature Reviews: From the Internet to Paper, Los Angeles, USA.

Fisher, M.; Ramdas, K.; Ulrich, K. (1999): Component Sharing in the Management of Product Variety: A Study of Automotive Braking Systems, in: Management Science, 45 (3), 297–315.

Fischer, T. (1993): Variantenvielfalt und Komplexität als betriebliche Kostenbestimmungsfaktoren?, in: krp Kostenmanagement, 37 (1), 27–31.

Fleck, A. (1995): Hybride Wettbewerbsstrategien: Zur Synthese von Kosten- und Differenzierungsvorteilen, Wiesbaden.

Flieder, K. (2010): Mit RFID und BPM zum ereignisgesteuerten Unternehmen, in: ZWF Zeitschrift für wirtschaftlichen Fabrikbetrieb, 105 (5), 494–502.

Flieder, K. (2012): Modularisierung in Automotive und SOA, in: Productivity Management, 17 (1), 32–35.

Flynn, B.; Sakakibara, S.; Schroeder, R.; Bates, K.; Flynn, E. (1990): Empirical Research Methods in Operations Management, in: Journal of Operations Management, 9 (2), 250–284.

Franke, H.-J.; Firchau, N. (2001): Variantenvielfalt in Produkten und Prozessen: Erfahrungen, Methoden und Instrumente zur erfolgreichen Beherrschung, in: VDI-Gesellschaft (Ed.): Variantenvielfalt in Produkten und Prozessen: Erfahrungen, Methoden und Instrumente, Düsseldorf.

Franke, H.-J.; Hesselbach, J.; Huch, B.; Firchau, N. (2002): Variantenmanagement in der Einzel- und Kleinserienfertigung, München.

Freund, M.; Braune, A. (2012): Multi-Platform User Interface Models by means of the Abstract Platform Concept, in: Proceedings of the International Conference on Industrial Technology 2012, Athens, Greece.

Friedrich, T. (2004): Strategische Produktprogrammplanung bei variantenreichen Produkten, Bamberg.

Gabath, C. (2008): Gewinngarant Einkauf: Nachhaltige Kostensenkung ohne Personalabbau, Wiesbaden.

Gausemeier, J.; Riepe, B. (2005): Komplexitätsbeherrschung in den frühen Phasen der Produktentwicklung, in: Industrie Management, 16 (5), 54–58.

Gebhardt, N.; Bahns, T.; Krause, D. (2014): An example of visually supported design of modular product families, in: Procedia CIRP, 21, 75–80.

Geimer, H. (2005): Komplexitätsmanagement globaler Supply Chains, in: HMD Praxis der Wirtschaftsinformatik, 42, 38–46.

Gemünden, H. G.; Schoper, Y.-G. (2014): Future Trends in Project Management: First Results of the New Expert Survey 2014, in: Project Management aktuell, 5, 6–16.

Gepp, M.; Foehr, M.; Vollmar, J.; Schertl, A.; Schaeffler, T. (2015): System integration in modularization and standardization programs, in: Proceedings of the 9th Annual IEEE Systems Conference (SysCon), Vancouver, Canada.

Gerberich, C. (2004): Managen von Komplexität und Dynamik – eine große Herausforderung für heutige Unternehmen, in: Maier, F. (Ed.): Komplexität und Dynamik als Herausforderung für das Management, Wiesbaden.

Gießmann, M. (2010): Komplexitätsmanagement in der Logistik – Kausalanalytische Untersuchung zum Einfluss der Beschaffungskomplexität auf den Logistikerfolg, Lohmar.

Gießmann, M.; Lasch, R. (2011): Komplexitätsmanagement in der Logistik: Empfehlungen für die praktische Durchführung und Umsetzung. Available at: http://www.gbv.de/dms/zbw/682216739.pdf (accessed: 20 May 2015).

Gomes, P.; Dahab, S. (2010): Bundling resources across supply chain dyads: The role of modularity and coordination capabilities, in: International Journal of Operations & Production Management, 30 (1), 57–74.

Göpfert, J. (1998): Modulare Produktentwicklung: Komplexitätsbewältigung durch die gemeinsame Modularisierung von Produkt und Entwicklungsorganisation, in: Franke, N.; Braun, C.-F. von (Eds.): Innovationsforschung und Technologiemanagement: Konzepte, Strategien, Fallbeispiele, Berlin.

Göpfert, I.; Schulz, M. (2013): Variantenmanagements als Bestandteil einer logistikgerechten Produktentwicklung – eine Untersuchung am Beispiel der Automobilindustrie, in: Göpfert, I.; Braun, D.; Schulz, M. (Eds.); Automobillogistik: Stand und Zukunftstrends, 2nd edition, Wiesbaden.

Göpfert, J.; Steinbrecher, M. (2001): Komplexitätsbeherrschung durch modulare Produktentwicklung, in: VDI-Gesellschaft Entwicklung Konstruktion Vertrieb (Ed.): Variantenvielfalt in Produkten und Prozessen: Erfahrungen, Methoden und Instrumente, Düsseldorf.

Götzfried, M. (2013): Managing Complexity Induced by Product-Variety in Manufacturing Companies: Complexity Evaluation and Integration in Decision-Making, Bamberg.

Gräßler, I. (2004): Kundenindividuelle Massenproduktion: Entwicklung, Vorbereitung der Herstellung, Veränderungsmanagement, Berlin.

Greitemeyer, J.; Ulrich, T. (2005): Umfassendes Komplexitätsmanagement – die optimale Komplexitätsbalance finden und kostengünstig halten. UNITY AG. Aailable at: http://unityag.de/fileadmin/files/Fachartikel/Komplexit_tsmanagement_lang_mitLogo.pdf (accessed: 20 May 2015).

Grimm, R.; Schuller, M.; Wilhelmer, R. (2014): Portfoliomanagement in Unternehmen: Leitfaden für Manager und Investoren, Wiesbaden.

Grösser, S. (2011): Projekte scheitern wegen dynamischer Komplexität: Qualitative Feedbackmodellierung zur Komplexitätsbewältigung, in: Project Management aktuell, 5, 18–25.

Grotkamp, S.; Franke, J. (2007): Produktstrukturierung bei hoher Variantenvielfalt, in: Industrie Management, 23 (6), 33–36.

Grübner, A. (2007): Bewältigung marktinduzierter Komplexität in der industriellen Fertigung: Theoretische Ansätze und empirische Ergebnisse des International Manufacturing Strategy Survey, Frankfurt am Main.

Grussenmeyer, R.; Blecker, T. (2013): Requirements for the design of a complexity management method in new product development of integral and modular products, in: International Journal of Engineering, Science and Technology, 5(2), 132–149.

Gumpinger, T.; Jonas, H.; Krause, D. (2009): New Approach for Lightweight Design: From Differential Design to Integration of Function, in: Proceedings of the International Conference on Engineering Design ICED '09, Standford, USA.

Haberfellner, R.; Nagel, P.; Becker, M.; Büchel, A.; Massow, H. (1999): Systems Engineering: Methodik und Praxis, Zürich.

Haf, H. (2001): Plattformbildung als Strategie zur Kostensenkung, in: VDI-Gesellschaft Entwicklung Konstruktion Vertrieb (Ed.): Variantenvielfalt in Produkten und Prozessen: Erfahrungen, Methoden und Instrumente, Düsseldorf.

Halman, J.; Hofer, A.; Vuuren, W. van (2003): Platform-Driven Development of Product Families: Linking Theory with Practice, in: Journal of Product Innovation Management, 20, 149–162.

Hanenkamp, N. (2004): Entwicklung des Geschäftsprozesses Komplexitätsmanagement in der kundenindividuellen Serienfertigung: Ein Beitrag zum Informationsmanagement in mehrdimensional modellierten Produktionssystemen, Aachen.

Hasenpusch, J.; Moos, C.; Schwellbach, U. (2004): Komplexität als Aktionsfeld industrieller Unternehmen, in: Maier, F. (Ed.): Komplexität und Dynamik als Herausforderung für das Management, Wiesbaden.

Haumann, M. (2011): Variantenmanagement in der Refabrikation, Aachen.

Heckmann, P. (2006): Wie gesund ist Ihre Supply Chain, in: Logistik Heute, 9, 46–48.

Helfrich, C. (2009): Das Prinzip Einfachheit: Reduzieren Sie die Komplexität, Renningen

Hellström. M.; Wikström, K. (2005): Project business concepts based on modularity – improved manoeuvrability through unstable structures, in: International Journal of Project Management, 23, 392–397.

Hellwig, M.; Sypli, V. (2014): Leit- und Sicherungstechnik mit drahtloser Datenübertragung: Sicherheit im drahtlosen Bahnbetrieb, Qualität in der Informationsverarbeitung, Methoden der Qualitätssicherung, Wiesbaden.

Herrmann, A.; Seilheimer, C. (2002): Variantenmanagement, in: Albers, S.; Herrmann, A. (Eds.): Handbuch Produktmanagement: Strategieentwicklung – Produktplanung – Organisation – Kontrolle, Wiesbaden.

Herrmann, C.; Reinhart, G.; Schuh, G.; Spengler, T.; Vietor, T.; Drescher, B.; Gäde, M.; Klein, T.; Richter, T.; Schönemann, M.; Spiegelberger, B.; Vogels, T. (2015): Strategien, Methoden und Werkzeuge für die Entwicklung mechatronischer Produkte: Ergebnisse und Synergiepotenziale aus den Forschungsprojekten GiB-Wert, MEPROMA und SynProd, in: ZWF Zeitschrift für wirtschaftlichen Fabrikbetrieb, 110 (5), 251–255.

Herzwurm, G. (2000): Kundenorientierte Softwareproduktentwicklung, Wiesbaden.

Hesse, L.; Fetzer, H.-J.; Warnecke, G. (2002): Plattformkonzepte – Herausforderung an die Unternehmensorganisation, in: ZWF Zeitschrift für wirtschaftlichen Fabrikbetrieb, 97 (10), 487–491.

Heydari, B.; Dalili, K. (2012): Optimal System's Complexity: An Architecture Perspective, in: Procedia Computer Science, 12, 63–68.

Hirzel, M. (1993): Komplexmanagement in der dynamischen Organisation, in: Hirzel Leder & Partner (Eds.): Synergiemanagement: Komplexität beherrschen – Verbundvorteile erzielen, Wiesbaden.

Hoek, R. van (2001): The rediscovery of postponement a literature review and directions for research, in: Journal of Operations Management, 19, 161–184.

Hofer, A. (2001): Management von Produktfamilien: Wettbewerbsvorteile durch Plattformen, Wiesbaden.

Homburg, C.; Daum, D. (1997): Wege aus der Komplexitätskostenfalle, in: ZWF Zeitschrift für wirtschaftlichen Fabrikbetrieb, 92 (7–8), 333–337.

Hoole, R. (2005): Five ways to simplify your supply chain, in: Supply Chain Management: An International Journal, 10 (1), 3–6.

Huang, Y.-Y.; Li, S.-J. (2008): Suitable application situations of different postponement approaches: Standardization vs. modularization, in: Journal of Manufacturing System, 27, 111–122.

Hyötyläinen, M.; Möller, K. (2007): Service packaging: key to successful provisioning of ICT business solutions, in: Journal of Services Marketing, 21 (5), 304–312.

Imori, M.; Shimamura, K.; Anraku, K.; Inaba, S.; Nozaki, M.; Yamagami, T.; Yoshida, T. (1990): Modular Construction of a Bolloon-Borne Apparatus, in: Proceedings of the IEEE Nuclear Science Symposium Conference Record, Arlington, USA.

Jacobs, M.; Swink, M. (2011): Product portfolio architectural complexity and operational performance: Incorporating the roles of learning and fixed assets, in: Journal of Operations Management, 29, 677–691.

Jäger, J. M.; Kluth, A.; Sauer, M.; Schatz, A. (2013): Komplexitätsbewirtschaftung: Die neue Managementdisziplin in Produktion und Supply Chain, in: ZWF Zeitschrift für wirtschaftlichen Fabrikbetrieb, 108 (5), 341–343.

Jäger, J.; Kluth, A.; Schatz, A.; Bauernhansl, T. (2014): Complexity patterns in the advanced Complexity Management of value networks, in: Procedia CIRP, 17, 645–650.

Jagersma, P. (2008): The hidden cost of doing business, in: Business Strategy Series, 9 (5), 238–242.

Jensen, T. C.; Bekdik, B.; Thuesen, C. (2014): Understanding Complex Construction Systems Through Modularity, in: Brunoe, T. D.; Nielsen, K.; Joergensen, K. A.; Taps, S. B. (Eds.): Proceedings of the 7th World Conference on Mass Customization, Personalization, and Co-Creation (MCPC 2014): Twenty Years of Mass Customization – Towards New Frontiers, Cham.

Jeschke, A. (1997): Beitrag zur wirtschaftlichen Bewertung von Standardisierungs-Maßnahmen in der Einzel- und Kleinserienfertigung durch die Konstruktion, Braunschweig.

Jina, J.; Bhattacharya, A.; Walton, A. (1997): Applying lean principles for high product variety and low volumes: some issues and propositions, in: Logistics Information Management, 10 (1), 5–13.

Joergensen, S.; Schou, C.; Madsen, O. (2014): Developing Modular Manufacturing Architectures – An Industrial Case Report, in: Zaeh, M. (Ed.) Enabling Manufacturing Competitiveness and Economic Sustainability: Proceedings of the 5th International Conference on Changeable, Agile, Reconfigurable and Virtual Production (CARV 2013) in Munich, October 6–9, Cham.

Junge, M. (2003): Modularisierung in der Automobilindustrie: Neu Trends erfordern neue Methoden, in: Junge, K.; Mildenberger, U.; Wittmann, J. (Eds.): Perspektiven und Facetten der Produktionswirtschaft: Schwerpunkte der Mainzer Forschung, Wiesbaden.

Kaiser, A. (1995): Integriertes Variantenmanagement mit Hilfe der Prozesskostenrechnung, Hallstadt.

Katzke, U.; Fischer, K.; Vogel-Heuser, B. (2003): Entwicklung und Evaluation eines Modells für modulare Automatisierung im Anlagenbau, in: Holleczek, P.; Vogel-Heuser, B. (Eds.): Verteilte Echtzeitsysteme, Berlin.

Kampker, A.; Maue, A.; Deutskens, C.; Förstmann, R. (2014): Standardization and Innovation: Dissolving the Contradiction with Modular Production Architectures, in: Proceedings of the 4th International Electric Drives Production Conference (EDPC), Nuremberg, Germany.

Keil, M. (2010): Die Reduktion von Komplexität: Hilfestellung für den Management-Alltag, in: Handbuch der Aus- und Weiterbildung, August, 1–18.

Kersten, W. (2011): Je komplexer, desto teurer und risikoreicher, in: io management, September/October, 14-19.

Kersten, W.; Hülle, J.; Möller, K.; Lammers, T. (2009): Kostenorientierte Analyse der Modularisierung, in: ZWF Zeitschrift für wirtschaftlichen Fabrikbetrieb, 104(12), 1136–1141.

Kersten, W.; Möller, K.; Sedlmeier, L.; Skirde, H. (2012): Analyzing the Cost Effects of Modularity – Requirements for the Development of a Methodology, in: Kersten, W.; Blecker, T.; Ringle, M. (Eds.): Managing the Future Supply Chain: Current Concepts and Solutions for Reliability and Robustness, Lohmar.

Kesper, H. (2012): Gestaltung von Produktvariantenspektren mittels matrixbasierter Methoden, München.

Keuper, F. (2004): Kybernetische Simultaneitätsstrategie: Systemtheoretisch-kybernetische Navigation im Effektivitäts-Effizienz-Dilemma, Berlin.

Keuper, F. (2014): Strategische Komplexitätssteuerung als Herausforderung für den CEO - eine systemtheoretisch-kybernetische Herangehensweise, in: Keuper, F.; Sauter, R. (Eds.): Unternehmenssteuerung in der produzierenden Industrie: Konzepte und Best Practices, Wiesbaden.

Kieviet, A. (2014): Implications of Additive Manufacturing on Complexity: Management within Supply Chains in a Production, Louisville, USA.

Kim, J.; Wilemon, D. (2009): An empirical investigation of complexity and its management in new product development, in: Technology Analysis & Strategic Management, 21 (4), 547–564.

Kim, J.; Wilemon, D. (2012): Complexity and the multiple impacts of new product development: Results from a field study, in: International Journal of Innovation and Technology Management, 9 (6.

Kippels, D. (1996): Entwicklung, Produktion und Verwaltung wachsen zusammen: Die Fabrik von morgen wird zum Innovationszentrum, in: VDI Nachrichten, 9, p. 3.

Kirchhof, R. (2003): Ganzheitliches Komplexitätsmanagement: Grundlagen und Methodik des Umgangs mit Komplexität im Unternehmen, Wiesbaden.

Klauke, A.; Schreiber, W.; Weißner, R. (2005): Neue Produktstrukturen erfordern angepasste Fabrikstrukturen, in: Wiendahl, H.-P.; Nofen, D.; Klußmann, J.; Breitenbach, F. (Eds.): Planung modularer Fabriken: Vorgehen und Beispiele aus der Praxis, München.

Klein, C. (2013): Raus aus dem IT-Dickicht, in: Automobil Produktion, Oktober 2013, 80–81.

Klepsch, B. (2004): Komplementäre Produkt- und Fabrikmodularisierung am Beispiel der Automobilindustrie, Düsseldorf.

Klinkner, R.; Risse, J. (2002): Time-to-Market-Management im Maschinenbau, in: Industrie Management, 18 (5), 23–26.

Klinkner, R.; Mayer, A.; Thom, A. (2005): Modulare Logistik: Ein Lösungskonzept zum Management von Komplexität in dynamischen Netzwerken, in: Industrie Management, 21 (5), 33–66.

Klug, F. (2010): Logistikmanagement in der Automobilindustrie: Grundlagen der Logistik im Automobilbau, Heidelberg.

Kluth, A.; Jäger, J.; Schatz, A.; Bauernhansl, T. (2014a): Evaluation of Complexity Management Systems – Systematical and Maturity-Based Approach, in: Procedia CIRP, 17, 224–229.

Kluth, A.; Jäger, J.; Schatz, A.; Bauernhansl, T. (2014b): Method for a Systematic Evaluation of advanced Complexity Management Maturity, in: Procedia CIRP, 19, 69–74.

Koch, M.; Renner, N. (2014): Gestaltung innovativer Baukasten- und Wertschöpfungssysteme: GiBWert – Wirtschaftliche Bewertung, in: ZWF Zeitschrift für wirtschaftlichen Fabrikbetrieb, 109 (12), 952–955.

Komorek, C. (1998): Integrierte Produktentwicklung: Der Entwicklungsprozess in mittelständischen Unternehmen der metallverarbeitenden Serienfertigung, München.

Königsreuther, P. (2015): Mit dem Faserverbund-Event des Jahres in die Adventszeit, in: MM Maschinenmarkt, 47, 32–33.

Köster, O. (1998): Komplexitätsmanagement in der Industrie: Kundennähe und Effizienz in der Leistungserstellung, Wiesbaden.

Koppenhagen, F. (2014): Modulare Produktarchitekturen – Komplexitätsmanagement in der frühen Phase der Produktentwicklung, in: Schoeneberg, K.-P. (Ed.): Komplexitätsmanagement in Unternehmen: Herausforderungen im Umgang mit Dynamik, Unsicherheit und Komplexität meistern, Wiesbaden.

Koppik, R.; Meier, M. (2009): F&E-Produktivitätssteigerung – mit Entwicklungsmanagement aus der Krise, in: ZWF Zeitschrift für wirtschaftlichen Fabrikbetrieb, 104 (12), 1172–1175.

Korreck, A. (2002): Methodik zur markt- und kostenorientierten Variantenplanung, Aachen.

Krause, F.-L.; Franke, H.-J.; Gausemeier, J. (2007): Innovationspotenziale in der Produktentwicklung, München.

Krieg, U. (2015): Regeln für schlanke Prozesse: Fünf Erfolgsfaktoren für ein Lean Supply Chain Management, in: ZulieferMarkt, Oktober 2015, 90–91.

Kroker, J.; Brüggemann, C.; Eilert, U.; Koschorrek, R. (2005): Zukünftige Ansätze für modulare Karosseriestrukturen, in: Gesamtzentrum für Verkehr Braunschweig e.V. (Ed.) Proceedings of the 2nd Symposium Fascination of Autobody in Braunschweig January 25, Braunschweig.

Krumm, S.; Schopf, K.; Rennekamp, M. (2014): Komplexitätsmanagement in der Automobilindustrie: optimaler Fit von Vielfalt am Markt, Produktstruktur, Wertstrom und Ressourcen, in: Ebel, B.; Hofer, M. (Eds.): Automotive Management: Strategie und Marketing in der Automobilwirtschaft, 2nd edition, Berlin.

Kruse, M.; Ripperda, S.; Krause, D. (2015): Platform Concept Development within the Integrated PKT-Approach, in: Proceedings of the 20th International Conference on Engineering Design ICED15, Milano, Italy.

Lammers, T. (2012): Komplexitätsmanagement für Distributionssysteme: Konzeption eines strategischen Ansatzes zur Komplexitätsbewertung und Ableitung von Gestaltungsempfehlungen, Lohmar.

Langlois, R. (2002): Modularity in technology and organization, in: Journal of Economic Behavior & Organization, 49, 19–37.

Laqua, I. (2008): Shop-floor IT – Wer sie braucht und was sie leistet!, in: PPS Management, 13 (1), 27–30.

Lasch, R. (2014): Strategisches und operatives Logistikmanagement: Prozesse, Wiesbaden.

Lasch, R.; Gießmann, M. (2009a): Ganzheitliche Ansätze zum Komplexitätsmanagement: Eine kritische Würdigung aus Sicht der Beschaffungslogistik, in: Bogaschewsky, R., et al. (Eds.): Supply Management Research: Aktuelle Forschungsergebnisse 2008, Wiesbaden.

Lasch, R.; Gießmann, M. (2009b): Qualitäts- und Komplexitätsmanagement: Parallelitäten und Interaktionen zweiter Managementdisziplinen, in: Hünerberg, R.; Mann, A. (Eds.): Ganzheitliche Unternehmensführung in dynamischen Märkten, Wiesbaden.

Lanza, G.; Peters, S.; Arndt, T.; Häfner, B.; Stricker, N. (2014): Die Produktion im Jahr 2025: Ein Zukunftsbild, in: Industrie Management, 30 (6), 64–66.

Ley, W.; Hofer, A. (1999): Produktplattformen: Ein strategischer Ansatz zur Beherrschung der Variantenvielfalt, in: io Management, 68 (7/8), 56–60.

Li, Y.; Li, L.; Liu, Y.; Wang, L. (2005): Linking management control system with product development and process decisions to cope with environment complexity, in: International Journal of Production Research, 43 (12), 2577–2591.

Lindemann, M.; Baumberger, G. (2006): Individualisierte Produkte, in: Lindemann, U.; Reichwald, R.; Zäh, M. (Eds.): Individualisierte Produkte – Komplexität beherrschen in Entwicklung und Produktion, Berlin.

Lindemann, M.; Maurer, M. (2006): Entwicklung und Strukturplanung individualisierter Produkte, in: Lindemann, U.; Reichwald, R.; Zäh, M. (Eds.): Individualisierte Produkte – Komplexität beherrschen in Entwicklung und Produktion, Berlin.

Lindemann, U.; Maurer, M.; Braun, T. (2009): Structural Complexity Management: An Approach for the Field of Product Design, Berlin.

Lübke, E. (2007): Lebenszyklusorientiertes Produktstrukturmanagement: Eine theoretische Untersuchung, München.

Luger, T.; Herrmann, C.; Steinborn, J.; Walther, G.; Spengler, T. (2008): Wertschöpfung durch Mehrfachnutzung: Potenziale, Herausforderungen, Lösungen, in: ZWF Zeitschrift für wirtschaftlichen Fabrikbetrieb, 103 (9), 602–606.

Madu, C. N. (1998): An empirical assessment of quality: research considerations, in: International Journal of Quality Science, 3 (4), 348–355.

Mahoney, R. M. (1997): Integrating Manufacturing Test Strategy with Manufacturing Production Strategy, in: Proceedings of the IEEE Systems Readiness Technology Conference Autotestcon '97, Anaheim, California, USA.

Manuj, I.; Sahin, F. (2011): A model of supply chain and supply chain decision-making complexity, in: International Journal of Physical Distribution & Logistics Management, 41 (5), 511–549.

Marshall, R. (1998): Design Modularisation: A Systems Engineering Based Methodology for Enhanced Product Realisation, Loughborough University.

Marshall, R.; Leaney, P. (1999): A systems engineering approach to product modularity. Proceedings of the Institution of Institution of Mechanical Engineers, Part B, in: Journal of Engineering Manufacture, 213 (8), 847–851.

Martensson, P.; Zenkert, D.; Akermo, M. (2015): Effects on manufacturing constraints on the cost and weight efficiency of integral and differential automotive composite structures, in: Composite Structures, 134, 572–578.

Marti, M. (2007): Complexity Management: Optimizing Architecture of Industrial Products, Wiesbaden.

Mattila, M. (2014): Managing Increasing Technological Complexity: Delivering Large System Products, in: Slepniov, D.; Waehrens, B.; Johansen, J. (Eds.): Global Operations Networks: Exploring New Perspectives and Agendas, Aalborg.

Mattsson, S.; Karlsson, M.; Fast-Berglund, A.; Hansson, I. (2014): Managing production complexity by empowering workers: six cases, in: Procedia CIRP, 17, 212–217.

Maune, G. (2001): Möglichkeiten des Komplexitätsmanagements für Automobilhersteller auf Basis IT-gestützter durchgängiger Systeme, Paderborn.

Mayer, A. (2007): Modularisierung der Logistik: Ein Gestaltungsmodell zum Management von Komplexität in der industriellen Logistik, Berlin.

Mayer, B.; Volk, F. (2013): 1800 Maßnahmen mit Einsparpotenzial, in: Automobil Produktion, Juli 2013, 16–18.

Mayer, B. (2014): Queen observiert JLRs Antrieb(e), in: Automobil Produktion, Dezember 2014, 26–27.

Mayer, H. (2013): Interview und schriftliche Befragung: Grundlagen und Methoden empirischer Sozialforschung, 6th edition, München.

Meffert, H. (1992): Marketingforschung und Käuferverhalten, 2nd edition, Wiesbaden.

Meffert, H.; Burmann, C.; Kirchgeorg, M. (2012): Marketing: Grundlangen marktorientierter Unternehmensführung, 11th edition, Wiesbaden.

Meier, B.; Bojarski, S. (2013): Ganzheitliches Modell zur Bewältigung vielfaltsinduzierter Komplexität, in: ZWF Zeitschrift für wirtschaftlichen Fabrikbetrieb, 108 (7), 547–551.

Meijer, B. (1998): To manage or not to manage complexity, in: IEMC '98 Proceedings of the International Conference on Engineering and Technology Management: Pioneering New Technologies: Management Issues and Challenges, in the Third Millennium, San Juan, Puerto Rico, USA.

Meyer, C. M. (2007): Integration des Komplexitätsmanagements in den strategischen Führungsprozess der Logistik, Bern, Switzerland.

Miragliotta, G.; Perona, M.; Pertioli-Staudacher, A. (2002): Complexity Management in the Supply Chain: Theoretical Model and Empirical Investigation in the Italian Household Appliance Industry, in: Seuring, S. et al. (Eds.): Cost Management in Supply Chains, Berlin.

Meyer, M.; Walber, B.; Schmidt, C. (2006): Produktionsplanung und -steuerung (PPS) in temporären Produktionsnetzwerken des Maschinen- und Anlagenbaus, in: Schuh, G. (Ed.): Produktionsplanung und -steuerung: Grundlagen, Gestaltung und Konzepte, 3rd edition, Berlin.

Moody, D. (2002): Empirical Research Methods. Available at: https://de.scribd.com/document/189136499/What-is-Empirical-Research1 (accessed: 15 August 2017).

Mogilner, C.; Rudnick, T.; Iyengar, S. (2008): The Mere Categorization Effect: How the Presence of Categories Increases Choosers' Perceptions of Assortment Variety and Outcome Satisfaction, in: Journal of Consumer Research, 35 (2), 202–215.

Möller, K.; Hülle, J.; Kahle, S. (2011): Kennzahlencockpits zur Steuerung und zum Monitoring der Standardisierung, in: ZWF Zeitschrift für wirtschaftlichen Fabrikbetrieb, 106 (10), 741–745.

Muffatto, M. (1999): Introducing a platform strategy in product development, in: International Journal of Production Economics, 60–61, 145–153.

Mühlenbruch, H. (2004): Technologie, in: Wiendahl, H.-P.; Gerst, D.; Keunecke, L. (Eds.): Variantenbeherrschung in der Montage: Konzept und Praxis der flexiblen Produktionsendstufe, Berlin.

Müller, M. (2005): Die Koordination von Supply Chains – eine transaktionskostentheoretische Untersuchung, in: Schmalenbachs Zeitschrift für betriebswirtschaftliche Forschung ZfbF, 57, 717–739.

Nagarur, N.; Azeem, A. (1999): Impact of commonality and flexibility on manufacturing performance: A simulation study, in: International Journal of Production Economics, 60–61, 125–134.

Nagengast, L.; Heidemann, C.; Rudolph, T. (2013): Der kombinierte Einsatz von Sortimentsreduktion und Regalkategorisierung zur Sortimentsoptimierung – eine empirische Untersuchung aus Konsumenten- und Händlersicht, in: Schmalenbachs Zeitschrift für betriebswirtschaftliche Forschung ZfbF, 65 (8), 666–687.

Neff, T.; Junge, M.; Virt, W.; Hertel, G.; Bellmann, K. (2001): An Approach for Evaluation of Modular Vehicle Concepts in the area of conflict between Standardization and Differentiation, in: VDI-Gesellschaft Entwicklung Konstruktion Vertrieb (Ed.): Variantenvielfalt in Produkten und Prozessen: Erfahrungen, Methoden und Instrumente, Düsseldorf.

Newman, J. (2009): Complexity Reduction: Managing the complexity of global product development to enable component reuse, http://lup.lub.lu.se/luur/download?func=downloadFile&recordOId=1482388&fileOId=1482389 (accessed: 11 August 2015).

Olbrich, R.; Battenfeld, D. (2000): Komplexitätsmanagement aus Sicht des Marketing und der Kostenrechnung. Available at: https://www.fernuni-hagen.de/marketing/download/forschungsberichte/fb03_web.pdf (accessed: 20 May 2015).

Oxford Living Dictionaries (2017a): Approach. Available at: https://en.oxforddictionaries.com/definition/approach (accessed: 26 November 2017).

Oxford Living Dictionaries (2017b): Strategy. Available at: https://en.oxforddictionaries.com/definition/strategy (accessed: 26 November 2017).

Pels, H.; Wortmann, J.; Zwegers, A. (1997): Flexibility in manufacturing: An architectural point of view, in: Computers in Industry, 33, 271–283.

Pero, M.; Abdelkafi, N.; Sianesi, A.; Blecker, T. (2010): A framework for the alignment of new product development and supply chains, in: Supply Chain Management: An International Journal, 15 (2), 115–128.

Perona, M.; Miragliotta, G. (2004): Complexity management and supply chain performance assessment: A field study and a conceptual framework, in: International Journal of Production Economics, 90, 103–115.

Peters, N.; Hofstetter, J. (2008): Konzepte und Erfolgsfaktoren für Anlaufstrategien in Netzwerken der Automobilindustrie, in: Schuh, G.; Stölzle, W.; Straube, F. (Eds.): Anlaufmanagement in der Automobilindustrie erfolgreich umsetzen: Ein Leitfaden für die Praxis, Wiesbaden.

Picot, A.; Baumann, O. (2007): Modularität in der verteilten Entwicklung komplexer Systeme: Chancen, Grenzen, Implikationen, in: Journal für Betriebswirtschaft, 27 (3-4), 221–246.

Piller, F. (1998): Kundenindividuelle Massenproduktion: Die Wettbewerbsstrategie der Zukunft, München.

Piller, F. (2001): Mass Customization: Ein wettbewerbsstrategisches Konzept im Informationszeitalter, 2nd edition, Wiesbaden.

Piller, F.; Waringer, D. (1999): Modularisierung in der Automobilindustrie – neue Formen und Prinzipien: Modular Sourcing, Plattformkonzept und Fertigungssegmentierung als Mittel des Komplexitätsmanagements, Aachen.

Ploom, T.; Glaser, A.; Scheit, S. (2013): Platform based Approach for Automation of Workflows in a System of Systems, in: Proceedings of the 7th IEEE International Symposium on the Maintenance and Evolution of Service-Oriented and Cloud-Based Systems (MESOCA), Eindhoven, The Netherlands.

Ponn, J.; Lindemann, U. (2008): Konzeptentwicklung und Gestaltung technischer Produkte: Optimierte Produkte – systematisch von Anforderungen zu Konzepten, Berlin.

Prillmann, M. (1996): Management der Variantenvielfalt: Ein Beitrag zur handlungsorientierten Erfolgsfaktorenforschung im Rahmen einer empirischen Studie in der Elektroindustrie, Frankfurt am Main.

Prodoehl, H. (2005): Synaptisches Management: Strategische Unternehmensführung im 21. Jahrhundert, Wiesbaden.

Proff, H.; Proff, H. (2013): Dynamisches Automobilmanagement: Strategien für international tätige Automobilunternehmen im Übergang in die Elektromobilität, Wiesbaden.

Puhl, H. (1999): Komplexitätsmanagement: Ein Konzept zur ganzheitlichen Erfassung, Planung und Regelung der Komplexität in Unternehmensprozessen, Kaiserslautern.

Raab, A.; Poost, A.; Eichhorn, S. (2009): Marketingforschung: Ein praxisorientierter Leitfaden, Stuttgart.

Rafele, C.; Cagliano, A. (2008): A tool for managing complexity in logistic systems under mass customization. Available at: http://porto.polito.it/1676098/1/Rafele_Cagliano_2007.pdf (accessed: 28 March 2017).

Rall, K.; Dalhöfer, J. (2004): Komplexität indirekter Prozesse bei der Erstellung variantenreicher Produkte, in: ZWF Zeitschrift für wirtschaftlichen Fabrikbetrieb, 99 (11), 623–630.

Rapp, T. (1999): Produktstrukturierung: Komplexitätsmanagement durch modulare Produktstrukturen und -plattformen, Wiesbaden.

Redlich, T.; Wulfsberg, J.; Bruhns, F.-L. (2009): Neue Kooperationsmuster in Entwicklung und Produktion: Open Production, in: ZWF Zeitschrift für wirtschaftlichen Fabrikbetrieb, 104 (7–8), 552–559.

Reiners, F.; Sasse, A. (1999): Komplexitätskostenmanagement, in: Kostenrechnungspraxis krp: Zeitschrift für Controlling, Accounting & System-Anwendungen, 43 (4), 222–232.

Reiß, M. (1993): Komplexität beherrschen durch Orga-Tuning, in: Reiß, M. (Ed.): Komplexität meistern – Wettbewerbsfähigkeit sichern, Stuttgart.

Reiss, M. (2011): Komplexitätsmanagement als Grundlage wandlungsfähiger Produktionssysteme, in: Industrie Management, 27 (3), 77–81.

Renner, I. (2007): Methodische Unterstützung funktionsorientierter Baukastenentwicklung am Beispiel Automobil, München.

Rosenberg, O. (2002): Kostensenkung durch Komplexitätsmanagement, in: Franz, K.-P.; Kajüter, P. (Eds.): Kostenmanagement: Wertsteigerung durch systematische Kostensteuerung, Stuttgart.

Ruppert, T. (2007): Modularisierung des Verbrennungsmotors als strategische Option in der Motorenindustrie, Kassel.

Rüßler, M. (2012): Management von Variantenvielfalt: Steigerung der Produktivität durch prozessorientierte Planung, in: Productivity Management, 17 (5), 12–15.

Sanchez, R. (1996): Strategic Product Creation: Managing New Interactions of Technology, Markets, and Organizations, in: European Management Journal, 14 (2), 121–138.

Sanchez, R.; Mahoney, J. (1996): Modularity, Flexibility, and Knowledge Management in Product and Organization Design, in: Strategic Management Journal, 17, 63–76.

Schaefer, S. (1999): Product design partitions with complementary components, in: Journal of Economic Behavior & Organization, 38, 311–330.

Schaffer, J.; Schleich, H.; Scavarda, L.; Parry, G. (2008): Automotive Production: Product Variety and how Emerging Economics can avoid Problems of Industrialised Countries, in: Proceedings of the 16th GERPISA International Colloquium, Turin, Italy.

Schapiro, S.; Henry, M. (2012): Engineering Agile Systems through Architectural Modularity, in: Proceedings of the IEEE International Systems Conference SysCon 2012, Vancouver, Canada.

Schatz, A.; Schöllhammer, O.; Jäger, J. (2014): Ansatz zum Umgang mit Komplexität in Unternehmen: Risiken aufdecken, Chancen erkennen und Potenziale heben, in: Controlling – Zeitschrift für erfolgsorientierte Unternehmenssteuerung, 26 (12), 686–693.

Schawel, C.; Billing, F. (2012): Top 100 Management Tools: Das wichtigste Buch eines Managers: Von ABC-Analyse bis Zielvereinbarung, 4th edition, Wiesbaden.

Scheer, A.-W.; Boczanski, M.; Muth, M.; Schmitz, W.-G.; Segelbacher, U. (2006): Prozessorientiertes Product Lifecycle Management, Berlin.

Schoeller, N. (2009): Internationales Komplexitätsmanagement am Beispiel der Automobilindustrie, Aachen.

Schoeneberg, K.-P. (2014a): Komplexität – Einführung in die Komplexitätsforschung und Herausforderung für die Praxis, in: Schoeneberg, K.-P. (Ed.): Komplexitätsmanagement in Unternehmen: Herausforderungen im Umgang mit Dynamik, Unsicherheit und Komplexität meistern, Wiesbaden.

Schoeneberg, K.-P. (2014b): Komplexität zwischen wissenschaftlichem Forschungsverständnis und praktischer Umsetzung, in: Schoeneberg, K.-P. (Ed.): Komplexitätsmanagement in Unternehmen: Herausforderungen im Umgang mit Dynamik, Unsicherheit und Komplexität meistern, Wiesbaden.

Schönsleben, P. (2011): Integrales Logistikmanagement: Operations und Supply Chain Management innerhalb des Unternehmens und unternehmensübergreifend, 6th edition, Heidelberg.

Schott, P.; Horstmann, F.; Bodendorf, F. (2015): Context Specific Complexity Management – A recommendation model for optimal corporate complexity, in: International Journal of Business Science and Applied Management, 10 (2), 32–46.

Schuh, G. (1989): Gestaltung und Bewertung von Produktvarianten: Ein Beitrag zur systematischen Planung von Serienprodukten, Düsseldorf.

Schuh, G.; Schwenk, U.; Speth, C. (1998a): Komplexitätsmanagement im St. Galler Management-Konzept, in: io Management, 67 (3), 78–85.

Schuh, G.; Schwenk, U.; Speth, C. (1998b): Komplexitätsmanagement als Trade-off aus Scale and Scope, in: Thexis 15 (2), 134–135.

Schuh, G. (2005): Produktkomplexität managen: Strategien, Methoden, Tools, München.

Schuh, G.; Schwenk, U. (2001): Produktkomplexität managen: Strategien, Methoden, Tools, München.

Schuh, G.; Canales, F.; Kubosch, A.; Paulukuhn, L. (2005): Lean Innovation – Less Complexity: Steigerung von Effektivität und Effizienz in der FuE, in: Industrie Management, 21 (3), 21–24.

Schuh, G.; Schmidt, A.; Gottschalk, S.; Schöning, S.; Gulden, A.; Augustin, R.; Rauhut, M.; Zancul, E.; Ring, T. (2007a): Effizient, schnell und erfolgreich: Strategien im Maschinen- und Anlagenbau, Frankfurt am Main.

Schuh, G.; Deger, R.; Jung, M.; Meier, J.; Schöning, S. (2007b): Managing Complexity in Automotive Engineering: Ergebnisse der Studie, Aachen.

Schuh, G.; Arnoscht, J.; Rudolf, S. (2010): Integrated Development of Modular Product Platforms, in: Kocaoglu, D. F.; Anderson, T. R.; Daim, T. (Eds.): Proceedings of International Center for Management of Engineering and Technology PICMET, Portland, USA.

Schuh, G.; Wentzel, D.; Rudolf, S.; Erkin, A.; Gerlach, M.; Schaffrath, K. (2015): Schnittstellenmanagement in der Business-to-Business-Praxis: Wie Unternehmen interne und externe Komplexität managen, in: ZWF Zeitschrift für wirtschaftlichen Fabrikbetrieb, 110 (11), 694–697.

Schulte, C. (1992): Komplexitätsmanagement, in: Schulte, C. (Ed.): Effektives Kostenmanagement: Methoden und Implementierung, Stuttgart.

Schulz, C. (2014a): Systemtheorie und Kybernetik als Grundlagen der Modellierung und des Controllings von Komplexität, in: Schoeneberg, K.-P. (Ed.): Komplexitätsmanagement in Unternehmen: Herausforderungen im Umgang mit Dynamik, Unsicherheit und Komplexität meistern, Wiesbaden.

Schulz, M. (2014b): Logistikintegrierte Produktentwicklung: Eine zukunftsorientierte Analyse am Beispiel der Automobilindustrie, Wiesbaden.

Schulze, L.; Mansky, S.; Klimek, J. (2009): Logistics Management of Late Product Individualisation: Application in the Automotive Industry, in: LogForum, 5 (1), 1–11. Available at: http://www.logforum.net/pdf/5_1_4_09.pdf (accessed: 28 March 2017).

Schwenk-Willi, U. (2001): Integriertes Komplexitätsmanagement: Anleitung und Methodik für die produzierende Industrie auf Basis einer typologischen Untersuchung, Bamberg.

Seibertz, A.; Brandstätter, M.; Schreiber, K. (2013): Kompositionales Variantenmanagement – Ganzheitlicher Ansatz zur Komplexitätsbeherrschung im Systems Engineering Umfeld, in: Maurer, M.; Schulze, S.-O. (Eds.): Tag des Systems Engineering, München.

Shamsuzzoha, A.; Helo, P.; Kekäle, T. (2008): Literature Overview of Modularity in World Automotive Industries, in: Proceedings of the Portland International Conference on Management of Engineering & Technology PICMET '08, Portland, USA.

Shamsuzzoha, A. (2011): Modular product architecture for productivity enhancement, in: Business Process Management Journal, 17 (1), 21–41.

Shamsuzzoha, A.; Helo, P. (2011): Information dependencies within product architecture: prospects of complexity reduction, in: Journal of Manufacturing Technology Management, 22 (3), 314–329.

Siddique, Z.; Rosen, D. (2001): Identifying Common Platform Architecture for a Set of Similar Products, in: Proceedings of the 1st Interdisciplinary World Congress on Mass Customization and Personalization MCPC 2001, Hong Kong, China.

Simon, H. (1962): The architecture of complexity, in: Proceedings of the American Philosophical Society, 106 (6), 467–482.

Simpson, T. (2004): Product platform design and customization: Status and promise, in: Artificial Intelligence for Engineering Design, Analysis and Manufacturing, 18, 3–20.

Slamanig, M. (2011): Produktwechsel als Problem im Konzept der Mass Customization: Theoretische Überlegungen und empirische Befunde, Wiesbaden.

Spath, D.; Demuß, L. (2006): Entwicklung hybrider Produkte – Gestaltung materieller und immaterieller Leistungsbündel, in: Bullinger, H.-J.; Scheer, A.-W. (Eds.): Service Engineering: Entwicklung und Gestaltung innovativer Dienstleistungen, 2nd edition, Berlin.

Springer, R. (2005): Flexible Standardisierung am Beispiel der Automobilindustrie, in: Antoni, C.; Eyer, E. (Eds.): Das flexible Unternehmen: Digitale Fachbibliothek, Düsseldorf.

Stang, S.; Hesse, L.; Warnecke, G. (2002): Plattformkonzepte: Eine strategische Gratwanderung zwischen Standardisierung und Individualität, in: ZWF Zeitschrift für wirtschaftlichen Fabrikbetrieb, 97 (3), 110–115.

Steffen, D.; Gausemeier, J. (2007): Modularisierung mechatronischer Systeme, in: Industrie Management, 23 (6), 9–12.

Stephan, D. (2015): Das fehlende Puzzlestück, in: PROCESS, 6, 36–38.

Stirzel, M. (2010): Controlling von Entwicklungsprojekten: Dargestellt am Beispiel mechatronischer Produkte, Wiesbaden.

Straube, F.; Mayer, A. (2007): Modularisierung logistischer Systeme, in: Industrie Management, 23 (6), 53–55.

Straube, F.; Doch, S.; Huynh, T. (2007): Logistikstrategien für die globalen Produktionsstrukturen der Automobilindustrie, in: Industrie Management, 23 (1), 35–38.

Stuhler, H.; Ricken, V.; Diener, R. (2010): Aufbau und Anpassung der Motorsteuerungs-Software für Otto- und Dieselmotoren, in: Isermann, R. (Ed.): Elektronisches Management motorischer Fahrzeugantriebe: Elektronik, Modellbildung, Regelung und Diagnose für Verbrennungsmotoren, Getriebe und Elektroantriebe, Wiesbaden.

Tamaskar, S.; Neema, K.; DeLaurentis, D. (2014): Framework for measuring complexity of aerospace systems, in: Research in Engineering Design, 25, 125–137.

Terada, Y.; Murata, S. (2008): Automatic Modular Assembly System and its Distributed Control, in: The International Journal of Robotics Research, 27 (3–4), 445–462.

Theuer, H. (2015): Serienprodukte ganz individuell, in: Productivity, 20 (3), p. 14.

Thiebes, F.; Plankert, N. (2014): Umgang mit Komplexität in der Produktentwicklung: Komplexitätsbeherrschung durch Variantenmanagement, in: Schoeneberg, K.-P. (Ed.): Komplexitätsmanagement in Unternehmen: Herausforderungen im Umgang mit Dynamik, Unsicherheit und Komplexität meistern, Wiesbaden.

Thomas, P. (2008): Mass Customization als Wettbewerbsstrategie in der Finanzdienstleistungsbranche, Wiesbaden.

Thorogood, A.; Yetton, P. (2004): Reducing the Technical Complexity and Business Risk of Major Systems Projects, in: Proceedings of the 37th Hawaii International Conference on System Sciences, Hawaii, USA.

Thun, J.-H.; Stumpfe, J. (2004): Integration von Produkt- und Prozessentwicklung – Zur Problematik von Komplexität und Dynamik bei der Innovation von Produkten und Prozessen, in: Maier, F. (Ed.): Komplexität und Dynamik als Herausforderung für das Management, Wiesbaden.

Ulrich, K.; Eppinger, D. (2000): Product Design and Development, 2nd edition, Boston, USA.

Viehweger, B.; Malikov, V. (2013): Leichtbau durch Produktionsinnovationen: Berichte aus der inpro-Innovationsakademie, in: ZWF Zeitschrift für wirtschaftlichen Fabrikbetrieb, 108 (4), 187–192.

Vogel, W. (2017): Complexity Management Approach for Resource Planning in Variant-rich Product Development, in: Bode, Ch.; Bogaschewsky, R.; Eßig, M.; Lasch, R.; Stölzle, W. (Eds.): Supply Management Research: Aktuelle Forschungs-ergebnisse 2017, Wiesbaden.

Vogel, W.; Lasch, R. (2016): Complexity drivers in manufacturing companies: a literature review, in: Logistics Research, 9 (25), 1–66.

Voigt, K.-I.; Baccarella, C.; Wassmus, A.; Meißner, O. (2011) The Effects of Customer Orientation on the Product Performance of Technological Innovations: A Comparison between SMEs and Large Companies, in: Proceedings of the International Conference on Technology Management in the Energy-Smart World (PICMET), Portland, USA.

Vollmar, J.; Gepp, M. (2015): Framework for Standardization Programs in the Engineer-To-Order Industry, in: Proceedings of the Portland International Conference on Management of Engineering and Technology (PICMET), Portland, USA.

Wallenburg, C.; Weber, J. (2005): Management von Produktion und Logistik bei Umweltdynamik, in: Industrie Management, 21 (5), 45–48.

Wangenheim, S. von (1998a): Integrationsbedarf im Serienanlauf dargestellt am Beispiel der Automobilindustrie, in: Horváth, P.; Fleig, G. (Eds.): Integrationsmanagement für neue Produkte, Stuttgart.

Warnecke, G. (2010): Komplexität: mit Kompetenz bewältigen, mit Technik beherrschen, in: ZWF Zeitschrift für wirtschaftlichen Fabrikbetrieb, 105 (7–8), 639–641.

Westphal, J. R. (2000): Komplexitätsmanagement in der Produktionslogistik. Available at: https://tu-dresden.de/bu/verkehr/ivw/ressourcen/dateien/diskuss/2000_4_diskusbtr_ivw.pdf (accessed: 15 August 2016).

Westphal, J. (2001): Komplexitätsmanagement in der Produktionslogistik: Entwicklung eines Ansatzes zur flußorientierten Gestaltung und Lenkung von heterogenen Produktionssystemen, Dresden.

Wiermeier, B.; Haberfellner, R. (2007): Referenzmodelle in der Automobilindustrie, in: Industrie Management, 23 (3), 47–50.

Wildemann, H. (1998): Komplexitätsmanagement durch Prozess- und Produktgestaltung, in: Adam, D. (Ed.): Komplexitätsmanagement, Wiesbaden.

Wildemann, H. (1999): Komplexität: Vermeiden oder beherrschen lernen, in: Harvard Business Manager, (6), 33–36.

Wildemann, H. (2000): Komplexitätsmanagement: Vertrieb, Produkte, Beschaffung, F&E, Produktion und Administration, München.

Wildemann, H. (2001): Supply Chain Management mit E-Technologien. Available at: http://wiwi.uniklu.ac.at/Forschung/07.pdf (accessed: 23 May 2015).

Wildemann, H. (2003): Produktordnungssysteme: Leitfaden zur Standardisierung und Individualisierung des Produktprogramms durch intelligente Plattformstrategien, München.

Wildemann, H. (2007): Weiterentwicklung von Produktionssystemen: Neue Methoden zur Produktionsoptimierung, in: Industrie Management, 23 (3), 19–22.

Wildemann, H. (2012): Komplexitätsmanagement in Vertrieb, Beschaffung, Produkt, Entwicklung und Produktion, 13th edition, München.

Wildemann, H. (2013): Komplexitätsmanagement in Vertrieb, Beschaffung, Produkt, Entwicklung und Produktion, 14th edition, München.

Wilke, J. (2012): Supply Chain Koordination durch Lieferverträge mit rollierender Mengenflexibilität: Eine Simulationsstudie am Beispiel von Lieferketten der deutschen Automobilindustrie, Wiesbaden.

Winkler, H.; Allmayer, S. (2012): Schnittstellenmanagement bei kundenindividueller Produktion, in: Productivity Management, 17 (1), 16–19.

Wleklinski, C. (2001): Methode zur Effektivitäts- und Effizienzbewertung der Entwicklung maschinenbaulicher Anlagen, Paderborn.

Wölfling, C. (2014): Komplexität im Anlagenbau. Available at: http://www.gfse.de/Dokumente_Mitglieder/studienpreis/sp_2014/P9900_Studienpreis_Komplexitaet_TdSE_2014_CW_R00_140921.pdf (accessed: 04 January 2017).

Wüpping, J. (2003): Praxiserfahrungen Variantenmanagement und Produktkonfiguration, in: Industrie Management, 19 (1), 49–52.

Wüpping, J. (2011): Renditekiller Komplexität: Vielfalt einfach – Nicht Einfalt vielfach, in: Controller Magazin, July/August 2011, 66–71.

Wüpping, J. (2013): Warum einfach? Es geht auch kompliziert! – Der kontrollierte Umgang mit Komplexität, in: Gleich, R.; Klein, A. (Eds.): Komplexitätscontrolling: Komplexität verstehen und beherrschen, Freiburg.

Yang, N.-D.; Ji, Y. (2010): Study of R&D Project Complexity's Influencing Mechanism on Organization Structure, in: Proceedings of the International Conference on Future Information Technology and Management Engineering FITME 2010, Changzhou, China.

Yang, B.; Yang, Y. (2010): Postponement in supply chain risk management: a complexity perspective, in: International Journal of Production Research, 48 (7), 1901–1912.

Zenner, C. (2006): Durchgängiges Variantenmanagement in der Technischen Produktionsplanung, Universität des Saarlandes.

Zerres, C. (2014): Notwendigkeit und Strategien eines Komplexitätsmanagements für variantenreiche Produkte – ein Beitrag am Beispiel der Automobilbranche, in: Schoeneberg, K.-P. (Ed.): Komplexitätsmanagement in Unternehmen: Herausforderungen im Umgang mit Dynamik, Unsicherheit und Komplexität meistern, Wiesbaden.

Zhou, D. (2002): An Empirical Study of the Role of Postponement Application in Reducing Supply Chain Complexity, in: Proceedings of the IEEE International Engineering Management Conference: Managing Technology for the New Economy IEMC-2002, Cambridge, UK.

Zich, C. (1996): Integrierte Typen- und Teileoptimierung: Neue Methoden des Produktprogramm-Managements, Wiesbaden.

Appendix

Table 6 – Part A: Overview of existing single approaches focused on product

Explanation according to complexity strategy: R Reduction of complexity M Mastering of complexity A Avoidance of complexity I Increasing of complexity O Outsourcing of complexity G General for complexity management	Single approaches focused on product						
	Modular concept	Modular system	Standardi-zation	Using same parts	Platform concept	Differential construction	Integral construction
Simon, 1962, p. 14	M						
Imori et al., 1990, p. 503	G						
Child et al., 1991a, p. 74	R		R				
Child et al., 1991b, p. 65	R						
Schulte, 1992, p. 90							R
Fischer, 1993, p. 30			R				
Ehrlenspiel, 1995, pp. 420–421						R, I	R
Fleck, 1995, p. 189	M	M					
Kaiser, 1995, p. 17	R						
Prillmann, 1996, p. 113			R				
Sanchez, 1996, p. 121	R						
Sanchez and Mahoney, 1996, p. 66	R						
Homburg and Daum, 1997, p. 335			A				
Jeschke, 1997, p. 22			R, A				
Jina, Bhattacharya and Walton, 1997, p. 8	R			R			
Mahoney, 1997, p. 395			R				
Pels, Wortmann and Zwegers, 1997, p. 274	M						
Adam, 1998, p. 59			R	R	R		
Bliss, 1998, pp. 155–156		R	R	R			
Bohne, 1998, p. 240	A	A	A	A			A
Eversheim, Schenke and Warnke, 1998, p. 32	R	R	R	R			
Göpfert, 1998, pp. 139–140	R, M						
Komorek, 1998, pp. 272–273	A	A	R	A			
Marshall, 1998, p. 65	G						
Piller, 1998, p. 195	R						
Schuh, Schwenk and Speth, 1998a, p. 82	R						
Schuh, Schwenk and Speth, 1998b, p. 134	R						

Table 6 – Part B: Overview of existing single approaches focused on product

Explanation according to complexity strategy: R Reduction of complexity M Mastering of complexity A Avoidance of complexity I Increasing of complexity O Outsourcing of complexity G General for complexity management	Modular concept	Modular system	Standardi-zation	Using same parts	Platform concept	Differential construction	Integral construction
Wangenheim, 1998a, pp. 73–74				R	R		
Wildemann, 1998, p. 58	R	R	R				
Benett, 1999, pp. 65–66, 133	R	R	R, A				
Fisher, Ramdas and Ulrich, 1999, p. 298				R	R		
Haberfellner et al., 1999, p. 23	R						
Marshall and Leaney, 1999, p. 847		G					
Muffatto, 1999, p. 145					R		
Nagarur and Azeem, 1999, p. 125			R				
Piller and Waringer, 1999, pp. 37, 64	R				R		
Reiners and Sasse, 1999, p. 230	A	A	R	R			
Schaefer, 1999, p. 312	R						
Wildemann, 1999, pp. 31, 34–36				R	R		
Baldwin and Clark, 2000, pp. 59, 64	R, A				R		
Bliss, 2000, pp. 42–44	R	R	R	R	R		
Herzwurm, 2000, p. 32	R		R				
Olbrich and Battenfeld, 2000, p. 17	R, M	R, M					
Ulrich and Eppinger, 2000, p. 200					R		
Westphal, 2000, p. 31		R	R	R			
Göpfert and Steinbrecher, 2001, p. 353	R						
Haf, 2001, p. 124	R		R				
Hofer, 2001, p. 46					R		
Maune, 2001, pp. 22–31	R		R	A	R	R, I	R
Neff et al., 2001, pp. 31–32			R	R			
Piller, 2001, p. 226	A	A	A	A	A		
Schuh and Schwenk, 2001, pp. 79–84	R	M				O	R
Schwenk-Willi, 2001, pp. 79–80, 143–146	R				R	O	R
Siddique and Rosen, 2001, p. 1					R		
Westphal, 2001, pp. 135, 154	R			R			

Table 6 – Part C: Overview of existing single approaches focused on product

Explanation according to complexity strategy: R Reduction of complexity M Mastering of complexity A Avoidance of complexity I Increasing of complexity O Outsourcing of complexity G General for complexity management	Modular concept	Modular system	Standardi-zation	Using same parts	Platform concept	Differential construction	Integral construction
Franke et al., 2002, pp. 55, 71–75	R, M	R, M	R, M		M	M	M
Herrmann and Seilheimer, 2002, p. 669				R	R		
Hesse, Fetzer and Warnecke, 2002, p. 487					M		
Klinkner and Risse, 2002, p. 25	M			M			
Korreck, 2002, p. 146			R				
Langlois, 2002, pp. 19–20		R					
Halman, Hofer and Vuuren, 2003, pp. 149, 155					R		
Junge, 2003, p. 90					R		
Katzke, Fischer and Vogel-Heuser, 2003, p. 69	R						
Wildemann, 2003, p. 58		R		R			
Wüpping, 2003, pp. 50–51	R		R		R		
Adam, 2004, p. 21				R			
A.T. Kearney, 2004, p. 11			R				
Dehnen, 2004, pp. 9, 62–69	R	R		R	R		
Ethiraj and Levinthal, 2004, pp. 159–161	R, M						
Friedrich, 2004, pp. 25–27	R, M		R, M		R, M		
Gerberich, 2004, p. 247	M	M		M	M		
Gräßler, 2004, p. 131							R
Keuper, 2004, pp. 177–179, 198–203	R	R	R	R	R	I	R
Klepsch, 2004, p. 15	R, M						
Mühlenbruch, 2004, p. 46	R	R	R	R	R	R	R
Perona and Miragliotta, 2004, p. 110	M						
Rall and Dalhöfer, 2004, p. 624	R		R				
Simpson, 2004, p. 4					R		
Thorogood and Yetton, 2004, p. 4			R	R			
Thun and Stumpfe, 2004, pp. 170–171			R		R		R
Blecker et al., 2005, p. 56	R		R				
Böckle, 2005, p. 12				R	R		

Anwendungsorientierte Forschungsbeiträge

Table 6 – Part D: Overview of existing single approaches focused on product

Explanation according to complexity strategy: R Reduction of complexity M Mastering of complexity A Avoidance of complexity I Increasing of complexity O Outsourcing of complexity G General for complexity management	Modular concept	Modular system	Standardi-zation	Using same parts	Platform concept	Differential construction	Integral construction
Böhmann and Krcmar, 2005, pp. 456–458	R		R	R			
Fettke and Loos, 2005, p. 21				M			
Gausemeier and Riepe, 2005, pp. 55–56	R						
Greitemeyer and Ulrich, 2005, p. 7					G		
Hellström and Wikström, 2005, p. 394		G					
Klauke, Schreiber and Weißner, 2005, p. 246					R		
Klinkner, Mayer and Thom, 2005, p. 34	R						
Kroker et al., 2005, pp. 77–78	R		R				
Schuh, 2005, p. 125-139	R	R			R	R, I	R
Schuh et al., 2005, p. 22					R		
Springer, 2005, pp. 10–14			R	R	R		
Anderson et al., 2006, pp. 22–25	R						
Blecker and Abdelkafi, 2006a, pp. 76–77	R						
Heckmann, 2006, p. 46				R			
Lindemann and Baumberger, 2006, p. 8	M	M	R	R	R		
Lindemann and Maurer, 2006, p. 43	R	R			R		
Scheer et al., 2006, p. 157	R	R	R				
Zenner, 2006, p. 2	R				R		
Adrian, 2007, p. 1					R		
Aurich, Grzegorski and Lehmann, 2007, p. 14	M			M	M		
Baumberger, 2007, p. 100	M	R	R	R	R		
Durst, 2007, p. 31	R		R				
Grotkamp and Franke, 2007, p. 35			A				
Grübner, 2007, p. 332	R						
Krause, Franke, Gausemeier, 2007, p. 23	R, M	R, M			R, M		
Lübke, 2007, pp. 252–254, 264–266				R	M	R	R, I
Marti, 2007, pp. 70, 77	R,M,A				R		
Mayer, 2007, pp. 40, 119	M			M	M		

Single approaches for complexity management in product development

Table 6 – Part E: Overview of existing single approaches focused on product

Explanation according to complexity strategy: R Reduction of complexity M Mastering of complexity A Avoidance of complexity I Increasing of complexity O Outsourcing of complexity G General for complexity management	Modular concept	Modular system	Standardi-zation	Using same parts	Platform concept	Differential construction	Integral construction
Meyer, 2007, pp. 63–65	R,M,A		R				
Picot and Baumann, 2007, pp. 222, 239	R						
Renner, 2007, pp. 15, 41	M	M	R		M	M	M
Ruppert, 2007, p. 68	R, M						
Schuh et al., 2007a, pp. 53-54	R		R				
Schuh et al., 2007b, pp. 3–4, 12	M	M					
Steffen and Gausemeier, 2007, p. 9	R						
Straube and Mayer, 2007, pp. 53-54	R, M			M	M		
Wiermeier and Haberfellner, 2007, p. 49	R						
Wildemann, 2007, p. 21	R		R				
Abdelkafi, 2008, pp. 148-149	R				R		
Aurich and Grzegorski, 2008, pp. 316–317	R,M,A		R,M,A				
Beetz, Grimm and Eickmeyer, 2008, p. 39	R						
Bick and Drexl-Wittbecker, 2008, pp. 61, 103	R	R	R				
El Haouzi, Thomas and Pétin, 2008, pp. 47–48	R	R					
Gabath, 2008, pp. 34–38	R	R	R		R		
Jagersma, 2008, p. 241			R				
Luger et al., 2008, p. 603			R				
Peters and Hofstetter, 2008, p. 16	A			R	R		
Ponn and Lindemann, 2008, pp. 150, 231, 240, 395–402	R		R	M			R
Rafele and Cagliano, 2008, p. 4			R				
Schaffer et al., 2008, p. 3					R		
Shamsuzzoha, Helo and Kekäle, 2008, p. 1595	G	G					
Terada and Murata, 2008, p. 445	R						
Thomas, 2008, p. 113	R				R		
Bohn, 2009, pp. 255–259	R		R				
Dombrowski et al., 2009, p. 257			R, M				
Gumpinger, Jonas and Krause, 2009, p. 202						R	I

Anwendungsorientierte Forschungsbeiträge

Table 6 – Part F: Overview of existing single approaches focused on product

Explanation according to complexity strategy: R Reduction of complexity M Mastering of complexity A Avoidance of complexity I Increasing of complexity O Outsourcing of complexity G General for complexity management	Modular concept	Modular system	Standardi-zation	Using same parts	Platform concept	Differential construction	Integral construction
Helfrich, 2009, p. 110	R			R	R		
Kersten et al., 2009, p. 1136	R		R				
Koppik and Meier, 2009, p. 1174			R				
Lasch and Gießmann, 2009a, p. 210	R						
Lasch and Gießmann, 2009b, pp. 106–108	R	R	R	R	R	R	R
Lindemann, Maurer and Braun, 2009, p. 35	R		G				
Newman, 2009, p. 3	R		R				
Redlich, Wulfsberg and Bruhns, 2009, p. 556	R						
Schöller, 2009, pp. 60-63	R				R		
Bayer, 2010, pp. 80-85	R	R		R	R		R,M,A
Caniato, Crippa and Größler, 2010, p. 63	R						
Duerre and Steger, 2010, p. 88	G				G		
Flieder, 2010, p. 497	R						
Gießmann, 2010, pp. 57–61	R,M,A	R	R	R	R	R	R
Gomes and Dahab, 2010, p. 59		G					
Klug, 2010, pp. 59–72	R		R	R			
Pero et al., 2010, p. 120	R						
Schuh, Arnoscht and Rudolf, 2010, p. 1					R		
Stirzel, 2010, pp. 131–132	R, M						
Stuhler, Ricken and Diener, 2010, p. 60			M				
Agrawalla, 2011, p. 157		G					
Brosch and Krause, 2011, p. 1		R			R		
Cao, Zhang and Liu, 2011, p. 786	R						
Gießmann and Lasch, 2011, pp. 11–14	R,M,A	R	R	R	R	R, I	R
Grösser, 2011, p. 19			R				
Haumann, 2011, pp. 12–13	A	A				A	A
Jacobs and Swink, 2011, p. 681					R		
Kersten, 2011, p. 17	R, A				R, A		

Single approaches for complexity management in product development

Table 6 – Part G: Overview of existing single approaches focused on product

Explanation according to complexity strategy: R Reduction of complexity M Mastering of complexity A Avoidance of complexity I Increasing of complexity O Outsourcing of complexity G General for complexity management	Single approaches focused on product						
	Modular concept	Modular system	Standardi-zation	Using same parts	Platform concept	Differential construction	Integral construction
Manuj and Sahin, 2011, p. 543			G		G		
Möller, Hülle and Kahle, 2011, p. 741	G		G	G			
Reiss, 2011, p. 78			R				
Shamsuzzoha, 2011, pp. 27, 35	R						R
Shamsuzzoha and Helo, 2011, pp. 318–319	R	R			R		
Slamaning, 2011, pp. 270–271	R				R		
Wüpping, 2011, p. 70	R						
Beckmann, 2012, p. 13	G		G		G		
Buchholz, 2012, pp. 213–214	R	R	A	A	R, A		
Eilmann and Nyhuis, 2012, p. 660	R						
Eitelwein, Malz and Weber, 2012, p. 79	R						
ElMaraghy et al., 2012, p. 801	R				R		
Flieder, 2012, p. 32	R						
Freund and Braune, 2012, p. 57					R		
Heydari and Dalili, 2012, p. 63		G					
Kersten et al., 2012, p. 156	R						
Kesper, 2012, p. 62	R	R			R		
Lammers, 2012, pp. 55–56	R		R				
Meffert, Burmann and Kirchgeorg, 2012, p. 449		R					
Rüßler, 2012, p. 12				R			
Schapiro and Henry, 2012, p. 3		R					
Schawel and Billing, 2012, p. 142			R				
Wildemann, 2012, pp. 143–149, 155–156	R,M,A	R,M,A		M, A	R,M,A		
Wilke, 2012, p. 70	R		R		R		
Winkler and Allmayer, 2012, p. 16	M			M	M		
Boyksen and Kotlik, 2013, p. 52			R				
Seibertz, Brandstätter and Schreiber, 2013, p. 165		M					
Göpfert and Schulz, 2013, p. 201					A		

Table 6 – Part H: Overview of existing single approaches focused on product

Explanation according to complexity strategy: R Reduction of complexity / M Mastering of complexity / A Avoidance of complexity / I Increasing of complexity / O Outsourcing of complexity / G General for complexity management	Single approaches focused on product						
	Modular concept	Modular system	Standardi-zation	Using same parts	Platform concept	Differential construction	Integral construction
Götzfried, 2013, pp. 43–45	R				R		
Jäger et al., 2013, p. 343	A		A				
Klein, 2013, p. 80					M		
Mayer and Volk, 2013, p. 17		M	M				
Meier and Bojarski, 2013, p. 547			R				
Ploom, Glaser and Scheit, 2013, p. 15					R		
Proff and Proff, 2013, p. 146			R				
Viehweger and Malikov, 2013, p. 187							I
Wildemann, 2013, pp. 143–147, 155–156	R,M,A	R,M,A		M, A	R,M,A		
Wüpping, 2013, p. 142	R		R				
Bauernhansl, Schatz and Jäger, 2014, p. 347	R, M		R, M				
Bittermann, 2014, p. 58					R		
Ehrlenspiel et al., 2014, pp. 359-361	R				R		
ElMaraghy and ElMaraghy, 2014, p. 4	R		R				
Gebhardt, Bahns and Krause, 2014, p. 75	R						
Gemünden and Schoper, 2014, p. 9	R		R				
Grimm, Schuller and Wilhelmer, 2014, p. 94	R		R				
Jäger et al., 2014, p. 649	A		A				
Jensen, Bekdik and Thuesen, 2014, pp. 541–554							G, I
Joergensen, Schou and Madsen, 2014, p. 58	R				R		
Kampker et al., 2014, p. 2	R						
Keuper, 2014, p. 56, 61			R			R	R
Kieviet, 2014, pp. 60, 64	R				R		
Kluth et al., 2014a, p. 226	A						
Kluth et al., 2014b, p. 72	A		A				
Koch and Renner, 2014, p. 953		R					
Koppenhagen, 2014, pp. 115, 119	R						
Krumm, Schopf and Rennekamp, 2014, p. 193		M			M		M

Table 6 – Part I: Overview of existing single approaches focused on product

Explanation according to complexity strategy: R Reduction of complexity / M Mastering of complexity / A Avoidance of complexity / I Increasing of complexity / O Outsourcing of complexity / G General for complexity management	Modular concept	Modular system	Standardi-zation	Using same parts	Platform concept	Differential construction	Integral construction
Lanza et al., 2014, p. 65		M	M				
Mattila, 2014, p. 145	G				G		
Mayer, 2014, p. 27	R						
Prodoehl, 2014, p. 45	R						
Schatz, Schöllhammer and Jäger, 2014, pp. 688–692	A		R, A				
Schoeneberg, 2014, pp. 18-21	M, R		R				
Schoeneberg, 2014b, p. 6			R				
Schulz, 2014a, p. 51	M						
Tamaskar, Neema and DeLaurentis, 2014, p. 125	R	R					
Thiebes and Plankert, 2014, pp. 180-183	M			M			M
Zerres, 2014, pp. 300–305	R		R	R, A	R	R, I	R
Gepp et al., 2015, p. 1	G		G				
Herrmann et al., 2015, p. 251	M	M					
Königsreuther, 2015, p. 33		R			R		
Krieg, 2015, p. 91			R				
Kruse, Ripperda and Krause, 2015, pp. 1-2	M				M		
Martensson, Zenkert and Akermo, 2015a, p. 577						R	
Schott, Horstmann and Bodendorf, 2015, p. 36	G		G		G	G	G
Schuh et al., 2015, p. 695	R				R		
Theuer, 2015, p. 3	R	R					
Vollmar and Gepp, 2015, p. 14				G			
Total amount of literature sources, which are concerned with the specific complexity management single approach:	158	60	90	56	87	19	29

Anwendungsorientierte Forschungsbeiträge

Table 7 – Part A: *Overview of existing single approaches focused on product portfolio, process and organization*

Explanation according to complexity strategy: R Reduction of complexity; M Mastering of complexity; A Avoidance of complexity; I Increasing of complexity; O Outsourcing of complexity; G General for complexity management	Single approaches focused on...							
	Product portfolio				Process		Organization	
	Packaging	Reducing product range	Reducing of customers	Postponement concept	Standardization of processes	Modularity of processes	Delayering	Empowerment
Child et al., 1991a, pp. 75, 78		R			R			M
Fischer, 1993, p. 30			R	M				
Hirzel, 1993, p. 182			R					
Reiß, 1993, pp. 8, 13–14, 21–22							R	
Coenenberg and Prillmann, 1995, p. 1245				R, A				
Crichton and Edgar, 1995, p. 13	R							
Fleck, 1995, p. 189		R						
Kippels, 1996, p. 3							M	
Dombkins, 1997, p. 428							G	
Homburg and Daum, 1997, pp. 335–336		R		M				
Jeschke, 1997, p. 27					R, A			
Bliss, 1998, p. 157	R							
Eversheim, Schenke and Warnke, 1998, p. 32				R				
Meijer, 1998, p. 279								R
Wildemann, 1998, p. 58	R							
Puhl, 1999, p. 37								R
Rapp, 1999, p. 61	R							
Baldwin and Clark, 2000, pp. 59, 64						R		
Battezzati and Magnani, 2000, p. 414				R				
Bliss, 2000, pp. 39–41, 46–49, 197–204	R	R	R	R				R
Olbrich and Battenfeld, 2000, p. 45								R
Westphal, 2000, p. 31				R				
Wildemann, 2000, p. 7		R	R					
Hoek, 2001, p. 163				R				
Maune, 2001, pp. 25, 31–39		R		R			M	
Piller, 2001, p. 226				R		R, A		
Schuh and Schwenk, 2001, p. 83	R							

Table 7 – Part B: *Overview of existing single approaches focused on product portfolio, process and organization*

Explanation according to complexity strategy: R Reduction of complexity / M Mastering of complexity / A Avoidance of complexity / I Increasing of complexity / O Outsourcing of complexity / G General for complexity management	Product portfolio			Process			Organization	
	Packaging	Reducing product range	Reducing of customers	Postponement concept	Standardization of processes	Modularity of processes	Delayering	Empowerment
Wildemann, 2001, p. 5				R				
Franke et al., 2002, pp. 21, 71	M				M			
Zhou, 2002, pp. 448-450				R	R	R		
Aurich, Barbian and Wagenknecht, 2003, p. 215						R		
Aurich and Wagenknecht, 2003, p. 662						A		
Armbruster and Kieser, 2003, p. 163								M
Dehnen, 2004, p. 155					R			
Gerberich, 2004, p. 247				M				
Hanenkamp, 2004, p. 69		R						
Keuper, 2004, pp. 184, 193	R							R
Mühlenbruch, 2004, pp. 46–48	R				R			
Böhmann and Krcmar, 2005, pp. 456, 459	R	R	R	R				
Geimer, 2005, p. 42		R						
Hoole, 2005, p. 4					R			
Müller, 2005, p. 720	M							
Schuh, 2005, p. 129	R							
Stephan, 2005, p. 36	R							
Wallenburg and Weber, 2005, p. 48					G			
Blecker and Abdelkafi, 2006a, p. 77						R		
Blecker and Abdelkafi, 2006b, p. 923						R		
Blecker and Abdelkafi, 2006c, p. 162					G			
Meyer, Walber and Schmidt, 2006, pp. 532, 535						R, M		
Spath and Demuß, 2006, p. 482					R			
Aurich, Grzegorski and Lehmann, 2007, p. 15						M		
Durst, 2007, p. 31			R	R				
Grotkamp and Franke, 2007, p. 35		R, A						

Anwendungsorientierte Forschungsbeiträge

Table 7 – Part C: *Overview of existing single approaches focused on product portfolio, process and organization*

Explanation according to complexity strategy: R Reduction of complexity / M Mastering of complexity / A Avoidance of complexity / I Increasing of complexity / O Outsourcing of complexity / G General for complexity management	Product portfolio			Process			Organization	
	Packaging	Reducing product range	Reducing of customers	Postponement concept	Standardization of processes	Modularity of processes	Delayering	Empowerment
Hyötyläinen and Möller, 2007, p. 305	R							
Lübke, 2007, pp. 254–255, 262	R			R				
Meyer, 2007, p. 64		R	M, A	R	M, A			
Straube, Doch and Huynh, 2007, p. 37					R			
Abdelkafi, 2008, p. 154					R			
Huang and Li, 2008, p. 111				R				
Laqua, 2008, p. 27		R						
Mogilner, Rudnick and Iyengar, 2008, p. 212		R						
Rafele and Cagliano, 2008, p. 4					R			
Thomas, 2008, p. 113						R		
Beimborn et al., 2009, p. 3					R			
Bohn, 2009, p. 261				M				
Lasch and Gießmann, 2009a, p. 210	R							
Lasch and Gießmann, 2009b, pp. 108–110	R	R	R	R	R			
Schulze, Mansky and Klimek, 2009, p. 1				M				
AlGeddawy and ElMaraghy, 2010, p. 5281				R				
Bayer, 2010, pp. 75–79	R	R		R, M				
Blockus, 2010, p. 287		G	G					G
Gießmann, 2010, pp. 62–70	R	R	R	R	R, A	R, A	R	R
Keil, 2010, p. 6								R
Klug, 2010, p. 55				R				
Yang and Ji, 2010, p. 183						R		
Yang and Yang, 2010, p. 1909				R				
Brosch and Krause, 2011, p. 1				R				
Gießmann and Lasch, 2011, pp. 15–20	R	R	R	R	R, A	R, A	R	R
Kersten, 2011, p. 17		R			R			
Kersten, 2011, p. 17		R			R			

Table 7 – Part D: Overview of existing single approaches focused on product portfolio, process and organization

Explanation according to complexity strategy: R Reduction of complexity M Mastering of complexity A Avoidance of complexity I Increasing of complexity O Outsourcing of complexity G General for complexity management	Single approaches focused on...							
	Product portfolio			Process			Organization	
	Packaging	Reducing product range	Reducing of customers	Postponement concept	Standardization of processes	Modularity of processes	Delayering	Empowerment
Reiss, 2011, p. 80				G				
Beckmann, 2012, p. 13		G		G				
ElMaraghy et al., 2012, p. 801						R		
Lammers, 2012, p. 55	R							
Winkler and Allmayer, 2012, p. 16				M				
Biedermann and Lindemann, 2013, p. 495	G							
Göpfert and Schulz, 2013, p. 202				M				
Jäger et al., 2013, p. 343					A			
Nagengast, Heidemann and Rudolph, 2013, p. 668		R						
ElMaraghy and ElMaraghy, 2014, p. 4				R				
Jäger et al., 2014, p. 649		R			A			
Keuper, 2014, p. 61								R
Kluth et al., 2014a, pp. 226–227		R			A			
Kluth et al., 2014b, p. 72		R			A			
Mattsson et al., 2014, p. 212								G
Schatz, Schöllhammer and Jäger, 2014, pp. 691–692		R					M	
Schulz, 2014b, pp. 218-220, 225				M				
Wölfling, 2014, p. 17				G	G	G	G	
Zerres, 2014, pp. 300, 306				R				
Braun, 2015, p. 308							R	
Schott, Horstmann, Bodendorf, 2015, p. 36	G	G						
Total amount of literature sources, which are concerned with the specific complexity management single approach:	23	25	11	40	20	15	9	14

Der Faktor Unsicherheit bei ersatzteillogistischen Kooperationen auf dem Drittanbietermarkt

Stefan Drechsler, Bastien Bodenstein, Rainer Lasch

Abstract

Die zunehmende Ersatzteilvielfalt – bedingt durch kürzer werdende Innovationszyklen bei gleichzeitig langanhaltender Lebensdauer komplexer Anlagen – und der Trend der Auslagerung von Dienstleistungen bewirken, dass der Drittanbietermarkt in der Ersatzteillogistik an Bedeutung gewinnt. Strategisch ausgerichtete Kooperationen zwischen Herstellern, Drittanbietern und Betreibern sind wichtig, um planungsintensive Prozesse nachhaltig zu optimieren. Unsicherheiten behindern jedoch die Bereitschaft, Allianzen einzugehen und sich gegenüber Innovationen in diesem Bereich zu öffnen. Durch eine qualitativ ausgerichtete Studie mit Akteuren des Drittanbietermarktes wurden die Relevanz aus der Literatur erarbeiteter Kooperationsmöglichkeiten erfasst und bestehende Unsicherheiten bzw. deren Ursache erforscht. Die Unsicherheit bezüglich verlässlicher Informationen erwies sich hier als zentraler Aspekt.

1 Einleitung

Die Verschiebung von Wertschöpfungsanteilen zugunsten produktbegleitender industrienaher Dienstleistungen ist ein deutlicher Indikator für die Veränderung der produzierenden Industrie. Lag der Bruttowertschöpfungsanteil im deutschen Dienstleistungssektor Anfang der 1990er Jahre noch bei 48%, stieg dieser bis zum Jahr 2012 auf 68%. Insbesondere im Maschinen- und Anlagenbau verzeichnet der Service einen signifikanten Bedeutungszuwachs (Eickelpasch, 2014, S. 1; Gröllich et al., 2015, S. 6 f.). Mit dem Trend der Auslagerung von Dienstleistungen gewinnen Drittanbieter an Wichtigkeit. Diese setzen sich dabei u.a. aus Herstellern, Servicedienstleistern und Lizenznehmern zusammen und sind sowohl für den Abnehmer der Ersatzteile als auch für den Hersteller ein entscheidender Faktor in der Ersatzteillogistik (IPRI (Hrsg.), 2013, S. 8). Drittanbieter haben den Vorteil, dass sie die Verfügbarkeit weder für alle Teile noch über die gesamte Lebensdauer der Primärprodukte hinweg sicherstellen müssen (Behfard et al., 2015, S. 498). In der Ersatzteillogistik übernehmen sie neben Dienstleistungen wie Beschaffung, Instandhaltung und Aufbereitung (Schuh, Stich, 2013, S. 168) häufig die Funktion von Zulieferern. Sie bilden somit ein entscheidendes Bindeglied zwischen Primärproduktherstellern und Abnehmern bzw. Betreibern einer Anlage (Liu, Lyons, 2011, S. 547).

Die Ersatzteilversorgung ist aus logistischer Sicht mit enormen Unsicherheiten verbunden. Die steigende Ersatzteilvielfalt und -komplexität bedingen schwer prognostizierbare Ersatzteilbedarfe und überdimensionierte Sicherheitsbestände (Dekker et al., 2013, S. 537 f.; Pawellek, 2016, S. 289). Durch Anlagenlebenszyklen von bis zu 30 Jahren können Folgekosten über den gesamten Nutzungszeitraum das Drei- bis Zehnfache der Anschaffungsinvestition betragen (Lanza et al., 2012, S. 514). Die koordinative Optimierung von Leistungen zwischen den Akteuren ist somit von signifikanter Wichtigkeit (Liu, Lyons, 2011, S. 547). Strategische Kooperationen mit Drittanbietern ermöglichen Effizienz und Effektivität im Bezug, in der Lagerung, dem Vertrieb, der Spedition und der Fertigung von Ersatzteilen, wobei es dem Auftraggeber ermöglicht wird, seine Risiken zu senken (Godoy et al., 2014, S. 103; Shi et al., 2016, S. 197). In der Praxis werden Synergien allerdings häufig nicht konsequent zielorientiert verfolgt, da Abhängigkeiten zwischen Akteuren und schlecht ausgestaltete Schnittstellen dies verhindern (Klostermann, 2007, S. 4).

In Anbetracht des Mangels an entsprechenden Untersuchungen soll im Folgenden die Frage beantwortet werden, wie in der Theorie behandelte Kooperationsansätze unter praktischen Gesichtspunkten zu bewerten sind. Außerdem ist zu klären, wo damit verbundene Unsicherheiten, die strategische Partnerschaften auf dem Drittanbietermarkt hemmen, ihre Ursprünge haben. Nach der Erläuterung von Kooperationsmöglichkeiten in Abschnitt 2 befasst sich Abschnitt 3 mit der Methodik der durchgeführten qualitativ ausgerichteten Fallstudien. Die theoretischen Annahmen erfahren in Abschnitt 4 einen Abgleich mit den Ergebnissen der Experteninterviews. Zusätzlich werden die Implikationen sowie die kritische Würdigung der Studien thematisiert. Abschnitt 5 schließt mit dem Fazit und gibt einen Ausblick auf den zukünftigen Forschungsbedarf.

2 Literaturüberblick

Veröffentlichungen auf dem Gebiet der Kooperationen auf dem Drittanbietermarkt lassen sich in zwei Ebenen teilen: Auf organisatorischer Ebene werden strategisch ausgerichtete Partnerschaften bezogen auf die Planung der Ersatzteillogistik behandelt. Auf technologischer Ebene stehen wiederum Innnovationen und Aspekte der Digitalisierung inklusive deren Einfluss auf die Ersatzteilplanung im Vordergrund.

2.1 Kooperationen auf organisatorischer Ebene

Auf Basis von Synergien zwischen den Akteuren sind organisatorische Kooperationen wie das Collaborative Management (CM) anzustreben. Liu und Jiang (2013, S. 3413 f.) beschreiben das Modell eines CM-Zentrums für Ersatzteile. Für dieses besteht die Hauptaufgabe in der zentralisierten Beschaffung, Lagerung und Verteilung von Komponenten. Das Konzept verbindet Ersatzteillieferanten (Hersteller und Drittanbieter) mit den Betreibern der Primärprodukte durch ein Zwei-Wege-Kommunikationsnetzwerk. Ziel des CM ist es, die Zusammenarbeit durch die kooperative Nutzung von Informationen und Ressourcen entlang der Supply Chain zu fördern. Durch die Zusammenarbeit der Unternehmen kann die Ersatzteilversorgung vereinfacht und präzisiert werden, bspw. durch gemeinsame Prognosen und eine Verkürzung der Reaktionszeiten, wodurch der Gesamtbestand und die Kapitalbindungs-, Lager- und Verwaltungskosten sinken. Die Zusammenarbeit und ein offener Informationsaustausch zwischen Kunden und Lieferanten ist dabei entscheidend für eine effektive und kooperative Planung der unternehmensübergreifenden Ersatzteillogistik (Huiskonen, 2001, S. 125). Das Konzept des Ersatzteilpoolings verfolgt eine gemeinsame Nutzung des Ersatzteillagers bzw. die Aufteilung der Bestände auf Drittanbieter. Die Verwaltung des Ersatzteil-Pools kann hierbei vom Betreiber oder vom Dienstleister ausgehen, wobei im Falle des Drittanbieters der Anreiz des Poolings bei gleichzeitiger Entscheidungsgewalt steigt (Godoy et al., 2014, S. 103; Karsten, Basten, 2013, S. 94 f.). Der Drittanbieter als Lagerverwalter erlangt somit eine größere Marktsicherheit und kann seine Losgrößen besser planen (Schuh et al., 2013, S. 196 f.). Als Hürde des Ersatzteilpoolings gilt allerdings die Kostenverteilung zwischen den Partnern (Wang et al., 2007, S. 371).

Infolge der bereits beschriebenen Ansätze ist es Betreibern mithilfe von Drittanbietern außerdem möglich, ein Obsoleszenz- bzw. Auslaufmanagement anzustreben. Insbesondere elektronische Komponenten sind in diesem Zusammenhang kritisch zu sehen, da hier der Primärprodukthersteller die Versorgung oft nicht über die gesamte Serviceperiode garantieren kann. Die Gründe hierfür sind zumeist in den immer kürzeren Innovationszyklen bei gleichzeitig länger anhaltender Produktlebensdauer zu finden (Dombrowski et al., 2005, S. 200 f.; Wagner et al., 2012, S. 69). Das Auslaufmanagement richtet den Fokus auf die Sicherstellung der Ersatzteilversorgung für langlebige Primärprodukte nach dem Ende der Serienproduktion. Diese Methode kommt vor allem dann zum Einsatz, wenn der Hersteller kritische Ersatzeile abkündigt. Zu denkbaren Strategien gehören u.a. die Verwendung kompatibler Teile, die Lagerung eines abschließenden Loses (Final Order) sowie die interne oder die externe Fertigung und Wiederaufbereitung durch Drittanbieter (Hesselbach et al., 2004, S. 113; Hong et al., 2008, S. 641). Erschwert wird das kooperative Auslaufmanagement durch die Dynamik des Ersatzteilbedarfs sowie das Wettstreben konkurrierender Produkte und Gebrauchtteile am Markt. Das so geförderte reaktive, kurzfristige Agieren von Unternehmen wird Ad-hoc-Management genannt und kann bedingen, dass den Abnehmer Abkündigungen unvorbereitet treffen (Schulze et al., 2012, S. 144).

Als erste theoretisch motivierte Annahme ist somit abzuleiten, dass das Ad-hoc-Management die Langzeitplanung und damit Kooperationen auf Drittanbieterseite erschwert. Die gezielte Sammlung und Auswertung von Informationen über Verfügbarkeiten schon in der Nachserienphase kann hierbei Abhilfe schaffen (Kim et al., 2017, S. 203). Der Mangel an belastbaren Daten und das unzureichende Datenmanagement stellen allerdings ein großes Hemmnis dar. Die Datenqualität und die Kommunikation zwischen den Akteuren sind oft als ungenügend einzustufen, insbesondere dann, wenn die Nachfrageseite nicht genügend Daten und Informationen über die geforderten Ersatzteile erhalten und die Versorgungsseite die Ersatzteilnachfrage nicht rechtzeitig befriedigen kann (Liu, Lyons, 2011, S. 548 ff.; Zanjani, Nourelfath, 2014, S. 44 ff.). Die große Anzahl an Einzelteilen und die Vielfalt der Komponenten aufseiten der Kunden verursachen hierbei eine schlechte Prognosezuverlässigkeit (Dekker et al., 2013, S. 544). Letztlich ist nicht nur die Qualität der Daten entscheidend, sondern auch ihre Verfügbarkeit. Vor allem Drittanbieter stehen vor der Herausforderung, die Daten vom Eigentümer zu erhalten, weshalb das Angebot technischer Dienstleistungen wie Fernwartungen nicht flächendeckend erfolgt. Als Grund für das Verhalten des Herstellers werden in der Literatur Datensicherheitsbedenken angegeben (Kurz, 2016, S. 466). Hier ist die zweite Annahme zu induzieren, dass dies ein Hindernis für das strategisch ausgerichtete Zusammenarbeiten auf dem Drittanbietermarkt darstellt.

2.2 Technologisch ermöglichte Kooperationen

Aufgrund des immer weiter steigenden Automatisierungsgrades erfahren Dienstleistungsangebote auf Basis technologischer Innovationen eine kontinuierliche Weiterentwicklung (Meyer et al., 2012, S. 69). Plattformen, bspw. E-Auktionen und E-Kataloge, werden dazu genutzt, um Zeit und Kosten bei der Beschaffung von Ersatzteilen einzusparen (Michelino, Caputo, 2011, S. 39). Derartige E-Purchasing-Systeme ermöglichen auf effiziente und kostengünstige Weise, Produkte und Dienstleistungen weltweit zu verkaufen (Nedelea, Baditoiu, 2010, S. 67 ff.). Die Gesamtheit an Plattformen wird zuweilen vereinfachend auch als E-Marketplace bezeichnet. Dieser soll eine Integration und langfristige Kooperation zwischen Akteuren fördern und kann deshalb auch als technologische Erweiterung des bereits beschriebenen CM angesehen werden (Eng, 2004, S. 101 ff.; Liu, Jiang, 2013, S. 3416).

Bisher existieren nur wenige Untersuchungen in Bezug auf E-Marketplaces im Rahmen technischer Dienstleistungen (Wang et al., 2011, S. 612 f.). So stellen Michelino und Caputo (2011, S. 41) in einer Studie fest, dass die Portale ihren Einsatz oft nur zur Reduzierung der Kosten innerhalb der Supply Chain erfahren. Sie dienen der Ausführung von Bestellungen, nicht aber der Förderung von Kooperationen, obwohl sie auf der Planungsebene Vorteile mit sich bringen. Beim On-demand Computing (Echtzeit-Bedarfsplanung) z.B. arbeiten alle Akteure gemeinsam in einem Cloud-basierten System, um die Belastungen von Produktionsanlagen durch Sensorik zu erfassen und anhand der gespeicherten Daten Ausfälle zu prognostizieren. Der Ansatz zielt darauf ab, die Kommunikation und die Auftragsabwicklungsprozesse zu vereinfachen sowie Engpässe in der Ersatzteilversorgung zu identifizieren (Fleischer et al., 2013, S. 124 ff.). Obwohl insbesondere die Versorgung der Supply Chain mit echtzeitfähigen Daten das Potenzial hat, die Ersatzteilversorgung zu optimieren, ist dies noch nicht weitverbreitet (Stich et al., 2015, S. 66 f.).

Daraus schlussfolgernd kann die dritte Annahme getroffen werden, dass E-Marketplaces nebst weiteren durch die Digitalisierung ermöglichten Kooperationsmöglichkeiten durch eine einseitige, nicht partnerschaftlich ausgelegte Nutzung noch einen geringen Stellenwert verzeichnen.

3 Methodik

Der Literaturüberblick verdeutlicht, dass ein Nachholbedarf bezüglich der praktischen Bewertung von Kooperationsmöglichkeiten besteht, denn zum Ursprung der Implementierungshemmnisse lassen sich bezogen auf die genannten Akteure nur wenige Aussagen aus der Literatur ableiten. Da der Drittanbietermarkt soziale, komplexe Einheiten von Unternehmen umfasst, wurde zur Überprüfung der gestellten Annahmen die Methodik der qualitativen Analyse in Form von Fallstudien mit Experteninterviews gewählt (Eisenhardt, Graebner, 2007, S. 25).

3.1 Qualitative Fallstudien und Experteninterviews

Im Allgemeinen werden in einer Fallstudie Detailinformationen gesammelt, die dem Forschenden einen tiefgreifenden Eindruck vom Forschungsobjekt verschaffen, weswegen oft nur ein oder wenige Projekte unter hohem Aufwand realisierbar sind (von Rimscha, Sommer, 2016, S. 369 ff.). Für die Konzeption des Forschungsdesigns gilt hierbei die Einhaltung bestimmter Gütekriterien. Konstruktvalidität hilft bei der Identifikation korrekter Maßnahmen zur Datensammlung, während die interne Validität die kausalen Beziehungen und Verknüpfungen zwischen den Erhebungsdaten sicherstellt. Externe Validität ist ein Kriterium zur Auswahl der untersuchten Fälle und Reliabilität wird wiederum durch eine sorgfältige Dokumentation sichergestellt, um Wiederholbarkeit zu garantieren (Stuart et al., 2002, S. 430).

Wir wählten das Experteninterview als Haupterhebungsinstrument, da es sich durch eine hohe inhaltliche Kausalität auszeichnet (Yin, 2009, S. 106 f.). Der Schwerpunkt sollte dabei vor allem auf der Generierung tieferer Erkenntnisse liegen (Flick, 2007, S. 193 ff.). Hierbei eignet sich besonders das halbstandardisierte bzw. semistrukturierte Leitfadeninterview. Auf diese Art soll dem Befragten zum einen die Freiheit gewährt werden, neue und zukunftsrelevante Aspekte zu äußern, und zum anderen ermöglicht werden, theoretische Vorüberlegungen als Diskussionsgrundlage einzubeziehen (Bortz, Döring, 2006, S. 314). Die Durchführung fundiert auf dem Interviewleitfaden, der die Übersetzung des Untersuchungsgegenstandes und der Annahmen repräsentiert (Kaiser, 2014, S. 52). In dessen Mittelpunkt stand somit, die Bekanntheit und Verbreitung der erarbeiteten Kooperationsmöglichkeiten zu erfassen sowie die entsprechenden Unsicherheiten und Umsetzungshemmnisse.

Die Auswahl von Fällen wird von den Forschungsfragen und dem Zugang zu potenziellen Daten, Interviewpartnern, Dokumenten und Beobachtungsmöglichkeiten beeinflusst (Yin, 2009, S. 30). Maßgebliches Kriterium für die Auswahl der Probanden stellte die Perspektive innerhalb der ersatzteillogistischen Lieferkette dar. Die Positionen Hersteller, Betreiber und Drittanbieter sollten durch mindestens einen Repräsentanten vertreten sein. Da der Fokus auf den Drittanbietern liegt, wurden hier zwei Unternehmen interviewt, die sich – zur Sicherstellung der externen Validität und Güte der Ergebnisse – im Kontext deutlich voneinander unterschieden. Zusätzlich stammen die Unternehmen aus investitionsintensiven Branchen mit einer Anlagen-Mindestnutzungsdauer von 20 Jahren. Die aktuelle Position und der Werdegang der Interviewten stellte deren Expertise auf dem behandelten Gebiet sicher (siehe **Tabelle 1**). Da der Hersteller U03H am Markt auch als technischer Dienstleister auftritt, konnte der Ansprechpartner ebenfalls Fragen zur Dienstleistungsperspektive beantworten.

Tabelle 1: Teilnehmende Unternehmen und Interviewpartner

ID	Perspektive	Branche	Mitarbeiter	Position Interviewter
U01D	Drittanbieter	Windenergieanlagen	40	Geschäftsführer
U02B	Betreiber	Glasverarbeitungsindustrie	200	Technischer Betriebsleiter
U03H	Hersteller	Sanitär und Klima	230	Planungsingenieur
U04D	Drittanbieter	Schwermaschinenbau	110	Leiter Einkauf

3.2 Inhaltsanalyse

Die im April und Mai 2017 bei den Unternehmen persönlich durchgeführten Interviews wurden transkribiert und ausgewertet. Da im Rahmen des Forschungsvorhabens die reine Häufigkeit von Nennungen nur von untergeordnetem Belang ist, diente die qualitative Inhaltsanalyse als Instrument zur Auswertung der Interviews. Die für die Beantwortung der Forschungsfrage relevanten Informationen aus den transkribierten Texten wurden aufbereitet, zusammengefasst und strukturiert (Mayring, 2010, S. 17 ff.). Das Programm MAXQDA (Version 12) unterstützte den Auswertungsprozess. Zunächst wurden sämtliche Aussagen in kurzen Oberbegriffen paraphrasiert sowie für die Bearbeitung der Forschungsfragen irrelevante Textstellen gestrichen. Der Interviewleitfaden diente als Grundlage zur deduktiven Ableitung der Auswertungskategorien.

Zentrales Instrument der anschließenden Zusammenfassung war die induktive Erweiterung des Kategorisierungsschemas. Die so gewonnenen Kategorien wurden in Haupt- und Unterkategorien eingeteilt und die entsprechenden Textstellen zugeordnet. Dies ermöglichte die inhaltliche Strukturierung zur Filterung spezifischer Themen und Aspekte. Enthielt eine Textstelle redundante Informationen, wurde nur die prägnanteste, ohne Sinnverlust kodierbare Stelle übertragen. Der Inhalt der Interviews konnte schließlich durch Abstrahieren und Generalisieren auf ein Minimum unterschiedlicher Ausprägungen komprimiert werden. Diese Vorgehensweise war im Zuge der Analyse von hoher Bedeutung, da neue Aspekte häufig erst nach mehrmaligem Lesen und nicht immer im Kontext der eigentlich gestellten Frage auftraten. Die Sortierung der Ausprägungen erfolgte im Sinne gemeinsamer Bedeutungsmerkmale. Die so gewonnenen Inferenzen wurden anschließend fallübergreifend mit den durch die Literaturanalyse gewonnenen Annahmen abgeglichen (Yin, 2009, S. 42 f.).

4 Resultate

Die Präsentation der Studienergebnisse erfolgt in drei Schritten: Zuerst wird die durch die Probanden wahrgenommene Bedeutung von Kooperationen im Allgemeinen herausgestellt, denn hier zeigt sich ein heterogenes Bild. Darauf folgt ein Abgleich der in Abschnitt 2 erläuterten Kooperationsansätze mit deren praktischer Umsetzung in den befragten Unternehmen. Hierbei ist wieder zwischen organisatorischer und technologischer Ebene zu unterscheiden. Abschließend werden die Implikationen und die kritische Würdigung der Studien behandelt.

4.1 Wahrgenommene Bedeutung von Kooperationen

Ersatzteillogistische Lieferanten-Kunden-Kooperationen wurden von den Befragten als wichtig erachtet: Demnach „[…] ist es schon sinnvoll, zwischen Betreiber und Hersteller eine Kooperation aufzubauen, aber auch eine Kooperation zwischen Zulieferer und Hersteller muss da sein […]" (U03H), jedoch kaum im Sinne des strategisch ausgerichteten CM. Für den Betreiber U02B ist so zwar der 24-Stunden-Lieferservice in Notfällen von besonderer Bedeutung, eine tiefer gehende Zusammenarbeit mit den Lieferanten im Hinblick auf ein gemeinsames Ersatzteilmanagement wurde von ihm aber noch nicht in Betracht gezogen. Drittanbieter U04D bietet Ersatzteile in kleinen Stückzahlen an, um sich vom Großhändler abzugrenzen: „Das geht in Richtung Kooperation mit Firmen, mit denen man auch zusammenarbeitet. Drei, vier Firmen, die da immer regelmäßig anrufen" (U04D). Drittanbieter U01D ist unzufrieden mit der derzeitigen Situation bezogen auf bestehende Partnerschaften entlang der Ersatzteillieferkette: „[…] Relevanz in der Vergangenheit gleich Null. Eben, weil im Markt sehr viel Geld dringesteckt hat. Aufgrund der Subventionierung" (U01D) und fügte hinzu: „Für die Zukunft nach vorn heraus denke ich, dass es ein notweniger Schritt ist zu kooperieren. Ansonsten können die ausgerufenen Preise und Vergütungen nicht mehr gehalten werden" (U01D).

Bezüglich der Diskrepanzen mit dem Lieferanten sind die beiden Drittanbieter klar voneinander abzugrenzen: U04D, der den Großteil der Ersatzteile über den Drittanbietermarkt im In- und Ausland bezieht, äußerte keine grundsätzlichen Konflikte, da eine bereits jahrzehntelang andauernde Partnerschaft besteht. Für U01D auf der anderen Seite stellen die Kosten in der Windenergiebranche einen großen Unsicherheitsfaktor dar. Die Ersatzteilbeschaffung macht hier 40% der Instandhaltungskosten aus, wobei das Unternehmen Teile überwiegend vom Originalhersteller erwirbt: „Wir haben eine Auswertung gefahren. Wir haben im Jahr 2016 87% des Ersatzteilaufwandes [bei dem Originalhersteller] bezogen. Der Rest lief über Dritte" (U01D). Dies betrifft überwiegend hochkomplexe elektronische Ersatzteile (75%), weshalb U01D im Vergleich zu den hauptsächlich mechanischen Ersatzteilen von U04D in der Beschaffung über Dritte sehr eingeschränkt ist. U01D sieht daher vor, direkt beim ursprünglichen Lieferanten zu bestellen, um die Unabhängigkeit vom Hersteller zu erlangen. Die entsprechenden Kontakte nebst weiteren für den Drittanbieter relevanten Informationen hält der Anlagenhersteller allerdings zurück und agiert laut Aussage des Interviewten bewusst als Blackbox. Entgegen der Aussage in Abschnitt 2.1 sieht er dabei weniger die Angst vor Datenmissbrauch als vielmehr die durch den Hersteller befürchteten Verluste von Marktanteilen als Ursache: „Auf einer Seite sind wir Marktbegleiter vom Hersteller, auf der anderen Seite sind wir Wettbewerber vom Hersteller und auf der dritten Seite sind wir Kooperationspartner vom Hersteller" (U01D). Die Sicherstellung des Absatzes wird in diesem Fall höher priorisiert als eine Kooperation. Um an ausführliche Informationen bezüglich des Ausfallverhaltens der Anlagen zu gelangen, arbeitet U01D deshalb mit erfahrenen Betreibern und anderen Drittanbietern auf dem Markt zusammen: „Für die älteren Anlagen […] haben wir jetzt eine Alternative, da greifen wir auch manchmal auf Dienstleister zurück" (U01D).

U04D sah eher einen Unsicherheitsfaktor bezogen auf die Qualität der gelieferten Daten, insbesondere hinsichtlich der diskontinuierlichen Nachfrage von Endkunden und deren Ad-hoc-Kommunikation im Fall einer Havarie. Ungünstig für den Drittanbieter ist in diesem Zusammenhang die teilweise sehr lange Vorlaufzeit: „Bei großen Pendelrollenlagern hat man schon eine Vorlaufzeit von vier bis sechs Monaten" (U04D). Dabei bemängelte er auch das Know-how der Lieferanten: „Die technischen Grundlagen, die Zeichnungen, die Informationen werden […] immer schlechter. Die Qualität und der technische Hintergrund" (U04D). Die frühzeitige Kommunikation entlang der Supply Chain könnte hier hilfreich sein: „Reden, reden, reden, […]. Dass jeder mit dem anderen redet. […] ihm das rechtzeitig mitzuteilen, um sich darauf vorbereiten zu können" (U04D).

Der Hersteller U03H stützt diese Aussage, bezog Mängel im Know-how jedoch auf die Drittanbieter: „Er braucht erstmal einen Tag, bis er alles versteht" (U03H). Dies ist seiner Meinung nach nur mithilfe einer intensiveren Zusammenarbeit zwischen Herstellern, Drittanbietern und Betreibern zu verbessern. Die Unsicherheit bezüglich der Verfügbarkeit und Qualität von Informationen ist hierbei als zentral anzusehen, da sie im Fall der befragten Unternehmen die wahrgenommene Relevanz von Kooperationsmöglichkeiten bedingt und beeinflusst.

4.2 Aktuelle Relevanz organisatorischer und technologischer Kooperationsmöglichkeiten

4.2.1 Ersatzteilpooling, Langzeitplanung und Auslaufmanagement

Hemmnisse in Bezug auf die Kostenverteilung beim Ersatzteilpooling konnten generell nicht identifiziert werden, denn diese Strategie spielt eine noch untergeordnete Rolle für die Unternehmen. Der Hersteller U03H besitzt ein Zentrallager und sah keine Notwendigkeit für eine geordnete Aufteilung der Ersatzteile. Der Betreiber U02B zeigte eine ähnliche Sichtweise. Der Dachkonzern verwaltet hier bereits ein internes Ersatzteilnetzwerk, wobei Material auch von anderen Unternehmen innerhalb des Konzerns angefordert werden kann: „Wir haben unser eigenes Zentrallager, aber innerhalb des Konzerns […], gerade für große Bauteile, Steuerungsbauteile, Frequenzumrichter […] wird das per Mail mit der technischen Zentrale kommuniziert" (U02B). Drittanbieter U01D bezeichnete Ersatzteilpooling zwar als relevant für seine Branche: „Ersatzteilpooling kommt mehr und mehr. Es gab schon Feldversuche […]" (U01D), allerdings ist dies noch nicht bei den Kunden angekommen: „Wir haben tatsächlich ein Ersatzteilpooling unseren Betreibern vorgeschlagen. […] Also die Idee fanden sie alle gut, aber keiner sagt: Ja, das machen wir" (U01D). Dies ist auch auf das Fehlen einer strategischen Langzeitplanung zurückzuführen: „Es ist hier eben das Ad-hoc-Management oder wie ich gesagt habe Hands-On-Mentalität. […] es ist hier nicht, dass ich einen strategischen Einkäufer habe, der sich hier nach und nach die Teile anschaut, um proaktiv tätig zu werden, eher reaktiv" (U01D).

Zwar äußerte der Hersteller U03H, dass eine kurzfristige Planung das Eingehen von Kooperationen erschwert, dennoch war eine proaktive Verbesserung dieser Umstände nicht in näherer Zukunft angedacht. So verlässt sich Drittanbieter U04D aus Gründen der diskontinuierlichen Nachfrage eher auf Erfahrungswerte als auf eine gezielte Prognose: „Ja, das wird nach Erfahrungswerten gekauft" (U04D). Sowohl U02B als auch U03H gaben an, dass die Einschätzung der Ersatzteilnachfrage im Unternehmen auf Erfahrungswissen beruht und die Unternehmen diese Unsicherheit mit einem ausreichend bestückten Lager ausgleichen. Dies trifft ebenfalls auf U01D zu, der derzeit noch keine ersatzteilspezifischen Prognosemodelle nutzen kann, da die relativ kurze Existenz des Unternehmens (seit 2015) den Gebrauch von Vergangenheitswerten verhindert. Das Management von obsoleten Ersatzteilen wird folglich erschwert: „[...] weil sie es einfach nicht sauber ermitteln konnten und dann noch hohe Ersatzteilbestände aus den Büchern abschreiben mussten, weil sie es einfach nicht mehr verwenden konnten" (U01D).

Abkündigungen zeigten sich bei allen Unternehmen als Herausforderung: „Anbieter bzw. Zulieferer stellen ihre Ersatzteilprogramme alle 5 bis 10 Jahre oder noch häufiger um, sodass du teilweise ganze Maschinen oder ganze Sanitäranlagen [...] ausbauen musst, da du nicht mehr das bekommst, was du als Ersatzteil dafür brauchst" (U03H). Hierbei sind die Drittanbieter stets auf der Suche nach Alternativen: „Das kam schon vor. [...] ein großer Abbruchhammer von [dem Hersteller] gibt es nicht mehr [...]. Irgendeine Firma […], eine Elektronikfirma, da sind wir rangekommen. Die konnten für diesen Bohrhammer noch Ersatzteile liefern" (U04D).

Ein kooperatives Auslaufmanagement konnte jedoch bei keinem Unternehmen identifiziert werden. Trotz vorhandener Problematiken bezüglich Obsoleszenz und Lieferengpässen agieren sie tendenziell eher reaktiv als proaktiv. Für die Zukunft strebt lediglich U01D eine Langzeitplanung für kritische Ersatzteile an. Das Unternehmen forciert einen strategischen Einkauf, um Lieferschwierigkeiten in windstarken Monaten zu überbrücken und der Veralterung von Teilen vorzubeugen. **Abbildung 1** fasst die geschilderten Erkenntnisse bezüglich der mit Informationsunsicherheit zusammenhängenden Kooperationshemmnisse zusammen.

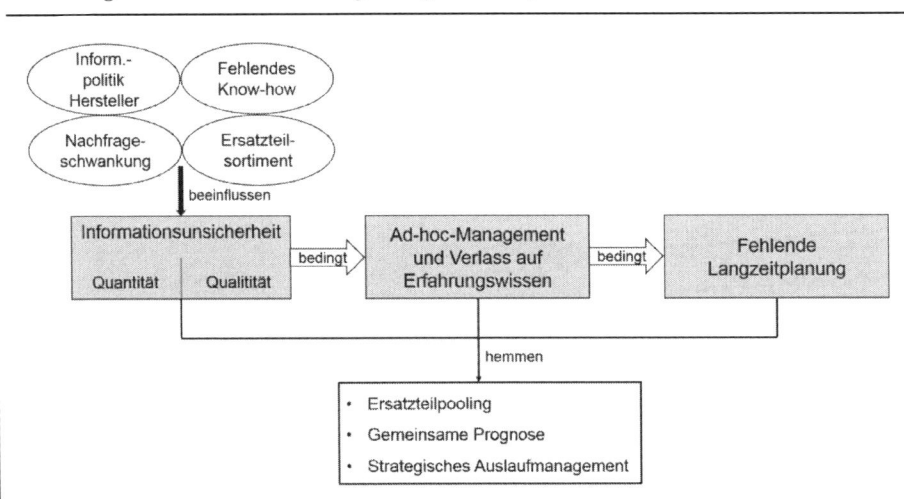

Abbildung 1: Kausalzusammenhänge bezüglich der Informationsunsicherheit

4.2.2 E-Marketplaces und innovative Technologien

E-Marketplaces waren zum Zeitpunkt der Interviews allen außer dem Experten der Betreiber-Perspektive bekannt: „Nein, habe ich noch nicht gesehen" (U02B). Der Drittanbieter U01D stand dem Thema sehr offen gegenüber: „Ja, wir nutzen es tatsächlich auch. Wenn wir merken, es gibt gewisse Ersatzteile, die kann ich dort gebraucht deutlich günstiger kaufen" (U01D). U03H nutzt ebenfalls bestimmte Portale seiner Zulieferer: „[...] unser Einkäufer macht das auch. [...] Der läuft da quasi virtuell durch das Internet und kauft dann im Warenkorb ein" (U03H). U04D sah keinen Mehrwert für die Ersatzteillogistik. Zum einen wies ihm eine in der Vergangenheit bereits genutzte Plattform für technische Dienstleistungen zu lange Reaktionszeiten auf. Zum anderen ging der Interviewte davon aus, dass es für seine benötigten Ersatzteile keine geeignete Plattform gibt, weshalb er einen persönlichen Ansprechpartner bevorzugt. Auch die Einseitigkeit der E-Marketplaces wurde als Hemmnis für die Nutzung angeführt: „Es ist sehr einseitig. Ich würde nicht sagen, dass das eine Kooperation ist. [...] Wenn du da draufgehst, dann suchst du was. Entweder findest du es oder nicht. Das ist eine einseitige Suche irgendwo" (U04D). U03H begründete dies mit dem geringen Level an Vorgangsautomatisierung, da trotz E-Marketplace nach wie vor die Erfragung von Angeboten und die umständliche Ersatzteilsuche erforderlich sind. Außerdem erwähnte er, dass Ersatzteile über entsprechende Portale bisher nur von Großhändlern bezogen werden können. U02B und U04D fügten hinzu, dass die Plattformen eher auf den Kundenkreis bezogen und nicht branchenübergreifend betrieben werden.

In Bezug auf Technologien, die eine kooperative Zusammenarbeit zwischen Akteuren fördern können, erachtete U01D Augmented Reality als Arbeits-, Zeit- und Kostenersparnis für Monteure: „(...) Google Glass als Zukunftstechnologie, um Materialbestellungen abzugeben und Zeit vor Ort zu sparen" (U01D). Zusätzlich ist U01D das einzige der vier Unternehmen, das in der Fernwartung tätig wird, indem es gemeinsam mit weiteren Dienstleistern der Branche ein eigenes System entwickelt.

4.3 Implikationen und kritische Würdigung

Auf Basis der Ergebnisse lässt sich implizieren, dass alle befragten Akteure zwar auf ersatzteillogistische Kooperationen angewiesen sind, die Verbreitung und aktive Nutzung von organisatorischen und technologischen Kooperationsmöglichkeiten jedoch als gering und nur eingeschränkt möglich eingeschätzt werden müssen. So kommen Ersatzteilpooling und E-Marketplaces im Fall der vier befragten Unternehmen nicht bzw. nicht unter strategisch-kooperativen Gesichtspunkten zum Einsatz. Dies lässt sich im Falle der untersuchten Partner zum einen darauf zurückführen, dass die Notwendigkeit noch nicht gesehen wird. Zum anderen existieren Unsicherheiten, die das Eingehen von Kooperationen hemmen. Dazu zählen Versorgungsunsicherheiten – hervorgerufen durch die diskontinuierliche Nachfrage – und hohe Beschaffungskosten nebst langen Lieferzeiten der Ersatzteile. Außerdem sind im ständig drohenden Auslauf und der unerwarteten Abkündigung von Komponenten Unsicherheitsfaktoren zu sehen. Schlecht einschätzbare Kosten bei der Implementierung von Innovationen bewirken zudem eine Übervorsichtigkeit der Unternehmen.

Maßgeblich ist die Problematik der nur unzureichend vorliegenden Informationen, wobei sich eine wichtige doppelte Kausalität ergibt: Die Informationsunsicherheit gilt als Hindernis für eine partnerschaftliche Ersatzteillogistik, da sie gleichzeitig die vorher genannten Unsicherheiten bedingt bzw. verursacht. Gleichzeitig sind Lieferanten-Abnehmer-Kooperationen aber eine wichtige Stellschraube zur Verbesserung der Informationspolitik und damit zur Beseitigung ebendieser Unsicherheitsfaktoren. Die drei eingangs gestellten Annahmen konnten somit bestätigt werden.

Es ist außerdem erkennbar, dass das Dienstleistungsangebot und die Abhängigkeiten entlang der Lieferkette nach Branche differenziert werden müssen. U01D ist mit 40 Mitarbeitern und einer Bestandszeit von zwei Jahren im Windenergiegeschäft recht neu auf dem Drittanbietermarkt, sieht jedoch neben den gravierend empfundenen Unsicherheiten auch die größten Veränderungspotenziale. Dieser Umstand bezog sich hierbei auf die allgemein schwierige Lage der Ersatzteillogistik in der Windenergiebranche, was der Befragte unter anderem auf vergangene und vorherrschende Subventionen zurückführte. Es wird daher empfohlen, in einer zukünftigen Studie mehrere Experten innerhalb einer Branche zu untersuchen, um spezifischere Aussagen bezüglich der Marktdynamiken zu treffen und deutlichere Abgrenzungen zu schaffen. Somit wäre es möglich, geeignete Industriezweige miteinander abzugleichen und herauszustellen, inwieweit Synergien zwischen diesen hergestellt werden können.

Die eingangs erwähnten Gütekriterien wurden eingehalten. Der auf Grundlage aus der Literatur gewonnener Erkenntnisse erstellte Interviewleitfaden bedingt die Beachtung der Konstruktvalidität. Die Sicherstellung der Validität basiert auf der qualitativen Auswertung und Prüfung der Ergebnisse auf Plausibilität durch den Abgleich mit den aus der Literatur gewonnenen Ausarbeitungen (Mayring, 2010, S. 117). Darüber hinaus fanden sowohl sich ähnelnde als auch sich unterscheidende Unternehmen mehrerer Perspektiven eine Beachtung (Yin, 2009, S. 40). Die Vorgehensweise wurde dokumentiert und mehrere Forscher in den Auswertungsprozess eingebunden, sodass auch die Reliabilität gewährleistet ist. Eine Limitation ergibt sich durch die Befragung von nur vier Unternehmen, denn somit sind die dargestellten Ergebnisse – wie dies häufig bei qualitativen Studien der Fall ist – nur bedingt generalisierbar. Innerhalb der Fallstudienforschung geht es allerdings weniger um die Gültigkeit von Messungen als vielmehr um die Validität der Interpretationen und der eingesetzten Methoden. Ein in diesem Zusammenhang verwendetes Gütekriterium ist die semantische Gültigkeit, welche die Prüfung der Bedeutungsrekonstruktion der kodierten Aussagen im Zuge der Kategorien zum Gegenstand hat. In dieser Studie wurden deshalb alle relevanten Textstellen gesammelt und miteinander verglichen sowie wiederholt geprüft. Dabei wurde darauf geachtet, dass das Analyseinstrument die Bedeutung der Originalaussage der Experten rekonstruieren kann (Mayring, 2010, S. 117 ff.).

5 Fazit und Ausblick

Zusammenfassend lässt sich festhalten, dass die Forschungsfragen beantwortet werden konnten. So wird die partnerschaftliche Zusammenarbeit auf dem Drittanbietermarkt von den Probanden nur bedingt als Element der strategischen Ersatzteilplanung erachtet, obwohl speziell Drittanbieter ihre Kosten und Risiken in Bezug auf die Ersatzteillogistik durch geeignete Partnerschaften minimieren können. Die Unternehmen der Investitionsgüterindustrie nehmen ihre ersatzteillogistischen Kooperationsmöglichen nicht in ausreichender Form bewusst wahr, obwohl die Potenziale vorhanden wären, die entsprechenden Prozesse durch eine kollaborative Planung effizienter zu gestalten. Dies betrifft sowohl die Zusammenarbeit auf organisatorischer Ebene, bspw. durch Ersatzteilpooling und Auslaufmanagement, als auch technologisch ermöglichte Kooperationen, etwa in Form von E-Marketplaces und Fernwartungen.

Die qualitative Untersuchung zeigt, dass insbesondere Unsicherheiten und Hemmnisse bedingt durch ein schlechtes Informationsmanagement zum derzeitigen Fehlen der langfristigen Sichtweise in den befragten Unternehmen beitragen. Dies wiederum verstärkt die vorhandenen Schwierigkeiten bezüglich der hohen Handlingkosten und der Ersatzteilversorgung, bspw. Unsicherheiten hervorgerufen durch unstete Bedarfe. Elektronische Ersatzteile mit kurzen Lebens- und Innovationszyklen in der Auslaufphase der Primärprodukte gelten hierbei als hauptsächliche Planungsherausforderung, denn deren Anbieter haben meist nur eine kleine Auswahl an Lieferanten. Dies fördert spezifische Abhängigkeiten, deren Auswirkungen auf die Ersatzteillogistik der Akteure in vertiefenden Studien zu erforschen sind.

Prognosen bezüglich der zukünftigen Ersatzteilversorgung und die langfristige Optimierung der Prozesse stehen bei allen untersuchten Unternehmen erst am Anfang, denn noch haben Erfahrungswerte und das Ad-hoc-Management den höheren Stellenwert. Zukünftige Forschungsanliegen sollten sich deshalb darauf konzentrieren, eine proaktive Leitkultur zu fördern und dazu beitragen, die intensivere Zusammenarbeit zwischen allen Akteuren attraktiver zu machen. Eine konsequente Langzeitplanung ebnet hierbei den Weg für die Akzeptanz von Innovationen, wobei mehr Studien, die entsprechende Erfolgsfaktoren identifizieren, notwendig sind. Auch quantitative empirische Untersuchungen sind in diesem Zusammenhang denkbar. Unsere Ergebnisse repräsentieren hierfür bereits eine thematische Weichenstellung.

Literatur

Behfard, S.; Heijden, M. C. van der; Al Hanbali, A; Zijm, W. H. M. (2015): Last time buy and repair decisions for spare parts, in: European Journal of Operational Research, 244, 498–510.

Bortz, J.; Döring, N. (2006): Forschungsmethoden und Evaluation für Human- und Sozialwissenschaftler, 4. Auflage, Heidelberg: Springer Medizin Verlag.

Dekker, R.; Pinçe, Ç.; Zuidwijk, R.; Jalil, M. N. (2013): On the use of installed base information for spare parts logistics: A review of ideas and industry practice, in: International Journal of Production Economics, 143(2), 536-545.

Dombrowski, U.; Horatzek, S.; Wrehde, J. (2005): Der Weg zu einem lebenszyklusorientierten Ersatzteilmanagement Teil II: Vergangenheitsbewältigung, in: Zeitschrift für wirtschaftlichen Fabrikbetrieb, 100(4), 197–201.

Eickelpasch, A. (2014): Industrielle Nachfrage nach Dienstleistungen, DIW Roundup: Politik im Fokus, No. 10.

Eisenhardt, K.; Graebner, M. (2007): Theory building from cases: Opportunities and challenges, in: Academy of Management Journal, 50(1), 25–32.

Eng, T. Y. (2004): The role of e-marketplaces in supply chain management, in: Industrial Marketing Management, 33(2), 97–105.

Fleischer J.; Lanza G.; Appel, D.; Stricker, N.; Hennrich, H.; Herder, S. (2013): Life Cycle Performance 4.0 – Strategische und technische Lösungen für den intelligenten Betrieb von Maschinen und Anlagen, in: Zeitschrift Werkstatttechnik online, 103(2), 124–129.

Flick, U. (2007): Qualitative Sozialforschung – eine Einführung, vollständig überarbeitete und erweiterte Neuausgabe, Reinbek bei Hamburg: Rowohlt.

Godoy, D. R.; Pascual, R.; Knights, P. (2014): A decision-making framework to integrate maintenance contract conditions with critical spares management, in: Reliability Engineering & System Safety, 131, 102–108.

Gröllich, D.; Lehmann, I.; Paritschkow, S.; Schmauder, M. (2015): Ein Leitfaden für produzierende KMU zur Analyse und Gestaltung von produktbegleitenden Dienstleistungen, Technische Universität Dresden, Projekt WEGANO.

Hesselbach, J.; Dombrowski, U.; Bothe, T.; Graf, R.; Wrehde, J.; Mansour, M. (2004): Planning process for the spare part management of automotive electronics, in: Production Engineering, 11(1), 113–118.

Hong, J. S.; Koo, H. Y.; Lee, C. S.; Ahn, J. (2008): Forecasting service parts demand for a discontinued product, in: IEE Transactions, 40(7), 640–649.

Huiskonen, J. (2001): Maintenance spare parts logistics: Special characteristics and strategic choices, in: International Journal of Production Economics, 71(1), 125–133.

Kaiser, R. (2014): Qualitative Experteninterviews: Konzeptionelle Grundlagen und praktische Durchführung, Wiesbaden: Springer VS.

Karsten, F.; Basten, R. J. (2014): Pooling of spare parts between multiple users: How to share the benefits?, in: European Journal of Operational Research, 233(1), 94–104.

Kim, T. Y.; Dekker, R.; Heij, C. (2017): Spare part demand forecasting for consumer goods using installed base information, in: Computers & Industrial Engineering, 103, 201–215.

Klostermann, T. (2007): Optimierung kooperativer Dienstleistungen im Technischen Kundendienst des Maschinenbaus, Wiesbaden: Gabler.

Kurz, J. (2016): Capacity planning for a maintenance service provider with advanced information, in: European Journal of Operational Research, 251(2), 466–477.

Lanza, G.; Fleischer, J.; Schulze, V.; Appel, D.; Behmann, B., Bertsch, D.; Braun, J.; Hennrich, H.; Herder, S.; Meier, H.; Peters, S.; Stoll, J.; Stricker, N. (2012): Life Cycle Performance in der Produktionstechnik – Ausgewählte Ansätze zur Steigerung von Zuverlässigkeit und Effizienz, in: Zeitschrift Werkstatttechnik online, 103(2), 513–517.

Liu, C. L.; Lyons, A. C. (2011): An analysis of third-party logistics performance and service provision, in: Transportation Research Part E: Logistics and Transportation Review, 47(4), 547–570.

Liu, J.; Jiang, T. (2013): Research on Collaborative Management Strategy of Spare Parts Based on E-Marketplaces, in: Advanced Materials Research, 694–697, 3412–3418.

Mayring, P. (2010): Qualitative Inhaltsanalyse: Grundlagen und Techniken, 11. aktualisierte und überarbeitete Auflage, Weinheim, Basel: Beltz.

Meyer, K.; Thieme, M.; Dijk, S. (2012): Ansatzpunkte, Maßnahmen und Handlungsempfehlungen für die Verzahnung von Dienstleistungen und Hochtechnologie, in: Meyer, K.; Thieme, M. (Hrsg.): High-Tech-Services, Clustermanagement und Dienstleistungsengineering: Potentiale, Trends und Perspektiven, Leipziger Beiträge zur Informatik: Band XXXV, 67–93.

Michelino, F.; Caputo, M. (2011): The Role of Internet-based Tools in Customer–Supplier Relationships, in: Marketing Review St. Gallen, 28(4), 38-43.

Nedelea, S.; Baditoiu, L. (2010): E-marketplaces and Their Importance for Logistic Networks, in: Internal Auditing and Risk Management, 1(17), 67–78.

Pawellek, G. (2016): Integrierte Instandhaltung und Ersatzteillogistik – Vorgehensweisen, Methoden, Tools, 2. Auflage, Berlin, Heidelberg: Springer Vieweg.

IPRI (Hrsg.) (2013): LeAnServ – Lebenszyklusorientierte Anpassung des logistischen Servicelevels in der Nachkaufphase für Maschinenkomponentenhersteller, Schlussbericht, Vorhaben 16724, IPRI – International Performance Research Institute gGmbh.

Rimscha, M. B. von; Sommer, C. (2016): Fallstudien in der Kommunikationswissenschaft, in: Averbeck-Lietz, S. (Hrsg.): Handbuch nicht standardisierte Methoden in der Kommunikationswissenschaft, Wiesbaden: Springer VS, 369–384.

Shi, Y.; Zhang, A.; Arthanari, T.; Liu, Y.; Cheng, T. C. E. (2016): Third-party purchase: An empirical study of third-party logistics providers in China, in: International Journal of Production Economics, 171, 189–200.

Schmidt, C. (2004): Analyse von Leitfadeninterviews, in: Flick, U.; von Kardorff, E.; von Steinke, I. (Hrsg.): Qualitative Forschung: ein Handbuch, 3. Auflage, Reinbek bei Hamburg: Rowohlt, 447–456.

Schuh, G.; Stich, V.; Wienholdt, H. (2013): Ersatzteillogistik, in: Schuh, G.; Stich, V. (Hrsg.): Logistikmanagement: Handbuch Produktion und Management 6, 2. vollständig neu bearbeitete und erweiterte Auflage, Berlin, Heidelberg: Springer, 165–208.

Schulze, S.; Engel, C.; Leichnitz, H. (2012): Obsolescence Management as a Tool for Effective Spare Parts Management, in: Dornfeld, D. A.; Linke, B. S. (Hrsg.): Leveraging Technology for a Sustainable World, Berlin, Heidelberg: Springer, 143–148.

Stich, V.; Adema, J.; Blum, M.; Reschke, J. (2015): Supply Chain 4.0: Logistikdienstleister im Kontext der vierten industriellen Revolution, in: Voß, P. H. (Hrsg.): Logistik – eine Industrie, die (sich) bewegt, Wiesbaden: Springer Gabler, 63–76.

Stuart, I.; McCutcheon, D.; Handfield, R.; McLachlin, R.; Samson, D. (2002): Effective case research in operations management: a process perspective, in: Journal of Operations Management, 20(5), 419–433.

Wagner, S. M.; Jönke, R.; Eisingerich, A. B. (2012): A strategic framework for spare parts logistics, in: California Management Review, 54(4), 69–92.

Wang, Y.; Potter, A.; Naim, M.; Beevor, D. (2011): A case study exploring drivers and implications of collaborative electronic logistics marketplaces, in: Industrial Marketing Management, 40(4), 612–623.

Wang, H.; Van Oudheusden, D.; Cattrysse, D. (2007): Cost allocation in spare parts inventory pooling, in: Transportation Research Part E: Logistics and Transportation Review, 43(4), 370–386.

Yin, R. K. (2009): Case Study Research: Design and Research, 4. Auflage, Los Angeles: Sage Publication.

Zanjani, M. K.; Nourelfath, M. (2014): Integrated spare parts logistics and operations planning for maintenance service providers, in: International Journal of Production Economics, 158, 44–53.

Erfolgsfaktoren zur zukünftigen Gestaltung resilienter Supply Chains – Konzeption eines Bezugsrahmens

Lukas Biedermann, Herbert Kotzab

Abstract

Ziel des vorliegenden Beitrages ist die Bestimmung von Erfolgsfaktoren und deren Wirkzusammenhängen, die zur zukünftigen Gestaltung resilienter Supply Chains beitragen. Im Rahmen einer systematischen Literaturanalyse wurden auf einer Datenbasis von 180 Publikationen 13 relevante Bezugsrahmen mit direktem Bezug zu insgesamt 34 verschiedenen Einflussfaktoren von Supply-Chain-Resilienz identifiziert. Aufgrund einer fehlenden Standardterminologie und eines mangelnden Verständnisses über Wirkzusammenhänge wird in der Literatur jedoch nicht deutlich, welche Erfolgsfaktoren eine bedeutende Rolle in der Gestaltung resilienter Supply Chains spielen. Mit dem hier entwickelten Bezugsrahmen soll dieses Defizit ausgeglichen werden, indem Erfolgsfaktoren anhand ihrer Wirkungszusammenhänge in einem logischen Ordnungsrahmen abgebildet werden. Durch seine inhaltliche Fülle stellt der konzeptionelle Bezugsrahmen ein provisorisches Erklärungsmodell dar, das als Grundlage für eine weitere empirische Überprüfung dienen kann.

1 Einleitung[10]

Eine zunehmende Vernetzungsdichte und eine steigende Volatilität in internationalen Wirtschaftsmärkten führen zu einer häufigeren Anfälligkeit von Supply Chains gegenüber nicht vorhersehbaren Störungen (Sahu, Datta, Mahapatra, 2016). Weitere Ursachen für die Störanfälligkeit von Versorgungsketten vieler Industrien können in der global vernetzten sowie komplexen Struktur von Wertschöpfungsketten gefunden werden (Thun, Hoenig, 2011). Vor diesem Hintergrund sind Unternehmen angehalten, Fähigkeiten zu entwickeln, die nach einem Störfall eine schnelle Rückkehr zur Ausgangssituation ermöglichen (Scholten et al., 2014, S. 211).

---

[10] Der vorliegende Beitrag basiert auf bisher nicht veröffentlichten Ausführungen von Biedermann.

Ponomarov und Holcomb bezeichnen dies im Kontext von Supply Chain Management als Supply-Chain-Resilienz und definieren diese als „die adaptive Fähigkeit einer Supply Chain, sich auf unvorhergesehene Ereignisse vorzubereiten, auf Störungen zu reagieren und durch die kontinuierliche Ausführung der Geschäftsprozesse auf das angestrebte Leistungsniveau, durch strukturelle und funktionale Kontrolle, zurückzukehren" (Ponomarov, Holcomb, 2009, S. 131).

Trotz des verstärkten Forschungsinteresses (Carvalho, Azevedo, Cruz-Machado, 2012) liegen in Bezug auf Resilienzforschung wenig Befunde vor (Scholten et al., 2014, S. 211). Dies betrifft vor allem die Frage, wie eine resiliente Supply Chain zu gestalten ist, um zukünftigen Störungen erfolgreich zu begegnen.

Der vorliegende Beitrag will sich damit befassen und setzt sich die Identifikation von Erfolgsfaktoren zur Gestaltung resilienter Supply Chains sowie deren zugrunde liegenden Wirkzusammenhänge zum Ziel. Dazu wird die relevante Literatur nach existierenden Bezugsrahmen sowie Erfolgsfaktoren und Wirkzusammenhängen inhaltlich analysiert. Anschließend folgt ein Vorschlag zu einem konzeptionellen Bezugsrahmen zur Identifikation und Darstellung von zukünftigen Erfolgsfaktoren zur Gestaltung resilienter Supply Chains vorgestellt.

2 Kritische Bestandsaufnahme der Literatur

2.1 Methodischer Zutritt

In Anlehnung an Denyer und Tranfield (2009) wurde die Untersuchung in mehreren Schritten durchgeführt. Die Literatur wurde in mehreren wissenschaftlichen Datenbanken gesucht (sciencedirect, emeraldinsight, tandofline, springerlink sowie ieeexplore.iie.org), wobei eine Suche im Titel und im Abstrakt nach den Begriffen „supply chain" und „resilien*" durchgeführt wurde. Als Untersuchungszeitraum für die zu sichtende Literatur wurde der Zeitraum von 2003 bis 2016 festgelegt (Kamalahmadi, Mellat-Parast, 2016, S. 117). Auf dieser Grundlage konnten zunächst knapp unter 500 Beiträge identifiziert werden, die in einem weiteren Schritt in Bezug auf deren Tauglichkeit für den Untersuchungszweck inhaltlich geprüft wurden. Dies führte zu einer weiteren Reduktion auf 180 Beiträge zur Supply-Chain-Resilienz, die in die Untersuchung gelangten. In diesen 180 Publikationen konnten wiederum 28 unterschiedliche Bezugsrahmen gefunden werden. Diese wurden dahingehend geprüft, ob Supply-Chain-Resilienz den zentralen Untersuchungsgegenstand zur Bildung des Bezugsrahmens bildet. Auf diese Weise wurden 13 Bezugsrahmen mit direktem Bezug zu Einflussfaktoren bzw. zu Elementen, Eigenschaften oder Voraussetzungen von Supply-Chain-Resilienz identifiziert.

2.2 Inhaltliche Schwerpunkte in der Literatur

Tabelle 1 stellt die relevanten Bezugsrahmen in Bezug auf den Forschungsgegenstand und den -fokus sowie die erkannten Forschungslücken kompakt dar. Insgesamt konnte festgestellt werden, dass die identifizierten Bezugsrahmen zwar strukturell stark unterschiedlich sind, sich aber inhaltlich ähneln. Die angeführten Eigenschaften, Einfluss- und Erfolgsfaktoren resilienter Supply Chains sind zahlreich genannt, doch es mangelt an einer Darstellung der Wirkzusammenhänge.

Tabelle 1: Kritische Bestandsaufnahme zu Bezugsrahmen zur Supply-Chain-Resilienz

Autor	Inhaltliche Analyse		
	Gegenstand der Forschung	Fokus der Forschung	Forschungsdefizite
Christopher, Peck (2004)	Einflussfaktoren zur Steigerung der Resilienz von Supply Chains in privaten und öffentlichen Sektoren	Erkennung von und Umgang mit Supply-Chain-Risiken aus Prozess-Perspektive Darstellung von Einflussfaktoren für den Ausbau resilienter Supply-Chain-Strukturen	unspezifischer/ generischer Bezugsrahmen keine klare Darstellung der Wirkzusammenhänge
Reichhart, Holweg (2007)	Zusammenhang zwischen Produktions- und Supply-Chain-Flexibilität und Reaktionsfähigkeit unter Berücksichtigung von bedarfsseitigen Anforderungen und internen Fähigkeiten	vier Typologien von Reaktionsfähigkeit: Produkt, Volumen, Mix und Lieferung Identifikation von Faktoren zur Steigerung der Reaktionsfähigkeit der Supply Chain	unvollständige Darstellung von Erfolgsfaktoren keine Betrachtung der Wirkzusammenhänge der Faktoren
Kong, Li (2008)	Risikoursachen zur Entwicklung eines Bezugsrahmens zur Gestaltung resilienter Supply Chains	Faktoren zur Steigerung der Supply-Chain-Resilienz	enger theoretischer Forschungszugang aus der Perspektive des Wissensmanagements mangelnde Berücksichtigung der Wirkzusammenhänge
Ponomarov, Holcomb (2009)	Literatur-Review zur Integration verschiedener Perspektiven zur Supply-Chain-Resilienz	Bezugsrahmen zur Darstellung von Erfolgsfaktoren, insb. der Bedeutung der logistischen Leistungsfähigkeit zur Gestaltung resilienter Supply-Chain-Strukturen und -Prozesse	starker Fokus auf logistische Leistungsfähigkeit keine Berücksichtigung von Erfolgsfaktoren

Anwendungsorientierte Forschungsbeiträge

Autor	Inhaltliche Analyse		
	Gegenstand der Forschung	Fokus der Forschung	Forschungsdefizite
Pettit et al. (2010)	Metaanalyse zum Umgang mit Supply-Chain-Störereignissen und deren Umgang	konzeptioneller Bezugsrahmen unternehmerischer Steuerungsmöglichkeiten zur Schwachstellenbekämpfung entlang einer Supply Chain	sehr breit gefasster konzeptioneller Bezugsrahmen keine Betrachtung von Wirkzusammenhängen
Blackhurst et al. (2011)	empirische Untersuchung von Eigenschaften resilienter Supply Chains	konzeptioneller Bezugsrahmen zur Bestimmung des Resilienz-Levels einer Supply Chain Darstellung von Erfolgsfaktoren und limitierenden Faktoren zur Gestaltung einer resilienten Supply Chain	keine Berücksichtigung der Wirkzusammenhänge der Erfolgsfaktoren
Soni, Jain (2011)	Untersuchung wesentlicher Treiber für Supply-Chain-Verletzlichkeit sowie daraus abgeleiteter Faktoren zur Gestaltung resilienter Supply-Chain-Fähigkeiten	Darstellung verschiedener Faktoren zur Gestaltung resilienter Supply Chains	unvollständiger Bezugsrahmen Wirkzusammenhänge nicht berücksichtigt
Pal et al. (2014)	empirische Untersuchung der Voraussetzungen für die Resilienz mittelständischer Unternehmen aus der schwedischen Textilindustrie	Erfolgsfaktoren zur Gestaltung von Resilienz	fokussiert auf einen Industriezweig und enger regionaler Untersuchungsrahmen keine Untersuchung von Wirkzusammenhängen der identifizierten Faktoren
Scholten et al. (2014)	Analyse der Abhängigkeiten zwischen dem Konzept der Supply-Chain-Resilienz auf Basis der strategischen Managementliteratur und der Erkenntnisse aus der anwendungsorientierten Katastrophen-Forschung	integrierter Bezugsrahmen als Management-Entscheidungshilfe in der Vorbereitung auf unvorhersehbare Störereignisse sowie der Störungsbeseitigung Zuordnung der Faktoren zu den einzelnen Phasen des Störungsverlaufs	retrospektiver Forschungsansatz auf Basis humanitärer Supply Chains sehr übergeordnete Betrachtungsebene Bezugsrahmen in Form einer Auflistung Wirkzusammenhänge nicht betrachtet

Autor	Inhaltliche Analyse		
	Gegenstand der Forschung	Fokus der Forschung	Forschungsdefizite
Pereira et al. (2014)	Untersuchung der Bedeutung der Einkaufsabteilung bei der Identifikation von unternehmensinternen und -übergreifenden Störungen mit Auswirkungen auf die Resilienz der Supply Chain	Untersuchung von limitierenden und Erfolgsfaktoren zur Gestaltung resilienter Supply Chains	allgemein gehaltener Bezugsrahmen ohne Berücksichtigung vorab identifizierter Erfolgs- und limitierenden Faktoren Wirkzusammenhänge nicht berücksichtigt
Hosseini et al. (2016)	Untersuchung der wesentlichen Elemente zum Design resilienter Supply Chains basierend auf Absorption, Anpassungsfähigkeit und Regeneration	mehrstufiges Vorgehensmodell für die Gestaltung resilienter Supply Chains Darstellung der Abhängigkeiten der wesentlichen Gestaltungseigenschaften	Vorgehensmodell mit leichtem Fokus auf die mathematische Bestimmung des Resilienz-Wertes der Supply-Chain-Struktur
Purvis et al. (2016)	Untersuchung der Unterschiede zwischen Theorie und Praxis zur Entwicklung von Strategien zur Gestaltung resilienter Supply Chains	Bezugsrahmen zur Darstellung verschiedener Elemente zur Gestaltung resilienter Supply Chains und Strategien	geringe externe Validität der Befunde aufgrund der geringen Stichprobe (n=1) mangelnde Nachvollziehbarkeit der Vorgehensweise
Kamalahmadi, Mellat-Parast (2016)	Untersuchung des aktuellen Forschungsstandes zur Supply-Chain-Resilienz	Bezugsrahmen mit mehreren Prinzipien zur Supply-Chain-Resilienz sowie deren Beziehungen	begrenzter Betrachtungsumfang der Literaturrecherche unvollständige Abbildung der wesentlichen Prinzipien und Erfolgsfaktoren für Supply-Chain-Resilienz im Vergleich zu früheren Veröffentlichungen

2.3 Literaturgestützte Erfolgsfaktoren zur Gestaltung resilienter Supply Chains

Summarisch konnten in der in **Tabelle 1** vorgestellten Literatur 34 unterschiedliche Erfolgsfaktoren zur Gestaltung resilienter Supply Chains gefunden werden. Dabei werden die von Christopher und Peck (2004) vorgeschlagenen Faktoren Supply-Chain-Reengineering, Kollaboration, Agilität und eine gemeinsame Supply-Chain-Risikomanagement-Kultur zwischen den beteiligten Akteuren als allgemeine Erfolgsfaktoren anerkannt. Diese bilden die Basis für das Grundlagenverständnis von Supply-Chain-Resilienz (Kamalahmadi, Mellat-Parast, 2016, S. 122). Scholten, Sharkey und Fynes (2014) fügen dabei das Wissensmanagement als fünften allgemeinen Erfolgsfaktor hinzu.

Neben diesen allgemein akzeptierten Erfolgsfaktoren konnten in der Literatur die Faktoren Flexibilität, Redundanz und Sichtbarkeit/Transparenz als spezifische Erfolgsfaktoren festgestellt werden.

Insgesamt lassen aber die Ergebnisse der Literaturanalyse keine Aussage darüber zu, welche wesentlichen Elemente, Erfolgsfaktoren oder Prinzipien maßgeblich zur zukünftigen Gestaltung einer resilienten Supply Chain beitragen. Beispielsweise wird der Faktor Agilität in mindestens sechs der dreizehn Bezugsrahmen genannt, jedoch lässt sich hieraus keine Aussage über ihre allgemeine Gültigkeit treffen, da ebenso 33 weitere Eigenschaften genannt werden. Mögliche Gründe für die beobachtete Vielfalt mögen in den verschiedenen zugrunde liegenden Forschungsperspektiven, der uneinheitlichen Verwendung der jeweiligen Begrifflichkeiten sowie in den unterschiedlichen Untersuchungsobjekten der untersuchten Publikationen liegen.

2.4 Kritische Würdigung der Befunde

Die in den vorangegangenen Abschnitten präsentierten Ergebnisse können wie folgt reflektiert werden:

- Insgesamt werden viele unterschiedliche Erfolgsfaktoren zur Gestaltung resilienter Supply Chains in den Bezugsrahmen genannt und beschrieben. Die am häufigsten genannten Eigenschaften sind Flexibilität, Transparenz/Sichtbarkeit, Agilität und Zusammenarbeit.

- Aufgrund einer fehlenden Standardterminologie und eines mangelnden Verständnisses über Wirkzusammenhänge ist nicht klar, welche Erfolgsfaktoren zur Gestaltung resilienter Supply Chains eine bedeutende oder weniger bedeutende Rolle spielen. Das begriffliche Verständnis der genannten Erfolgsfaktoren unterscheidet sich teilweise stark.

- Wirkzusammenhänge zwischen den Erfolgsfaktoren zur Supply-Chain-Resilienz werden nur in zwei Bezugsrahmen beschrieben.

- Die in der Literatur identifizierten Erfolgsfaktoren sind Ergebnisse retrospektiver Forschungsarbeiten.

Vor diesem Hintergrund soll die Gültigkeit der Erfolgsfaktoren für zukünftige Herausforderungen im Supply Chain Management im Zuge der Ausarbeitung im folgenden Abschnitt überprüft werden.

3 Aufbau und Struktur eines konzeptionellen Bezugsrahmens

Abbildung 1 bildet den für die vorliegende Arbeit relevanten konzeptionellen Bezugsrahmen zur Darstellung von Erfolgsfaktoren zur Gestaltung resilienter Supply Chains ab. Gemäß den Darstellungsvorgaben von Kleiner (2011) und Kubicek (1977, S. 18) umfasst die Abbildung Kästchen und Pfeile. Die Kästchen repräsentieren die relevanten Analyseeinheiten. Die Pfeile stellen die identifizierten Wirkzusammenhänge zwischen den Analyseeinheiten dar. Der Bezugsrahmen wird in drei strukturelle Ebenen unterteilt: Auf der untersten Ebene sind die wesentlichen Erfolgsfaktoren berücksichtigt. Agilität und Robustheit als Gestaltungsansätze sind auf der mittleren Ebene dargestellt. Auf der obersten Ebene wird der Zielzustand als Ergebniseben gezeigt.

3.1 Gestaltungsansätze für resiliente Supply Chains

3.1.1 Agilität

Eine agile Supply Chain zeichnet sich durch die Fähigkeit aus, schnell auf unvorhersehbare Störereignisse reagieren zu können (Carvalho, Duarte, Cruz-Machado, 2011; Braunscheidel, Suresh, 2009; Christopher, Peck, Towill, 2006, S. 281). In diesem Zusammenhang spielt die Fähigkeit einer schnellen Ressourcenallokation eine entscheidende Rolle (Li, Chung, Goldsby, Holsapple, 2008, S. 411). Somit zeichnet sich die agile Supply Chain durch eine hohe Transparenz an Information sowie Informationsweitergabe aus (Hohenstein, Feisel, Hartmann, Giunipero, 2015; Braunscheidel, Suresh, 2009; Swafford, Gosh, Murthy, 2006).

Agilität bedeutet ebenso hohe Geschwindigkeit und Reaktionsfähigkeit der Supply Chain (Christopher, Peck, 2004; Wieland, Wallenburg, 2013), damit Prozesse rasch neu gestaltet werden können und reaktive Maßnahmen zur Reduktion von Schäden bei unvorhersehbaren Störungen rasch eingeleitet werden (Wieland, 2013, S. 654; Blackhurst et al., 2011; Agarwal, Shankar, Tiwari, 2007; Christopher, 2000).

3.1.2 Robustheit

Robustheit gilt als Kapazität des Netzwerks, interne oder externe Störereignisse auszuhalten (Ponnambalam, Long, Sarawgi, Fu, Goh, 2014, S. 8; Meepetchdee, Shah, 2007; Dekker, Colbert, 2004). Es handelt sich um die Fähigkeit der Supply Chain, während und infolge logistischer Prozessstörungen adäquat leistungsfähig zu bleiben (Vlajic, van der Vorst, Haijema, 2012). Im Sinne eines End-to-End-Gestaltungsansatzes soll Robustheit proaktiv die kapazitive Widerstandsfähigkeit einer Supply Chain gegenüber potenziellen Störereignissen erhöhen, damit negative Leistungsauswirkungen während und infolge von Prozessstörungen vermieden werden.

Anwendungsorientierte Forschungsbeiträge

Abbildung 1: Konzeptioneller Bezugsrahmen zur Gestaltung resilienter Supply Chains

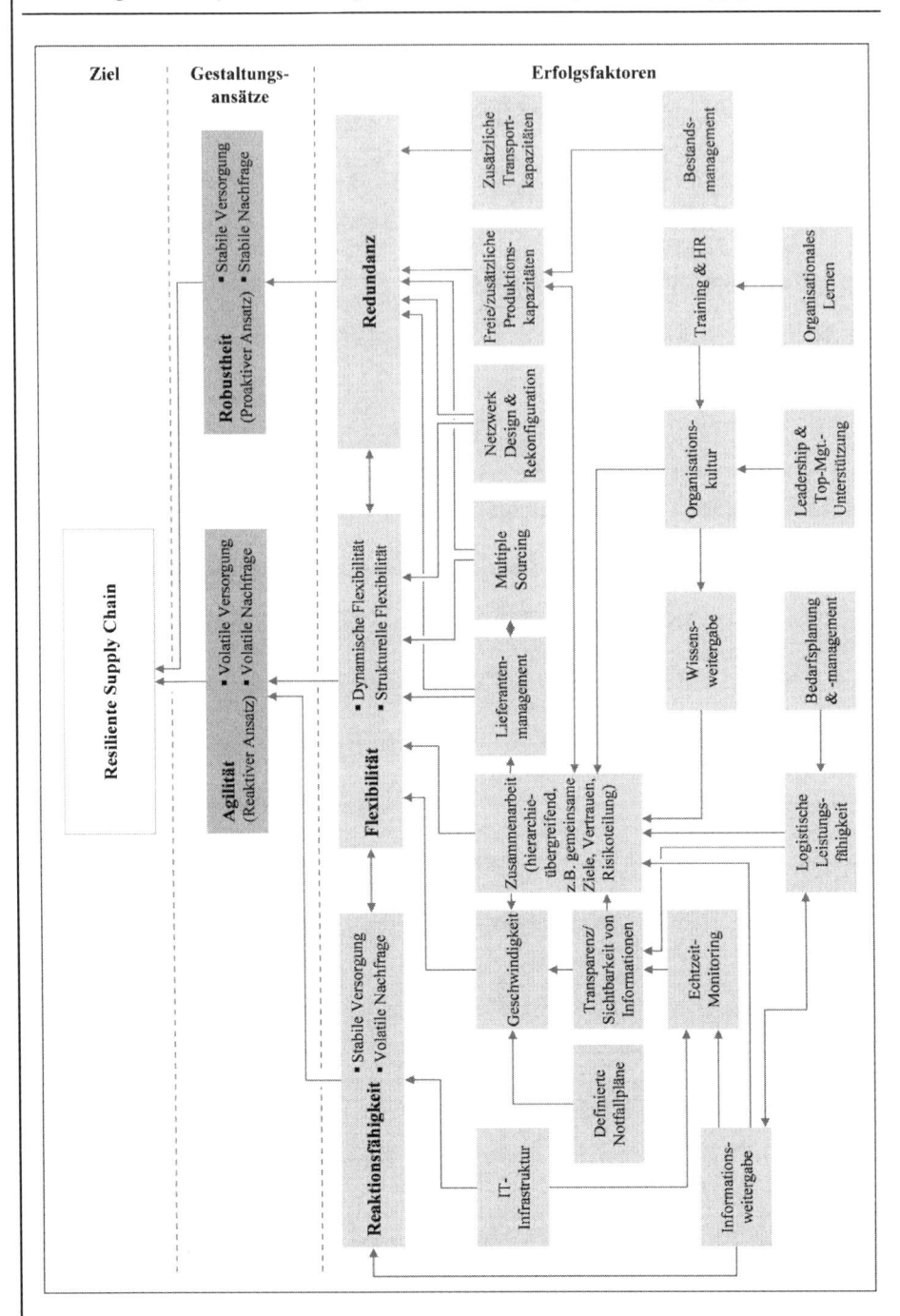

3.2 Erfolgsfaktoren und deren Wirkzusammenhänge

3.2.1 Proaktive Erfolgsfaktoren[11]

Redundanz

Mehrere Autoren sehen Redundanz als Mittel zur Supply-Chain-Resilienz (Stewart, Kolluru, Smith, 2009; Sheffi, Rice, 2005; Rice, Caniato, 2003). Redundanzen beziehen sich dabei auf Sicherheitsbestände, Multiple Sourcing sowie ungenutzte Kapazitätsreserven (Sheffi, Rice, 2005; Rice, Caniato, 2003). Redundanz gilt dabei als maßgeblicher Einflussfaktor der Supply-Chain-Robustheit (Wieland, 2013; Albert, Barabási, 2002).

Zusammenarbeit/Kooperation/Kollaborative Partnerschaften

Supply-Chain-Resilienz erfordert ein hohes Maß an Zusammenarbeit, Kooperation und partnerschaftlichen Beziehungen. Ohne ein solches kann Risikomanagement in einer stark vernetzten Supply Chain nicht funktionieren (Kamalahmadi, Mellat-Parast, 2016, S. 124; Soni, Jain, Kumar, 2014, S. 14). Vor diesem Hintergrund versteht sich Zusammenarbeit als die Fähigkeit zum unternehmensübergreifenden Informationsaustausch, zur Ressourcennutzung, zur offenen Kommunikation, zum aktiven Wissensaustausch sowie zur gemeinsamen Entscheidungsfindung auf Basis kongruenter Zielvorstellungen und Anreize. Ein höheres Maß an Zusammenarbeit führt somit indirekt zu einer erhöhten Supply-Chain-Resilienz.

Informationsweitergabe

Informationsaustausch stellt eine Grundvoraussetzung zum Ausbau kooperativer und partnerschaftlicher Zusammenarbeit dar (Wilding, 2013; Christopher, Holweg, 2011; Kamalahmadi, Mellat-Parast, 2016, S. 124; Mandal, 2012).Wesentliche Informationen, die in diesem Zusammenhang als End-to-End-relevant erscheinen, umfassen beispielsweise Kundenbedarfe (Ponomarov, 2012), Auftragsdaten, Lagerbestandsinformationen, Versand- und Transportlogistische Informationen, Informationen über Störvorfälle (Soni, Jain, 2011, S. 935) sowie Informationen zu aktuellen Supply-Chain-Risiken (Saghafian, van Oyen, 2012). Auf diese Weise kommt der IT-Infrastruktur eine bedeutende Rolle zu.

Kultur und Wissensweitergabe

Die Unternehmenskultur ist ebenso ein Erfolgsfaktor für Supply-Chain-Resilienz (Kamalahmadi, Mellat-Parast, 2016, S. 120) und trägt damit zur Gestaltung einer flexiblen und resilienten Supply Chain bei (Sheffi, Rice, 2005, S. 47; Tan, Kannan, Handfield, 1998). Dabei spielen ein gemeinsames Verständnis und Sensitivität für potenziel-

---

[11] In Anlehnung an Ponis und Koronis entsprechen proaktive Erfolgsfaktoren einem vorausschauenden Planungselement, als Teil einer antizipativen bzw. vorbereitenden Tätigkeit sich auf potenzielle, unerwartete Ereignisse einzustellen (Ponis, Koronis, 2012, S. 921).

le Supply-Chain-Risiken bei den beteiligten Partnern eine wichtige Rolle (Scholten, Sharkey, Fynes, 2014, S. 215; Faisal et al., 2006).

Die gezielte Entwicklung und der Ausbau konsistenter unternehmensübergreifender Unternehmenskulturen werden als wesentlicher Erfolgsfaktor für die Entwicklung langfristig stabiler Beziehungen zwischen kooperierenden Supply-Chain-Partnern betrachtet (McAfee, Glassman, Honeycutt, 2002). Ebenso bildet das Wissen über Umwelteinflüsse und Gegebenheiten des Marktes einen entscheidenden Erfolgsfaktor auf dem Weg zu resilienten Supply-Chain-Strukturen und -Prozessen (Kamalahmadi, Mellat-Parast, 2016). Dabei spielen die proaktive Einstellung, die Anpassungsfähigkeit an neue Rahmenbedingungen sowie die Fähigkeit, unter Zeitdruck innovative Lösungskonzepte erarbeiten zu können, eine besondere Rolle (Kamalahmadi, Mellat-Parast, 2016, S. 121).

Personalmanagement, Training und organisationales Lernen
Die Mitarbeiterqualifikation sowie Trainings- und Fortbildungsmaßnahmen sind bestimmende Maßnahmen, um positiv auf die Entwicklung einer Resilienz fördernden Unternehmenskultur hinzuwirken. Dies ist eng verknüpft mit dem Konzept des organisationalen Lernens, um die Fähigkeit zu entwickeln, aus vergangenen Störereignissen und deren Bewältigung zu lernen und für zukünftige Ereignisse besser gerüstet zu sein (Ponomarov, Holcomb, 2009).

Führung und Top-Management-Support
In Zusammenhang mit der Gestaltung einer Resilienz fördernden Organisationskultur spielt die Unterstützung durch das Top-Management eine wichtige Rolle (Ponomarov, Holcomb, 2009; Christopher, Peck, 2004). Insbesondere sind Managementrichtlinien und Aktionen einzuführen, die eine kontinuierliche Erfassung von End-to-End-Supply-Chain-Risiken verfolgen und die hierfür notwendige Ressourcenallokation bei den beteiligten Akteuren koordinieren (Kleindorfer, Saad, 2005; Sheffi, Rice, 2005).

Netzwerkdesign und Re-Konfiguration
Blackhurst, Kaitlin und Graighead (2011, S. 383) argumentieren, dass sich die Netzwerkdichte und die -komplexität gegenläufig zu Supply-Chain-Resilienz verhalten: Je größer die Zahl der Knoten und Verknüpfungen, desto anfälliger ist die Supply Chain gegenüber Störungen und desto geringer ist ihre Resilienz (Kamalahmadi, Mellat-Parast, 2016, S. 123; Sheffi, 2005). Gleichzeitig steige hierdurch die Robustheit des Systems (Ponnambalam, Long, Sarawgi, Fu, Goh, 2014, S. 8). Konträr hierzu stellen Cardoso, Barbosa-Póvoa, Relvas, Novais (2014b) fest: Je höher die Anzahl an Knoten und deren Verflechtungen, desto größer ist die Flexibilität und desto größer ist die Resilienz der Supply Chain.

Unter Berücksichtigung dieser gegensätzlichen Untersuchungsergebnisse lässt sich daher zusammenfassen, dass allein die Anzahl der Verknüpfungen zwischen den

Knoten kein verlässlicher Indikator für das Maß an Supply-Chain-Resilienz ist. Offensichtlich ist die Konfiguration aller drei Faktoren (Dichte, Komplexität und Kritikalität von Knoten) entscheidend für das Maß an Supply-Chain-Resilienz, wobei sich je nach Netzwerkstruktur unterschiedliche Level von Supply-Chain-Resilienz ergeben können (Kim, Chen, Linderman, 2015, S. 55). Unbestritten ist, dass die gezielte Gestaltung der Netzwerkstruktur die Resilienz einer Supply Chain beeinflusst (Christopher, Peck, 2004) und somit als ein Erfolgsfaktor zur Gestaltung resilienter Supply Chains angesehen werden kann.

Logistische Leistungsfähigkeit

Die logistische Leistungsfähigkeit einer Organisation wird ebenso als Erfolgsfaktor für die Entwicklung einer resilienten Supply Chain angesehen (Ponomarov, Holcomb, 2009, S. 135 ff.) sowie als Voraussetzung für die Erlangung von nachhaltigen Wettbewerbsvorteilen gegenüber Mitbewerbern. Wang, Jie und Abareshi (2015) belegen, dass sich Prozessausfallrisiken in der Supply Chain durch eine hohe operative logistische Leistungsfähigkeit reduzieren lassen. Dabei spielen insbesondere die prozessualen Anbindungen, die Kooperation sowie der Informationsaustausch mit den beteiligten Supply-Chain-Partnern eine entscheidende Rolle.

Echtzeit-Monitoring und IT-Infrastruktur

Ein kontinuierliches Echtzeit-Monitoring der Supply Chain trägt zu einer erhöhten Informationstransparenz bei und steigert dadurch die Risikobereitschaft der beteiligten Akteure. Auf diese Weise wird eine schnellere Geschwindigkeit) im Falle von Supply-Chain-Störereignissen erzielt (Macdonald, 2008). Voraussetzung für ein Echtzeit-Monitoring ist eine entsprechende IT-Infrastruktur, die unternehmensübergreifende Material- und Informationsflüsse abbildet (Gunasekaran, Subramanian, Rahman, 2015).

Bedarfsmanagement

Das Bedarfsmanagement beinhaltet die enge Abstimmung mit Downstream-Partnern, wie zum Beispiel Händlern und Dienstleistern, um Kundennachfragen in die gewünschte Richtung beeinflussen zu können. Da Lieferanten- und Produktionskapazitäten in ihrer Obergrenze nur bedingt flexibel auf Nachfrageschwankungen reagieren können, erscheint ein wirksames Bedarfsmanagement notwendig, um dynamische Nachfrageschwankungen zu glätten und an gegebene Kapazitätsgrenzen anzupassen. Dies kann zeitlich, räumlich und produktspezifisch erfolgen (Tang, 2006, S. 465). Ponomarov und Holcomb (2009) sehen das Bedarfsmanagement als direkten Einflussfaktor für die logistische Leistungsfähigkeit eines Unternehmens und begründen dieses als indirekten Erfolgsfaktor zur Gestaltung resilienter Supply-Chain-Strukturen.

Produktions- und Transportschlupfkapazitäten

Schlupfkapazitäten in der Produktion sowie im Transport gelten als Möglichkeiten, die Redundanz der betrachteten Supply Chain direkt zu erhöhen (Macdonald, 2008, S. 45). Allerdings laufen die Kosten zur Sicherung überschüssiger Kapazitäten etwaigen Effizienz- und Kostenzielen zuwider (Sheffi, Rice, 2005, S. 41). Mit Eintreffen eines Störereignisses tritt der Mehrwert der redundanten Produktions- oder Transportkapazitäten zutage. Unter Berücksichtigung des jeweiligen Geschäftsmodells sowie der jeweiligen Supply-Chain-Strategie eines Unternehmens ist zu entscheiden, bis zu welchem Grad zusätzliche Produktions- und Transportkapazitäten vorgehalten werden sollen (Kamalahmadi, Mellat-Parast, 2016, S. 122).

Bestandsmanagement

Zusätzliche Sicherheitsbestände tragen ebenso wie zusätzliche Produktions- und Transportkapazitäten unmittelbar zu einer erhöhten Redundanz in der Supply Chain bei (Sheffi, Rice, 2005). Gleichzeitig steigen aber auch die Kapitalbindungskosten sowie die Durchlaufzeit, was angesichts der oben aufgeführten Definition des Erfolgsfaktors Flexibilität als konträrer Effekt angesehen werden kann.

Lieferantenmanagement und Multiple Sourcing

Der Ausfall eines einzigen Lieferanten kann die Funktions- und Leistungsfähigkeit des gesamten Supply-Chain-Netzwerks beeinträchtigen (Wannenwetsch, 2005, S. 10). Offensichtlich können Lieferanten als unausweichliche Risikoquellen angesehen werden (Rajesh, Ravi, 2015, S. 343). Abhilfe verschaffen einerseits die intensivierte Koordination und Kollaboration mit Lieferanten (Upstream-Partnerschaften), um so die effiziente Materialversorgung im Krisenfalle sicherzustellen (Tang, 2006, S. 454). Andererseits stellen Multiple-Sourcing-Ansätze eine strategische Option zur Steigerung der Redundanz in der Supply Chain dar. Tatsächlich bildet Multiple Sourcing neben Sicherheitsbeständen und ungenutzten Kapazitätsreserven eine der häufigsten Formen von Redundanz (Sheffi, Rice, 2005; Rice, Caniato, 2003).

3.2.2 Reaktive Erfolgsfaktoren[12]

Flexibilität

Flexibilität ist die Fähigkeit, im Störfall verschiedene Maßnahmen ergreifen zu können, die eine Reaktion und Anpassung an die Störeinflüsse in der Supply Chain ermöglichen (Kamalahmadi, Mellat-Parast, 2016, S. 122; Peck, 2005; Lee, 2004). Flexibilität kann durch Transportmittel, Produktionsanlagen- und -einrichtungen, Arbeitszeitmodelle oder vertragliche Vereinbarungen mit Kunden, Lieferanten

---

[12] Reaktive Erfolgsfaktoren können als solche Elemente und Maßnahmen verstanden werden, die unmittelbar nach einem Störereignis zu einer schnellen Beseitigung der Störungsauswirkungen beitragen (Ponomarov, Holcomb, 2009).

und/oder Dienstleistern erreicht werden (Kamalahmadi, Mellat-Parast, 2016, S. 122; Yang, Yang, 2010; Colicchia, Dallari, Melacini, 2010; Tang, Tomlin, 2008; Tang, 2006; Scholten, Schilder, 2015; Sheffi, Rice, 2005). Flexibilität betrifft die Möglichkeiten einer schnellen Reaktion und Anpassung an Störeinflüsse entlang der gesamten Supply Chain (upstream und downstream) und ist auf der strategischen sowie auf einer unternehmensübergreifenden prozessualen Ebene zu verankern.

Geschwindigkeit und vorgegebene Notfallkonzepte
Geschwindigkeit bezieht sich auf die Zeitspanne, die eine Supply Chain benötigt, um auf Störereignisse (kurzfristig) zu reagieren (Mandal, Sarathy, Rao Korasiga, Bhattacharya, Ghosh Dastidar, 2016; Johnson, Elliott, Drake, 2013; Jüttner, Maklan, 2011; Stevenson, Spring, 2007). Im Kontext von Supply-Chain-Resilienz trägt die Geschwindigkeit vor, während und auch nach einem Störereignis zur Anpassungsfähigkeit und somit zur Flexibilität einer Supply Chain bei (Jüttner, Maklan, 2011, S. 248). Deswegen wird eine hohe Geschwindigkeit im Falle eines Störereignisses auf Unternehmensseite als Hebel zum Ausbau der Wettbewerbsfähigkeit angesehen (Hohenstein, Feisel, Hartmann, Giunipero, 2015, S. 105; Bakshi, Kleindorfer, 2008; (Sheffi, Rice, 2005; Christopher, Peck, 2004).

Reaktionsfähigkeit
Reaktionsfähigkeit beschreibt eine zum Kunden gerichtete Fähigkeit einer Supply Chain, unmittelbar auf Bedarfsänderungen reagieren zu können, basierend auf der Fähigkeit, Marktbewegungen in Echtzeit zu erkennen, zu verstehen und Informationen ausgehend vom Kunden rückwärts in die Supply Chain verarbeiten zu können (Ramakrishnan, 2002; Catalan, Kotzab, 2003). Brusset und Teller (2017) sehen eine derart verstandene Reaktionsfähigkeit als Grundlage für die dynamische und strukturelle Flexibilität eines Unternehmens an.

Transparenz/Sichtbarkeit von Informationen
Informationstransparenz ist ebenso ein wesentlicher Erfolgsfaktor zum Ausbau von Supply-Chain-Flexibilität und -Geschwindigkeit (Mandal, Sarathy, Rao Korasiga, Bhattacharya, Ghosh Dastidar, 2016) und trägt somit indirekt zur Supply-Chain-Resilienz bei (Scholten, Schilder, 2015). Es geht dabei um den Grad des Zugangs zu betrieblichen und überbetrieblich-strategischen Informationen der beteiligten Akteure (Mandal, Sarathy, Rao Korasiga, Bhattacharya, Ghosh Dastidar, 2016; Wie, Wang, 2010; Barratt, Oke, 2007).

3.3 Kritische Würdigung des konzeptionellen Bezugsrahmens

Der in **Abbildung 1** vorgestellte Bezugsrahmen versteht sich im Sinne von Scherm (1999, S. 15) als theoretisches Minimalkonzept und fasst die auf der Grundlage der analysierten Literatur festgestellten Erfolgsfaktoren sowie Annahmen über deren Wirkzusammenhänge zur Gestaltung einer resilienten Supply Chain zusammen. Somit dient er als eine Art provisorisches Erklärungsmodell (Kubicek, 1979) und ermöglicht die Plausibilitätsprüfung der konzeptionellen Ergebnisse (Scherm, 1999). Einschränkend ist jedoch festzuhalten, dass er damit nicht die Anforderungen an ein Hypothesensystem (Kleiner, 2011; Welge, 1980) erfüllt.

Vor diesem Hintergrund dient der Bezugsrahmen als Ergebnis einer theoriebasierten Vorgehensweise und bildet in konzentrierter Art und Weise die Kernelemente des Untersuchungsgegenstandes ab. Er erlaubt daher eine nachvollziehbare Strukturierung des Untersuchungsfeldes.

4 Zusammenfassung und Ausblick

Das primäre Ziel des vorliegenden Beitrages war die Bestimmung von Erfolgsfaktoren, die zur zukünftigen Gestaltung resilienter Supply Chains beitragen. Dazu wurde die wissenschaftliche Supply-Chain-Resilienz-Literatur analysiert, aufbereitet und darauf aufbauend ein konzeptioneller Bezugsrahmen entwickelt. Dieser verknüpft die erkannten Erfolgsfaktoren anhand ihrer Wirkzusammenhänge in einem logischen Ordnungsrahmen. Durch seine inhaltliche Fülle stellt der konzeptionelle Bezugsrahmen ein *provisorisches Erklärungsmodell* dar, das als Grundlage für eine weitere empirische Überprüfung dienen kann.

Insbesondere erscheint für zukünftige Forschungsbemühungen die Fragestellung interessant, inwieweit die ermittelten Erfolgsfaktoren in der Praxis umsetzbar sind. Diesbezüglich sind kontextbedingte Aspekte zu berücksichtigen, wie bspw. die Reichweite der betrachteten Supply Chain, industriespezifische Besonderheiten oder die Intensität der beobachteten Störungen. Herauszufinden ist ebenso, ob die identifizierten Erfolgsfaktoren vom Systemzustand einer Supply Chain abhängig sind. Die Beantwortung derartiger weiterführender Forschungsfragen lässt interessante Erkenntnisse zur Lösung kontextbezogener Probleme bei der Implementierung von Erfolgsfaktoren zur Gestaltung resilienter Supply Chains in der Unternehmenspraxis erwarten.

Literatur

Agarwal, A.; Shankar, R.; Tiwari, M. (2007): Modeling agility of supply chain, in: Industrial Marketing Management, 36(4), 443–457.

Albert, R.; Barabási, A.-L. (2002): Statistical mechanics of complex networks, in: Review of Modern Physics, 74(1), 47–97.

Bakshi, N.; Kleindorfer, P. (2008): Co-opetition and Investment for Supply-Chain Resilience, in: Production and Operations Management, 18(6), 583–603.

Barratt, M.; Oke, A. (2007): Antecedents of supply chain visibility in retail supply chains: a resource-based theory perspective, in: Journal of Operations Management, 25(6), 1217–1233.

Biedermann, L. (n.V.): Supply Chain Resilienz – Konzeptioneller Bezugsrahmen und Identifikation zukünftiger Erfolgsfaktoren. Unveröffentlichtes Manuskript.

Blackhurst, J.; Kaitlin, S.; Graighead, C. (2011): An empirically derived framework of global supply resiliency, in: Journal of Business Logistics, 32(4), 374–391.

Braunscheidel, M.; Suresh, N. (2009): The organizational antecedents of a firm's supply chain agility for risk mitigation and response, in: Journal of Operations Management, 27(2), 119–140.

Brusset, X.; Teller, C. (2017): Supply Chain Capabilities, Risks, and Resilience, in: International Journal of Production Economics, 184, 59-68.

Cardoso, S.; Barbosa-Póvoa, A.; Relvas, S.; Novais, A. (2014): Resilience assessment of supply chains under different types of disruption, in: J. D. Mario R. Eden (Hrsg.): Proceedings of the 8th International Conference on Foundations of Computer-Aided Process Design – FOCAPD 2014, Cle Elum, Washington, USA: Elsevier B.V., 759–764.

Carvalho, H.; Azevedo, S.; Cruz-Machado, V. (2012): Agile and resilient approaches to supply chain management: influence on performance and competitiveness, in: Logistics Research, 48(22), 49–62.

Carvalho, H.; Duarte, S.; Cruz-Machado, V. (2011): Lean, agile, resilient and green: divergencies and synergies, in: International Journal of Lean Six Sigma, 2(2), 151–179.

Catalan, M.; Kotzab, H. (2003): Assessing the responsiveness in the Danish mobile phone supply chain, in: International Journal of Physical Distribution & Logistics Management, 33(8), 668–685.

Christopher, M. (2000): The agile supply chain, competing in volatile markets, in: Industrial Marketing Management, 29, 37–44.

Christopher, M.; Holweg, M. (2011): "Supply Chain 2.0": managing supply chains in the era of turbulence, in: International Journal of Physical Distribution and Logistics Management, 41(1), 63–82.

Christopher, M.; Peck, H. (2004): Building the resilient supply chain, in: The International Journal of Logistics Management, 15(2), 1–13.

Christopher, M.; Peck, H.; Towill, D. (2006): A taxonomy for selecting global supply chain, in: The International Journal of Logistics Management, 17(2), 277–287.

Colicchia, C.; Dallari, F.; Melacini, M. (2010): Increasing supply chain resilience in a global sourcing context, in: Production Planning & Control: the Management of Operations, 21(7), 680–694.

Dekker, A.; Colbert, B. (2004): Network robustness and graph topology, Proceedings of the Twenty-Seventh Australasian Computer Science Conference (ACSC2004), Dunedin, New Zealand, Sydney: Australian Computer Society, 359–368.

Denyer, D.; Tranfield, D. (2009): Producing a systematic review, in: Buchanan, D.; Bryman, A.: The Sage Handbook of Organizational Research Methods, London: Sage Publications Ltd., 671–689.

Faisal, M.; Banwet, D.; Shankar, R. (2006): Supply chain risk mitigation: modeling the enablers, in: Business Process Management, 12(4), 535–552.

Gunasekaran, A.; Subramanian, N.; Rahman, S. (2015): Supply chain resilience: role of complexities and strategies, in: International Journal of Production Research, 53(22), 6809–6819.

Hohenstein, N.-O.; Feisel, E.; Hartmann, E.; Giunipero, L. (2015): Research on the phenomenon of supply chain resilience – a systematic review and paths for further investigation, in: International Journal of Physical Distribution & Logistics Management, 45(1/2), 90–117.

Hosseini, S.; Al Khaled, A.; Sarder, M. (2016): A general framework for assessing system resilience using Bayesian networks: A case study of sulfuric acid manufacturer, in: Journal of Manufacturing Systems, 41, 211–227.

Johnson, N.; Elliott, D.; Drake, P. (2013): Exploring the role of social capital in facilitating supply chain resilience, in: Supply Chain Management: An International Journal, 18(3), 324–336.

Jüttner, U.; Maklan, S. (2011): Supply chain resilience in the global financial crisis: an empirical study, in: Supply Chain Management: An International Journal, 16(4), 246–259.

Kamalahmadi, M.; Mellat-Parast, M. (2016): A review of the literature on the principles of enterprise and supply chain resilience: Major findings and directions for future research, in: International Journal of Production Economics, 117, 116–133.

Kim, Y.; Chen, Y.-S.; Linderman, K. (2015): Supply network disruption and resilience: A network structural perspective, in: Journal of Operations Management, 33(34), 43–59.

Kleindorfer, P.; Saad, G. (2005): Managing disruption risks in supply chains, in: Production and Operations Management, 14(1), 53–68.

Kleiner, M. (2011): Strategisches Entscheiden in Unternehmen, Berlin: Logos Verlag.

Kong, X.-Y.; Li, X.-Y. (2008): Creating the Resilient Supply Chain: The Role of Knowledge Management Resources. 4th International Conference on Wireless Communications, Networking and Mobile Computing (WiCOM), Dalian, China: The Institute of Electrical and Electronics Engineers, Inc. (IEEE), 1–4

Kubicek, H. (1977): Heuristische Bezugsrahmen und heuristisch angelegte Forschungsdesigns als Elemente einer Konstruktionsstrategie empirischer Forschung, in: Köhler, R.: Empirische und handlungstheoretische Forschungskonzeptionen in der Betriebswirtschaftslehre: Bericht über die Tagung in Aachen, März 1976, Stuttgart: Poeschel Verlag, 3–36.

Kubicek, H. (1979): Informationstechnologie und Organisationsforschung – eine kritische Bestandsaufnahme der Forschungsergebnisse, in: Hansen, H.; Schröder, K.; Weihe, H.: Mensch und Computer, München, Wien: Oldenbourg Verlag, 53–79.

Lee, H. (2004): The triple-A supply chain, in: Harvard Business Review, 2–12. Verfügbar unter: https://hbr.org/2004/10/the-triple-a-supply-chain (abgerufen am 27. Oktober 2016).

Li, X.; Chung, C.; Goldsby, T.; Holsapple, C. (2008): A unified model of supply chain agility: the work-design perspective, in: The International Journal of Logistics Management, 19(3), 408–435.

Macdonald, J. R. (2008): Supply Chain Disruption Management: A Conceptual Framework and Theoretical Model, College Park, Maryland (USA): Graduate School of the University of Maryland. Verfügbar unter: http://drum.lib.umd.edu/bitstream/handle/1903/8803/umi-umd-5824.pdf?sequence=1&isAllowed=y.

Mandal, S. (2012): An empirical investigation into supply chain resilience, in: IUP Journal of Supply Chain Management, 9(4), 46–61.

Mandal, S.; Sarathy, R.; Rao Korasiga, V.; Bhattacharya, S.; Ghosh Dastidar, S. (2016): Achieving supply chain resilience: The contribution of logistics and supply chain capabilities, in: International Journal of Disaster Resilience in the Built Environment, 7(5), 544–562.

McAfee, R.; Glassman, M.; Honeycutt, E. J. (2002): The effects of culture and human resource management policies on supply chain management, in: Journal of Business Logistics, 23(1), 1–17.

Meepetchdee, Y.; Shah, N. (2007): Logistical network design with robustness and complexity considerations, in: International Journal of Physical Distribution & Logistics Management, 37(2), 201–222.

Pal, R.; Torstensson, H.; Mattila, H. (2014): Antecedents of organizational resilience in economic crises – an empirical study of Swedish textile and clothing SMEs, in: International Journal of Production Economics, 147, 410–428.

Peck, H. (2005): Drivers of supply chain vulnerability: an integrated framework, in: International Journal of Physical Distribution & Logistics Management, 35(4), 210–232.

Pereira, C. R.; Christopher, M.; Da Silva, A. L. (2014): Achieving supply chain resilience: the role of procurement, in: Supply Chain Management: An International Journal, 19(5/6), 626–642.

Pettit, T. J.; Fiksel, J.; Croxton, K. L. (2010): Ensuring Supply Chain Resilience: Development of a Conceptual Framework, in: Journal of Business Logistics, 31(1), 1–21.

Ponnambalam, L.; Long, D.; Sarawgi, D.; Fu, X.; Goh, R. S. (2014): Multi-Agent Models to Study the Robustness and Resilience of Complex Supply Chain Networks, 2014 International Conference on Intelligent Autonomous Agents, Networks and Systems, Bandung, Indonesia: IEEE, 7–12.

Ponomarov, S. (2012): Antecedents and Consequences of Supply Chain Resilience: A Dynamic Capabilities Perspective, Dissertation at University of Tennessee. Verfügbar unter: http://trace.tennessee.edu/utk_graddiss/1338 (abgerufen am 8. August 2015).

Ponomarov, S.; Holcomb, M. (2009): Understanding the concept of supply chain resilience, in: The International Journal of Logistics Management, 20(1), 124–143.

Purvis, L.; Spall, S.; Naim, M.; Spiegler, V. (2016): Developing a resilient supply chain strategy during 'boom' and 'bust', in: Production Planning & Control, 27(7–8), 579–590.

Rajesh, R.; Ravi, V. (2015): Supplier selection in resilient supply chains: a grey relational analysis approach, in: Journal of Cleaner Production, 86, 343–359.

Ramakrishnan, R. (2002): Performance measurement of supply chain management, in: DILF Orientering, 39(2), 16–18.

Reichhart, A.; Holweg, M. (2007): Creating the customer-responsive supply chain: a reconciliation of concepts, in: International Journal of Operations & Production Management, 27(11), 1144–1172.

Rice, J.; Caniato, F. (2003): Building a secure and resilient supply network, in: Supply Chain Management Review, 7(5), 22–30.

Saghafian, S.; Oyen, M. van (2012): The value of flexible backup suppliers and disruption risk information: newsvendor analysis with recourse, in: IIE Transactions, 44, 834–867.

Sahu, A. K.; Datta, S.; Mahapatra, S. (2016): Evaluation and selection of resilient suppliers in fuzzy environment: Exploration of fuzzy-VIKOR, in: Benchmarking: An International Journal, 23(3), 651–673.

Scherm, E. (1999): Internationales Personalmanagement, Berlin: Oldenbourg Wissenschaftsverlag.

Scholten, K.; Schilder, S. (2015): The role of collaboration in supply chain resilience, in: Supply Chain Management: An International Journal, 20(4), 471–484.

Scholten, K.; Sharkey, P.; Fynes, S. B. (2014): Mitigation processes – antecedents for building supply chain resilience, in: Supply Chain Management: An International Journal, 19(2), 211–228.

Sheffi, Y. (2005): The Resilient Enterprise: Overcoming Vulnerability for Competitive Advantage (Bd. 2), Cambridge, MA, USA: MIT University Press Group Ltd.

Sheffi, Y.; Rice, J. (2005): A supply chain view of the resilient enterprise, in: MIT Sloan Management Review, 47(1), 41–48.

Soni, U.; Jain, V. (2011): Minimizing the vulnerabilities of supply chain: a new framework for enhancing the resilience, in: Proceeding of the 2011 IEEE (IEEM), Singapur, 933–939.

Soni, U.; Jain, V.; Kumar, S. (2014): Measuring supply chain resilience using a deterministic modeling approach, in: Computers & Industrial Engineering, 74, 11–25.

Stevenson, M.; Spring, M. (2007): Flexibility from a supply chain perspective: definition and review, in: International Journal of Operations & Production Management, 27(7), 685–713.

Stewart, G.; Kolluru, R.; Smith, M. (2009): Leveraging public-private partnerships to improve community resilience in times of disaster, in: International Journal of Physical Distribution & Logistics Management, 39(5), 343–364.

Swafford, P.; Gosh, S.; Murthy, N. (2006): The antecedents of supply chain agility of a firm: scale development and model testing, in: Journal of Operations Management, 24(2), 170–188.

Tan, K.; Kannan, K.; Handfield, R. (1998): Supply chain management: supplier performance and firm performance, in: International Journal of Purchasing & Materials Management, 34(3), 2–9.

Tang, C. (2006): Perspectives in supply chain risk management, in: International Journal of Production Economics, 103(2), 451–488.

Tang, C.; Tomlin, B. (2008): The power of flexibility for mitigating supply chain risks, in: International Journal of Production Economics, 12–27.

Thun, J.-H.; Hoenig, D. (2011): An empirical analysis of supply chain risk management in the German automotive industry, in: International Journal of Production Economics, 131, 242–249.

Vlajic, J.; Vorst, J. van der; Haijema, R. (2012): A framework for designing robust food supply chains, in: International Journal of Production Economics, 137(1), 176–189.

Wang, M.; Jie, F.; Abareshi, A. (2015): Evaluating logistics capability for mitigation of supply chain uncertainty and risk in the Australian courier firms, in: Asia Pacific Journal of Marketing and Logistics, 27(3), 486–498.

Wannenwetsch, H. (2005): Vernetztes Supply Chain Management, Berlin, Heidelberg, New York: Springer Verlag.

Wei, H. L.; Wang, E. T. (2010). The strategic value of supply chain visibility: increasing the ability to reconfigure, in: European Journal of Information Systems, 19(2), 238–249.

Welge, M. (1980): Management in deutschen multinationalen Unternehmungen: Ergebnisse einer empirischen Untersuchung, Stuttgart.

Wieland, A. (2013): Selecting the right Supply Chain based on risks, in: Journal of Manufacturing Technology Management, 24(5), 652–668.

Wieland, A.; Wallenburg, C. (2013): The influence of relational competencies on supply chain resilience: a relational view, in: International Journal of Physical Distribution & Logistics Management, 43(4), 300–320.

Wilding, R. (2013): Supply chain temple of resilience, in: Logistics and Transportation Focus, 15(11), 54–59.

Yang, B.; Yang, Y. (2010). Postponement in supply chain risk management: a complexity perspective, in: International Journal of Production Research, 48(7), 1901–1912.

Supply-Chain-Risiken in der Textilindustrie

Tessa Sarnow, Meike Schröder

Abstract

Die Textil- und Bekleidungsindustrie ist gekennzeichnet durch eine starke Abhängigkeit der einzelnen Produktionsschritte untereinander. Gleichzeitig stellen immer kürzere Kollektionsrhythmen sowie global verteilte Wertschöpfungspartner Risiken für die Unternehmen dar. Ziel dieses Beitrages ist die Identifikation von Risiken in diesem Kontext. Zur Erfassung aller relevanten Supply-Chain-Risiken wurden Experteninterviews durchgeführt. Dabei standen die Analyse der branchenspezifischen Struktur der Supply Chain sowie die Einbettung des Risikomanagements in den unternehmerischen Kontext an erster Stelle. Anschließend wurde ein Risikokatalog zusammengestellt. Erweitert wurde die erstellte Liste durch Berichte z.B. von Unternehmensberatungen und der Weltbank. Auf diese Weise konnten im Rahmen einer Branchenanalyse unternehmensinterne, supply-chain-interne, brancheninterne und globale Risiken aufgedeckt und in die genannten Kategorien eingeordnet werden, die für die Textil- und Bekleidungsindustrie von besonderem Interesse sind.

1 Einleitung

Die Notwendigkeit einer Analyse von Supply-Chain-Risiken im Bereich der Textilindustrie ergibt sich aus der spezifischen Struktur der Wertschöpfungskette, die starken Einfluss auf die Risikolandschaft hat und somit die alleinige Nutzung generischer Risikomanagement-Methoden verbietet. Außerdem werden durch die Verortung im Markt der Konsumgüter vielfältige Risiken für die zumeist global verteilten Supply Chains dargestellt.

Charakteristisch für den Produktionsprozess der Textil- und Bekleidungsindustrie ist eine linear verkettete statt einer netzartigen Struktur. Die einzelnen Prozessschritte müssen sequenziell durchlaufen werden. Gleichzeitig verkürzen sich die Kollektionsrhythmen zunehmend und zur Kostenkontrolle werden Zulieferbetriebe an weltweit verteilten Standorten integriert. Hieraus entstehen Risiken, denen im Rahmen des Risikomanagements durch Einleiten geeigneter Maßnahmen begegnet werden muss.

Die betrachtete Forschungslücke wirft die folgenden Forschungsfragen auf:

- Was sind die wesentlichen Merkmale der Textilindustrie und der zugehörigen Supply Chains?
- Welche Herausforderungen und Chancen bestehen aktuell und in Zukunft für das Risikomanagement in der Textilindustrie?

Zur Beantwortung der Forschungsfragen ist die Anwendung verschiedener Analysen notwendig. Zunächst ist es nötig, Charakteristika der Textilindustrie aufzuzeigen und die Besonderheiten textiler Supply Chains zu untersuchen. Anschließend werden die Strukturen und die Verankerung des Risikomanagements im Bereich der Textilindustrie erfasst. Neben der Verwendung von Fachliteratur werden hierzu die Aussagen der in Experteninterviews befragten Personen ausgewertet. Zur Analyse der aktuellen Stärken der Textilindustrie und den sich bietenden Chancen wird neben einer Literaturrecherche auf Experteninterviews zurückgegriffen. Äquivalent hierzu werden auch die sich aktuell präsentierenden Schwächen und drohende Risiken analysiert.

2 Forschungsgegenstand und -design

2.1 Wertschöpfung in der „textilen Kette"

Im Allgemeinen wird in der Textilindustrie nicht zwischen Herstellern und Händlern unterschieden, da zumeist eine vertikale Integration vollzogen wurde, die eine solche Unterscheidung irrelevant macht. Im Bereich der Bekleidungsindustrie ist dies nur zum Teil der Fall, weshalb eine Differenzierung der Begriffe Bekleidungshersteller und -händler vorgenommen werden soll.

Breitkopf (1999, S. 162) zählt zu den Bekleidungsherstellern sowohl Unternehmen, die ihre eigenen Kollektionen produzieren, als auch Unternehmen, die zu 100% fremdfertigen lassen. Demgegenüber definiert Loock (2008, S. 41) als Bekleidungshersteller solche Unternehmen, die dem Bekleidungshandel vorgelagert sind. Aufgrund der zunehmenden vertikalen Integration schlägt er vor, Hersteller und Händler unter dem Begriff der Bekleidungsbranche zusammenzufassen (Loock, 2008, S. 44). Des Weiteren führen er (2008, S. 53) und weitere Autoren (Nothardt, Schmitter, Trede, 2007, S. 682 ff.; Horstmann, 1997, S. 4 f.; Hoyndorff et al., 2010, S. 20) den Begriff der „Vertikalisierten Unternehmen" ein und stellen dar, dass diese sich nicht durch eine einfache Zusammenführung der Wertschöpfungsketten von Hersteller und Handel auszeichnen, sondern dass vielmehr eine neue, optimierte Wertschöpfungskette entsteht (siehe **Abbildung 1**).

Abbildung 1: Traditionelle Wertschöpfungsketten der Bekleidungsbranche (eigene Darstellung nach Loock ‚2008, S. 52 f.)

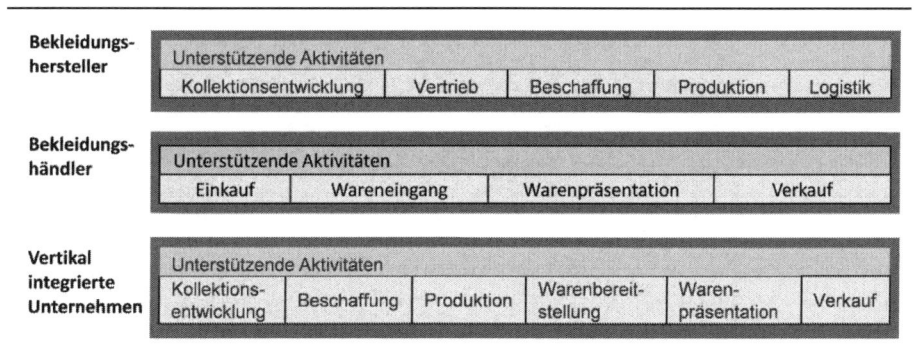

Bekleidungs-hersteller	Unterstützende Aktivitäten				
	Kollektionsentwicklung	Vertrieb	Beschaffung	Produktion	Logistik

Bekleidungs-händler	Unterstützende Aktivitäten			
	Einkauf	Wareneingang	Warenpräsentation	Verkauf

Vertikal integrierte Unternehmen	Unterstützende Aktivitäten					
	Kollektionsentwicklung	Beschaffung	Produktion	Warenbereitstellung	Warenpräsentation	Verkauf

Fernie und Grant (2015, S. 37) argumentieren, dass sich Supply Chains zunehmend vom Modell der vertikalen Integration weg zu einem „Design/Source/Distribute"-Modell entwickeln, um eine Fokussierung der Modeunternehmen auf Kernkompetenzen zu ermöglichen. Eine grafische Darstellung des Modells findet sich in **Abbildung 2**.

Abbildung 2: Moderne Wertschöpfungsketten der Bekleidungsbranche (eigene Darstellung nach Fernie, Grant, 2015, S. 37)

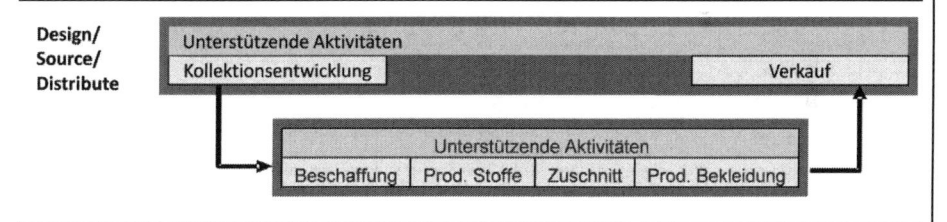

Design/ Source/ Distribute	Unterstützende Aktivitäten	
	Kollektionsentwicklung	Verkauf

	Unterstützende Aktivitäten			
	Beschaffung	Prod. Stoffe	Zuschnitt	Prod. Bekleidung

Ein weiterer häufig verwendeter Begriff in diesem Bereich ist der der Fashion- oder Modebranche. Hoyndorff et al. (2010, S. 12) charakterisieren die Fashionbranche dadurch, dass sie Produktion und Vertrieb von Bekleidung umfasst. Der Begriff stellt demzufolge ein Synonym zur Bekleidungsindustrie dar. Unter Beachtung des Verständnisses von „Fashion" kann gesagt werden, dass die Fashionbranche ein Segment der Bekleidungsindustrie ist. Andere Segmente sind z.B. Sport- sowie Arbeits- und Schutzbekleidung, wobei hier der Übergang zur Mode einerseits und technischen Textilien andererseits fließend ist. An die Fashionbranche schließt sich der Endverbraucher und im Folgenden die Entsorgung an.

Abbildung 3: Textile Kette
(eigene Darstellung nach Loock, 2008, S. 40, und ÖkoMedia PR, 2001, S. 5)

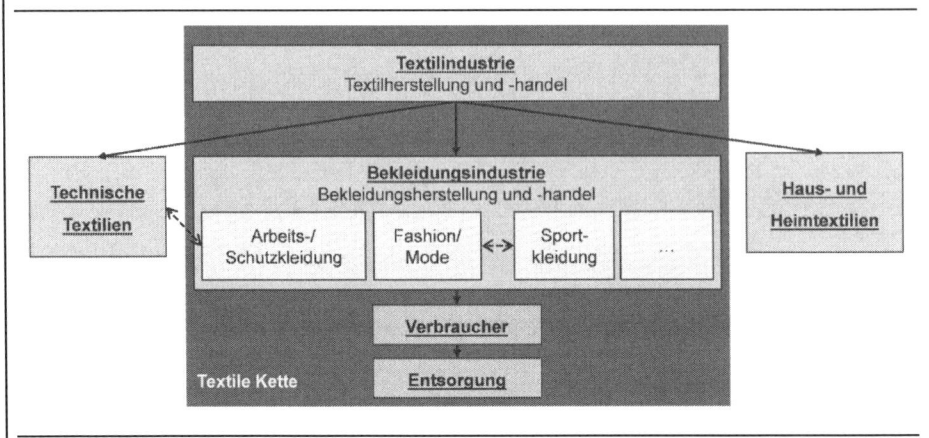

Der gesamte Weg von der Gewinnung der Rohstoffe, die durch die Textilindustrie verarbeitet werden, bis hin zur Entsorgung der Bekleidung wird als „textile Kette" bezeichnet (Loock, 2008, S. 40) und ist in **Abbildung 3** dargestellt.

Die Art der Kooperationen innerhalb der textilen Kette nimmt verschiedenste Formen an und ist einem stetigen Wandel unterworfen. Im betrachteten Bereich der Textilindustrie handelt es sich zumeist um eine auf den Produktionsprozess bezogene Kooperation. Die Kooperationsrichtung ist dabei, bedingt durch die sequenzielle Art der textilen Supply Chain, als vertikal zu bezeichnen. Eine Kooperation zwischen Unternehmen der gleichen Wertschöpfungsstufe erfolgt in der Regel nicht. Häufig ist das Größenverhältnis zwischen Bekleidungshändlern und Textilunternehmen nicht ausgeglichen, sondern inhomogen (Krippendorf, 2009, S. 4). Dies hat auch Einfluss auf eine stark hierarchische Orientierung. Während die Bekleidungsunternehmen zumeist in westlichen Industrieländern angesiedelt sind, handelt es sich bei den Zulieferern oft um kleine Betriebe in Entwicklungsländern (Krippendort, 2009, S. 5 f.). Das Konkurrenzverhältnis variiert, da für Standardprodukte und die Sortimente von Low-Budget-Herstellern häufig Multi-Sourcing-Strategien vorzufinden sind, wohingegen High-Value-Produkte meist über Single Sourcing beschafft werden, um eine möglichst intensive Kooperation möglich zu machen. Auch die zeitliche Perspektive ist je nach Unternehmensstrategie stark unterschiedlich. Bei der Art der Bindung ist eine klare Tendenz der vertraglichen Festschreibung zu erkennen. Vertrauen und Intensität sind stark abhängig von der einzelnen Kooperation. Ebenso variiert die Anzahl der Partner innerhalb einer Kooperation.

Die Charakteristika der Textil- und Bekleidungsindustrie sind im Wesentlichen die relativ kurzen Produktlebenszyklen und eine sehr hohe Volatilität des Kundenverhaltens. Die Häufigkeit der Kollektionswechsel und Entwicklungsrhythmen ist innerhalb der Bekleidungsbranche sehr unterschiedlich und hat sich in den vergangenen Jahren stark in Richtung schneller Kollektionswechsel entwickelt. Eine Darstellung gängiger Kollektionsrhythmen findet sich in **Abbildung 4**.

Abbildung 4: *Verschiedene Kollektionsrhythmen über zwölf Monate (eigene Darstellung nach Deloitte & Touch GmbH Wirtschaftsprüfungsgesellschaft, 2014, S. 13)*

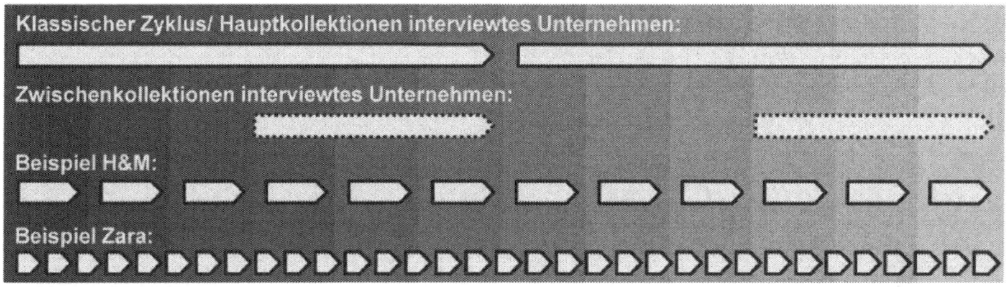

Weitere Herausforderungen stellen die geringe Vorhersagegenauigkeit und die vergleichsweise hohen Impulskaufraten dar (Abernathy et al., 1999, S. 8; Christopher, Lowson, Peck, 2009, S. 102 f.).

Eine Besonderheit, die der Branche zu eigen ist, betrifft die bereits erwähnte Linearität des Produktionsprozesses. Der größte Teil der Herstellung von Bekleidung erfolgt in Prozessschritten, die voneinander abhängig sind und nur in sequenzieller Abfolge durchgeführt werden können (Horstmann, 1997, S. 17).

2.2 Forschungsdesign und -struktur

Da sich der vorliegende Beitrag mit einem unstrukturierten Forschungsproblem beschäftigt, ist ein qualitativer Ansatz für das Untersuchungsdesign gut geeignet. Das Erkenntnisinteresse ist explorativ, das Erkenntnisziel die Erweiterung des Anwendungswissens. Zur Erreichung dieses Ziels werden Primärdaten in einer empirischen Studie erhoben. In Verbindung mit einer Datenerhebung durch Interviews wird somit die Verwendung von teilstrukturierten oder unstrukturierten Interviews festgelegt. Da durch die Forschungsfelder Risikomanagement und Textilindustrie ein tiefgehendes Verständnis und Wissen bei den befragten Personen vorausgesetzt wird, eignet sich ein Experteninterview am besten als Erhebungsmethode (Ghauri, 2010, S. 56 f.; Döring, Bortz, 2016, S. 183).

Der entwickelte Interviewleitfaden gliedert sich in drei Blöcke: Zunächst werden Informationen zur Struktur und Organisation der Supply Chain erfasst. Dabei liegt der Fokus insbesondere auf der Anzahl und auf Abhängigkeiten von Lieferanten verschiedener Stufen sowie dem Management von Beständen und Schwankungen. Im zweiten Fragenblock werden der Umgang mit Supply-Chain-Risiken und die Positionierung des Supply Chain Managements im Unternehmen abgefragt. Der letzte Block dient dazu, die Umsetzung der verschiedenen Stufen des Risikomanagement-Prozesses im Unternehmen zu erfassen. Der komplette Interviewleitfaden ist in **Anhang A** dargestellt.

Es wurden vier Interviews mit Akteuren verschiedener Bereiche der textilen Supply Chain geführt. Dabei lag der Fokus darauf, möglichst umfassende Informationen zu erhalten, sodass die Inhalte in mehrstündigen Gesprächen erarbeitet wurden. Eine Übersicht der Interviewpartner gibt **Tabelle 1**.

Tabelle 1:   *Interviewteilnehmer (eigene Darstellung)*

Nr.	Branche	Position
1	vertikal integriertes Unternehmen der Bekleidungsbranche	Leiter im Bereich Supply Chain und Logistik
2	Logistikdienstleister	Unternehmensentwicklung im Bereich Fashion
3	Logistikdienstleister	Risikomanagement auf Corporate Level
4	(Textil-)Logistikdienstleister	Leiter des Qualitätsmanagements

Die mithilfe der Interviews gewonnenen Daten werden zur Erstellung eines Risikokatalogs genutzt. Die Struktur dieses Katalogs ist angelehnt an die Differenzierung von Supply-Chain-Risiken nach dem Modell von Christopher und Peck (2004, S. 4), erweitert durch Pfohl (2008, S. 23). Eine vereinfachte Darstellung findet sich in **Abbildung 5**.

Abbildung 5:   *Supply-Chain-Risiken nach Christopher, 2004 (eigene Darstellung)*

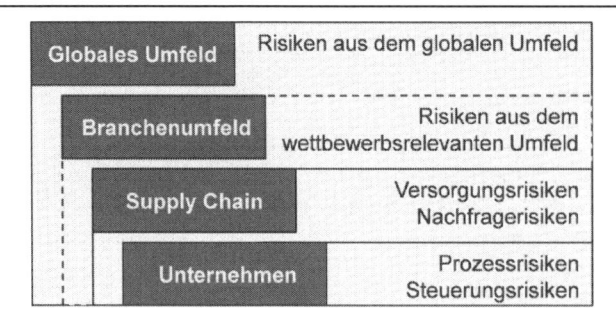

Globales Umfeld	Risiken aus dem globalen Umfeld
Branchenumfeld	Risiken aus dem wettbewerbsrelevanten Umfeld
Supply Chain	Versorgungsrisiken / Nachfragerisiken
Unternehmen	Prozessrisiken / Steuerungsrisiken

Der Bereich des wettbewerbsrelevanten Umfelds, in dem Fall der Branche, ist vergleichsweise groß und kann durch das Modell einer Branchenanalyse, wie sie durch Porters Modell der „Five Forces" gegeben ist, weiter untergliedert und somit strukturiert werden. Wie der Name impliziert, werden dabei fünf sogenannte Treiber identifiziert. Dies sind: Bedrohung durch neue Anbieter, Bedrohung durch Substitute, Verhandlungsmacht der Lieferanten, Verhandlungsmacht der Abnehmer und Rivalität innerhalb der Branche (Porter, 1992, S. 26).

3 Supply-Chain-Risiken in der Textilindustrie

Basierend auf den aus Experteninterviews und Literaturüberblick gewonnenen Daten wurden die im Folgenden beschriebenen Risiken identifiziert. Eine Übersicht findet sich in **Anhang B**.

3.1 Prozessrisiken

Prozessrisiken beziehen sich auf die Unterbrechung des Wertschöpfungsprozesses sowie zugehöriger Managementaufgaben. Laut Christopher und Peck (2004, S. 5) muss daher dafür gesorgt werden, dass Transportnetz, Kommunikationsmittel und Infrastruktur die Prozesse unterstützen und einen Ausfall von Teilsystemen verhindern. Eines der interviewten Unternehmen bietet Maßanfertigungen an. Dies kann zwar nicht als „fast fashion" in seiner eigentlichen Bedeutung bezeichnet werden, nichtsdestotrotz wird durch das Versprechen einer Lieferfrist von zwei Wochen bei globalen Warenströmen und individualisierten Produkten eine Herausforderung kreiert. Alle wertschöpfenden Prozesse müssen ohne Verzögerungen ablaufen, damit der Liefertermin eingehalten werden kann.

Prozessrisiken sind z.B. alle denkbaren Maschinenausfälle, Krankheit von Mitarbeitern oder ein Stromausfall im Produktionsstandort und hierdurch das Zusammenbrechen der elektronischen Kommunikation. Eine weitere genannte Risikoursache ist in komplexen Unternehmensstrukturen zu finden. Viele Hierarchieebenen und Abhängigkeiten können die Reaktionsfähigkeit in Entscheidungssituationen mindern. Ebenso werden die Prozesse verzögert, wenn z.B. das Warenwirtschaftssystem nicht durchgängig ist und viele Schnittstellen aufweist.

Im Bereich Mitarbeiter gibt es mehrere Risiken, die in den Interviews angesprochen wurden. Neben krankheitsbedingtem Ausfall bedeuten auch Fluktuation und mangelnde Zuverlässigkeit ein Risiko für Unternehmen.

Im weiteren Sinne gehört auch der Transport der fertigen Bekleidungsprodukte vom Produktionsstandort bis ins Lager in Zentraleuropa zu den Prozessrisiken, da es sich um einen Transport innerhalb des Unternehmens handelt. Solche transportbedingten

Risiken sollen jedoch unter die Versorgungsrisiken gezählt und der Standort des Zentrallagers als fokaler Standort angenommen werden.

3.2 Steuerungsrisiken

Die in einer Supply Chain auftretenden Steuerungsrisiken stehen in engem Zusammenhang mit den Regelungen und Systemen, die die Wertschöpfungsprozesse in einer Supply Chain steuern. Beispielhaft nennen Christopher und Peck (2004, S. 5) Regeln zur Höhe von Bestellmengen und Sicherheitsbeständen, aber auch Abläufe zur Steuerung und Kontrolle der durchgeführten Transporte und zum Management der Anlagen. Seitens der Interviewpartner wurde das Risiko genannt, dass mit einem Joint-Venture-Partner Probleme auftreten können. Diese können verschiedener Art sein – von Vertragsverletzungen über missverstandene Weisungen bis hin zu Insolvenzen – und alle Bereiche der Kooperation betreffen. Solche Probleme können nicht nur bei Joint Ventures auftreten, sondern bei jeder Art der Unternehmenskooperation, die in einer Supply Chain vertreten ist.

An vielen Stellen gehen Risiken, die mit Kooperationspartnern und der Steuerung der Waren- und Informationsflüsse zu tun haben, in Versorgungsrisiken über. Während diese auf die Unterbrechung der Flüsse ausgerichtet sind, fokussieren die Steuerungsrisiken auf die zugrunde liegenden Normen und Abläufe. Die Interviewpartner machten deutlich, dass insbesondere in Bereichen, die sensible Daten involvieren, die Zusammenarbeit durch Standardarbeitsanweisungen und Normen geregelt werden muss. So müssen beispielsweise Maßnahmen zum Schutz des Designs bzw. der Kollektion ergriffen werden. Es bestehen jedoch auch außerhalb des direkten Einflussbereichs von Kooperationspartnern gewisse Risiken, die zu den Steuerungsrisiken zählen. Dies sind z.B. Ausfälle oder Verzögerungen von Transporten sowie Out-of-Stock-Situationen durch saisonale Schwankungen.

Ein weiteres Steuerungsrisiko wird durch global verteilte Standorte ausgelöst, indem bei der Steuerung der Flüsse zwischen diesen Standorten verschiedenste rechtliche Rahmenbedingungen zu beachten sind. Eine Übertretung ist durch die Komplexität der Situation möglich. Ebenso kann es durch Unaufmerksamkeit dazu kommen, dass Miet- oder Charterverträge unbemerkt auslaufen.

Außerdem können bedeutende Risiken auftreten, wenn keine Standards für die Kommunikationsbeziehungen mit Partnern etabliert werden. Es kann durch ein solches Versäumnis zu Kontrollverlust und somit verstärkt zum Eintritt einer Risikosituation innerhalb der Supply Chain kommen.

3.3 Versorgungsrisiken

Weg von der Steuerungsebene und hin zur konkreten Durchführung der Güter- und Informationsflüsse zwischen Lieferanten und fokalem Unternehmen treten sogenannte Versorgungsrisiken auf (Christopher, Peck, 2004, S. 5 f.). Der Bereich der Informationsflüsse wird im Besonderen geprägt von der Zuverlässigkeit des IT-Systems und der zugrunde liegenden Infrastruktur. Eine Unterbrechung der Stromversorgung, ein Hackerangriff, Fehlfunktionen, Anwenderfehler oder Inkompatibilitäten stellen mögliche Risiken dar, die eine Unterbrechung der Informationsflüsse auslösen können.

Es wurde von den Interviewpartnern bemängelt, dass im Textilbereich zum einen eine Vielzahl von Lieferanten eingebunden werden muss, was die Durchsetzung eines Standards erschwert. Zum anderen sind diese Lieferanten häufig kleine Betriebe, die nicht in die notwendige Infrastruktur investieren wollen oder können. In den Interviews wurde z.B. erwähnt, dass in einem Fall nur ein Terminal zur Übertragung der Transportpapiere zur Verfügung steht. Ist ein Konkurrenzunternehmen zuerst vor Ort und belegt das Terminal, so bleibt nur die Möglichkeit, alle Daten manuell ins System einzugeben. Die hierdurch entstehenden Zeitverluste sowie die erhöhte Fehleranfälligkeit stellen Risiken für den Informationsfluss dar.

Eine hohe Anzahl an Lieferanten stellt außerdem einen Komplexitätstreiber dar, der die Transparenz in der Supply Chain deutlich verringert (Zierul, 2017, Minute 19:31). Es müssen außerdem Risiken bedacht werden, die durch die mangelnde Qualität der kommunizierten Informationen hervorgerufen werden. Die Interviewpartner merkten an, dass in den vergangenen Jahren trotz eines großen technischen Fortschritts die Vorhersagegenauigkeit in Bezug auf Kapazitätsbedarfe kaum erhöht werden konnte. Durch den Mangel an frühzeitig verfügbaren zuverlässigen Daten können Lieferengpässe auftreten. Dies stellt die Schnittstelle zum Güterfluss dar, dem zweiten großen Bereich, in dem Versorgungsrisiken entstehen können.

Neben dem Risiko, dass die benötigten Güter vom Lieferanten nicht bereitgestellt werden können, kann es auch zu Transportrisiken kommen. Je nachdem, welcher Verkehrsträger gewählt wird, können verschiedene Risiken relevant werden. Beispielhaft wurden der Ausbruch des Eyjafjallajökull auf Island im Jahr 2010 und die Insolvenz der südkoreanischen Reederei Hanjin 2016 genannt. Ersteres hatte zur Folge, dass der Flugverkehr über Europa zeitweise zum Erliegen kam, was sich weniger auf die Textilindustrie, als auf die Automobilbranche auswirkte. Im zweiten Fall hingegen war vor allem der Bekleidungshandel betroffen, wie einer der Interviewpartner berichtete. Dies liegt daran, dass Hanjin als Low-Cost-Carrier galt und daher große Volumina an Bekleidung und Textilien transportierte, die in der Folge nicht umgeschlagen werden konnten (Förster, 2016).

Neben den direkten Folgen aus der Verzögerung eines Transportes kann es zu Beschädigungen oder zum Verlust der Güter kommen. In diesem Fall ist die Möglichkeit zur Nachlieferung davon abhängig, wie spezifisch das verlorene Gut war. Insbesondere im Hochpreissegment, in dem Designs für jede Kollektion extra hergestellt werden, kann ein Zwischenfall, der zum Verlust der Stoffe führt, eine große Verzögerung für die Bekleidungsherstellung bedeuten. Neben solchen Transportrisiken sind auch Qualitätsrisiken zu beachten. Im Bereich von Textilien bzw. Bekleidung kann in den meisten Fällen keine Nachbesserung erfolgen, wenn Qualitätsmängel am Produkt festgestellt werden. Das Auftreten eines solchen Mangels hat daher oft sehr weitreichende Folgen.

3.4 Nachfragerisiken

Den Versorgungsrisiken stehen die Nachfragerisiken gegenüber. Sie betrachten neben den Güter- und Informationsflüssen auch die Finanzflüsse, die die Supply Chain vonseiten des Marktes durchströmen (Christopher, Peck, 2004, S. 5). Wie schon bei der Betrachtung der Upstream-gerichteten Flüsse ist auch hier die Insolvenz von Partnern bzw. Kunden ein großes Risiko. Es können hierdurch wichtige strategische Partner und Lieferanten wegfallen, die nicht leicht zu ersetzen sind. Ebenso ist im Falle des Verlusts von Kunden durch Insolvenz auch das fokale Unternehmen einem gewissen Risiko ausgesetzt, da unter Umständen große Umsatzanteile mit dem Kunden verlorengehen. Ähnliche Risiken können beim Verlust von Key Accounts auftreten.

Informationsdefizite können nicht nur zu Versorgungsrisiken führen, sondern auch auf der Nachfrageseite Risiken entstehen lassen. So wurde von den Interviewpartnern angemerkt, dass die Prognosen der Kunden zumeist zwar in Bezug auf die Gesamtmenge der in der Saison abgerufenen Volumina stimmen, aber häufig die zeitliche Verteilung sehr variabel und schwer einschätzbar ist. Im Bekleidungsbereich spielen vor allem Wetter und Impulse durch Trendsetter aus Film, Fernsehen und Musikindustrie eine große Rolle bei der Entwicklung der Verkaufszahlen.

Doch nicht nur der reguläre Güterfluss in Richtung Kunde muss betrachtet werden, sondern auch die anfallenden Retouren. Laut Aussage der Interviewpartner haben diese in den vergangenen Jahren immer mehr zugenommen, was im wachsenden Stellenwert des E-Commerce begründet ist. Allgemein wurde geäußert, dass die Veränderungen in der Wahl der Versandoption durch den Kunden eine ernst zu nehmende Herausforderung darstellen, die Risiken mit sich bringt. Als Beispiele wurden In-Store-Delivery bzw. In-Store-Return, Same-Day-Delivery oder Evening-Express genannt. Im Zuge der Einführung neuer Strukturen zur Abwicklung der rückwärts gerichteten Warenströme müssen die entsprechenden Risiken behandelt werden.

Ein weiteres Risiko, das explizit genannt wurde, ist teilweise den Nachfrage- und teilweise den Umfeldrisiken zuzurechnen. Es handelt sich um die Entwicklung neuer Stoffe, die eine weniger aufwendige Handhabung erfordern und z.B. nicht mehr hängend transportiert werden müssen. Daraus ergibt sich für Textillogistiker, die auf den Transport von Hängeware spezialisiert sind, das Risiko, dass ihre Leistungen weniger stark nachgefragt werden. Schon jetzt ist ein Trend erkennbar, dass pro Jahr ca. 5% weniger Hängeware transportiert werden. Andererseits können solche Entwicklungen auch als Marktentwicklungen eingeordnet und die daraus resultierenden Risiken als Umfeldrisiken eingestuft werden.

3.5 Umfeldrisiken

Unter die Umfeldrisiken fallen solche Risiken, die ihren Ursprung außerhalb der Supply Chain haben, aber mindestens ein Element derselben direkt beeinflussen. Christopher und Peck (2004, S. 6) führen als Beispiele neben der Produktkontamination auch Unfälle oder extreme Wetterbedingungen an. Einer der Experten wies darauf hin, dass politische und soziale Unruhen an den Standorten der Produktionsbetriebe ein Risiko darstellen können, da diese häufig in Regionen liegen, die durch Unruhen beeinträchtigt werden. Im konkreten Fall stellten die Entwicklungen des arabischen Frühlings ein sehr großes Risiko für den Produktionsbetrieb vor Ort dar.

Setzt man den Gedankengang fort, so sind im Rahmen der Umfeldrisiken nicht nur politische und soziale Risiken zu betrachten, sondern auch ökonomische, ökologische, technologische und legislative Entwicklungen. Durch die Experten wurde insbesondere der Stellenwert der Legislative hervorgehoben. So wurde mehrfach betont, dass durch Änderungen der rechtlichen Rahmenbedingungen multiple Risiken auftreten können. Zum einen kann durch Unwissenheit insbesondere im internationalen Umfeld unbeabsichtigt gegen lokales Gesetz verstoßen werden. Außerdem kann es zu Wettbewerbs- und Kartellrechtsverstößen kommen. Ebenso haben (makro-)ökonomische Veränderungen Auswirkungen auf eine Supply Chain. Beispiele für Risiken in diesem Bereich, die in den Interviews genannt wurden, sind Protektionismus, Handelsbeschränkungen und Embargobeschlüsse der Vereinten Nationen.

In den sozialen Bereich fallen die Themen der ordnungsgemäßen Buchführung und Compliance. Oft bewegen sich Unternehmen gerade in diesem Bereich in einer unsicheren Situation. Konkret wurde von einem der Interviewpartner berichtet, dass das Unternehmen seine Geschäftstätigkeit in Russland auf einem sehr geringen Niveau hält, da einerseits kein Risiko durch die erzwungene Teilnahme an korrupten Geschäftspraktiken eingegangen werden soll, andererseits aber die Zollformalitäten ohne die Zahlung von Schmiergeldern kaum in einem vertretbaren und vom Kunden akzeptierten Zeitrahmen abgewickelt werden könnten. Ein weiteres wichtiges Thema in diesem Bereich ist die Corporate Social Responsibility. Durch zahlreiche Negativbeispiele ist die Textilindustrie in den vergangenen Jahren in Verruf geraten, sodass heutzutage die Kunden vermehrt auf entsprechende Programme der Unternehmen achten. Risiken entstehen in diesem Fall dadurch, dass die Kunden die Bemühungen des Unternehmens nicht für ausreichend befinden. Außer der Forderung nach der Einhaltung von Sozialstandards ist auch die Nachhaltigkeit der Produktion von zunehmendem Interesse für Kunden. Zumindest wird heutzutage ein gewisses Maß an Interesse von der Gesellschaft erwartet. Dies führte in letzter Zeit dazu, dass verschiedenste Labels und Zertifikate eingeführt wurden, die teilweise nur geringe Aussagekraft besitzen.

Auch wurde in den Interviews bestätigt, dass Kunden bspw. im Hochpreissegment nicht explizit Nachhaltigkeit fordern. Um keine Risiken einzugehen, werden allerdings Maßnahmen getroffen, die schnell umgesetzt werden können, wenn sich die Kundennachfrage verstärkt. Wie bereits beschrieben, lassen High-Value- und Low-Budget-Hersteller häufig im selben Betrieb mit den gleichen Sozialstandards fertigen. Sofern dies den Kunden nicht explizit bekannt wird, sind kaum negative Konsequenzen zu befürchten. Ändert sich allerdings die Akzeptanz der Kunden tiefgreifend, so sind deutliche Reputationsrisiken zu befürchten.

Außer bei Sozialstandards wird auch in Bereichen der Nachhaltigkeit heute eher oberflächlich gearbeitet. Sogenanntes Greenwashing ist häufig anzutreffen. Auch die Interviewpartner bestätigten, dass zwar „grüne" Transportlösungen vorhanden sind, aber wegen der höheren Kosten nur sehr selten angefragt werden (Fernie, Grant, 2015, S. 74). Einige Unternehmen sind in Fragen der Corporate Social Responsibility jedoch sehr aktiv und bspw. nach der ISO 14001 zertifiziert. Auch werden laut Interviewpartner der Carbon-Footprint ermittelt und auf Kundenwunsch Elektroautos bei der Auslieferung eingesetzt. Der gesamte Bereich der Corporate Social Responsibility ist eng verknüpft mit Reputationsrisiken. Ein weiteres Risiko für das Image eines Unternehmens ist, dass Terrorakte mithilfe des Transportequipments eines Logistikdienstleisters, bspw. Sprengstoff in Container, durchgeführt werden könnten.

Je nachdem, wie sich in Zukunft die Ansichten der Gesellschaft und somit die Anforderungen der Kunden verändern, werden die Unternehmen in diesem Bereich vor immense Herausforderungen gestellt. Neben einem solchen Umschwung in den gesellschaftlichen Normen können auch andere Marktveränderungen Risiken hervorrufen. Als Beispiel hierfür wurde der Trend weg von Hängeware hin zu Liegeware genannt. Da die Umfeldrisiken alle Bereiche umfassen, die außerhalb einer Supply Chain liegen, fallen hierunter multiple und teilweise sehr verschiedene Risiken.

4 Situation und Entwicklung der Textilindustrie

Stellt man den zuvor identifizierten Risiken jeweils – auf einen Treiber bezogen – mögliche Chance gegenüber, so wird deutlich, in welchen Bereichen die Risiken besonders präsent sind und verstärkt betrachtet werden müssen. Gleichzeitig können Chancen ergriffen werden. Da das Ausnutzen von Chancen eine mögliche Reaktion auf bestehende Risiken darstellt, ist auf ihre Darstellung im Folgenden nicht zu verzichten. Eine detaillierte Diskussion der einzelnen Chancen kann an dieser Stelle jedoch nicht erfolgen. Die entsprechenden Quellen zu den Chancen der fünf Treiber nach Porter sind **Tabelle 2** zu entnehmen.

Tabelle 2: Quellen zu identifizierten Chancen in der Textilbranche nach Porters „Five Forces" (eigene Darstellung)

Treiber	Quellen
Neue Anbieter	Bundesministerium für Wirtschaft und Energie, 2016; Bundesverband der Deutschen Volksbanken und Raiffeisenbanken, 2013, S. 4; Ewald et al., 2013, S. 10 und S. 17; inditex.com, 2016; Interviewpartner; Krippendorf, Holst, Richter 2009, S. 20, 34–38, 42 ff.
Lieferanten	Interviewpartner
Abnehmer	Christopher et al., 2009, S. 105; Ewald et al., 2013, S. 4, 16, 18–21; Interviewpartner
Substitute	Interviewpartner
Branchenrivalität	Bundesministerium für Wirtschaft und Energie, 2016; Ewald et al., 2013, S. 8, 19f.; Krippendorf, Holst, Richter, 2009, S. 40; Porter, 2011, S. 12

Eine zusammenfassende Darstellung sowohl der positiven als auch der negativen Einflussfaktoren findet sich in **Abbildung 6**. Es wurden im Wesentlichen alle zuvor genannten Faktoren aufgegriffen. Einzig solche Faktoren, die je nach äußeren Umständen entweder eine Chance oder ein Risiko darstellen, wurden nicht aufgenommen. Dies sind für den Treiber „Verhandlungsmacht der Kunden" eine kurze Time-to-Market, die Nutzung von Siegeln und Zertifikaten sowie die zunehmende Nutzung sozialer Medien. Für den Treiber „Rivalität innerhalb der Branche" handelt es sich um die Differenzierung und die Sortimentsbreite bzw. -tiefe.

Die Bedrohung, die neue Anbieter für die etablierten Unternehmen darstellen, ist durchaus ernst. Insbesondere die Marktöffnung und somit das Wegfallen von Handelsbeschränkungen machen es neuen Marktteilnehmern oder etablierten Unternehmen aus dem Ausland leicht, im deutschen Markt Fuß zu fassen. Einzig der stark innovations- und technologiegetriebene Bereich der Technischen Textilien ist nicht akut bedroht.

Im Bereich der Verhandlungsmacht der Lieferanten gleichen sich die positiv und die negativ wirkenden Faktoren weitestgehend aus. Je nachdem, ob die Lieferanten eines Bekleidungshändlers eher im Bereich der Standardprodukte oder sehr spezifischer Produkte aktiv sind, verändert sich das Machtverhältnis. Eine allgemein gültige Aussage kann somit nicht getroffen werden.

Anwendungsorientierte Forschungsbeiträge

Abbildung 6: *Analyse der Bekleidungsbranche sowie ihres Umfelds (eigene Darstellung nach Porter, 1992, S. 26)*

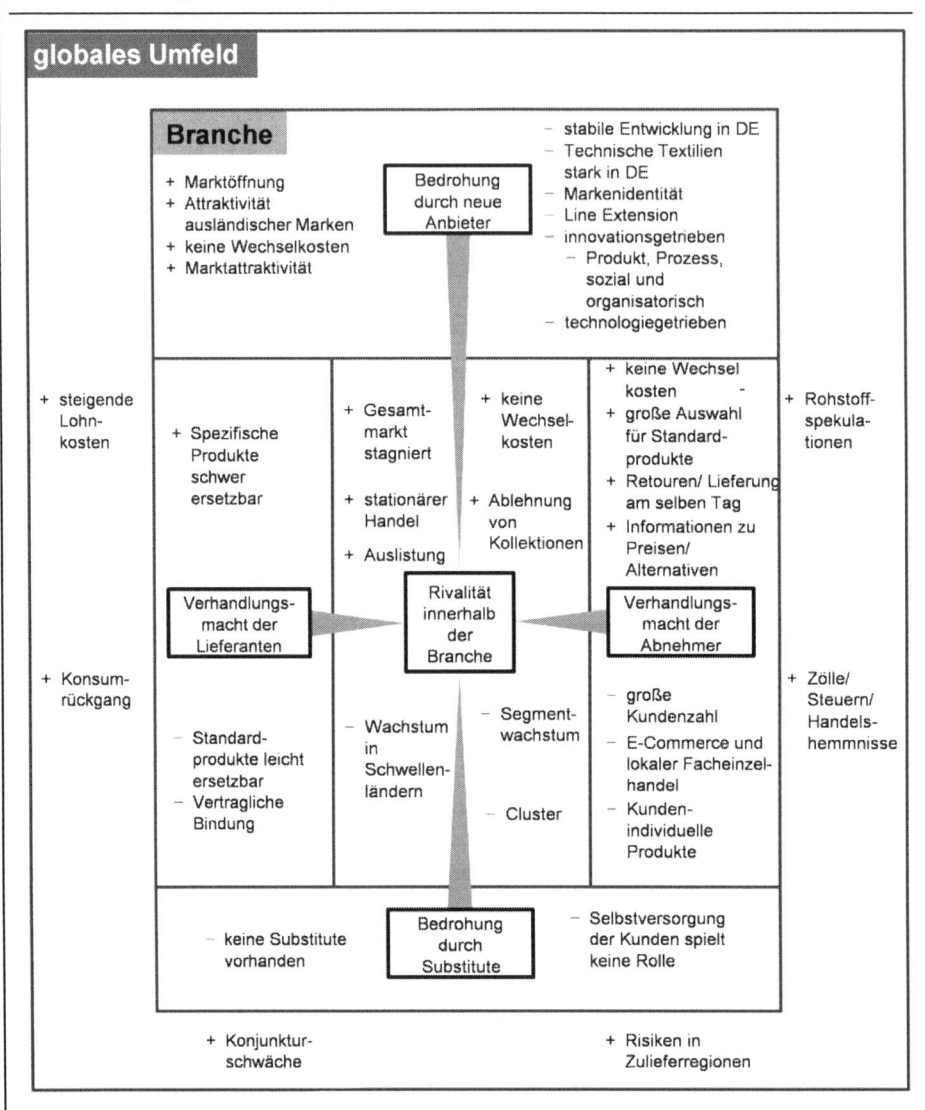

```
globales Umfeld
┌─────────────────────────────────────────────────────────────┐
│  Branche                                                    │
│                              – stabile Entwicklung in DE    │
│                              – Technische Textilien         │
│   + Marktöffnung    Bedrohung  stark in DE                  │
│   + Attraktivität   durch neue – Markenidentität            │
│     ausländischer   Anbieter   – Line Extension             │
│     Marken                     – innovationsgetrieben       │
│   + keine Wechselkosten          – Produkt, Prozess,        │
│   + Marktattraktivität              sozial und              │
│                                     organisatorisch         │
│                                – technologiegetrieben       │
└─────────────────────────────────────────────────────────────┘
```

(Darstellung der fünf Kräfte nach Porter mit umliegenden Faktoren: Verhandlungsmacht der Lieferanten, Rivalität innerhalb der Branche, Verhandlungsmacht der Abnehmer, Bedrohung durch neue Anbieter, Bedrohung durch Substitute)

Links außen (globales Umfeld):
+ steigende Lohnkosten
+ Konsumrückgang

Rechts außen (globales Umfeld):
+ Rohstoffspekulationen
+ Zölle/ Steuern/ Handelshemmnisse

Unten (globales Umfeld):
+ Konjunkturschwäche
+ Risiken in Zulieferregionen

Verhandlungsmacht der Lieferanten:
+ Spezifische Produkte schwer ersetzbar
– Standardprodukte leicht ersetzbar
– Vertragliche Bindung

Rivalität innerhalb der Branche:
+ Gesamtmarkt stagniert
+ stationärer Handel
+ Auslistung
– Wachstum in Schwellenländern
– Segmentwachstum
– Cluster
+ keine Wechselkosten
+ Ablehnung von Kollektionen

Verhandlungsmacht der Abnehmer:
+ keine Wechselkosten
+ große Auswahl für Standardprodukte
+ Retouren/ Lieferung am selben Tag
+ Informationen zu Preisen/ Alternativen
– große Kundenzahl
– E-Commerce und lokaler Facheinzelhandel
– Kundenindividuelle Produkte

Bedrohung durch Substitute:
– keine Substitute vorhanden
– Selbstversorgung der Kunden spielt keine Rolle

Eine sehr starke Tendenz ist hingegen für den Treiber „Verhandlungsmacht der Abnehmer" zu sehen. Hier ist deutlich zu erkennen, dass es sich im Bekleidungshandel um einen Käufer- statt einen Verkäufermarkt handelt (Helm, 2006; Kreutzer, 2013). Durch diverse Faktoren kann der Kunde Macht über Bekleidungsunternehmen ausüben. Der Mangel an Wechselkosten und die große Auswahl an Alternativen übertrumpfen die Unabhängigkeit der Unternehmen von einzelnen Individuen. Zwar fällt eine Jeans mehr oder weniger im Jahresumsatz nicht auf, doch auch einzelne Kunden, die wegfallen, haben Einfluss auf das wirtschaftliche Ergebnis.

Eindeutig positiv ist der Treiber „Bedrohung durch Substitute" zu bewerten. Da keine Substitute für Bekleidung existieren und kaum jemand Kleidung selbst herstellt, sind für diesen Bereich keine Risiken zu nennen. Anderes ergibt sich bei der Betrachtung der Rivalität innerhalb der Branche. Durch Stagnation des Marktes und die starke Position der Kunden entwickelt sich ein heftiger Wettbewerb in der Branche. Immer kürzere Kollektionsrhythmen und die steigenden Serviceanforderungen durch die Kunden stellen die Unternehmen stets vor neue Herausforderungen.

Ebenso negativ wirken sich die Einflussfaktoren des globalen Umfelds aus. Vielfältige Risiken ergeben sich in wirtschaftlicher Hinsicht. Außerdem sind in den typischen Zulieferregionen des Nahen Ostens und Nordafrikas multiple Risiken politischer und technologischer Natur zu erwarten.

Abschließend bleibt zu sagen, dass die Bedrohung durch neue Anbieter und die Verhandlungsmacht der Lieferanten ein ausgeglichenes Verhältnis von Chancen und Risiken aufweisen. Im Bereich der Substitute sind keine Risiken zu nennen, während sowohl die Verhandlungsmacht der Abnehmer als auch die Rivalität in der Branche sowie Risiken aus dem globalen Umfeld eine deutliche Bedrohung für Unternehmen des Bekleidungshandels darstellen und entsprechend im Rahmen des Risikomanagements gehandhabt werden müssen.

5 Zusammenfassung und Ausblick

Der Umgang mit Risiken, die in der textilen Supply Chain auftreten können, erfordert eine mehrstufige Betrachtung derselben. So können Supply-Chain-Risiken auf allen Einflussebenen identifiziert und mit geeigneten Risikomaßnahmen behandelt werden.

Zur Erreichung dieses Ziels wurde die Textil- und Bekleidungsindustrie mit der zugehörigen Supply Chain betrachtet, sodass die erste Forschungsfrage beantwortet werden konnte. Neben dieser inhaltlichen Grundlagenarbeit wurden methodische Grundlagen durch die Auseinandersetzung mit empirischen Erhebungsmethoden festgelegt. Die Expertenbefragung wurde als geeignete Methode identifiziert und entsprechende Interviews durchgeführt. Dabei wurden einerseits Strukturen von Textil-Supply-Chains und des zugehörigen Risikomanagements untersucht. Andererseits wurden Risiken im Umfeld von Textil- und Bekleidungsunternehmen identifiziert und in strukturierter Form gesammelt. Unter Zuhilfenahme von Literaturquellen wurde die Liste der Risiken erweitert und mittels Branchenanalyse ein Bild der aktuellen Situation der Textil- und Bekleidungsindustrie gezeichnet, was die Beantwortung von Forschungsfrage zwei darstellt. Abhängig vom Integrationsgrad und den Supply-Chain-Strukturen ist eine Ausarbeitung einzelner Risikobereiche an anderer Stelle notwendig.

Für die fünf Risikokategorien können – basierend auf den identifizierten Supply-Chain-Risiken – folgende generische Aussagen zusammengefasst werden: Je nach konkreter Risikosituation und -bewertung durch das Unternehmen ergeben sich Handlungsnotwendigkeiten, die die Auswahl und Priorisierung von Maßnahmen zur Handhabung von Prozessrisiken bestimmen. Wie im Falle der Prozessrisiken ist die genaue Ausgestaltung der Maßnahmen für Steuerungsrisiken abhängig von der Situation im Unternehmen. Generische Maßnahmen dienen der Orientierung und dem Einstieg ins Thema und sind nicht als umfassende Risikobehandlung zu betrachten. Wie die Branchenanalyse schon gezeigt hat, geht im Allgemeinen kein großes Risiko vonseiten der Lieferanten aus. Allerdings trägt auch die Beherrschung geringer Risiken zur Verbesserung der Situation bei. Es ist eine verstärkte Integration der Lieferanten zur Begegnung der Versorgungsrisiken generell zu empfehlen. Durch den großen Einfluss, den der Kunde hat, sowie eine stagnierende Marktentwicklung geraten Bekleidungsunternehmen zunehmend in Bedrängnis. Die Risikolandschaft in Bezug auf Nachfragerisiken ist generell wenig positiv und muss nach Möglichkeit durch Risikomaßnahmen beeinflusst werden. Aufgrund des hohen Drucks in der Branche durch immer neue Konkurrenten aus dem In- und Ausland sowie aufgrund zahlreicher schwer zu beeinflussender globaler Einflussfaktoren ist die Bewertung der Risikosituation im Hinblick auf Umfeldrisiken kritisch. Zur Vermeidung existenzbedrohender Situationen sind Maßnahmen einzuleiten und deren Erfolg zu überwachen.

In dem vorliegenden Beitrag werden wichtige Einflussfaktoren für die Textil-Supply-Chain dargestellt. Je nach konkreter Situation eines Unternehmens und der individuellen Risikobewertung sind der Risikokatalog zu erweitern und entsprechende Maßnahmen zu entwickeln.

Literatur

Abernathy, F. H.; Dunlop, J. T.; Hammond, J. H.; Weil, D. (1999): A stitch in time: lean retailing and the transformation of manufacturing – lessons from the apparel and textile industries, New York: Oxford University Press.

Breitkopf, S. K. (1999): Externes Controlling: eine konzeptionelle und empirische Analyse am Beispiel des marktorientierten Kostenmanagements in der Bekleidungsindustrie, Frankfurt am Main: Lang.

Bundesministerium für Wirtschaft und Energie (2016): Textil und Bekleidung. Verfügbar unter: http://www.bmwi.de/DE/Themen/Wirtschaft/branchenfokus,did=196528.html (abgerufen am 21. November 2016).

Bundesverband der Deutschen Volksbanken und Raiffeisenbanken (2013): VR Branchen special – Textilgewerbe, Deutscher Genossenschafts-Verlag.

Christopher, M.; Peck, H. (2004): Building the Resilient Supply Chain, in: The International Journal of Logistics Management, 15(2), 1–13.

Christopher, M.; Lowson, B.; Peck, H. (2009): Fashion Logistics and Quick Response, in: Fernie, J.; Sparks, L. (Eds.): Logistics and Retail Management, 3rd edition, London, Philadelphia: Kogan Page Ltd., 102–120.

Döring, N.; Bortz, J. (2016): Forschungsmethoden und Evaluation in den Sozial- und Humanwissenschaften, 5. vollständig überarbeitete, aktualisierte und erweiterte Auflage, Berlin und Heidelberg: Springer.

Ewald, O.; Hunger-Siegler, C.; Janßen, P.; Vos, G.; Hinz, J.; Grebe, J. (2013): Deutsche Bekleidungshersteller. Branchenbericht – Corporate Sector Report No. 80680316, Frankfurt am Main: Commerzbank AG.

Fernie, J.; Grant, D. B. (2015): Fashion logistics: insights into the fashion retail supply chain, London, Philadelphia: Kogan Page.

Förster, K. (2016): Hanjin-Pleite wird ein Fall für die Gerichte. Verfügbar unter: http://www.hansa-online.de/hanjin-pleite-wird-ein-fall-fuer-gerichte/?p=43563 (abgerufen am 31. Oktober 2016).

Ghauri, S. N. (2010): Research methods in business studies, 4th edition, Financial Times Prentice Hall.

Helm, R. (2006): Marketing als Pendant der betrieblichen Wertschöpfung, in: Bea, F. X.; Friedl, B.; Schweitzer, M. (Eds.): Allgemeine Betriebswirtschaftslehre. Bd. 3: Leistungsprozess, 9., neu bearbeitete und erweiterte Auflage, Stuttgart: Lucius/Lucius.

Horstmann, S. (1997): Vertikale Vertriebskooperationen in der Bekleidungswirtschaft: eine Analyse innovativer Distributionskonzepte US-amerikanischer und deutscher Bekleidungshersteller, Frankfurt am Main, New York: S. Lang.

Hoyndorff, K.; Hülsmann, S.; Spee, D.; Hompel, M. ten (2010): Fashion logistics. 2. Auflage, München: Huss-Verlag.

inditex.com (2016): Brands. Verfügbar unter: https://www.inditex.com/en/brands (abgerufen am 02. Dezember 2016).

Kreutzer, R. T. (2013): Praxisorientiertes Marketing: Grundlagen – Instrumente – Fallbeispiele, 4., vollständig überarbeitete und erweiterte Aufl., Wiesbaden: Springer Gabler.

Krippendorf, W.; Holst, G.; Richter, U. (2009): Branchenanalyse Textilindustrie. Untersuchungen zur Situation und Entwicklung der Branchen „Textilgewerbe", Projektbericht No. S-2008-201-1, Berlin: IMU-Institut Berlin GmbH.

Loock, H. (2008): Kollektionsentwicklung in der Bekleidungsbranche unter besonderer Berücksichtigung empirischer Erfolgsfaktoren, 1. Auflage, München, Mering: Rainer Hampp Verlag.

Nothardt, F.; Schmitter, F.; Trede, T. (2007): Logistik in der Bekleidungsbranche – quo vadis, in: Stölzle, W.; Weber, J.; Hofmann, E.; Wallenburg, C. M. (Eds.): Handbuch Kontraktlogistik. Management komplexer Logistikdienstleistungen, 1. Auflage, Weinheim: Wiley.

ÖkoMedia PR (2001): Lebenslauf von Textilien: von der Faser zum Recycling, 1. Auflage, Eschborn: Gesamttextil.

Pfohl, H.-C. (2008): Sicherheit und Risikomanagement in der Supply Chain, Hamburg: Deutscher Verkehrs-Verlag.

Porter, M. E. (1992): Wettbewerbsstrategie: Methoden zur Analyse von Branchen und Konkurrenten (Competitive Strategy), 7. Auflage, Frankfurt/Main: Campus-Verlag.

Zierul, S. (2017): Mode schlägt Moral – Wie fair ist unsere Kleidung. Video verfügbar unter: http://www1.wdr.de/mediathek/video/sendungen/tag-sieben/video-mode-schlaegt-moral-100.html (abgerufen am 05. Februar 2017).

Anhang A

1. <u>Struktur und Organisation der Supply Chain</u>
   a. Wie viele Lieferanten welcher Stufen haben Sie? Wie sind diese global verteilt und in welcher Beziehung stehen Sie zu ihnen?
   b. Wo liegen Engpässe und wie werden sie gehandhabt?
   c. Welche „Ausweichrouten" gibt es?
   d. Wie hoch ist der Lieferbereitschaftsgrad?
   e. Arbeiten Sie „lean" oder gibt es hohe Bestände?
   f. Wie werden Schwankungen im Auftragsvolumen abgefangen/ verhindert?
   g. Wie lang ist die durchschnittliche „Lebensdauer" von Kooperationen und welcher Art sind diese?

2. <u>Supply-Chain-Risiken und deren Management allgemein</u>
   a. Wie transparent ist Ihre Supply Chain?
   b. Sind Abhängigkeiten zwischen den Kooperationspartnern/zu Wettbewerbern bekannt?
   c. Wie wird mit Notfällen umgegangen?
   d. Wo ist das Supply-Chain-Risikomanagement bei Ihnen angesiedelt?
   e. Wie wird die Supply Chain gesteuert?
   f. Spielt „Industrie 4.0" im Rahmen des Supply-Chain-Risikomanagements eine Rolle?
   g. Werden identifizierte Risiken entlang der Supply Chain kommuniziert?
   h. Wie wird Reputationsrisiken begegnet?
   i. Welche Trends und Herausforderungen sehen Sie für die Zukunft der Textillogistik?

3. <u>Risikomanagementprozess konkret</u>
   a. Wie läuft die Risikoidentifikation ab?
   b. Wie läuft die Risikoanalyse ab?
   c. Wie läuft die Risikobewertung ab?
   d. Wie läuft die Risikosteuerung ab?
   e. Wie läuft die Risikokontrolle ab?

Anhang B

	Stärken und Chancen	Risiken
Prozessrisiken		Maschinenausfälle
		Mitarbeiterausfall
		Mangelnde Mitarbeiterzuverlässigkeit
		Mitarbeiterfluktuation
		Lange Reaktionszeit durch steile Hierarchie
		Stromausfälle
		undurchgängiges Warenwirtschaftssystem
Steuerungsrisiken	IT-Integration zur Informationsweiterleitung	Transportausfälle/-verzögerungen
		Out-of-Stock-Situationen
		Compliancerisiken
		Schutz des Designs
		Mängel in Kommunikationsstandards
		Probleme mit Partnern (Vertragsverletzungen)
		Probleme mit Partnern (missverstandene Weisungen)
		Probleme mit Partnern (Insolvenz)
		Auslaufen von Verträgen
Versorgungsrisiken	Viele Lieferanten für Standardprodukte	Wenige Lieferanten für High-Quality
		Qualitätsmängel
	Vertikale Integration bindet Lieferanten	Mangelnde Prognosezuverlässigkeit
		Transportrisiken
		Lieferschwierigkeiten
		Inkompatibilität der IT-Systeme
		Anwenderfehler
		Fehlfunktionen des IT-Systems
		Hackerangriffe
		Unterbrechung der Stromversorgung

Supply-Chain-Risiken in der Textilindustrie

	Stärken und Chancen	Risiken
Nachfragerisiken	Trends erfassen und umsetzen	Keine Wechselkosten für Kunden
	Stärke des E-Commerce und lokalen Facheinzelhandel	Große Auswahl für Standardprodukte
	strategische Positionierung, Sortimentsbreite und -tiefe	Lieferbereitschaft kritisch, Time-to-Market
	kundenindividuelle Produkte	Forecast der Nachfrage schwierig
	internationaler Markt kann für Absatz genutzt werden	Sonderaktionen beeinflussen Preisempfinden
	techn. Fortschritt ermöglicht innovative E-Commerce Konzepte	Retouren bewältigen
		Insolvenz von Kunden
	Konsumethik	Neue Vertriebskanäle
		Ungünstige Entwicklung der klassischen Vertriebskanäle
		Siegel und Zertifikate oft nur für Teilbereiche
		Line Extensions beeinflussen Markenidentität
		Entwicklung neuer Materialien
Risiken des wettbewerbsrelevanten Umfelds	Wachstum in Schwellenländern	Stagnation des Gesamtmarktes
	Wachstum in Segmenten	Marktattraktivität
	lokaler Facheinzelhandel schafft Identität	Ausländische Wettbewerber
	Cluster und Vernetzung	Marktöffnung
	stabile Entwicklung in DE	Kosten im stationären Facheinzelhandel
	Innovation (Sozial, Produkt, Prozess)	Wegfallen einzelner Verkaufsstellen
	Stärke der Markenidentität	Kollektion verfehlt den Markt
	starkes SCM, kurze Time-to-Market	Sortimentsbreite und -tiefe
	Technologiegetriebenheit	Wetterbedingungen
	Keine Substitute	
	Technische Textilien stark in Deutschland	
	Selbstversorgung spielt keine Rolle	

	Stärken und Chancen	Risiken
Risiken des globalen Umfelds		Politische Instabilität, Korruption, Elektrizitätsversorgung
		Disconnect mit Finanzsektor
		Kaum Nutzung des Innovationspotentials
		Mangel an qualifizierten Arbeitern
		Konjunkturschwäche
		Lohnsteigerungen in Zulieferländern
		Steigen der Rohstoffpreise
		Bekleidungskonsum sinkt; immaterielle Konsumgüter im Trend
		Zölle, Handelshemmnisse

Autorenverzeichnis

Lukas Biedermann
Lukas Biedermann studierte Wirtschaftsingenieurwesen an der Universität Bremen in den Vertiefungsrichtungen Luft- & Raumfahrt (B.Sc.) sowie Logistik und Produktionswirtschaft (M.Sc.). Im Rahmen seiner laufenden Promotion am Lehrstuhl für ABWL und Logistikmanagement an der Universität Bremen untersucht Biedermann zukünftige Erfolgsfaktoren zur Gestaltung resilienter Supply Chains. Seit 2014 ist Lukas Biedermann als Unternehmensberater für die Porsche Consulting GmbH tätig. Zu seinen Fachgebieten zählen die integrierte Planung und Steuerung von Wertschöpfungsnetzwerken, Supply Chain Management, Lieferantenmanagement sowie Supply Chain Leadership-Coaching. Lukas Biedermann ist Autor einiger internationaler wissenschaftlicher Publikationen und Mitglied in verschiedenen Industrie- und Wissenschaftsverbänden.

Christoph Bode
Prof. Dr. Christoph Bode leitet seit 2014 den Stiftungslehrstuhl für Procurement an der Universität Mannheim. Der Lehrstuhl wurde auf Initiative der Industrie eingerichtet und wird von einem Stifterkreis – bestehend aus Bilfinger SE, BME e.V., Dietmar Hopp Stiftung, Heidelberger Druckmaschinen AG, Hilti AG, KSB AG, Roche Diagnostics GmbH, Saint-Gobain Building Distribution Deutschland GmbH, SAP SE sowie SEW-EURODRIVE – finanziert und gefördert. In Forschung und Lehre beschäftigt er sich mit Einkauf, Logistik und Supply Chain Management mit Fokus auf Risiken, Innovationen, Nachhaltigkeit und der Gestaltung von Lieferantenbeziehungen.

Christoph Bode studierte Wirtschaftsingenieurwesen mit Abschlüssen an der Universität Karlsruhe (heute: KIT) und dem Grenoble INP (Frankreich). Die Promotion erfolgte an der WHU – Otto Beisheim School of Management in Vallendar und die Habilitation an der Eidgenössischen Technischen Hochschule Zürich (Schweiz). Vor seinem Wechsel an die Universität Mannheim arbeitete er am Department of Organization and Strategy der Tilburg University (Niederlande).

Seine Arbeiten wurden sowohl in multidisziplinären Managementzeitschriften (*Academy of Management Journal, Organizational Research Methods*) als auch in führenden Zeitschriften im Feld des Operations Managements (*European Journal of Operational Research, Journal of Operations Management*) publiziert.

Christoph Bode ist Associate Editor (*International Journal Operations & Production Management, Journal of Business Logistics, Journal of Purchasing and Supply Management, Journal of Supply Chain Management*), Mitglied in Editorial Review Boards (*Journal of Opera-*

tions Management, Journal of Management Studies) und regelmäßiger Gutachter für renommierte Fachzeitschriften und Konferenzen.

Bastien Bodenstein

Bastien Bodenstein studierte Wirtschaftsingenieurwesen für Maschinenbau und Energietechnik an der Hochschule für Technik, Wirtschaft und Kultur in Leipzig und anschließend Wirtschaftsingenieurwesen an der Technischen Universität Dresden. Während seiner Studienzeit arbeitete er für den Automobilproduzenten BMW, die Industriekonzerne Saint-Gobain und Thyssen Krupp sowie das Luft- und Raumfahrtunternehmen Fokker Elmo in Beijing/China. Darüber hinaus verbrachte er ein akademisches Auslandssemester an der Siam University in Bangkok/Thailand.

Dr. Marie Katharina Brüning

Dr. Marie Katharina Brüning studierte International Business and Management mit dem Schwerpunkt Operations and Supply Chain an der University of Groningen (Niederlande) und an der Hanken School of Economics (Finnland). 2010 schloss sie den Master of Science mit cum laude ab. Danach arbeitete sie als Projektmanagerin in der Automobilindustrie. Von 2013 bis 2017 war sie wissenschaftliche Mitarbeiterin an der Jacobs University Bremen in der Arbeitsgruppe Produktions- und Logistiknetzwerke unter der Leitung von Prof. Dr. Julia Bendul. Im gleichen Zeitraum promovierte sie zum Thema Supply-Chain-Risikomanagement ebenfalls an der Jacobs University Bremen. Marie Katharina Brüning ist Autorin von mehreren international veröffentlichten Publikationen.

Julia Burkhardt

Julia Burkhardt studierte informationsorientierte Betriebswirtschaftslehre an der Universität Augsburg. Im Anschluss daran besuchte sie die EBS Universität für Wirtschaft und Recht in Oestrich-Winkel und die Deusto Business School in San Sebastián/Spanien, um ihren Masterabschluss zu erlangen. Seit September 2015 arbeitet Julia Burkhardt am Institut für Supply Chain Management der Universität St. Gallen und forscht zum Thema „Vorlieferantenmanagement".

Stefan Drechsler

Stefan Drechsler studierte Wirtschaftswissenschaften und Betriebswirtschaftslehre mit der Vertiefung Operations and Logistics Management an der Technischen Universität Dresden. Während und nach dem Studium arbeitete er vor allem in der Maschinenbaubranche und absolvierte unter anderem ein Praktikum bei der Homag GmbH, dem führenden Hersteller von Holzbearbeitungsmaschinen. Er ist seit 2014 als wissenschaftlicher Mitarbeiter am Lehrstuhl für BWL, insb. Logistik an der Fakultät Wirtschaftswissenschaften der TU Dresden tätig. Seine Forschungsinteressen liegen im Bereich der Ersatzteillogistik, wobei er betrachtet, wie sich Informationsmängel auf die Nutzung von praktischem Wissen und die Einstellung gegenüber Innovationen auswirken.

Dr. Nicolas Fugger

Dr. Nicolas Fugger studierte Volkswirtschaftslehre an der Rheinischen Friedrich-Wilhelms-Universität Bonn und der Universität zu Köln. Im Anschluss promovierte er an der Universität zu Köln. Während seiner Promotion erforschte er als Mitglied der DFG-Forschergruppe (FOR 1371) „Design & Behavior – Economic Engineering of Firms and Markets" die optimale Gestaltung von Auktionen, Verhandlungen und hybrider Mechanismen im Einkauf und absolvierte einen Forschungsaufenthalt am Smeal College of Business der Pennsylvania State University. Seit 2016 arbeitet Nicolas Fugger in der Forschungsgruppe „Marktdesign" am Zentrum für Europäische Wirtschaftsforschung (ZEW) in Mannheim. Dort leitet er den Forschungsschwerpunkt „Regeldesign für die öffentliche Beschaffung". Seine Forschungsinteressen umfassen alle Gebiete des Marktdesigns mit Schwerpunkten in der angewandten Auktionstheorie und im Einkaufsdesign. Eine seiner Forschungsarbeiten veröffentlichte er in *Management Science*.

Dr. Martin Grunewald

Dr. Martin Grunewald arbeitet derzeit als Akademischer Rat am Lehrstuhl für Produktion und Logistik der Technischen Universität Braunschweig von Prof. Dr. Thomas S. Spengler. Nach dem Studium der Wirtschaftsmathematik an der Universität Magdeburg promovierte er zur Beschaffungslogistik in der Automobilindustrie an der Technischen Universität Braunschweig. Seine Forschungsinteressen liegen in der (Automobil-)Logistik und der Digitalisierung der Produktion, mit speziellem Fokus auf die betriebswirtschaftliche Bewertung von neuen Technologien.

Dr. Tobias Kosmol

Dr. Tobias Kosmol absolvierte ein Duales Studium der Betriebswirtschaftslehre an der Friedrich-Alexander-Universität Erlangen-Nürnberg und den Master in Management an der Universität Mannheim. 2017 promovierte er an der WHU – Otto Beisheim School of Management zum Dr. rer. pol. (summa cum laude). Tobias Kosmol beschäftigt sich in seiner Forschung mit der Beschaffung in Schwellenländern, dem Risikomanagement in der Lieferkette, der Kognition von Managern und der digitalen Transformation des Einkaufs. Seine Arbeiten sind unter anderem im *Journal of Supply Chain Management* und im *Journal of Purchasing & Supply Management* erschienen. Als DAAD-Stipendiat verbrachte er ein Jahr an der Sichuan University in Chengdu/China, wo er das höchste chinesische Sprachniveau (HSK 6) erlangte. Tobias Kosmol ist Mitglied in zahlreichen wissenschaftlichen Institutionen, wie der IPSERA, und Verbänden, wie dem BME. Seit 2017 ist Tobias Kosmol als Senior Consultant für die INVERTO GmbH tätig, einer spezialisierten Unternehmensberatung für Einkauf und Supply Chain Management.

Autorenverzeichnis

Prof. Dr. Herbert Kotzab

Prof. Dr. Herbert Kotzab studierte Marketing und Management an der Wirtschaftsuniversität Wien, an der er auch zum Dr. rer. soc. oec promovierte (1996) sowie mit der Venia in Betriebswirtschaftslehre habilitierte (2002). Zwischen 1999 und 2011 war er Universitätsprofessor an der Copenhagen Business School. Seit 2011 ist er Inhaber des Lehrstuhls für ABWL und Logistikmanagement an der Universität Bremen. Seine Forschungsresultate sind in zahlreichen wissenschaftlichen Artikel in international anerkannten Zeitschriften erschienen. Seine Forschungsinteressen gelten dem Supply Chain Management im Handel sowie der Theoriebildung im Supply Chain Management. Er ist Mitglied in zahlreichen wissenschaftlichen Gesellschaften und Verbänden. Seit 2013 ist Herbert Kotzab Editor-in-Chief der Zeitschrift *Logistics Research*.

Prof. Dr. Rainer Lasch

Prof. Dr. habil. Rainer Lasch ist Inhaber des Lehrstuhls für BWL, insbes. Logistik an der Fakultät Wirtschaftswissenschaften der TU Dresden, seit 2002 Gastprofessor an der Università degli studi di Trento und seit 2006 wissenschaftlicher Leiter des Kompetenzzentrums Logistik und Unternehmensführung der Dresden International University. Er ist Autor von zahlreichen Lehrbüchern und von international anerkannten Publikationen sowie Gutachter für mehrere internationale Zeitschriften. Darüber hinaus ist Rainer Lasch profilierter Forschungspartner des BMBF und der Wirtschaft, insbesondere bei den Themen Benchmarking in der Logistik, marktorientierte Prozessgestaltung, Lieferantenbewertung, Supply Chain Management, Risikomanagement, Ersatzteillogistik sowie quantitative Planungsverfahren in der Logistik. Zudem ist er Mitglied in zahlreichen wissenschaftlichen Gesellschaften und Verbänden sowie im wissenschaftlichen Beirat des Bundesvorstands des BME tätig.

Maximilian Merath

Maximilian Merath arbeitet seit Mitte August 2015 als wissenschaftlicher Mitarbeiter am Stiftungslehrstuhl für Procurement der Universität Mannheim, nachdem er dort zuvor bereits sein Masterstudium (M.Sc.) im Studiengang „Mannheim Master in Management" abgeschlossen hat. Er befasst sich in seiner Forschung vor allem mit der Bewältigung von Störungen im vorgelagerten Liefernetzwerk. Hierbei untersucht er besonders, welche Entscheidungprozesse mit dem reaktiven Risikomanagement in Verbindung stehen, wie diese strukturiert sind und durch welche Faktoren diese beeinflusst werden. Mithilfe von Simulationsexperimenten untersucht er zum Beispiel den Reaktionsprozess von Unternehmen im Anschluss an Störungen in der Lieferkette unter verschiedenen Bedingungen. Er geht damit der Frage nach, unter welchen Umständen Unternehmen sofort reagieren sollten und wann eine Reaktion besser aufgeschoben werden sollte. Außerdem betrachtet er die Auswirkungen von CSR-Engagement auf Stakeholder-Reaktionen nach unethischem Verhalten von Unternehmen. Einer seiner aktuellen Forschungsbeiträge (in Zusammenarbeit mit Christoph Bode) wurde im August 2017 mit dem renommierten „Chan Hahn Best Paper Award" der Operations & Supply Chain Management (OSCM) Division der Academy of Management ausgezeichnet.

Dr. Marc Müller

Dr. Marc Müller studierte von 2008 bis 2012 Betriebswirtschaftslehre an der Westfälischen Wilhelms-Universität Münster und International Management an der University of Strathclyde. Im Anschluss promovierte er bei Prof. Dr. Wolfgang Stölzle zum Dr. oec. HSG. Der Forschungsschwerpunkt seiner Dissertation ist die soziale Verantwortung in globalen Supply Chains. Während seiner Promotion war Marc Müller als Projektmanager und wissenschaftlicher Mitarbeiter an der Universität St. Gallen angestellt, wo er zahlreiche Praxisprojekte zu aktuellen Fragestellungen des Einkaufs und Supply Chain Managements (u.a. Engpassmanagement, Nachhaltigkeit im Einkauf, Vorlieferantenmanagement) begleitete. Seit 2016 ist Marc Müller für die Dr. Ing. h. c. F. Porsche AG im Bereich Beschaffung Interieur und als Teammitglied der Strategie 2025 tätig.

Dr. Christian Paul

Christian Paul promovierte nach seinem Studium der Betriebswirtschaftslehre in Saarbrücken an der Universität Karlsruhe/Karlsruhe Institute of Technology in Volkswirtschaftslehre. Dabei lag sein Fokus in der Lehre bzw. Forschung in den Bereichen Spieltheorie, Industrieökonomik und experimentelle Ökonomik. Seit 2010 unterstützt er für TWS Partners international tätige Kunden bei Einkaufsverhandlungen und im Bereich der angewandten Industrieökonomik. Außerdem berät er bei Transformationsprojekten, wie etwa der Entwicklung innovativer Einkaufsprozesse oder Procurement-4.0-Anwendungen.

Tessa Sarnow

Tessa Sarnow studierte Logistik & Mobilität sowie Internationales Wirtschaftsingenieurwesen an der Technischen Universität Hamburg. Seit 2017 ist sie wissenschaftliche Mitarbeiterin am Fachgebiet für Unternehmensführung und Logistik der Technischen Universität Darmstadt. Der Forschungsschwerpunkt von Tessa Sarnow lag in der Vergangenheit vor allem in den Gebieten des Supply Chain Managements sowie des Qualitäts- und Risikomanagements in der Logistik. Aktuell beschäftigt sie sich neben der Forschung an Potenzialen und Anwendungsmöglichkeiten von Datenbrillen mit vielfältigen weiteren Fragestellungen der Intralogistik.

Dr. rer. pol. Meike Schröder

Dr. Meike Schröder ist Oberingenieurin am Institut für Logistik und Unternehmensführung an der Technischen Universität Hamburg (TUHH). Zu ihren Forschungsschwerpunkten zählen Logistik, Supply Chain Management und Unternehmensführung. Meike Schröder studierte Betriebswirtschaftslehre an der Westfälischen Wilhelms-Universität Münster, promovierte an der Helmut-Schmidt-Universität Hamburg zum Dr. rer. pol. und habilitiert zum Thema Supply Chain Risikomanage-

Autorenverzeichnis

ment am Institut für Logistik und Unternehmensführung (TUHH). Sie verfügt über jahrelange Erfahrung in nationalen und internationalen Projekten in den Themenbereichen Logistik, Risikomanagement und Human Resource Management. Darüber hinaus ist sie Mitglied in verschiedenen Arbeitskreisen, wissenschaftlichen Gesellschaften und Verbänden (u.a. VHB, DSI, RMA, BVL).

Dr. Benedikt Schulte

Dr. Benedikt Schulte studierte Mathematik an der Universität Bonn. Sein Studium schloss er mit einer Arbeit über optimalen Massentransport auf Alexandrov-Räumen ab. Bei seiner anschließenden Tätigkeit als Unternehmensberater sammelte er breite Erfahrungen in den Bereichen Supply Chain Management und Logistik. Mit Unterstützung eines Promotionsstipendiums der Stiftung der Deutschen Wirtschaft (sdw) und unter der Betreuung von Prof. Dr. Richard Pibernik promovierte er in der Zeit von 2012 bis 2015 am Lehrstuhl für Logistik und Quantitative Methoden der Universität Würzburg. Teile seiner Dissertationsschrift, die den Titel „Integrated Segmentation of Supply and Demand with Service Differentiation" trägt, wurden in namhaften internationalen Zeitschriften publiziert. Seit 2017 arbeitet er im Bereich Operations der REWE Digital GmbH in Köln.

Prof. Dr. Thomas S. Spengler

Prof. Dr. Thomas S. Spengler ist seit 1998 Inhaber des Lehrstuhls für Produktion und Logistik der Technischen Universität Braunschweig. Er studierte Wirtschaftsingenieurwesen an der Universität Karlsruhe (TH), promovierte und habilitierte sich dort im Fach Betriebswirtschaftslehre. Seine Habilitationsschrift zum industriellen Stoffstrommanagement wurde mit dem Werner-Kern-Preis ausgezeichnet. Von 2007 bis 2008 war Thomas S. Spengler Vorsitzender der Gesellschaft für Operations Research (GOR). Im Jahr 2008 übernahm er den Vorstand des neu gegründeten Instituts für Automobilwirtschaft und Industrielle Produktion (AIP). Von 2008 bis 2012 war er Vizepräsident der Technischen Universität Braunschweig für Forschung, wissenschaftlichen Nachwuchs und Technologietransfer. Er ist Gründungsvorstand des Niedersächsischen Forschungszentrums für Fahrzeugtechnik (NFF) und Mitbegründer des Produktionstechnischen Zentrums Niedersachsen (PZN). Thomas S. Spengler ist Autor von mehr als 50 begutachteten Zeitschriftenbeiträgen. Darüber hinaus ist er Mitglied im Editorial Board verschiedener hochrangiger Zeitschriften.

Wolfgang Vogel

Wolfgang Vogel studierte Wirtschaftsingenieurwesen an den Hochschulen Ulm, Neu-Ulm und Mannheim (2006–2010) mit dem Abschluss Diplom-Wirtschaftsingenieur (FH). Im Anschluss erwarb er einen Master of Science in Maschinenbau an der Hochschule Mannheim (2010–2012). Seit August 2011 ist Wolfgang Vogel externer Doktorand am Lehrstuhl für Betriebswirtschaftslehre, insbesondere Logistik an der Fakultät Wirtschaftswissenschaften der Technischen Universität Dresden. Im Rahmen seiner Dissertation und in Zusammenarbeit mit einem Unternehmen aus der Automobilindustrie beschäftigt er sich mit dem Themengebiet Komplexitätsmanagement in der Produktentwicklung. Seit 2016 ist Wolfgang Vogel als Projektleiter für Komplexitätsmanagement im Bereich Produktentwicklung in der Automobilindustrie tätig.

Prof. Dr. Achim Wambach
Achim Wambach ist seit April 2016 Präsident des Zentrums für Europäische Wirtschaftsforschung (ZEW) in Mannheim. Vor seinem Wechsel an das ZEW war er Direktor des Instituts für Wirtschaftspolitik (iwp) an der Universität zu Köln und Co-Direktor des Europäischen Zentrums für freie Berufe der Universität zu Köln.

Achim Wambach hat in Köln Physik und Mathematik studiert und anschließend an der Universität Oxford promoviert. Nach einem Master of Science in Economics an der London School of Economics hat er in München in Volkswirtschaftslehre habilitiert. Von 2001 bis 2005 war er Professor für Volkswirtschaftslehre an der Universität Erlangen-Nürnberg. In seiner Forschung beschäftigt sich Achim Wambach unter anderem mit Fragen der Wettbewerbspolitik sowie Informationsproblemen auf Märkten. Dabei arbeitet er mit Methoden des Marktdesigns und der Industrieökonomik.

Sönke Wieczorrek
Sönke Wieczorrek ist Doktorand bei der Volkswagen Konzernlogistik in Kooperation mit dem Lehrstuhl für Produktion und Logistik der Technischen Universität Braunschweig von Prof. Dr. Thomas S. Spengler. Zuvor studierte er dort Wirtschaftsingenieurwesen. In seiner Forschung beschäftigt er sich mit der Lieferantenentwicklung in der Automobilindustrie, insbesondere vor dem Hintergrund großer Lieferanten- und Transportnetzwerke.

Druck:
Canon Deutschland Business Services GmbH
im Auftrag der KNV-Gruppe
Ferdinand-Jühlke-Str. 7
99095 Erfurt